THE HOMEOWNER'S COMPLETE HANDBOOK FOR

ADD-ON SOLAR

GREENHOUSES & SUNSPACES

PLANNING DESIGN CONSTRUCTION

by Andrew M. Shapiro

Illustrations by Carolyn D. Shapiro

 Rodale Press, Emmaus, Pa.

Printed in the United States of America on recycled paper
containing a high percentage of de-inked fiber.

Cover and book design: Anita Noble
Art direction: Karen A. Schell
Cover photographs: top, courtesy of Creative Structures, Inc.; bottom, green-
    house design by Paul Russell and Creative Structures, Inc.
Cover photography: Mitchell T. Mandel
Interior photography: Kelly Gloger (except as noted)
Copy editing: Cristina Negrón Whyte

Library of Congress Cataloging in Publication Data

Shapiro, Andrew M.
    The homeowner's complete handbook for add-on solar
greenhouses & sunspaces.

    Bibliography: p.
    Includes index.
    1. Solar greenhouses—Design and construction.
I. Title.
SB416.S47 1984   690'.89   84-18361

ISBN 0-87857-507-3 hardcover
ISBN 0-87857-508-1 paperback

2 4 6 8 10 9 7 5 3 1 hardcover
2 4 6 8 10 9 7 5 3 1 paperback

To Norman B. Saunders and to my daughter Sarah
Alexandra Shapiro, in hopes that she will grow up in
the energy-efficient and equitable world Norman en-
visions

CONTENTS

ACKNOWLEDGMENTS

I am deeply indebted to all the solar greenhouse designers and builders who have laid so much of the groundwork in what is presented here, and who have shared their experiences, either in print or in conversations with me. Special thanks go to Mark Ward and Jeremy Coleman, who was also a technical editor of the book. Much thanks is also due to Miriam Klein and Miranda Smith for teaching me about plants and their needs for growth, as well as for astounding me with the quantity of food that can actually be grown in a greenhouse and for reviewing chapter 4.

Thanks also goes to Vernon Henderson for his important help in the chapter on economics. Norman B. Saunders has provided me with many hours of teaching and guidance, as well as inspiration, and I owe all of what I have learned about passive solar heating to him. He also kindly reviewed most of the technical aspects of the manuscript. My gratitude also goes to Phil and Phyllis Morrison for their helpful guidance and encouragement throughout this project. And much appreciation is due to Kelly Gloger for his fine photographs and to Carolyn Shapiro who has completed wonderful illustrations despite many changes and much nit-picking about construction details. Thanks are also due to the technical research and sales departments of the manufacturers of the various products discussed, for their kind help and review of pertinent parts of the manuscript.

And thanks to my editor at Rodale, Joe Carter, for his insights into both form and content, and his gentle prodding to make this book more readable. Thanks, too, to Margaret J. Balitas for the organization and assistance that she provided.

INTRODUCTION

In only a few years solar greenhouses have evolved from the experimental efforts of a few pioneers to become fairly commonplace add-on solutions to the needs for solar heat, for year-round or extended-season plant and food growing and for sunny winter environments. Much knowledge has been gained in this time about what makes solar greenhouses work and what makes them *not* work. The purpose of this book is to bring together the information and techniques that owners and builders need to avoid repeating past mistakes and to take advantage of what is truly a wealth of accumulated experience.

I became interested in solar greenhouses in 1977, while working at the National Center for Appropriate Technology (NCAT), an organization devoted to assisting low-income families meet basic needs for shelter, food and heat with energy-related approaches. This was at the beginning of the "solar greenhouse movement," when the whole idea of getting heat and food from the same structure was just beginning to become popular. We built a research greenhouse and began experimenting at NCAT and funding solar greenhouse projects around the country. When I began a project to monitor the food and heat production of attached solar greenhouses in New England, it quickly became apparent that there wasn't enough information available to people outside of the Southwest and Rocky Mountain states, where the solar greenhouse movement started. So I became involved with giving design assistance and producing an NCAT publication on solar greenhouse design.

Since then greenhouse construction has grown from backyard projects into an industry, with over 40 solar greenhouse manufacturers offering their products where there were perhaps only 10 just a few years ago. Much has been learned in this time—about designing the greenhouse as both an effective solar heater for the house and an effective greenhouse for plants, and about putting together the right materials into a tight, long-lasting structure. I, too, have learned from the greenhouses I've designed and built, and I've felt it important, with this boom in greenhouse construction, to meet the prospective greenhouse owners' and builders' needs for specific answers to their many questions about design and construction.

The first question that often comes up is What is a *solar* greenhouse? There isn't one exclusive shape or size that defines this type, but by design and function it might better be called "energy conserving and heat storing." All greenhouses use solar energy to provide warmth and daylight for plant growth. Traditional greenhouses, however, are designed and built primarily for providing the proper environment for plant growth. These greenhouses do little to minimize the energy needed to maintain this environment. When the weather outside is less than ideal, an auxiliary heating or cooling system is needed to maintain the desired inside climate. An important emphasis in traditional greenhouse design has been mainly to maximize the amount of light available to the plants. This is accomplished by having the structure totally glazed, and often by using only one layer of glazing. The angle and orientation of the glazing are based on delivering maximum light levels for the plants. In short, traditional greenhouses rely on low-cost energy. But, in the space of less than ten years, in the face of high-cost energy, greenhouse design has evolved rapidly. New shapes, materials and controls have emerged to meet the needs of the new energy-efficient greenhouses.

Solar greenhouse design and construction combines concern for the plant-growing environment with energy conservation. Glazing orientation and angle are set to capture the heat value of solar energy while providing sufficient light for plant growth. Solar heat that is collected during the day is stored for use at night. Energy-conserving double glazing is commonly used. Areas of the greenhouse skin that aren't glazed are insulated to minimize heat loss. The whole greenhouse shell is built very carefully to minimize heat-robbing air infiltration. Because of these design improvements, the energy use of solar greenhouses is but a fraction of that for traditional designs.

These design improvements have gone hand in hand with the surge in interest in residential solar heating. Today's solar greenhouse is most commonly an "attached" solar greenhouse fastened to the south wall of a home. An attached solar greenhouse has a unique relationship with its house: During a sunny winter day it transfers warm air to the house; at night it can take heat back from the house as needed. A properly designed attached greenhouse is a net energy producer, giving more energy to the house than it takes back. And it contributes much more than heat: It provides fresh, moist air to the house, a place to grow vegetables and houseplants and a place to enjoy a sunbath year-round, all without the heating bills of a conventional greenhouse. An attached greenhouse is also a buffer for the house, sheltering the area it covers from wind and temperature extremes, essentially eliminating heat loss through the common wall in addition to providing solar heat.

Energy-efficient greenhouse design has given rise to some new words and phrases. *Sunspace* is often used interchangeably with solar greenhouse. To avoid confusion I will use *solar greenhouse* to mean a space that is designed to provide an optimum, or near optimum, environment for plants, along with producing solar heat for the house and providing some amount of space for lounging in the sun. I'll define a sunspace as being a glazed enclosure built onto the south side of the house. It would be used just for solar heating and living space, though not to the complete exclusion of plant or food growing. There isn't a huge difference between a solar greenhouse and a sunspace, but you will find that there are stricter design requirements for a greenhouse intended for serious food growing. A sunspace design, on the other hand, can conform more to your desire for a certain appearance and shape. The difference is a matter of emphasis: The greenhouse has plant growth as a primary consideration, with living space being secondary, while in a sunspace living space is the primary concern, with plant growth being secondary. Both combine these uses with solar heating the house, and both require tight construction to ensure they will be energy efficient.

An attached solar greenhouse is a multipurpose structure. During the design and construction attention is paid to each function: growing plants, solar heating and living space. Designing and building a structure devoted only to one or two of the functions is a simpler job, since you have to juggle fewer requirements. If, for example, the structure won't be used for growing plants, the increased illumination and ventilation required for good plant growth becomes somewhat less important, although glazing for solar heating and ventilation for natural cooling will be important. As I present various aspects of design, I'll concentrate on incorporating the features required for all three purposes. But if your goals are different, you can choose the features that are most appropriate for accomplishing them.

Using This Book

The purpose of this book is threefold. The first is to give you enough information to decide whether or not an attached solar greenhouse is right for you and if you have a suitable location for one. The second is to guide you through a total design process that will result in an efficient greenhouse that is well matched to your house and your needs for solar heat, plant-growing space and solarium space, and that also holds costs within your budget. There is no single design presented that is supposed to be appropriate for all houses, all people and all climates. Even for one situation, there are likely to be several possible designs. Greenhouses are wonderfully flexible, not requiring the degree of design precision that other solar heating systems can require. If a solar greenhouse is designed with a little too much glazing, for example, some extra heat can be dumped "overboard" by opening a greenhouse vent or a house window. But an oversized passive system consisting of south-facing windows

might make the house uncomfortably warm. There are design limits and rules of thumb, though—which I'll be presenting as we go along—but they are not as strict as with other types of solar heating systems. This design process is both a map and a set of tools that will enable you to design the best greenhouse for your situation.

The third purpose is to provide precise construction details for all aspects of solar greenhouse construction that differ significantly from ordinary house construction. I have not included instructions for conventional building techniques, such as pouring a concrete foundation or building a stud wall, since this information is available in many places. Actual step-by-step explanations are included when the drawings of the details are not fully self-explanatory or where I have found that a particular technique makes the job easier or makes it come out better. Of course, not all possible techniques and details are included, but I have tried to include a wide enough range of details to present at least one possible solution to most design requirements.

I have more than once been asked if it is really possible for a do-it-yourselfer to design and build an effective solar greenhouse. My experience has been that problems are mostly a result of a lack of information about design or about proper use of materials. The purpose of this book is to gather together enough information for you to begin a solar greenhouse project with confidence and to answer this question with a resolute "Yes!"

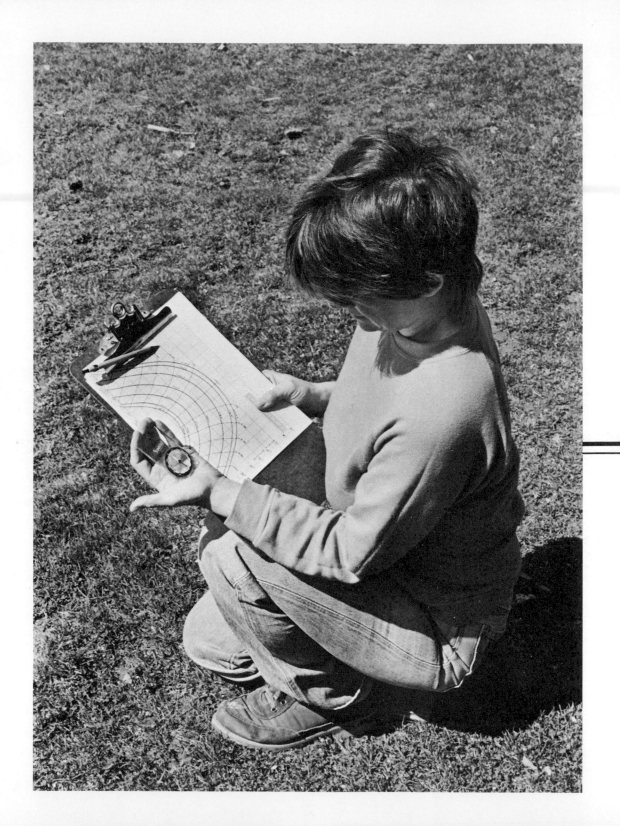

Section I:

PLANNING THE SOLAR GREENHOUSE

In this section you'll get a first look at attached solar greenhouses. We'll explore their uses: for growing plants, for adding solar heat to your house and for having a place to sit in the sun and enjoy the good company of plants. Some alternatives to a greenhouse you may want to consider are also covered, as well as the skills you should have to build a greenhouse yourself. We'll look at your house and its potential greenhouse sites, then locate the best spot and find out with a solar site survey just how much sun that spot will get. The costs of building a greenhouse and a procedure that you can use to refine the cost figure are presented first in general terms and then in some detail. And the greenhouse is examined from an investment point of view, balancing costs against returns. All of this will get you acquainted with greenhouses, with what they can and can't do, and will help you sort through and refine your own goals and expectations. Once you've done this, you'll be ready for "Section II: Designing the Greenhouse," where we'll actually design a greenhouse that meets your particular needs.

A GREENHOUSE FOR YOUR HOME

Chapter 1 looks at the uses for an attached solar greenhouse, and how they can mesh with your needs and desires, to see if a greenhouse is an appropriate solution. We'll also take a quick look at construction costs (which are discussed in more detail in chapter 3), and at the skills required to build a greenhouse. This survey should give you a pretty good idea about how a solar greenhouse can work with your house and your life-style, and it raises issues and questions that will be explored more fully in subsequent chapters.

A Multi-Use Structure

Attached solar greenhouses make the best use of the effort and expense put into building them when they can be put to their maximum use: heating the house, providing a place to grow food and houseplants, and providing some amount of living space. A greenhouse can easily perform all these functions, as long as careful attention is paid to integrating them into the overall design. These three

functions can be thought of as a triangle (see figure 1-1). You can locate your particular needs on this triangle and your priorities for each. If you are primarily interested in having a sunspace for solar heating and a sunny living space, you would be located between these two corners but away from the food growing corner. If you want all three functions, in some order of priority, you would put your mark somewhere inside the borders of the triangle.

An attached greenhouse will give you the most benefit for its cost if your needs fall somewhere inside the triangle. If they fall on one of the lines or at one of the corners, an attached greenhouse may still be appropriate, but there is less benefit for the cost, and there may be cheaper or better ways to meet your needs.

As we cover the benefits, the costs and the alternatives, keep this triangle in mind. You don't have to put an absolute fix on your priorities right away, since your ideas are likely to change as you go through this book and see what is and isn't possible. The green-

Figure 1-1: An attached solar greenhouse is most cost-effective as a multipurpose structure, providing solar heat for the house, a place to grow vegetables, fruits and other plants and a place in the sun. If you want all three of these, a greenhouse is for you. If you want only two of these, a greenhouse is one choice among a few options: Your needs can be met in other ways, perhaps less expensively. If your goal is to gain just one of the uses, there are definitely some less expensive options to consider.

houses that work best are the ones where the owners knew their needs *before* they began building.

Solar Heating

An attached greenhouse with a good solar exposure can contribute a substantial amount to a house's heating needs. (Checking the solar exposure of a site is covered in chapter 2.) When the winter sun is shining, solar heated air from the greenhouse is brought into the house, either by simply opening a door, window or other vent in the common wall, or by an automatic fan. If the greenhouse is attached to a living area where you spend a lot of time during the day, the solar heat can be used to heat just that area, allowing you to run the rest of the house at a lower temperature by lowering the thermostat. The solar heat can be more broadly distributed around the house, if needed, depending on the interior layout and your heating needs. In some cases, the house heating system can be kept off when the sun shines. With larger greenhouses, auxiliary heating may not even be needed for hours after the sun has gone down because of the solar heat stored in the house.

Your actual fuel savings depend on several factors: on the area of the south-facing greenhouse glazing relative to the size of the house, on how well the house is insulated, on the local climate and on how the greenhouse is used. If the greenhouse is operated strictly as a place to grow plants, some of the collected solar heat will be needed to keep the plants warm at night. If it is empty of plants, much more heat is available to the house. "Section II: Designing the Greenhouse" takes a closer look at these and other more subtle factors involved in determining the amount of solar heat available. This section also goes through a method for determining the *solar heating fraction* you could expect from a greenhouse attached to your house. Solar heating fraction is the percentage of the heating fuel used in the house that is displaced by solar heat from the greenhouse. The numbers for attached solar greenhouses generally range from 10 to 50 percent for greenhouses built onto existing houses. They can, of course, be higher, and they often are in energy-efficient new construction that includes tighter construction, higher levels of insulation and extra heat storage.

The energy efficiency of the existing house naturally has a great effect on the solar heating fraction. You can't expect a solar greenhouse to significantly reduce the fuel bills of an uninsulated or poorly insulated house. One of the primary rules of solar space heating is "Insulation first—solar heating second." Insulating and tightening up the house is a must. If the choice is between the two, tightening up is definitely a more cost-effective way to reduce heating bills. Chapter 6 looks at how the level of insulation in a house affects the solar heating fraction.

Growing Vegetables, Fruits and Other Plants

The solar greenhouse provides a wonderful, protected environment in which to *grow food*. It can be used to provide fresh vegetables year-round, or it can be used to simply extend the growing season for a couple of months on either end of the outdoor season. But whether the greenhouse is used for season extension or as a year-round producer, substantial amounts of food can be grown. The graph in figure 1-2 shows the food yields from an 8-by-18-foot greenhouse (with 90 square feet of actual growing area) at the Rodale Research Center in Maxatawny, Pennsylvania. The food you grow in the winter not only saves you money and energy, it also saves energy for society as a whole. Your greenhouse produce only has to travel a few feet to your kitchen, rather than the hundreds or thousands of miles from California, the southern United States or Mexico.

Another important benefit of growing your own food is nutrition. Food grown in a greenhouse can be picked and eaten at the height of ripeness, when its vitamin content is highest. And you control what's in the soil and what is sprayed on the plants. Growing food organically in a greenhouse is a little more difficult than using chemical fertilizers and chemical pest control, but for many people it is worth the effort. In an attached greenhouse, which shares air with your living space, the arguments against chemical fertilizers and pest controls are even more compelling than in a freestanding greenhouse or outdoor garden. In economic terms, if you eat organic vegetables, your savings from growing your own will be increased, since organically grown produce is typically more expensive than conventionally grown vegetables. And organically grown vegetables are often unavailable during the winter. Even if you grow very little to eat in the greenhouse, you can bring delightful flavorings to your winter cooking with freshly picked herbs. They may not make a dent in your food budget, but they can make simple food sparkle.

As previously mentioned, some growers use their greenhouses all year for food production, while others use them to extend the growing season a couple of months on either end. A typical season-extension sequence usually leaves out the December through February crop, when both light levels and temperatures are lowest. Some owners find that after growing a spring greenhouse crop of seedlings (for the outside garden) and early tomatoes, maintaining an outside garden all summer and raising fall crops back in the greenhouse, that they want the midwinter break. During this period they use the greenhouse only as a solar heater and a solarium. They can let the nighttime greenhouse temperature fall as low as it will, since back-up heat isn't needed to protect plants. Other growers enjoy putting in the extra effort for the bonus of having fresh salads in midwinter.

A common misconception about solar greenhouses is that the greenhouse grows food. But it's not quite so automatic. The greenhouse provides a controlled environment in which *you* help the plants grow. Those tomatoes won't plant, water and fertilize themselves and then come rolling through the door three months later. Growing food in a greenhouse requires some getting used to, even for accomplished outdoor gardeners. Success comes with your time and attention given for managing the greenhouse and gener- ally learning the ropes. Even seasoned greenhouse gardeners expect to see insect pests and diseases from time to time, and controlling them requires immediate and continuing

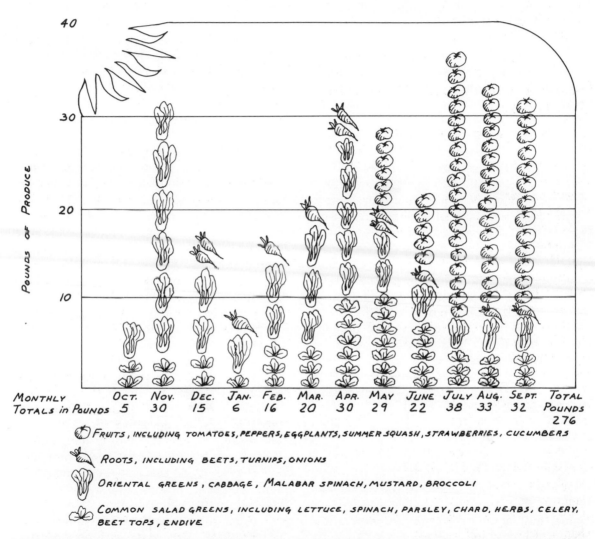

FRUITS, INCLUDING TOMATOES, PEPPERS, EGGPLANTS, SUMMER SQUASH, STRAWBERRIES, CUCUMBERS

ROOTS, INCLUDING BEETS, TURNIPS, ONIONS

ORIENTAL GREENS, CABBAGE, MALABAR SPINACH, MUSTARD, BROCCOLI

COMMON SALAD GREENS, INCLUDING LETTUCE, SPINACH, PARSLEY, CHARD, HERBS, CELERY, BEET TOPS, ENDIVE

Figure 1-2: This data, taken from a solar greenhouse at the Rodale Research Center, shows a typical year of harvest from year-round growing. Note that yields are lower in midwinter, due to cooler temperatures and shorter days with less light, but that substantial quantities were still grown right through the winter. This greenhouse was also used through the summer for hot-weather crops. It has 91 square feet of growing space in a total space of about 150 square feet.

attention. From soil preparation to harvest, greenhouse growing is an ongoing job, though most greenhouse owners wouldn't call it work.

The greenhouse horticulture books listed in the bibliography (see Further Reading) can help you learn this skill. Chapter 4 discusses features that can be built in to decrease the need for daily attention.

Having a place to grow your garden *seedlings* is another advantage of having a solar greenhouse. Greenhouse seedlings tend to be much healthier and stronger than those grown indoors next to a window (unless you use indoor grow-lights to increase the available light). If you have a big garden, producing your own seedlings can save quite a bit of money. It is not difficult to produce over 1,000 seedlings in a 200-square-foot greenhouse. There are some greenhouse owners who supply a whole neighborhood with seedlings; others make seedlings a pocket-money business venture. Most houseplants also thrive in the light-filled environment of the greenhouse. Many greenhouse owners grow only ornamental plants, finding their interests more in this area than in home food production. With a little planning something can be in bloom for much of the year. And a greenhouse can do wonders for houseplants that tend to droop and be miserable in the house in the winter.

Your Place in the Sun

Having a place to bask in the winter sun may or may not have a monetary payback value, but for many greenhouse owners it's the most important aspect of having a greenhouse. For others, the solarium aspect is secondary, and they fill the greenhouse as much as possible with growing beds and benches for potted plants. But even in the most plant-filled space, a chair or a hammock always seems to find its way into a sunny corner or nook.

One new greenhouse owner I talked with had just relocated from sunny California to frostier Massachusetts. In his delight over his greenhouse, he said, "It's transformed our winter. We sunbathe in the hammock. . . . It's a place where you can get really hot, and the coolness of the house is quite enjoyable." Using the greenhouse as a solarium, then, can save heating fuel in addition to what is saved by heat transfer from the greenhouse, as long as you turn down the thermostat in the house.

Of course, a greenhouse isn't always going to be warm and comfortable. Much depends on how you use it. For example, one of the ways to increase its energy contribution to the house is to allow its temperature to fall somewhat at night (using less back-up heat) and rise somewhat during the day. When plants are being grown, they will determine the acceptable temperature extremes. Plants can tolerate higher and lower temperatures than you can. (Many vegetables are quite "comfortable" between 50 and 85°F.) When there are no plants present, the requirements of solar heating the house determine the extremes. The daytime temperature may rise to 80 or 85°F, at which point warm air is brought into the house. The nighttime temperature may be allowed to "float" or fall as low as it will without adding any back-up heat. If, on the other hand, you want more living space from the greenhouse, temperature changes or "swings" would be reduced to stay within the comfort range.

Some solar greenhouses have been built as part of the living room, with no separation between greenhouse and the existing living space. This scheme can be architecturally stunning, but it also subjects the living areas to cold temperatures at night and high tem-

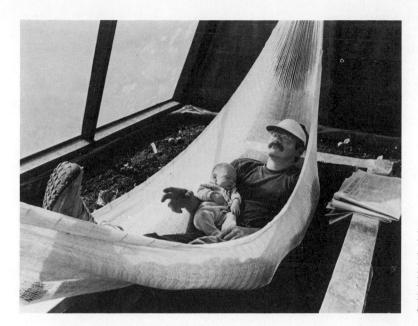

Photo 1-1: No matter how small the greenhouse or how little attention was paid to creating a living space when the greenhouse was built, people usually manage to find a place for a chair or a hammock.

peratures on sunny days. This can mean extra house heating and cooling costs, decreasing the net fuel savings from the greenhouse. Separating the two spaces is a much better strategy for preserving comfort and saving energy. Glass doors give the best of both worlds, providing both a view into the greenhouse and a sizable opening when you want it. (A screen door for this opening will keep pets out of the growing beds.)

Other Benefits, Other Options

In addition to providing heat, a greenhouse full of plants generates moisture and oxygen from plant transpiration. This fresh air can be a welcome addition in winter, particularly in cold climates where the air in the house tends to get dry. The pleasure you can gain just from being inside a plant-filled greenhouse can make it a valuable addition to any house. In the city, a greenhouse can trans-

form an unwanted view into a view of plants and flowers. And the pleasure of sitting in a lush warm spot in the winter is really beyond monetary value—it simply makes life more pleasant.

A well-built solar greenhouse can increase the resale value of the house, sometimes by as much as or more than the greenhouse cost to build. A good-looking space added onto the house will appeal to all buyers, while the lower heating bills and a place to grow plants may appeal only to some. The extent to which the resale value is increased varies quite a bit, depending on the particular house, the neighborhood and other factors, but shouldn't be ignored in your decision to build, or in deciding what type of greenhouse to build.

If you're looking for a better return on your investment in extended season food production, you might consider some alternatives. They may not be as glamorous or as fun

Photo 1-2: A greenhouse intended for maximum food production can be literally filled with foliage at the height of its growing season.

as a greenhouse, but they are certainly cheaper and may well satisfy your needs. Cold frames as simple as polyethylene row covers, made of simple wire hoops covered with clear polyethylene, or old windows covering a partially buried box, can add a month or two on either end of the growing season. More elaborate cold frames such as Rodale's Solar Growing Frame or the Solar Pod by Solar Survival can support hardy salad crops through fairly cold winters. (Addresses for obtaining the

plans for both of these systems or the kit for the Solar Pod are in Appendix 2.)

Lowering Heating Bills

If your main purpose for a solar greenhouse is to reduce your heating bills you should first make certain that your house is ready for solar heat. To save space heating energy, you should always work to conserve energy first, before adding a solar heating system. A wide variety of energy conservation techniques has been proven to be more cost-effective than solar heating. If you are not familiar with the many sneaky paths for heat to be lost from a house, consult with a professional home *energy auditor* to determine the most effective energy conservation strategies for your house. The best approach to tightening up a particular house depends heavily on the particular situation, so it is usually worth the investment in an experienced auditor's time to assess the situation. It is safe to say, though, that it is not worth the cost and effort to build any solar heating device without first tightening up a house's air leaks as much as possible, followed by additions of ceiling and wall insulation.

Once the house is tight and better insulated, the added solar heat can take care of a greater portion of the reduced heating needs. But if you mainly want solar heat, there are less expensive alternatives to building a greenhouse, such as adding double glazed, south-facing windows or solar air-heating collector systems.

A Space in the Sun

If your only purpose in building a solar greenhouse is to have a place to sit in the sun, the structure (we'll call it a solarium) need not be as elaborate or as expensive as one intended for solar heating and plant growing.

A solarium doesn't need sloped overhead glazing to provide illumination for plant growth. The winter sun will be low enough in the sky to shine on you through vertical glazing, which is easier to build than sloped glazing. Vertical glazing also provides more protection from the higher angle summer sun, making it easier to prevent overheating. If you have a south-facing porch, removable glazing panels can be a very inexpensive way to turn it into a winter solarium while still having an open-air porch in summer. The panels can be as expensive as removable glass panels or as inexpensive as clear vinyl or polyethylene covered wood frames. One scheme for building removable panels is detailed in chapter 11.

Greenhouse Construction Costs

One of the first questions asked by prospective greenhouse owners is How much will it cost? In this section, we'll take a first look at this question to give you a general idea of costs. Chapter 3 takes a closer look, breaking the costs down in more detail and looking at a few examples. There is, of course, no single answer to cost questions. Cost depends on size, location, the quality of materials used, the cost of labor and how many automatic features are included. This discussion looks at materials cost only, for people who want to build their own, and materials plus labor, for those who want to have a greenhouse built for them.

Table 1-1 shows the ranges of both the above costs: materials only and materials plus labor. The wide range shows that you can build a greenhouse to fit your budget. The higher-cost greenhouses tend to cost as much as or more than room additions of similar sizes, while simpler owner-built greenhouses can be quite inexpensive. For example, the materials costs for a 200-square-foot (floor area) greenhouse tend to fall between $800 and $7,000. Total costs for materials and labor, not including any contractor or designer fees, can run from $2,500 to $16,000. The lower figures are for a greenhouse built with recycled lumber, with the very lowest-cost glazing (polyethylene) and no automatic features, such as ventilation fans. The higher figures include the use of new materials, fac-

TABLE 1-1:
TYPICAL GREENHOUSE CONSTRUCTION COSTS

| FLOOR AREA (ft²) | LOW COST | | HIGH COST | |
	MATERIALS ONLY ($)	MATERIALS AND LABOR ($)	MATERIALS ONLY ($)	MATERIALS AND LABOR ($)
100	500	1,500	4,000	10,000
200	800	2,500	7,000	16,000
300	1,000	3,000	9,000	20,000

NOTE: Prices are as of early 1984.

tory-sealed double-glass glazing, fully automatic venting and back-up heating systems and a finished floor. Greenhouses with costs in the middle of this range usually include new materials of moderate quality, standard-size glass or moderate lifespan plastic glazing materials, a moderate level of interior finish and some automatic features. Kit greenhouses tend toward the upper price ranges, but there are a few lower-priced kits available (see Appendix 2).

Labor costs vary quite a bit with location and skill of the builder. The amount of labor and skill required depends on how polished the greenhouse is to be. Fifty hours of labor is not uncommon for a 100- or 200-square-foot greenhouse made of very low cost materials, with an earth or gravel floor. On the other hand, a more polished, more automatic greenhouse of the same size can require 200 or 300 hours. Larger greenhouses don't usually require proportionally more labor. Changing a 10-by-10-foot greenhouse to a 10-by-20-foot one won't double the labor, but might add only 50 percent to the labor cost. Increasing the size can be thought of as adding sections into the middle of the greenhouse. The end-walls are the same, all the same openings are required, all the same construction stages are required and all the head-scratching over difficult details is the same. There is essentially just more foundation, framing and glazing.

In estimating your costs at this early stage, start by choosing what seems to be a reasonably sized greenhouse. If you have a small house and modest plans for growing plants, start with 100 to 150 square feet. If you intend to do more serious greenhouse gardening, you might start a little larger, perhaps 150 to 200 square feet. If you want to capture enough solar heat to make a noticeable difference in your fuel bills, start with a greenhouse whose south-facing glazed area is around 20 percent of the floor area of your house. For

example, a lowest-cost 200-square-foot greenhouse would cost about $800 for materials. Materials plus labor might run as low as $2,500. A moderately priced greenhouse of the same size might run $2,500 for materials or $6,000 for materials and labor. (All prices are as of early 1984.)

Can You Build One?

Anyone with basic carpentry skills can build a greenhouse. To a certain extent, the greenhouse you build can be matched to your construction skills. A simple, low-cost greenhouse can be built with average construction skills. Materials requiring high precision can be avoided. On the other hand, building a "top-of-the-line" all-automatic greenhouse with the highest-quality materials takes about the same level of skill that any building addition would require, from footings to finish work. But no matter how fancy or plain, the greenhouse will need to be tight in order to conserve energy and contain solar heat. The information provided in "Section III: Construction Detailing" will give you an idea of how your building skills are matched to the job.

If you do build it yourself, or if you hire a carpenter to work with you, an essential requirement is *organization*. Once you settle on a design, materials lists must be made and prices collected to arrive at a cost. Building permits must be obtained. Materials must be ready at the building site when you need them, particularly if you are hiring labor. For some people, organizing a project is second nature, while for others it's a struggle. If the greenhouse of your dreams is beyond your experience and skills, consider hiring a skilled builder for those parts of the job where you need the most help. This approach can combine your labor with higher skills where needed and can teach you something as well.

Chapter 2

SITE PLANNING

To get the best heating performance from your solar greenhouse, it must be located where the sun will shine on it for at least three hours before and after noon, 9:00 A.M. to 3:00 P.M. During this period the sun delivers more than 90 percent of the total energy available over the whole day (when there are no clouds). Ideally the greenhouse should face as close to south as possible, but anywhere within 45 degrees of south, from southeast to southwest, is acceptable. Within this range, the sun's rays will be fairly perpendicular to tilted glazing during the middle of the day, for good light and heat penetration into the greenhouse. A greenhouse that faces further away from south, even approaching due east or west, can capture enough solar heat to take care of itself for much of the year, as long as the end wall of the greenhouse that faces south is fully glazed and is reasonably unshaded. A way-off-south greenhouse, however, generally won't capture enough solar heat to do much more than balance the back-up heat it will require. But it can be an excellent solar-heated growing and living space. However, any east- or west-facing expanse of glazing is going to be suscep-

tible to summer overheating and will need additional attention to summer shading. For a greenhouse that is used for growing as much food as possible, morning light should be considered in your site planning, as it helps the plants get an early start on growing for the day. If your choice is between southeast- and southwest-facing sites, the southeastern exposure will encourage better plant growth and will also bring solar heat into the house earlier in the morning, when it is usually needed, more than later in the day.

Attaching the greenhouse to a much-used living space in the house is another important element of site planning. If the greenhouse is attached to a kitchen, dining or living area in which you spend a lot of time, heat from the greenhouse only has to enter this small area in order for you to be able to turn off the furnace on a sunny day. If, however, the solar heat were vented into an empty bedroom, the energy collected would not be nearly so useful. It is possible to use a fan and duct to move heat from a greenhouse to a more distant living area, and indeed this is the only choice in some situations, but it is much

Photo 2-1: This greenhouse takes advantage of the shelter provided by the east wing of the building.

simpler and more direct if the greenhouse actually adjoins a living area. Some greenhouse owners have converted south-facing bedrooms to studies or living areas to take advantage of the warmth in that room on sunny days.

The sheltering immediately around the greenhouse will also affect the greenhouse's performance. At windy sites it is a good idea to nestle the greenhouse into any shelter that the house or the surrounding vegetation provides, as long as these don't shade the greenhouse excessively. The terrain will also affect your planning, in that you don't want to place the greenhouse where the drainage is poor. Legal requirements also enter into site planning. Many localities have set-back requirements that force you to maintain a minimum distance between any addition to a house and the lot lines.

Checking Your Solar Access

The first step in checking the available sun on your site is simple observation. Check how sunny the south side of your house is over the course of a day. Make notes about where shadows are cast and for how long. Note what time the morning sun first hits the south side and when it finally leaves in the evening. On a windy day go outside and find the least windy area. If you do your planning during the heating season check these conditions more than once to see how they change. You may already know some of these things about your house, if you stop to think about them. It might be helpful to sketch out a site plan that shows prevailing wind direction, sheltered areas and shaded areas. An example of this is shown in figure 2-1.

If you like to follow natural events, such as the cycles of the moon and the rise and fall of the sun's path through the course of the year, you may know the sun's position on the shortest and longest days of the year. But you may not know when, during the different months of the year, the sun will hit your greenhouse location. This information is fairly easy to develop and is indispensable for determining if your site has good solar access. The procedure, a *solar survey,* requires only

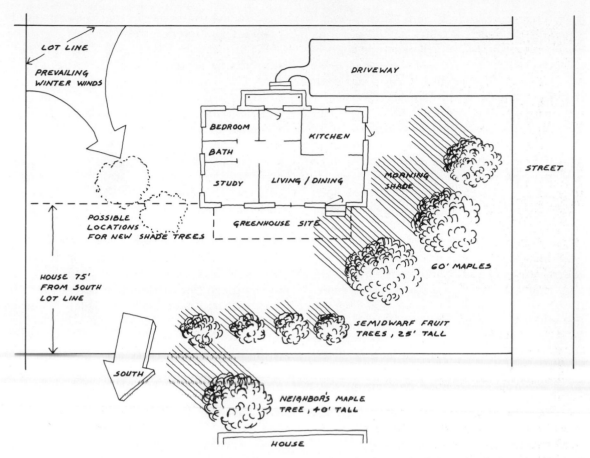

Figure 2-1: A sketch of your house site will help define possible greenhouse locations and pinpoint obstructions to the sun. It should show the house with its major living areas, lot lines, trees and other shadow-casting objects, prevailing winter winds, true south and any other significant features.

simple tools and a chart of the sun's path throughout the year, and it takes little time to perform.

Figures A-2 through A-9 in Appendix 3 are sun path charts, which show the position of the sun in the sky at any time of the day for any day of the year for 28 to 56 degrees north latitude (NL) in intervals of 4 degrees. Along the bottom of each sun path chart the *azimuth angles* are marked. These indicate the

angle of the sun's position, in a horizontal plane, relative to south. If you are standing on your prospective greenhouse site, looking due south, your azimuth is 0 degrees. If you look toward the southwest, you have rotated 45 degrees, and the azimuth you are siting along is 45 degrees west of south. Along the vertical sides of the charts are shown the *altitude angles*, which are a measure of the sun's angular height above the horizon. If the sun were directly overhead, its altitude angle would be 90 degrees. Halfway between this position and the horizon the altitude angle is 45 degrees.

The solid curved lines in the sun path charts represent the sun's path through the sky on the twenty-first day of each month. Note that the sun's path is the same on 21 May and 21 July, 21 April and 21 August, and so on. The dashed lines crossing the sun's path are the hours of the day. The sun is always south at *solar noon,* so the noon hour line corresponds with the 0-degree azimuth line.

Solar noon is different from clock noon (standard time) by up to a half hour, unless you are in the center of your time zone, where solar time and clock time are about the same. If you are on the east side of the time zone the sun reaches its high point in the sky after noon on the clock, and before noon on the west side. If you are near the border of the time zone, solar time and clock time can be off by as much as a half hour. And during day-

light saving time the sun reaches its highest point an hour later on the clock.

For example, Providence, Rhode Island, is on the far eastern side of the eastern time zone. If you are checking the sun's azimuth at clock noon during daylight saving time, you will find the sun is still in the eastern sky by as much as 40 or 50 degrees east of south. It won't reach due south until somewhere around 1:20 or 1:30 P.M. clock time. During standard-time months, it will be due south between 12:20 and 12:30 P.M. Thus in this case solar noon comes 20 to 30 minutes after clock noon during standard time and an hour and 20 to 30 minutes after clock noon during daylight saving time. The easiest way to check the variation between clock and solar time is to check the clock time when the sun is at 0 degrees azimuth, or due south. Once you have completed your solar survey, you will want to reconcile clock and solar time, so you can check to see if your survey is accurate. You will be able to predict from your survey when a shadow will fall on your potential green-

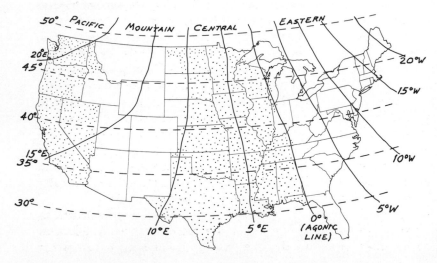

Figure 2-2: This map shows the deviation of true south from magnetic south, along with latitude and the time zones (Pacific, Mountain, Central and Eastern) that span the country. At the agonic line, magnetic and true south are equal because there is no magnetic deviation. *(Source: Redrawn from the Isogonic Chart of the United States, United States Department of Commerce, Coast and Geodetic Survey, 1965.)*

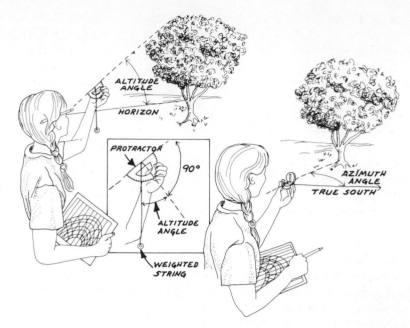

Figure 2-3: The altitude angle of the top of an obstruction is easily found with a protractor with a weighted string attached to its center. Site across the flat side of the protractor and read the altitude angle on the side. The azimuth is found with the compass, taking variation from true south into account.

house site, and then check it by the clock. Don't worry if you are a half hour off one way or the other, but if you are farther off than that, you should go back to your survey and find your error.

The site survey involves plotting on the sun path chart the azimuth and altitude angles of any obstructions to the sun. There are three main steps:

First, determine the latitude of your site (see figure 2-2) and choose the appropriate sun path chart. Next, you must determine *true south.* A common magnetic compass will tell you *magnetic south,* as long as you are careful to keep it away from steel objects, such as belt buckles, pocketknives or sneakier things like paint-covered nails in a wooden railing on which you might set the compass. Even overhead wires or underground pipes can affect compass readings, so in urban or

suburban areas it is a good idea to check compass readings from more than one spot.

Even if your compass isn't biased by steel or if your lot map is well marked, you probably still need to adjust for magnetic variation from true south, based on your location, as shown in figure 2-2. If you live along the line running through Chicago down towards Florida (which is marked "0°") magnetic south is the same as true south. If you live to the east of this line, true south is west of magnetic south by the degrees shown on the various deviation lines. If you live to the west of the 0-degree line, true south is to the east of magnetic south. For example, if you live in Providence, Rhode Island, true south is fully 15 degrees west of magnetic south.

The final step is to plot any obstructions to the sun on the sun path chart. In addition to the compass, you will need a protractor

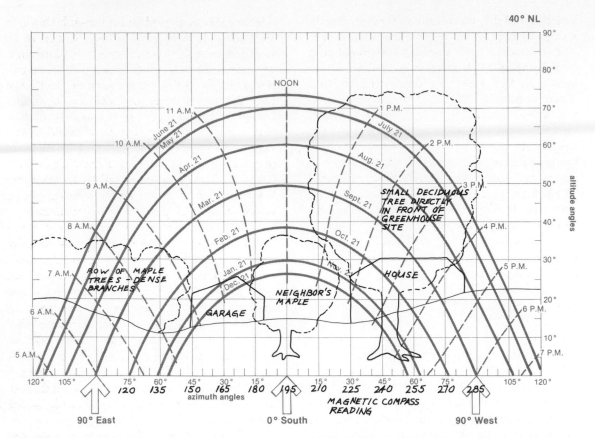

40° NL

Figure 2-4: This solar survey shows a site that is unshaded for a little more than half the day in the winter. The row of trees on the east and the neighbor's buildings don't present any substantial shading, but the small, close-by maple tree on the west will cast a major shadow, even in the winter, since its branches are fairly dense. If the greenhouse could be moved to the east a few feet, or if the tree were cut down, the site would have excellent sun. When the neighbor's maple tree grows, it will someday interfere with midday sun in February and October. Perhaps some agreement should be made with the neighbor to preserve your solar access.

with a weighted string suspended from its center point, as shown in figure 2-3. This simple tool will tell you the altitude angles of the tops of the obstructions. You have to site along the straight edge and carefully read the angle crossed by the string on the face of the protractor. Your compass will tell you the azimuth angle of the obstruction. In order to avoid confusion between true and magnetic south, you can write your compass reading below each of the azimuth angles on the sun path chart before you begin the survey. For example (assuming your compass has 0- to 360-degree markings), if true south is 15 degrees west of magnetic south, true south will be at 195 degrees (whereas magnetic south is 180 degrees on the compass). On the sun path chart you would then write "195" under south, "210" under 15 degrees west, "225" under 30 degrees west, and so on, as shown in figure 2-4. By doing this you can avoid wondering later if you really did compensate correctly.

Since the purpose of the site survey is to predict the amount of sun that will shine into the greenhouse, the survey must be done from where you think the glazing will be. Ideally you should place your eyes in the center of where the main plane of the glazing would be. This is critical if objects shading the site are close by, since moving the greenhouse a few feet up or down or sideways can make the difference between a good site and an obscured one. If all the shadows are cast by distant objects, your exact placement is less critical. If you are planning a tall greenhouse, you may need to sit on a stepladder or look out a second story window to position yourself.

Once you are positioned, find true south (0 degrees azimuth) with your compass. Then site the altitude angle of the horizon, marking this point on the sun path chart. Move along the horizon, siting and marking azimuth and altitude, as far as you can, to the east and west. Then go back and site each object that rises above the horizon. Use dashed lines to indicate the outline of deciduous trees, to indicate their partial shading in winter. If you have more than one possible site, do a survey for each one to find the sunniest spot. Or if it looks like raising the height of the greenhouse will give you additional sun, make a comparison survey from higher up.

Evaluating the Completed Survey

As previously discussed, the critical part of the sun's path for solar heating is the 9:00 A.M. to 3:00 P.M. period (solar time). If this area shows up clear on your survey, you have an excellent site. If it is somewhere around half-obscured, the greenhouse may be able to collect enough heat to take care of itself, but probably won't make any real heat contribution to the house. On sunny winter days it would contribute heat, but then would need a similar amount of back-up heat at night to protect plants. If the site is more than half-obscured, the greenhouse will be a net energy loser, requiring more heat to keep plants warm than it will contribute to the house.

Deciduous trees cast deceptively dense shadows when they are bare of leaves, usually cutting out about 50 percent of the sun's energy. Densely branching trees can cut out even more: 60 to 70 percent blockage is not unusual for maples or other dense trees. In evaluating your site survey, consider that areas shaded by deciduous trees are at least 50 percent shaded. The site shown in the example survey (figure 2-4) falls somewhere between being half-obscured and unshaded. The deciduous tree on the west side is the main culprit.

There are just a few ways to make the best of a shaded site: move the shade, move the greenhouse or adapt your expectations to what you have. If the main shading problem is caused by a single tree or a few trees that are on your property, you can cut them down or have them topped or accept their shading. One objection to cutting trees is losing summer shade, not to mention the aesthetic loss of a tree. If the trees are within 45 degrees of south, they are usually below the sun's path in summer and won't provide summer shading unless they are quite close to the house and rather tall. (You can check this with a solar survey.) These trees will of course shade the yard, which is often no small benefit in the heat of summer. Pruning a tree to gain sun will, obviously, have to be done again every few years, depending on how deeply you prune and how fast the tree grows, but at least you still have the tree. Moving the greenhouse is a choice for some sites, though there is often little choice of appropriate attachments to a house. But it is possible that moving the greenhouse just 5 or 10 feet one way or the other can change a marginal site into a pretty good one. This is particularly true if shifting the site allows you to take advantage of one more hour of sun in the 9:00 A.M. to 3:00 P.M. period.

Sometimes raising the greenhouse up a few feet can improve a marginal site. This could be accomplished by building on a platform or deck rather than directly on the ground. In some cases, it may be necessary to build on the second floor to reach the sun. If this were your situation, you would have to evaluate whether the increased expense is justified. In the example site survey, the greenhouse could be moved to the east (to the left) to get out from under the shadow of the small deciduous tree, or the tree could be cut down. This would give more sun to the greenhouse during the critical afternoon hours. It is now blocked by the tree after about 12:30 P.M., particularly in February, March, September and October. If the greenhouse could be moved to the east enough that the tree were at 60 degrees west azimuth, the early afternoon sun could get to the greenhouse in winter but late afternoon summer sun would be blocked. The right decision depends on if the tree is important for other reasons, and if moving the greenhouse would be desirable or practical.

The other approach is changing your expectations. If, for example, your survey shows good sun all year except for November, December and January, you might decide to use the greenhouse only for solar heating and for a sunspace during whatever sunny hours you have in these months, concentrating your growing efforts during the fall and spring.

One thing to remember is that trees grow. If trees to the south are just below the path of

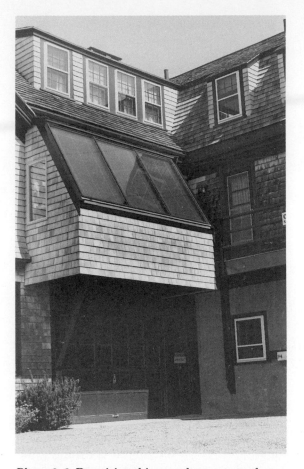

Photo 2–2: By raising this greenhouse up to the second floor, solar access and garage access were both preserved. *(Photo courtesy of WES Contracting, Pocasset, Mass.)*

the sun, within a few years they will be blocking it, unless they are a slow-growing or self-limiting variety that only reaches a certain height. If the trees are on a neighbor's property, the situation is a little sticky if they shade your only possible site. In the example solar survey, the neighbor's maple tree will probably start to shade the greenhouse in February and October in a few years. Only a few states have solar access rights, which protect your right to the sun shining on your greenhouse.

Check with your state energy office for information. But simply talking to your neighbor and reaching some type of agreement that will protect your sunshine is what is needed even if solar access laws are on the books. Perhaps you can provide the pruning to keep the trees down below the sun path. Or perhaps the neighbor would be willing to let you replace existing trees with a short, self-limiting variety that will provide privacy without growing tall enough to shade your greenhouse.

If your view of the sun is dependent on your neighbor's not planting anything in certain areas of his yard, a written agreement may be in order, even if he isn't currently planning to plant anything. It is legally possible for a neighbor to attach your sun rights to his deed, so that if the house is sold, the next owners can't plant a row of fast-growing pines in front of your greenhouse, but this can be complicated and costly. Friendly diplomacy is what is really needed to sort out these kinds of situations.

Your solar survey is also useful in preventing overheating problems in the summer. You can see the number of hours of summer sun that the greenhouse will receive, and plan accordingly. If the greenhouse is in direct sun all afternoon, you may need some type of shading. This subject is covered in detail in "Section II: Designing the Greenhouse."

Microclimate and Terrain

Microclimate is generally defined as the local climate in a small area, as opposed to the overall regional climate. An area bordering a large lake, for example, will have more moderate temperatures than an area farther away. An area that is downwind from the lake will receive more moisture than an upwind zone. In choosing a location for an attached greenhouse, consider microclimate on an even smaller scale: The objective is to place the greenhouse in the most sheltered spot where it will still receive the best sun. In windy areas, a sheltered location will significantly decrease winter heat loss. In very windy places it can even be worth creating a windbreak with trees, hedges or fencelines. The south side of the house naturally has a warmer winter microclimate than other sides. Houses that offer a south-facing nook or corner or that have hedges blocking easterly or westerly winds give you a natural location. Where there are no existing windbreaks, consider the prevailing winter winds. If you are unfamiliar with their direction as they move around your house, you can make them visible by placing a few sticks or poles with ribbons tied on the top at potential greenhouse locations and observing the motion of the ribbons. In warmer climates, it's a good idea to find a location that combines winter wind sheltering with an openness to prevailing summer breezes. This will help keep the greenhouse cool in summer.

As you narrow down your choices for a site, you should look into whether or not there are any underground obstructions. There may be a septic tank, a dry well, water supply or drain lines, underground electric or gas service or other elements that aren't deep enough to be out of the way of foundation work. And you probably don't want to build over something like a septic tank that you might have to get to later on. Your choice for a site may also be affected by the structural condition of the house wall to which the greenhouse would be attached. A greenhouse can exert a pretty substantial load on a house wall, so the wall should be thoroughly checked, especially on older homes, for stud spacing and condition. The walls of older post-and-beam houses, for example, may need revamping to make them ready for a greenhouse because there may be no studs at all.

Locations that have poor drainage should be avoided, unless you can cure the problem or are willing to build the greenhouse up on a platform and let the water run underneath. A waterlogged foundation and floor will rob heat, be a mess and keep the humidity level in the greenhouse higher than it should be. Water or excess moisture in your basement may be an indication of drainage problems. In general, it is best to choose a spot where you will be able to slope the earth away from both the house and greenhouse. If gutters and downspouts from the roof empty at the greenhouse location, these will have to be moved, or the downspouts extended. Sites where groundwater is anywhere near the surface will need to be improved with some kind of drainage technique. But choosing a spot that requires minimal earth work can help keep construction costs down. The details of the various foundation types are covered in chapter 9.

Legal Requirements and Other Considerations

Setbacks from the lot line are a primary consideration in urban or suburban locations. You should always check your local zoning board or building inspector for applicable ordinances. If it turns out that the south side of your house is too close to the lot line it may be possible to build the greenhouse off the east or west end of the house. A site plan showing the size and location of the greenhouse relative to the house and the lot lines is usually required when applying for a building permit. Sometimes you can get a variance from the regulations, if your neighbors don't object, in order to be able to build a little closer to the line.

Building permits are a legal necessity in most cities, towns and counties. These often require a set of drawings, not only including a site plan but also a foundation and floorplan, front and side views, and, in some cases, framing plans, so the inspector can check for structural integrity. It is important that you comply with local building regulations, even if they are more stringent than the ideas given in this book, in order to be sure your insurance will cover the structure. A building inspector can also be a very useful source of information about local building practices, such as choosing a foundation type to match local soil conditions and specifying snow loads on roofs.

Chapter 3

GREENHOUSE COSTS AND BENEFITS

An integral part of planning an attached solar greenhouse is looking at the economics—the costs and the benefits. This chapter first explores all the costs associated with building, maintaining and operating a greenhouse and then looks at the tangible benefits of solar heat, food and plant production, and resale value. With this information we will create a cost/benefit balance sheet that will aid in comparing expenses with income. These cost/benefit estimates will give you a reasonably accurate idea of the overall financial impact of a greenhouse addition, which should help to steer you to the type of greenhouse that best suits your needs and your budget.

You will be able to use the information in this chapter to do a cost/benefit analysis of the greenhouse you actually intend to build. This final round of calculations will require a complete design so that you can do more accurate cost estimating and solar performance calculating. "Section II: Designing the Greenhouse" will help you come up with a design on which to base these more detailed calculations.

In examining the economics of building and owning a greenhouse, you will encounter a lot of ambiguity. There will be some things you will be able to estimate with some degree of certainty, like the construction costs and the amount of solar heat you can expect. Other factors, however, will be less certain. How much will the greenhouse increase the resale value of the house? How much food will you really grow in it? How fast will fuel costs rise in the next few years? Will the rate of inflation be higher or lower than the cost of the money required to build? For these factors you'll have to make some educated guesses that will allow you to look at the long-term costs and benefits of being a greenhouse owner.

And there is a larger question that may well override strong concerns about having a positive cost benefit picture: Should the greenhouse only be valued as a supplier of food, solar heat, tax credits and high resale value? How do you value sitting in the sun, looking out your window at lush greenery or having a supply of fresh, humidified air in the house in midwinter? Some people feel that calculating a payback on a greenhouse is like calculating a payback on the cost of taking a vacation or remodeling a kitchen: There is another level of less tangible, life-enhancing value that would never show up on a balance sheet. This isn't a rationale for making an imprudent investment, but it is something to keep in mind, something that can balance purely economic decision making.

If the economic return question isn't that important for making decisions about your own project, you will still want to know construction costs, and you may want to get at least a rough idea of solar heating performance. This chapter will give you estimates of these and other factors. We'll use as an example a 10-by-16-foot greenhouse for developing estimates. You will also find guidelines for adjusting the costs and benefits of this greenhouse to other sizes that you might choose.

Construction Costs

As table 1-1 shows, greenhouse construction costs can vary greatly. Inexpensive greenhouses can be built with recycled lumber, low-cost glazing material and hardware, and your own labor. At the other extreme, the whole job can be turned over to a professional architect or builder, with orders for complete automation, top-quality materials, tiled floors and planting beds and room for a table with several chairs. Most projects will fall somewhere in the middle, with trade-offs being made between what you'd like and what you can afford. There are also trade-offs between cost and longevity of materials, since cheaper materials often don't last as long and can require more maintenance.

You will have to decide how much automation you can afford. Automatic exhaust venting, automatic transfer of solar heat to the house and automatic back-up heating all

make the job of running the greenhouse much easier, but since they add to the cost, you may choose just one or two automatic features. If you have to leave the greenhouse unattended with plants growing in it, automation for temperature control is usually a necessity.

Another trade-off is between initial cost and resale value. If you want to recoup the cost of the greenhouse when the house is sold, you will probably want the workmanship and materials of the greenhouse to at least match those of the house.

The example 10-by-16-foot greenhouse used for this cost analysis is intended for solar heating and plant growing and also includes a small sitting area. Three versions of this greenhouse will be considered: very low cost, medium cost and relatively high cost. As was discussed in chapter 1, larger and smaller greenhouses will not cost proportionally more or less. For example, a 10-by-32-foot greenhouse would not cost twice as much as our example unit, but might cost 1⅔ to 1¾ times as much. By the same token, an 8-by-10-foot greenhouse might be three-quarters the cost of the example, not half as much.

Table 3-1 describes the three example greenhouses and shows construction costs. Costs are broken down into materials, labor (at $10 per hour) and a total cost for a professional builder to do the job. This contractor price includes 20 percent on top of the price of materials and labor, to reflect the builder's costs in organizing and running the building job. Design fees, such as for an architect or professional designer, are not included. These can range from $100 to $200 for a basic set of drawings, up to $500 for drawings good enough for construction bidding. If supervision by the designer is needed, the cost can go somewhat higher. It is also becoming more common for contractors to offer design services.

The costs in the table represent the middle of a range, since materials and labor costs vary so much from place to place. These ranges are shown in parentheses below the various materials, labor and total contracted costs that are listed. They are expressed in terms of cost per square foot of greenhouse floor area, which allows you to make your own estimates for different size greenhouses. The lower end of the range is appropriate for lower-cost labor and materials and for larger sizes; the higher end for higher-cost materials and labor and for smaller sizes. The wide range in the hours of labor required reflects varying experience and skills, both in actual carpentry and in running the building project.

When looking at the top end of the cost range, note that the highest-cost example shown is not necessarily the maximum that you could spend. A fancy structure with tile floors, growing beds and a hot tub can easily cost over $100 per square foot. Note also that if you are estimating the cost of a greenhouse not intended for any plant growing, your costs will be less, since some features associated with keeping the indoor climate appropriate for plants are not required. Remember when using this chart that costs are for 1983 and don't include any sales tax, and that the cost of building materials tends to inflate faster than the general rate of inflation.

To estimate what your greenhouse will cost to build, you have to decide about its size. Until you have gone through "Section II: Designing the Greenhouse" and have determined more closely the right size for your greenhouse, you can use the guidelines from chapter 1: 100 to 150 square feet of floor area for small plant-growing ambitions and minimal solar heating; 150 to 200 square feet for more growing and slightly more solar heating; or 20 percent of the floor area of your house for more serious solar heating, assuming that your house is well insulated and tight.

If the greenhouse size is to be based on the area required for growing vegetables, you can figure on needing 20 to 40 square feet of growing area per person. Often the growing area in attached greenhouses is 50 or 60 percent of the floor area, if you want to leave some space for sitting. For this round of estimating size and cost, figure 50 square feet of floor area (growing area plus walkways and sitting area) per person if you want to grow vegetables through all or most of the year.

As an example, let's estimate the construction cost for a medium-priced greenhouse that will be used for solar heating and for extensive winter vegetable growing. Even though the medium price range cuts out some features, there is still some automation and double-glass glazing, the latter for a clear view out and to minimize maintenance. The house has 1,000 square feet of floor area and isn't well insulated. Only *after* insulating the house should a greenhouse be built with any intention of solar heating; so the first step will be insulating and tightening up the house. In sizing for solar heating, 20 percent of the floor area is 200 square feet ($1,000 \times 0.20 = 200$). There are four people in the family, so there will be adequate growing area for vegetables, based on the rule of thumb of 50 square feet of floor area per person. The medium-priced greenhouse could be built for about $15 per square foot for materials, or $3,000, plus $9 per square foot for labor, or about $1,800 labor, for a total of $4,800 ($24 per square foot). The cost could be trimmed with less expensive materials and with the owner providing some of the labor. The lower end of the materials cost range is $10 per square foot, so the lowest materials price would be about $2,000. If you supplied half the labor, using a skilled greenhouse builder only for those parts of the construction with which you are not familiar, the labor might be around $1,000, for a total cost of $3,000.

TABLE 3-1: TYPICAL GREENHOUSE CONSTRUCTION COSTS

COST RANGE	MATERIALS	FOUNDATION/ FLOOR	GLAZING	GROWING AREA
Low	Recycled lumber; other materials new but low cost	Treated wood-post foundation; dirt floor with gravel paths	Polyethylene; 1- to 2-year life span	Growing beds in ground, or of recycled lumber; free soil mixture of locally available soil, manure, sand and compost
Medium	Low and moderate cost new materials	Post, pier or continuous concrete block foundation; gravel floor	Fiberglass with inner polyethylene layer; outer layer 5- to 10-year life span, inner 2 to 5 year; glass where standard sizes fit	Aboveground beds of new materials; soil mixture materials purchased and delivered
High	All new, top-quality materials	Continuous poured concrete foundation; slab floor	All glass; 10- to 20-year life span	Aboveground beds of new materials; soil mixture materials purchased and delivered

NOTE: *The construction costs are 1983 prices and include everything you will need, short of seeds, a watering hose and gardening tools.*

*Figured at $10 per hour.

†Labor varies quite a bit depending on condition of recycled materials.

Zeroing In on Construction Costs

When you get close to actually building your greenhouse, you will doubtless want as precise an estimate of costs as possible. There is nothing more discouraging then getting halfway into a construction project and running out of money. With some careful planning this can be avoided. Of course, there will always be some unforeseen costs during construction, but we will add a "contingency fund" to the final estimate to take care of them. If you have never estimated the materials used in a building project before, you may want to take your completed plans and mate-

LEVEL OF AUTOMATION	TYPICAL CONSTRUCTION COSTS FOR 10-BY-16-FOOT GREENHOUSE		
	MATERIALS ($)	LABOR* ($)	CONTRACTOR BUILT ($)
All manual: Open doors/windows to house for *solar heat* from greenhouse on sunny winter days Open doors/windows for *back-up heat* for greenhouse on cold nights Open manual vents and outside door for *summer cooling*	600 (4 to 8 per ft²)	Usually owner built; 1,000 for hired labor (50 to 200 hours)†	
Some manual, some automatic: Open doors/windows to house for *solar heat* from greenhouse on sunny winter days Open doors/windows plus automatic heater for *back-up heat* Open manual vents plus automatic fan for *summer cooling*	2,500 (10 to 20 per ft²)	1,500 (6 to 12 per ft²) (100 to 200 hours)	5,400 (20 to 40 per ft²)
All automatic: Open doors/windows plus automatic fan for *solar heat* Open doors/windows plus automatic fan plus automatic heater for *back-up heat* Automatically operated vents for *summer cooling*	4,100 (20 to 35 per ft²)	3,600 (12 to 50 per ft²) (200 to 400 hours)	9,200 (40 to 100 per ft²)

rials list to an experienced greenhouse builder or designer for review. Another way to check your estimate is to compare your list with the materials list in a set of commercially available plans. (The plans listed in Appendix 2 indicate which include materials lists.)

To estimate the materials cost, you begin by counting up literally every piece that goes into the greenhouse, which means that you'll need a complete design. The procedure for using the information in this book to develop a confidence-inspiring estimate goes something like this:

Read through "Section II: Designing the Greenhouse" and follow the procedures outlined there to develop a size and shape for

TABLE 3-2: SAMPLE COMPONENT MATERIALS LIST: GLAZING

MATERIAL	WHERE USED	QUANTITY	SIZE
Filon shiplap-type glass fiber-reinforced polyester glazing	Roof and walls	5	4' 6⁵/₁₆" × 14' 4" (covers about 4' 2" × 14')
Filon vertical closure strips	To seal stepped edges of Filon	15	36"
Horizontal closure strips	To seal straight edges	12	36"
Gasketed aluminum ring-shank nails	To attach Filon to rafters	1 box of 500	1¼" length
Silicone sealant	To seal edges and joints	5 tubes	standard size
Drip edge	East and west edges of roof glazing	2	8'
1 × 4 trim	To cover top of vertical glazing on east and west sides	2	8'
1 × 3 strapping	To shim out 1 × 4 trim	2	8'
Aluminum flashing	Between house siding and top glazing	1	16' × 1'
Pop-rivets	To seal unsupported horizontal glazing joints	1 box of 100	⅛" × ½"
Back-up washers for pop-rivets	Same as above	1 box of 100	for ⅛" rivets

NOTE: *This component materials list is used to take materials quantities from sketches of each component of the greenhouse. This example shows the glazing materials for a Filon (glass fiber-reinforced plastic) glazing system, a moderate- to low-cost glazing. "Shiplap-type" refers to a particular corrugation pattern.*

your greenhouse. As you go through that section, you will also be making choices about the type of venting, house/greenhouse air exchange and back-up heating systems that you want.

Consult "Section III: Construction Detailing," which involves designing all the components of the greenhouse. This will include the foundation, framing, glazing, vents, fans, floor, growing areas, heat storage,

TABLE 3-3: SAMPLE MASTER MATERIALS LIST

MATERIAL	SIZE (linear ft)	QUANTITY	SOURCE*	UNIT PRICE ($)	TOTAL PRICE† ($)
4 × 4, pressure treated	12	5	Brewster Harris	7.68 8.27	38.40
2 × 4, pressure treated (1 for growing beds)	16	2	Harris Grossman Brewster	5.65 4.75 5.75	9.50
2 × 6, pressure treated (for growing beds)	12 10	12 4	Brewster Brewster	4.14 3.45	49.68 13.80
1 × 4, pressure treated (special order, Harris only)	12	3	Harris	2.26	6.78
2 × 6 (Use Harris: can choose pieces)	12 8	1 1	Brewster Harris Harris	4.14 5.25 3.25	5.25 3.25
2 × 4	12 10	11 6	Brewster Harris Brewster	2.76 3.00 2.30	30.36 13.80
1 × 4 (5 of these for ripping down into ³/₄" stops)	12	11	Brewster Harris	1.99 2.23	21.89

NOTE: *The master list is used for obtaining prices from materials suppliers and for your actual shopping list. The materials, sizes and quantities are a collection of all the materials in the various component materials lists. For example, lumber would come from component lists for framing, glazing (for stops or shims), growing beds, solid walls and roof, and foundation. Hardware would come from vents, doors and glazing, and would include nails and screws from just about every component list. This example is part of a lumber list for a greenhouse using a pressure-treated wood-post foundation system. Where a material's use is not obvious—for example, using a 1 × 4 to rip down into ³/₄-inch square window stops—it is a good idea to note what the material is for, so a proper grade can be chosen. Materials for parts of the greenhouse that might not get built right away—growing beds in this example—can be noted so that these costs can be separated from the total initial cost. By leaving space for three sources, you can compare prices. The "Total Price," (unit price times quantity) is listed only for the chosen supplier.*

The names Brewster, Harris and Grossman are used here as examples. They do not refer to actual companies.

†Generally the lowest cost source. Sometimes the needed quality is worth a premium.

back-up heating and the connection to the house. For each of these components, you will develop a set of sketches, showing all the materials and how they go together. (This task may seem like a tall order at first glance, but when you get to "Section III: Construction Detailing," you'll see how it all breaks down into various parts and components.)

From the component sketches, you will develop a list of the materials required, and this is where the counting begins. A typical listing for materials for one of these components is shown in table 3-2. You will also list any labor that you may have to subcontract, such as foundation digging and electrical or plumbing work.

Consolidate all the materials lists into a master materials list that separates lumber, hardware, glazing materials, insulation, soil and gravel, windows and doors, fans and other equipment. An example of a master list is shown in table 3-3.

Contact suppliers for prices using the master list to obtain prices. You would be wise to obtain prices from two or three suppliers. On big items, you can ask the suppliers how long they will hold a particular price for you. Make written notes of all pricing conversations, including people's names and the date. And its's always a good idea to shop around for both quality and price. You may even find that discounts can be had for the asking, especially if you present yourself as "Jones Builders" rather than "Bob Jones." It will always be important to get actual prices for the more expensive items, such as glazing and lumber. If your estimate is 50 percent low on $40 worth of nails, it is no catastrophe, but if it is even 20 percent low on $700 worth of glazing you won't be pleased.

Add up all the figures and add a contingency fund to take care of the unknowns that you are bound to encounter. These can include anything from lumber store price increases to unearthing a rotten sill on the house when you go to attach the greenhouse framing. A minimum contingency fund, if you are confident in your estimate, is 20 percent of the total. If you are a novice estimator and you don't have any experienced eyes looking over your shoulder, it might be a good idea to increase the percentage, but it would be a very good idea to have the estimate checked by a professional. Many people do careful estimates and then double the total. A contingency fund can be thought of as money that you don't really want to spend, but that won't upset you if you have to.

Labor estimates involve somewhat more uncertainty than materials estimates. About the best you can do is to take the set of sketches for each component and work through the construction process in your mind, step by step. List all the steps, in order, and how long each will take (see table 3-4). Some steps will require two people, such as installing big double-glass units or lifting up framing. Note the number of people required for each step, especially if you are hiring help, so that you can plan a schedule. If you are planning to hire a carpenter to work with you, consult with him over your drawings and lists.

Don't be discouraged by the time involved or by the piles of paper that this process will generate. It is well worth the effort to have confidence in your design, materials list and cost estimates. It is, of course, quite easy and inexpensive to change the design while the greenhouse is still on paper, but it can be difficult and expensive once you've begun building.

Photo 3-1: The labor required to build this greenhouse is detailed in table 3-4.

TABLE 3-4: SAMPLE LABOR ESTIMATE

Task	Labor Required (person-days)	Task	Labor Required (person-days)
Demolish small porch over back door	1	Install both vents (2 people, 1 day)	2
Foundation		Install vent openers	1
Digging for foundation and pouring concrete subcontracted out ($1,100)—allow 2 weeks for completion; install foundation insulation, flashing and rigid insulation covering; smooth out backfill after backhoe done (2 people for 1 day)	2	Exterior exhaust fan	
		Install fan and intake shutter	0.5
		Build and install insulated doors for fan and intake	1.5
		Heat exchange fan	
		Cut holes in wall for fan and return	0.5
		Build backdraft damper for return	0.25
Framing		Install fan and damper	1
Install sill and ledger plates (2 people, 1.5 days)	3	Make foam push-in plugs for fan and return	0.25
Make preformed trusses (2 people, 1.5 days)	3	Hang exterior door and trim (prehung door and screen door)	0.5
Install trusses, brace and block (2 people, 2 days)	4	Electrical	
Frame endwalls	2	Install 1 track light, 2 outlets and wire fans	2
Frame curb for roof vents	1	Plumbing	
Sheathing and siding		Install 1 hose bib	0.5
Sheath and side solid walls and roof	0.5	Final trim	
		Interior trim	1
Install insulation and vapor barrier	0.5	Exterior trim	2
Glazing		Paint	
		Paint frame before glazing (1 primer and 2 finish coats, each separated by 48 hours)	1.5
Pick up and deliver glass, Exolite and hardware	1		
Install glass support hardware	1	Finish exterior painting after greenhouse completed (same 3 coats)	1.5
Install glass (2 people, 1.5 days)	3	Build growing bed(s)	2
Install Exolite hardware	0.5	Install heat storage	
Install Exolite (2 people, 0.5 day)	1	Gather barrels	1
Exterior vents		Clean	0.25
Make flashing	0.5	Install	0.25
Build upper solid vent	1	Fill (while doing other things)	0.25
Build lower glazed vent	1	Total	45.75 days

NOTE: *The labor estimate is made by mentally going through each stage of construction and estimating how long each will take. Consult with any carpenter or subcontractor that you may hire for estimates of their time or to help you check estimates of your time. This example is for a 10-by-21-foot greenhouse with a poured concrete foundation, concrete slab floor, preformed truss framing, combined Exolite and double-glass glazing. The labor estimates, for the Kitchell greenhouse shown in photo 3-2, are for two experienced carpenters.*

If you are going to hire a professional to build the greenhouse for you, he or she will do all the estimating. The amount of designing you do and the amount the builder does will depend on the agreement you both reach. You can use this book to develop an overall size, shape and design that you can turn over to the builder for detailing. In fact, the builder may be interested in looking at some of the construction detailing in "Section III: Construction Detailing." You may want to work out all the details yourself, but be prepared for some give and take with an experienced builder, as he or she will probably have ideas about how the greenhouse should be built, based on experience. An experienced builder can work with you to develop a final design or to modify your plans to keep them within your budget. If you get an estimate from a builder, but then decide to build it yourself, you will need to reestimate the materials costs, since the builder may have access to materials at below retail prices.

Manufactured Greenhouses

In recent years there has been a surge in prefabricated attached greenhouses and sunspaces. The costs for these units vary almost as much as on-site building costs, depending on the type and quality of materials used. Some are made of high-grade aluminum extrusions with baked on enamel finishes and sealed double-glass glazing and have such visual amenities as curved eaves, while others are made with lower-cost framing and glazings. The ultimate cost also depends on how much of the finished greenhouse is actually provided by the manufacturer. Some packages are available with everything short of the foundation and the growing beds and soil, while others include only those pieces of the structure that would be difficult to fabricate

Photo 3-2: The clean, aesthetic finish details are attractive features of many prefabricated greenhouses. *(Photo courtesy of Lindahl Cedar Homes.)*

on site, or to find locally. Virtually all manufactured greenhouse packages don't include floors or foundations, but that is about the only generality you can make. If you look into prefabricated units, check carefully to see just what is and what isn't included. Installation costs will, of course, be in addition to the cost of the unit, and that cost also varies quite a bit. Some brands are sold directly from the factory to the retail customer, while other manufacturers have established dealer/installer networks. Appendix 2 lists numerous sources for manufactured greenhouses.

Manufactured greenhouses have the following advantages. They are:
• ready to be quickly installed over a prepared foundation
• often very good looking
• low in maintenance if the framing is aluminum
• available in a variety of lengths, widths, heights, and roof slopes

There are often some serious disadvantages. Manufactured greenhouses:

- don't always meet the exact requirements of a particular site
- are frequently designed with the luxury market in mind
- sometimes have inadequate venting and therefore require excessive use of fans
- can be inappropriate for the aesthetics of your house
- are not always energy efficient
- often are designed for only horticulture *or* solar heating, rather than a combination of the two
- usually are higher in cost than site-built greenhouses
- are very high in heat loss if they have aluminum framing without thermal breaks

In general, the important features to look for in a manufactured greenhouse are the same as the ones you would include in a site-built unit:

- A unit with the overall shape and slope to meet your solar heating needs, to fit the available space on your house and to make a good architectural blend with the look of your house
- Adequate overhead glazing for plant growing, if you're planning for a primarily horticultural greenhouse
- Adequately sized and properly placed vents for good ventilation
- Energy-conserving construction features and details
- Good installation instructions and factory or dealer support; a good indication of both of these is to ask the manufacturer to send you a copy of the installation instructions before you buy

All of these design features are discussed in detail (with regard to site-built greenhouses) in "Section II: Designing the Greenhouse."

To obtain a realistic estimate of the *installed* cost of a kit, the foundation, floor and whatever else isn't included must be added onto the kit price. The costs for a delivered package of materials vary from under $10 per square foot of floor area to $80. The lowest-cost models are mostly single glazed, or are built of low-cost materials. The final installed cost, including things like a floor, growing beds or benches, a door into the house, and so forth, can range from $15 to over $100 per square foot.

Operating Costs

Once the greenhouse is built there will be some ongoing costs for maintenance, increased property taxes and insurance, purchasing plant-growing supplies, and, if you have fans or a back-up heater, the cost of electricity or other fuel.

When the right materials are used, the maintenance of a solar greenhouse is similar to that for the rest of the house, but it is even more important that the integrity of the greenhouse skin be kept intact. Air leaks through worn-out weather stripping or other seals will waste valuable solar heat and will needlessly cool down the greenhouse. If the first rule of solar construction is "build it tight," the second is "keep it tight." All caulking and weather stripping should be checked every fall to be sure that the greenhouse will be tight for the winter.

In general, exterior restaining or resealing (paint is not recommended for the exterior) will be needed about as often as it's needed on the rest of the house, although greenhouse finishes and caulking may deteriorate faster because they are exposed to so much sunlight. Interior repainting will probably be required more frequently in a plant-growing greenhouse than in the house, unless a very good quality, washable paint is used.

Plant-growing greenhouses are usually painted white (or at least light colored) inside to maximize reflected light for the plants. The moist environment tends to deteriorate some paints faster, and with the white paint, the deterioration is more noticeable. When the paint grays, the light level to the plants is decreased.

Your property taxes may or may not be increased by the addition of a solar greenhouse. Many states exclude solar heating equipment from both sales and property taxes. The definition of solar heating equipment varies from state to state, so you should check with your state energy and tax offices for the exact rules. Homeowners' insurance will probably not cover your greenhouse without an increase in the premium, so check with your insurance agent.

The amount of back-up fuel required to keep the desired winter temperatures at night and during cloudy spells will vary quite a bit with climate and the sunniness of the site, with how tightly the shell is built and with the way you operate the greenhouse. Unless the greenhouse is shaded or is kept very warm all winter, back-up heating energy use should be small. If the greenhouse is not used for growing plants during midwinter, back-up energy use will be even less. In order to simplify our look at solar greenhouse economics, back-up energy use has already been subtracted from the total solar heat delivery to the house. The solar contribution is thus a net contribution. For example, where a savings of 100 gallons of fuel oil is predicted, the equivalent of 150 gallons' worth of solar heat may actually have been transferred to the house, but 50 gallons' worth was needed to keep the greenhouse warm on cold winter nights.

Some electricity is required to run any fans that you may have, which exchange air between the house and the greenhouse and exhaust hot air to the outdoors in summer. Unless the exhaust fan runs all summer (which it shouldn't if you have adequate vents and shading), the increased energy use will be unnoticeable on your electric bill, adding up to about $10 per year.

If growing plants is an ongoing project in the greenhouse, there will be expenses for supplies, including seeds, fertilizers and other soil amendments, pest control products, tools and pots. The cost of these will vary with your involvement in growing plants and with the availability of free resources. In some places many of the ingredients of a good soil mix or a good natural fertilizer are available for the hauling. There are lots of wonderful greenhouse tools you can buy: some are essential, some save time and some are just fun gadgets. You will have to spend a small amount every year for supplies, around $20 to $30, but you can keep this figure to a minimum if you need to. For example, seed from nonhybrids can be saved from year to year. The greenhouse horticulture books listed in the bibliography (see Further Reading) have hints for keeping operating costs down.

A Multitude of Benefits

The primary ongoing benefits from a greenhouse are solar heat and food, to the extent that you use the greenhouse for food production. Of these two benefits of greenhouse ownership, the solar heat contributed to the house will usually be of greater financial value. To get a reasonable estimate of this benefit, we will use this general rule of thumb: *The greenhouse will contribute the equivalent of 1 gallon of fuel oil during the heating season for each square foot of south-facing glazing.* In sunnier, colder climates, the heat contributed may be 20 to 40 percent greater, or 1.2 to 1.4 gallons saved per square foot of glazing. In cloudier, warmer climates, where there are fewer months in the heating season and less sunshine in those months, the heat contribution may be 20 to 40 percent lower providing a savings of 0.6 to 0.8 gallons. In "Section II: Designing the Greenhouse," we will develop a more precise method for estimating the value of the heat, based on your climate, house, the greenhouse design and how you use the greenhouse. But for now this rule of thumb will be sufficient.

This general rule of thumb assumes that the greenhouse faces within 30 degrees of south, that it isn't shaded at all during the winter and that all of the solar heat transferred to the house is "useful" heat. If, for example, the house already has a lot of south-facing windows to heat part of the house on a sunny winter day, the heat from the greenhouse won't all be useful. Or if the greenhouse has so much south-facing glass that it contributes more heat than the house can use, then some of the solar heat is wasted if it can't be stored in an added heat storage component. The rule of thumb also assumes that the greenhouse is kept just above freezing in midwinter, rather than at some higher temperature. In the design section we will deal with these factors in more detail. For now we'll assume that a properly sized, properly oriented greenhouse is attached to a house that is caulked, weather-stripped and insulated.

How much solar heat you get from your greenhouse depends strongly on how you operate it. If you are growing plants that require high nighttime temperatures, a good bit of the solar heat collected during the day will be needed to keep the greenhouse at the desired temperature at night. Growing orchids all winter in Vermont might take more heat than the greenhouse can collect. On the other hand, if only cold-hardy crops are grown during the colder months, energy use for back-up heating will be much less. Many people find that operating the greenhouse to grow anything during the midwinter months (mid-December through February) in cold, cloudy climates takes more heat than the produce is actually worth. Consequently, they use the greenhouse only as a solar heater during this time, growing nothing and supplying only enough back-up heat to keep any water containers in the greenhouse from freezing. The general rule of thumb assumes that the greenhouse isn't used for growing during midwinter in cold climates (with over 6,000 degree-days), except where winters are very sunny, such as in the southwest United States.

As an example, take the 10-by-16-foot greenhouse used in the cost estimating discussion. We'll assume that it has 150 square feet of south-facing glazing, which means it will contribute the heating equivalent of about 150 gallons of fuel oil worth about $150. If you don't use oil, table 3–5 shows how to convert this to equivalent amounts of other fuels. For example, if you use natural gas for heating, each square foot of south-facing greenhouse glazing will contribute the same amount of heat as 1.4 therms or 0.14 thousand cubic feet (mcf) of natural gas.

These figures can be adjusted based on the efficiency of your heating system. The efficiency of old, untuned heating systems can be as low as 50 percent, while older tuned up systems will be between 60 and 70 percent. Some of the new high-efficiency systems will be as high as 80 to 90 percent. Consult your heating fuel dealer for an estimate of your heating system efficiency.

For efficiencies other than those listed in table 3-5, the fuel saved by each square foot of south-facing greenhouse glazing is equal to the listed efficiency divided by your actual efficiency times the listed fuel savings per square foot of glazing.

$$\frac{\text{listed efficiency}}{\text{actual efficiency}} \times \begin{array}{c}\text{listed fuel savings per ft}^2\\\text{of glazing}\end{array}$$

= savings per ft² of south-facing glazing

For example, if you have an old gas furnace that operates at 60 percent efficiency, the fuel savings would be:

(70% ÷ 60%) × 1.4 therms = 1.6 therms gas

Note that the lower the efficiency of your heating system, the more fuel will be displaced by solar heat.

Food and Plants

The value of the food grown in the greenhouse depends on several factors. For one thing, it takes some time to get the hang of growing plants in a greenhouse, so it might be a year or two before you get maximum yields. How much will these yields be worth? If you manage your greenhouse organically, you will be growing "premium price" food. Would you have actually paid this premium price for organic produce or would you have gone to the supermarket and bought lower-cost, "nonorganic" produce? Will you grow food all year or let the greenhouse lie fallow in midwinter, using it only as a solar heater during that time? How many starter seedlings will you grow for outdoor gardening? In colder climates, where food can't be grown outdoors for a large part of the year, greenhouse food production can go on for much of the year, bringing in a larger return than in warmer climates. In cold climates the greenhouse will allow you to grow fruits and vegetables (such as tomatoes, melons, eggplants, peppers) you couldn't grow or wouldn't buy otherwise.

The many variables associated with food production make food output and value less certain than heat output and value, but it is

TABLE 3-5: FUEL SAVINGS PER SQUARE FOOT OF GREENHOUSE GLAZING

FUEL	AMOUNT	ASSUMED DELIVERED PERCENTAGE OF HEATING VALUE OF FUEL
Oil	1 gal	70
Electricity	29 kwh	100
Gas	0.14 mcf	70
Gas	1.4 therms	70
Propane	1.6 gal	70
Propane	0.06 mcf	70
Propane	6.6 lbs	70
Seasoned hardwood	0.01 cords	50

NOTE: *The heat delivered from 1 square foot of south-facing greenhouse glazing is equivalent to the heat delivered by the quantity of fuels listed above.*

nevertheless possible to make a reasonable estimate of what you can expect to grow and what that produce will be worth. Based on yield data taken from several solar greenhouses, including a greenhouse at the Rodale Research Center and several home greenhouses in New England, the following annual yields are possible:

• Vegetable yields: 1 to 2½ or 3 pounds per square foot of growing bed; includes greens and other vegetables, as well as fruits such as tomatoes and cucumbers

• Seedlings: 2 to 8 seedlings per square foot of growing area

Vegetable yields will depend, to a large extent, on your desires and goals for productivity. If you put in the time and effort to learn the ins and outs of growing plants in a greenhouse, and you keep up good plant maintenance practices, you will be able to achieve the higher yields. If you grow plants year-round, the yield may go as high as 3 pounds per square foot. If the greenhouse is dormant during midwinter or midsummer, the yields could still go as high as 2 or 2½ pounds per square foot of growing area.

Seedling yields can be pretty high, even in a small greenhouse, since they don't take up much space. They can be grown on benches, on top of growing beds, on shelves or in just about any unoccupied corner. Since seedlings are rather expensive to buy— usually a dollar or more for a six-pack—it is worthwhile to grow as many as you, and your friends, can use. In terms of space requirements, it isn't difficult to grow 1,000 seedlings in a 10-by-24-foot greenhouse.

Yields will also depend on your needs. Some people simply don't use much produce or don't have the time or inclination to grow it. If you want to use much of the floor area as a living space, the growing area will of course be limited. If you want to use the growing areas for house plants or flowers, it is difficult to assign these economic value.

As an example, let's use again the 160-square-foot greenhouse. Let's say that 80 square feet, half the floor area, is devoted to growing beds for vegetables and fruits, leaving 80 square feet for an ample sunspace. In the spring, shelves and temporary tables are used for raising seedlings. The greenhouse isn't used for growing plants in midwinter, but is intensively used the rest of the year. Assume an annual yield of 2 pounds per square foot for a total of 160 pounds. Valuing the produce conservatively at $0.50 per pound, this yield is worth $80.00. We'll also assume that 400 seedlings are grown. Valuing these at 6 for $1.00, 400 seedings are worth $67.00. Thus the value of the total yield is about $150.00 per year.

These values will of course have to be adjusted if you work up a projection for your greenhouse. Perhaps you don't have an out-

Photo 3-3: For many people, year-round or extended season food production is the most important feature of a solar greenhouse. *(Photo courtesy of Rodale Press Photography Department.)*

side garden, so you won't be growing seed-lings, but you would grow more produce year-round. Or perhaps you will concentrate on growing vegetables and fruits with higher economic values, such as herbs or European cucumbers. Perhaps you will grow house-plants and flowers, which you would other-wise be buying. Or perhaps you can sell seed-lings out of your greenhouse. The possibilities are many, but it will be useful to make projections if greenhouse gardening is your goal and you want to see an economic return from your greenhouse investment. Remember that these savings don't reflect the time you have to put in to get back the yields.

Tax Incentives

Unfortunately, the federal Internal Revenue Service (IRS) specifically excludes greenhouses from the 40 percent renewable energy tax credit (40 percent of the cost of qualifying systems is subtracted from your tax bill), because the greenhouse is said to serve a dual purpose—solar heating and growing plants, or solar heating and a living space. The credit typically applies only to solar heating systems consisting of a solar collection area, an absorber, a storage mass, a heat distribution method and heat regulating devices. Dual-purpose elements of the system are specifically excluded. (Clearly the IRS does not embrace the wisdom of using some-thing for two purposes.) You may be able to successfully argue that some components of a solar greenhouse, such as a fan and controls for distributing solar heat to the house, have the required single purpose. Or, if the green-house is actually used *only* as a solar heating system, you can write the IRS about your circumstances and request a "private ruling." Many kit manufacturers claim that you can get the full federal tax credit for their kit, but this can be misleading, if not untrue.

State tax incentives include credits and other benefits, so it is worth checking with your state energy office for details. Some states allow a tax credit on any solar green-house; others have certain requirements that must be met for the structure to be eligible for the credit. Vermont, for example, requires night insulation with a combined glazing and insulation value of R-4. Some states have sales tax rebates for solar heating equipment, in which the state reimburses you for sales tax on solar-heating-related materials. Some states, counties and municipalities also exclude solar equipment from property taxes, meaning that the town or county can't raise your property taxes because of the addition of a solar greenhouse. Many tax incentives are changing or are soon to expire, so check on the expiration date as well as the details. It is hoped that both federal and state incentives will be continued at least through this decade.

Resale Value

The value that an attached solar green-house adds to your house is often underrated. Assuming that you will sell your house at some point, the greenhouse can be thought of as a real-estate investment, similar to the increased value, for example, that an extra room would add to your house. How much value the greenhouse will add is hard to quantify, since it depends on so many factors. The quality of construction and design are two important factors. For best resale value, the greenhouse should fit in as well as possible with the house, with matching siding and color, and with matching trim and detailing, such as door and window styles.

A major factor affecting the resale value of the greenhouse is the value of your house relative to the going prices in the neighbor-hood. If you have a $65,000 house in a neighborhood of $50,000 houses, you may have difficulty selling the house for its full value, let alone increase the selling price by adding a greenhouse. On the other hand, if your house is undervalued for the neighborhood, it is much more likely that the greenhouse will increase the selling price of the house.

A greenhouse that either includes living space or that can be rearranged to include living space will probably have the broadest appeal to buyers. If the greenhouse supplies a significant amount of solar heat to the house, and it does so automatically, with fans or automatic vents, this will also appeal to many buyers. Documenting your fuel use before and after the greenhouse was built will help prove to prospective buyers that the greenhouse actually saves fuel. Ease of maintenance, durability of materials and glass glazing are preferable features for increasing the resale value.

A Sample Cost/Benefit Analysis

Now that we've looked at the individual costs and the benefits that can be quantified, we'll do a cost/benefit analysis based on the 10-by-16-foot greenhouse used in the discussion of construction costs. Table 3-6 summarizes this analysis. For our example greenhouse, let's work with a ten-year time frame. The assumption is that the house is sold at the end of ten years, but even if it isn't, the greenhouse is considered to be worth the resale value at that time. So the resale value is counted as a return, even if you don't actually sell at that time. All three construction cost levels (the same as those in table 3-1) are included in the analysis, so you can see the strong effect of construction cost on the final balance between cost and return.

This analysis is based on the economics of a greenhouse as a choice between putting your money in the bank or in the greenhouse. You add up the present value of the returns, including the resale value, and subtract the present value of the costs, to get the *net present value* (see table 3-6 note for a definition of net present value). The result tells you the financial difference between building the greenhouse and leaving your money in the bank. A positive net present value tells you how much more the greenhouse is worth to you than leaving the money in the bank. A negative net present value shows you what the greenhouse is costing you (or how much you have to otherwise justify its existence on aesthetics, pleasure or increased living space).

What do the numbers in table 3-6 tell us? One way to interpret the projection is to look at the net present value versus the present value of costs. For the low-cost greenhouse, you'd put $842 into the greenhouse for a net present value of $1,713, more than doubling your money. This is clearly a very good return. The fact of the matter is that very low cost owner-built greenhouses really are a great investment, particularly if you don't count your labor as a cost. The medium-cost greenhouse has a net present value of $573 for the $5,654 cost, profitable, though at a much lower rate. The high-cost unit shows a net present *cost* of $641 for the more than $9,000 present value of the costs. Financially speaking, you'd be better off to leave your money in the bank. But note that we have taken a somewhat conservative resale value, assuming the greenhouse did not appreciate in value along with the house. It might also be possible, in some states, to take a higher tax credit. As it stands now, the loss is small enough that only a minor change in the projection will change the outcome from a loss to a break even or a profit. And a break-even proposition is by no means undesirable for a building addition that also gives you a place to grow the freshest of food and flowers, not to mention sunbathing. You just can't get these from a nonsolar addition, or from leaving your money in the bank.

TABLE 3-6: SAMPLE COST/BENEFIT PROJECTION (Time Frame: 10 Years)

Costs	Greenhouse Cost Range			Comments
	Low ($)	Medium ($)	High ($)	
Construction (one time)	(600)	(5,400)	(9,200)	These are the same costs in table 3-1; the low-cost figure doesn't include labor costs, since the greenhouse is assumed to be owner built
Tax credit* (one time)	(60)	(540)	(920)	Assumes that a 10% state tax credit is taken, but no federal tax credit
Net construction cost (one time)	540	4,860	8,280	Construction cost after tax credit; this figure is used in subsequent calculations
Maintenance (ongoing)	151	189	189	Low-cost maintenance is materials cost for annual new glazing: $20 per year; medium and high include labor but maintenance is needed much less frequently: $25 per year; the figure shown is the *present value* of the 10 years of maintenance costs, as explained in the text
Property taxes (ongoing)	0	189	378	In some states, property taxes are waived for solar property; here it's assumed that taxes don't go up for the low-cost greenhouse, which is assumed to have no value in the assessor's eyes, up $25 per year for the medium and $50 per year for the high-cost unit; present value of the cost is shown
Insurance (ongoing)	0	189	378	We assume no increase in insurance for the low cost, $25 per year increase for the medium, and $50 per year increase for the high-cost unit; present value is shown
Electricity (ongoing)	0	76	76	This is the present value of the $10 annual energy cost to operate fans; the low-cost greenhouse has no fans
Growing supplies (ongoing)	151	151	151	Present value of cost of seeds, fertilizer, tools, pest remedies: $20 per year
Total	842	5,654	9,452	Present cost for 10 years of operation; total of above costs

For the purposes of this example, a 10 percent state tax credit but no federal credit is assumed, so the net cost is 10 percent less than the actual construction cost.

RETURNS	GREENHOUSE COST RANGE			COMMENTS
	LOW ($)	MEDIUM ($)	HIGH ($)	
Solar heat† (ongoing)	1,421	1,421	1,421	150 gallons of fuel oil at $1.25 per gallon = $188 annual return; assumes some back-up heat for plants except in midwinter; $1,421 is the *present value* of 10 years of savings
Food production (ongoing)	1,134	1,134	1,134	Season-extension food growing and seedling harvest, with $150 annual return, as discussed in text, with greenhouse dormant in midwinter; $1,134 is the present value of 10 years of harvests.
Resale value‡ (one time)	0	3,672	6,256	Assuming the resale value is 0 for the low-cost greenhouse and equal to the dollar amount of construction cost for the medium- and high-cost units, discounted to the present.
Total	2,555	6,227	8,811	This is the total of the above, or the present value of all the returns for 10 years

TOTAL OF COSTS AND RETURNS (10 years)	GREENHOUSE COST RANGE			COMMENTS
	LOW ($)	MEDIUM ($)	HIGH ($)	
Present value of costs	842	5,654	9,452	Total of all present value of costs
Present value of returns	2,555	6,227	8,811	Total of all present value of returns
Net present value	1,713	573	−641	Total returns minus total costs

†*The present value of ongoing costs is determined as follows, assuming a real inflation rate (the interest rate at the bank minus the inflation rate) of 4 percent:*

$$\text{Net present cost} = \frac{annual\ cost}{1.04} + \frac{annual\ cost}{(1.04)2} + \frac{annual\ cost}{(1.04)3} + \frac{annual\ cost}{(1.04)9} = (approximately)\ 7.55 \times annual\ cost$$

The present value of ongoing returns is determined in the same way.

‡*The assumption is that the low-cost greenhouse has no resale value since the glazing will need periodic replacement and is not finished enough to be considered as extra living area. Another assumption is that the medium- and high-cost greenhouses increase the resale value by the same dollar amount they cost to build—considering the present value of that resale, which is figured by taking the resale amount and dividing by 1.04 to the tenth power. This is the discounted value of the resale, or the value now of the future sale.*

Section II:

DESIGNING THE GREENHOUSE

Now that you have a basic idea of what greenhouses are all about, you're ready to begin designing a greenhouse that meets your requirements. First we'll take an in-depth look at greenhouse design requirements from three points of view: horticulture, solar heating the greenhouse itself and solar heating the house. We'll explore these approaches almost as if each were the sole purpose for the greenhouse in order to fully understand the optimum and minimum design requirements. Then we'll look at integrating these various uses, molding the design toward your particular uses for the structure, your house, site and climate and your budget, without sacrificing performance in areas that are important to you. And finally, we'll look at a few examples of how people have juggled these various factors for their particular situation. The Kemble/Flannigan greenhouse is primarily used to produce seedlings and to extend the growing season. The Badeau greenhouse, a pleasant sitting "room," also provides space for growing plants and food, and solar heat for the house. The Del Porto greenhouse is used to drastically reduce heating bills, and the Baerg greenhouse is for total solar heating and food production. The Pea greenhouse, a moderately priced structure, provides food and solar heat, and the Russell greenhouse, while it provides heat and space for plants, was built as an elegant addition.

Chapter 4

DESIGNING THE GREENHOUSE FOR HORTICULTURE

The design of a horticultural greenhouse revolves around the needs of the plants occupying it, much as the design of a house revolves around the needs of its occupants. Attached solar greenhouse design compromises the plants' needs with those of energy conservation and solar heating and of the people using part of the greenhouse as a living space. In this chapter, the plants' needs and the greenhouse features that respond to those needs are explored. A subsequent chapter, "Design Integration," deals with combining all the design elements of energy, horticulture and living space to create a structure that satisfies your individual requirements.

In order to maintain growth, all plants need certain amounts of air (carbon dioxide and oxygen), water, light and minerals from the soil. The rate at which plants grow is governed by what is called *the principle of the limiting factor*. This principle states that the yield of any crop is limited by deficiencies in one or more of the essential ingredients: air, water, light or soil. Take, for example, a plant in a beautiful soil mix that is watered regu-

larly and placed in a well-ventilated but completely dark closet. It won't grow properly at all. A greenhouse that is perfect in all respects except for having insufficient ventilation and air circulation will limit plant growth. Another "perfect" greenhouse that has too much shading will lead to spindly plants stretching toward whatever light they can find. Proper temperature of both the greenhouse soil and air can be considered as a fifth nutritive ingredient in that temperatures above or below a certain range can slow growth considerably.

In an outdoor environment, where the balance of ingredients for growth isn't always optimal, wild plants grow and multiply in response to the availability of the various ingredients. In a greenhouse, however, all the factors are controlled and hopefully optimized, creating a vigorous growing environment for a great variety of plants. Achieving an optimum environment requires both proper design and proper operation of the greenhouse. While this book does not cover greenhouse operation, it will guide you in

Figure 4-1: Good plant growth requires a balance of the four essential ingredients—light, air, water and nutrients—and the right temperature regime. The principle of the limiting factor of plant growth states that even if one of these is in short supply, growth will be limited.

arriving at a greenhouse design that promotes a balanced, productive environment.

A greenhouse that was designed exclusively for the benefit of the plants would result in exuberant plant growth. But it could also be very expensive to build and to heat and probably wouldn't be suitable for contributing solar heat to the adjacent house. Such a greenhouse might look like a clear plastic bubble over a garden, with elaborate heating, cooling, ventilation, irrigation, humidification and dehumidification systems. It would be similar, in some respects, to existing commercial greenhouses, with similar high costs for back-up heating. The attached solar greenhouse is designed to be a *net energy producer* in that it contributes more heat to the house than it uses in back-up heat. We are concerned, therefore, with reaching a good com-

promise between design requirements for plant growth and those for solar heating—and with controlling construction costs in the process. So, it is important to understand the limits of the various factors that contribute to growth. For example, we must consider not only how light levels can be maximized inside the greenhouse, but we need also to understand how much light can be *excluded* before growth is limited.

Let There Be Light

Of the four factors necessary for plant growth—air, water, light and nutrients—light and ventilation (air) are the most often neglected elements in solar greenhouse design. But they are, in fact, the elements that must be the most thoroughly planned before construction begins. Problems of inadequate light and ventilation are difficult and expensive to remedy after the greenhouse is built.

In order to understand the effect on a plant of being inside a solar greenhouse, imagine for a moment a healthy tomato plant in the middle of an open garden in midsummer. On clear days it receives full light directly from the sun, and when it's cloudy it gets diffuse light from the whole "sky dome" above. Now we are going to decrease the available light dramatically by moving this plant into the greenhouse. Right away the early morning and late afternoon summer sun are blocked by the house, assuming the wall faces south. On cloudy days, when the available sunlight is fairly evenly distributed over the whole sky, the plant is only looking at half the sky dome and is receiving perhaps only half the light it would in an open field.

Further reductions are caused by the greenhouse structure and glazing. Some glazing materials transmit more than 90 percent of the incoming light, the remainder being either absorbed or reflected. Teflon film, for example, transmits 96 percent (though it is a difficult material to work with). Low-iron glass transmits 92 percent and is a standard construction material, making it a good glazing choice. Common 3/16-inch tempered plate glass transmits closer to 85 percent of the available light because of its slightly higher iron content. (Maximum transmittance is usually measured when the sun is at right angles to the glazing. In other positions, actual transmittance can be somewhat lower because as the sun's angle becomes more oblique to the glazing, reflection from the glazing increases. This brings more emphasis to the importance of facing the greenhouse as close as possible to true south.) Double glazing transmits even less, usually the product of two single-layer transmittances. For example, two layers of low-iron glass transmit about 85 percent of the available light ($0.92 \times 0.92 = 0.85$). As the glazing gets dirty, and, in the case of plastics, as it ages, transmission decreases further still. More blockage is caused by solid roof or endwall sections, rafters and other solid members, and when it's all added up, there is quite a reduction in light when we take our tomato plant out of the real world and into the greenhouse.

Measurements of light levels in one double-glazed solar greenhouse showed that light levels were about half the outside levels, even within 3 feet of the south glazing. Deeper inside this greenhouse (about halfway between the south glazing and north wall), below a solid portion of the roof, light levels were only one-fourth the outside levels. Close to the north wall there was only one-sixth the outside light.[1] In general, light levels in a double-glazed greenhouse will average around one-half the outside levels at growing beds that aren't too far from the glazing. In a single-glazed greenhouse there can be as much as two-thirds the available outside light.

How much is enough for productive growth? It has been found that light one-half as intense as outside light will be sufficient to promote the growth of most vegetables. When light levels are much lower, *phototropism*, or bending towards the light, coupled with spindly growth will be noticed in many vegetables. On the other hand, many shade-loving houseplants can do quite well with considerably less light. And even though many vegetable plants can survive on much less light than one-half outdoor levels, their growth will be considerably slowed, so the enclosure must be designed to admit as much light as possible to the growing areas. Within the limits of the compromise between horticulture, solar heating and energy conservation, the following principles should be applied to the greenhouse design to ensure luxuriant and healthy plant growth.

Choose the least shaded site. The greenhouse should be located on the southernmost-facing side of the house, in a spot where

[1] Measurements were taken of photosynthetically active radiation (400 to 700 nanometer wavelength) on the horizontal in the National Center for Appropriate Technology's solar greenhouse on a sunny spring day. The NCAT greenhouse is freestanding, but only the south face is glazed. This glazing is 15 feet wide by 12 feet high at an angle of about 70 degrees from horizontal, facing due south. The glazing is Exolite, supported on 2 × 4s spaced on 24-inch centers. The roof and all other walls were solid at the time the measurements were taken. The measurement directly behind the glazing was taken near the center of the glazing. Measurements farther north in the greenhouse were taken on the (east-west) center line of the greenhouse. All interior walls are gloss-white. Measurements taken next to east and west walls showed even less light than those cited in the text. This greenhouse design represents far from the optimum light situation, as evidenced by the low-light level in the center and rear of the greenhouse, and the light levels directly behind the glazing are lower than a first guess might indicate.

it will be subject to the least amount of shading. (See chapter 2.) Remember that the shadow of a typical deciduous tree that is bare of leaves still blocks 50 percent of the available sunlight.

Glaze as much area as possible. This can somewhat compromise winter energy conservation and summer cooling, but various techniques will be discussed in chapters 5 and 6 to

limit this effect. The primary limiting factor to growth in a greenhouse is very often inadequate light.

Minimize glazing framing. Too often the greenhouse builder does not use the minimum sized rafter necessary to support the glazing against snow and wind loads. This results in unnecessary blockage of light. Rafters that are too wide or too thick block much early

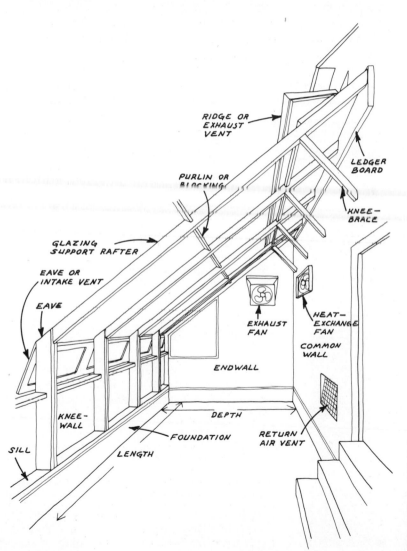

Figure 4-2: Shown here are the names and locations of the basic parts of the greenhouse, as they are used in this book. There are, of course, many other parts that go into the various construction details, all of which are covered in "Section III: Construction Detailing."

Photos 4-1 and 4-2: Small, light-weight rafters block much less of the sky than thicker, heavier ones. The size of glazing framing members should be minimized for best plant growth.

morning and late afternoon light from the plants. See chapter 10 for information on determining minimum safe rafter sizes and on framing systems that minimize shading.

Paint the interior of the greenhouse white. All framing and all other interior surfaces should be white to reflect light. White paint will minimize the rafters' early morning and late afternoon shading effect by reflecting the light that hits them. A white north wall is very important for evenly distributing the predominantly southern light in the greenhouse. While a plant in the greenhouse sees, at best, only the southern half of the sky dome, a north wall that is bright with reflected light will both increase the overall amount of light available to the plants and distribute that light more evenly.

When heat storage elements are placed along the north wall, this color requirement will probably be compromised so that the heat storage will absorb more heat. But where possible, dark-colored heat storage elements should be placed below the level of the growing areas. Heat storage that is placed above the planting level, to take advantage of direct sun and the warmer air higher up, should be painted a lighter color instead of flat black. A primary blue or red color will absorb very nearly as much heat as black and will reflect some light in parts of the spectrum that are useful to the plants.

Specular reflectors—reflectors such as aluminum foil, in which either a clear or distorted image is reflected—are not recommended inside the greenhouse. They can concentrate light into "hot spots" that can burn the plants while leaving other areas in relative shade. The diffuse reflection from white or even a reflective silver paint gives a more evenly distributed light throughout the greenhouse.

Place growing beds under glazing. The most effective growing beds in the greenhouse will be those directly beside or directly under glazing. Many vegetable crops use as much light as they can possibly get in a greenhouse. In warm climates where a partially solid roof is used to minimize summer overheating, the areas under the solid roof can be used for heat storage elements, for benches to carry shade-loving plants and seed germinating trays, for work tables or for your place for sitting in the sun.

You should also consider glazing the endwalls of the greenhouse next to the growing bed. Early morning light will help the plants get a good start on their growing day. Completely solid endwalls are useful because they provide shading from morning and afternoon summer sun, but they leave the adjacent interior areas shaded for half the day. To compromise this shading requirement with the need for light, endwall glazing can be limited to those areas directly adjacent to the plants, which is likely to be the southernmost side of the wall.

The top of the planting bed should be above the bottom of the glazing. The top of the soil in planting beds should be at least as high as the bottom of the glazing; otherwise, small seedlings sprouting in the soil will be shaded, resulting in poor, spindly growth.

Ventilation

Plants take in carbon dioxide (CO_2) and give off oxygen during photosynthesis. This "breathing" process accelerates during periods when all other growth requirements—sun, water and nutrients—are in adequate supply. Since plants don't have lungs, they rely on the movement of the air around them to carry away moist, oxygen-laden air and to supply air richer in carbon dioxide. The thin layer of air that is in direct contact with the leaf, known as the boundary layer, becomes very rich in oxygen and moisture if there is no air movement to disturb it. Even though air only a fraction of an inch away may be rich in carbon dioxide, a stagnant boundary layer surrounding the leaf will slow growth. Outdoor plants are much less subject to these boundary layers since there is almost always a slight breeze. The overall carbon dioxide levels in a greenhouse are rapidly depleted on a sunny day, even with thorough mixing of the air within the greenhouse. By midmorning on a sunny day the lowered levels of carbon dioxide in the air can actually become a limiting factor to growth.

Inadequate movement of air around a plant also results in excessive moisture in the boundary layer, which interferes with evaporation of water from the leaves. This creates an ideal environment for mold and fungus growth. Additionally, the canopy of plant leaves over a growing bed traps moisture evaporating from the soil, forming a moist microenvironment that is also ideal for growth of plant pests and disease unless adequate air movement is provided. And even with adequate air movement the air itself must be changed frequently to prevent the entire greenhouse from becoming too humid and to maintain adequate levels of carbon dioxide. Humidity levels in a greenhouse can reach well over 90 percent relative humidity, again creating an ideal environment for disease and pests.

Ventilation is also very important in controlling overheating in the greenhouse. Hot air must have an easy path out and fresh air an easy path in, whether by fan or natural convection or both, to maintain reasonable temperatures for plant growth. A single afternoon of severe overheating can ruin a crop that has taken weeks of work to grow. The ventilation system alone doesn't do all the temperature controlling. Other parts of the greenhouse that assist in cooling include heat storage elements (including the soil in the growing beds), solid portions of roof and walls, which cut down the amount of sun penetrating the greenhouse, and various shading devices such as shade cloth, which control heat gain. A good exhaust ventilation system, however, is the primary controller and will keep the air temperature in the greenhouse to within 5°F of the outside temperature even on a hot, sunny day, and without shading devices. Controlling temperature with greenhouse-to-house ventilation is as important in winter as exhaust ventilation is in summer. Winter temperatures can easily reach 100°F if the greenhouse is closed tight, which is too hot for almost all plants. Also, letting a greenhouse get that hot means that the surplus heat isn't being used for heating the house.

An attached solar greenhouse is in a unique, rather complex relationship with both the outside environment and the adjacent house. Depending on the season and the weather, the greenhouse provides ventilation to the plants in one or more of a variety of ways. On winter days, the majority of the fresh air is supplied from the house, with air leakage in the greenhouse supplying a fairly small amount (it is hoped) of outdoor air. The exchange of warm, moist, oxygenated air from the greenhouse with cooler, dry, carbon dioxide-rich air from the house is of great benefit to occupants of both the house and the greenhouse. The warmth is an obvious benefit, lowering fuel bills, but the extra moisture is useful, too. It makes you feel more comfortable, since there is less evaporative cooling from your body, allowing you to run the house a little cooler. And it is healthful, helping avoid dry skin and dry nasal passageways without an electric humidifier.

On cold nights when the heat storage in the greenhouse is depleted, warm air may be drawn from the house to keep the greenhouse warm. As described in chapter 5, heat exchange with the house can be as simple as leaving windows and doors ajar or as elaborate as a thermostatically controlled fan.

If the air exchange with the house is via natural convection—without the use of a fan—a small circulating fan inside the greenhouse is useful for disturbing the boundary layers of air around the plant leaves. The circulating fan should run during daylight hours, when photosynthetic activity is highest. One or two small tabletop fans are usually adequate. These may be hung from a wall or rafter to spread their effect evenly or you can use an oscillating fan. A little experimentation with placement will be needed in each greenhouse. A very gentle movement of most of the leaves in the greenhouse is a good indication that there is adequate air circulation. If the air exchange with the house is via a fan, it will also mix the air inside the greenhouse and eliminate the need for an additional circulator. (In winter try to direct fans to minimize air movement along the glass, since this increases heat loss through it.)

In the summer the greenhouse is simply

left wide open. Once nighttime temperatures are staying above a relatively warm 55°F, all the vents to the outdoors can be left open day and night. In northern climates, where short summers make greenhouse crops like melons, tomatoes and peppers attractive, the greenhouse must be well ventilated to prevent damage to these crops. In climates with longer summers, the greenhouse is often abandoned in summer in favor of outdoor gardening. In this case, good ventilation is important to minimize overheating of the house. Where garden space is limited, warm-climate greenhouses can be built with removable glazing to convert the greenhouse to an outdoor container garden for the summer.

In the spring and fall—or "swing seasons"—the situation is a little more complex. Some days will be like winter with the greenhouse operating in the winter mode; others will be like summer, with all exterior vents open. Some days, however, are warm enough that the house does not require solar heat from the greenhouse but the nights are cold enough that the greenhouse may require some heat from the house. In this case, the greenhouse must be vented to the exterior during the day and be shut tight to the outside at night. Some days will be cool in the morning and warm in the afternoon, requiring afternoon venting. All these conditions have implications for the design of both the greenhouse and its ventilation system.

If, for example, it is at all likely that you will be away from the greenhouse for blocks of time, it is best to plan for some type of automatic venting. Many greenhouses, however, do operate successfully with all-manual venting. Exterior vents can be cracked open slightly, or, if it is too cool outside, doors and windows between the house and greenhouse can be left open. The manual approach requires more attention from the operator—and a good eye for impending changes in the weather—but is less costly to build.

Ventilation Systems

This section covers the design of the *exhaust system*—for exchanging greenhouse air with outdoor air—and the *air exchange system*—for exchanging greenhouse air with air from the house. Part of the design of the air exchange system, specifically the sizing of the vents and fans, is covered in chapter 6, since this sizing is dictated by solar heating, rather than horticultural considerations. Placement and control, however, need to be considered from the perspective of plant growth, and are therefore covered here.

Exhaust Systems

The best natural ventilation scheme, as far as the plants are concerned, is the kind used in all the old-style, glass commercial greenhouses—continuous vents along the entire eave, or kneewall, and along the entire ridge. In this system, cool air is brought in through the vents at the eaves, just at planting bed level. The air is warmed as it flows across the bed, where it both absorbs moisture and oxygen from the plants and gives them carbon dioxide. As the air warms, it becomes lighter and rises out the ridge vent by what is called *natural convection*. This airflow occurs when air is provided a pathway with an inlet, a way to warm the air above the outside temperature, and an outlet higher than the inlet. Further, the greater the difference in height between inlet and outlet, the greater the airflow will be. (The same is true for temperature difference between inside and out: A greater difference increases flow rate.) The old greenhouse system maximizes airflow by letting the air in as low as is practical and letting it out as high as possible.

Vents have several advantages over fans. They are silent, require no electricity to operate and can distribute the incoming air as well as, or better than, fans. The following are

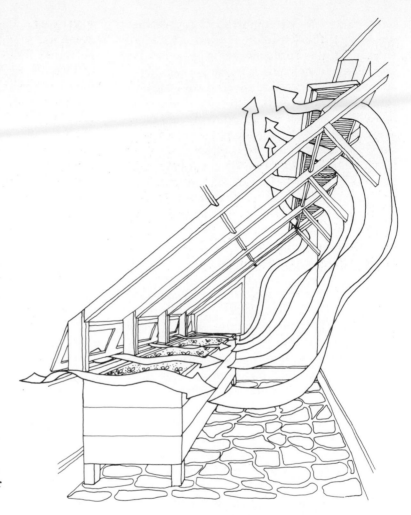

Figure 4-3: In late spring, summer and early fall, full eave and ridge vents wash cool, fresh air over the growing beds, eliminating hot spots that can cause poor growth.

basic principles of exhaust vent design to ensure that the greenhouse will be well ventilated.

Distribute the intake vent area as much as possible along the growing areas of the greenhouse to avoid hot spots. This may be done with a continuous vent along the kneewall, or by several smaller independently operated vents. Vents can be in solid or glazed areas.

Place an equal or larger area of exhaust vents as high as possible in the greenhouse. The exhaust vents should be as large as, or larger than, the lower vents.

Make the vents large enough. The total vent area should be one-fourth to one-third the area of the south-facing glazing. The larger vent area should be used for greenhouses with up to an 8-foot difference in height between the centers of the upper and

Photo 4-3: Heat piston vent openers use expanding paraffin to push open the vent above a certain temperature. They are available in several sizes and configurations, as discussed in chapter 12. *(Photo courtesy of Superior Autovents, Ltd., Huntington Beach, Calif.)*

lower vents. The smaller vent area is for taller greenhouses with more than 8 feet between the vents. The area of an exterior door may be counted as vent area, as long as it can be left open in the summer. The top half of the door counts as part of the upper vents, the lower half as part of the lower vents. But if a door accounts for more than one-third of the required area, air distribution may suffer. For example, a greenhouse with a south-facing glazing area of 120 square feet, by the one-quarter to one-third rule, requires a total vent area of 30 to 40 square feet. An exterior door, 2 feet 8 inches by 6 feet 8 inches, has an area of 17.8 square feet, but should be counted for only 10 to 13 square feet (one-third the total required) to avoid having too much vent area in one location. Therefore 20 to 30 square feet of vent area is needed in addition to the door.

Vents should be designed and built with care to prevent leaks. Leaking air will chill plants and waste energy. And leaking water

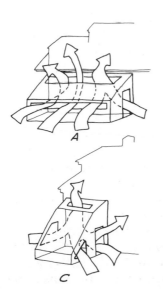

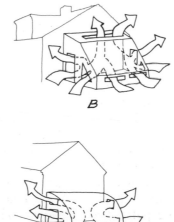

Figure 4-4: There are many ways to design for the necessary vent area. Full eave and ridge vents, shown in A, give the most even ventilation, though the several smaller vents grouped together in B are adequate. In shorter greenhouses, vents in the endwalls and roof, as in C, can provide sufficient ventilation. If the greenhouse structure only permits endwall vents, as in D, be sure you have allowed for enough area.

will tend to warp the vents and could eventually rot framing members.

Screen the vents, exterior doors, interior doors and fans. Screens prevent harmful insects and pests from invading the greenhouse and keep any beneficial insects you introduce inside. (Note that if you don't have self-pollinating varieties of fruiting plants, you'll have to do the pollinating or open the screens to let the bees do it when you have flowers.)

Vents should be easy to operate. If they are difficult to open they won't be used as often as they should be.

It is as important to have easily operated vents as it is to have properly designed vents. Vents will need adjustment at least twice a day in spring and fall. A few of the many

TABLE 4-1: SUMMARY OF EXHAUST VENTILATION OPTIONS

System	Control Mode	Controls	Comments	Relative Costs
Vents in roof, eave and/or endwalls	All manual	Props, cranks or pulleys	Requires operator attention to prevent overheating	Low for materials; medium to high for labor
Vents (in roof, eave and/or endwalls) plus exhaust fan	Manual and automatic	Manual vents; thermostat for fan	Allows manual venting when people are home, and automatic venting when they're away	Medium for materials; high for labor
Exhaust fan only	Automatic	Thermostat	Automatic operation; consumes electricity; makes some noise	Medium for materials; low for labor
Vents (in roof, eave and/or endwalls) with motorized vent opener for roof vent	Automatic	Thermostat	Automatic operation; low electricity consumption; no noise	High for materials; high for labor
Vents (in roof, eave and/or endwalls) with heat piston vent opener for roof vent	Automatic	Heat piston	Automatic operation; no noise; no electricity required; requires careful installation to ensure tight closure and ability to override piston	Medium for materials; high for labor

possible mechanisms, including manual operators, heat pistons and manual and motorized gear-driven systems, are described in detail in chapter 12.

Table 4-1 compares the various exhaust ventilation options (both vents and fans) and gives some guidelines for selecting an appropriate system or combination of systems.

Exhaust Fans

With a few exceptions, most attached greenhouses need an exhaust fan. If the greenhouse is well shaded or if a large area of automatic vents is incorporated, the need for a fan can be avoided. But if the main ventilation is via manually operated vents, a thermostatically controlled fan is great insurance against wilted crops on that one sunny day when the vents are mistakenly left closed. When no one is home, the exhaust fan system ensures proper temperature control. The annual electricity use for such a "back-up" fan will usually be less than 100 kilowatt-hours (kwh).

If construction labor costs are high, and the construction budget is tight, an exhaust fan system can be the only exhaust system, eliminating the need for vents. Fans are less expensive to install than vents because they involve a smaller penetration of the greenhouse skin. They are also more easily sealed in the winter. The electricity needed to run a fan-powered exhaust system is not as great as might be expected—on the order of 100 to 300 kilowatt-hours (kwh) per year, depending on greenhouse size, climate and other factors. And while an exhaust fan will never be silent, its noise can be reduced greatly, as will be discussed in chapter 12. There are many greenhouses that operate quite successfully with fans as the only exhaust system, but if it is at all possible to incorporate a vent system, the house and greenhouse will be quieter and more pleasant.

The design of an exhaust fan system follows the same principles as exhaust vent design. The natural flow of air in the greenhouse must be considered, even though the fan has the power to overcome natural convection. Working against prevailing winds or natural convection makes the fan work harder and use more energy than it should, shortening the life of the motor. Since fans concentrate in a small area all the ventilation that would occur in vents 20 or 30 times their size, the air moves very rapidly through the fan. Consequently, care must be taken with air inlet and outlet placement to avoid subjecting the plants to strong drafts, which can chill or dehydrate them. And exhaust fans, like vents, should be easy to seal tightly in cold weather. The following lists the important aspects of exhaust fan design:

The fan should provide 5 to 8 cubic feet per minute (cfm) of air per square foot of south-facing glazing. The 8-cfm rating should be used for greenhouses where the fan is the only exhaust system, and hence will be needed during summer. It is also used for greenhouses where there is little or no thermal storage to absorb the sun's heat, and for greenhouses in warm climates, meaning fewer than 4,000 degree-days (dd).

A larger slower-moving fan is preferable to a smaller high-speed fan for a number of reasons. Slower fans are much quieter and consume less energy. A standard two- or three-speed fan is an easy solution. Choose the rating of the lowest speed of the fan to match the required rating of 5 to 8 cfm per square foot of glazing.

For example, a greenhouse with 200 square feet of south-facing glazing should have a 1,000 to 1,600 cfm exhaust fan. If the greenhouse is also equipped with exhaust vents, 1,000 to 1,300 cfm are needed. A three-speed fan with 1,000, 1,500, and 2,000 cfm ratings would be appropriate and would give you more venting power for very hot days. If

Photo 4-4: Louvers are good for keeping rain and lighter breezes out of the fan, but they shouldn't be thought of as winter protection against infiltration.

Photo 4-5: Air intake louvers are opened when the exhaust fan goes on. If the fan power is insufficient, a motorized louver can be used as shown here.

the greenhouse has little thermal storage, is in a warm climate or has no exhaust vents, 1,300 to 1,600 cfm are needed.

Use exhaust louvers on the fan. Louvers keep rain out and keep breezes from blowing through the greenhouse when the fan isn't on. Most fans are available with matching exterior louvers that open by the fan's air pressure when it comes on.

Provide air intake louvers the same size as those on the fan. For example, a fan with a 28-inch frame should have a 28-inch-square intake louver. Pressure-operated louvers are the least expensive and easiest to install, but in some situations where the fan is drawing

only a small volume of air, a motor-actuated intake louver may be required.

Fan and intake louver placement should take advantage of natural convection and prevailing winds and should avoid strong drafts on the plants. Place the fan as near to the peak as is convenient and the intake louvers as near the ground as is convenient and at the opposite side of the greenhouse.

Insulating doors on fan and louver openings will minimize cold air leaks in winter. These will be used often during the colder parts of the swing seasons, when the nights are cold enough to warrant a tight closure, but the days are warm enough that some air leakage around the louvers is acceptable when the fan is not running.

Screen the fan and air intake louvers. This keeps hostile insects out and friendly ones in.

Exhaust Fan Controls

While it is possible to control a fan with a manual switch, it's not advisable. A simple, inexpensive line-voltage cooling thermostat costing about $25 helps ensure (automatically) that the greenhouse will not overheat.[2] This thermostat activates the fan at or above a certain temperature setpoint, which you can adjust. This keeps the greenhouse temperature from rising above the optimum for plant growth, 80 to 85°F for many vegetable crops.

---

[2] Line voltage means that the thermostat is wired right into the 120-volt power line, without the need for transformers. Thermostats that use transformers are called low-voltage thermostats.

If the fan is a multispeed unit, a speed control is also needed. This control is used to set the fan to the lowest speed at which it will adequately cool the greenhouse, although the right speed may be different for different seasons. Two-speed fans can also be controlled by a two-stage thermostat, which will turn on the lower speed of the fan at the setpoint and turn on the higher speed if the temperature rises a certain number of degrees above the setpoint. While the two-stage thermostat offers more precise control of the greenhouse temperature, a single-speed or multispeed fan with a manual-speed switch can give you adequate control over ventilation. Be sure that any speed controller or thermostat you get is compatible with your fan; mismatched controls can quickly destroy the fan motor.

Motor-operated air intake louvers may be necessary if the fan suction isn't enough to open unpowered louvers. With some simple wiring these louvers are opened whenever the

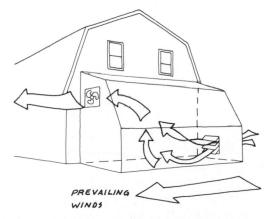

Figure 4-5: Exhaust fans should be placed high, with the intake louvers low on the opposite end-wall, to take advantage of natural convection. You can let any prevailing winds help the fan, by placing it on the leeward side, with the intake louver to windward.

Photo 4-6: Having an insulated door over a fan exhaust vent is a must for keeping the greenhouse tight in the winter.

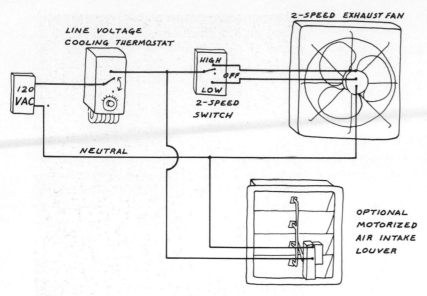

Figure 4-6: This schematic shows the wiring and components for controlling an exhaust fan with a line-voltage thermostat and a two-speed switch. The fan should be sized for adequate cooling on low speed. The two-speed switch allows the fan to be run at the higher speed if needed. Some fans can also be controlled with a variable-speed or rheostatic controller.

fan is turned on, and they close automatically when the thermostat turns off the fan. Exhaust fan wiring is very straightforward, as shown in figure 4-6. The fan should be wired to a new or existing circuit, depending on the current draw of the fan and other loads on the circuit. A ground fault interrupter, or GFI, is recommended for all greenhouse wiring.

The thermostat should be located about at the height of the planting beds, in order to respond to the temperature that the plants are experiencing. Shading the thermostat is essential to prevent the sun from directly heating it, which can cause the fan to turn on prematurely and overly cool the greenhouse. If there isn't a spot in the greenhouse that is always shaded, such as under a shelf, a shield must be constructed. A very simple shield can be constructed by tacking a curved piece of aluminum flashing around the thermostat, as shown in figure 4-7. The aluminum is nailed

down on one side and latched on the other. (Be sure to sand down or bend over the sharp edges of the aluminum.)

Temperature Control

Maintaining temperatures conducive to good plant growth is one of the most important functions of a horticultural greenhouse. Proper temperature is so critical that it can be considered a fifth essential ingredient for plant growth, along with air, water, light and soil. Most vegetable plants grow well between 50 and 85°F, with growth slowing down considerably if the temperature goes 10 degrees above or below this range. Most plants will suffer permanent damage at greater extremes, wilting above 95°F and, of course, freezing below 32°F.

Within this 50 to 85°F "comfort range" different crops prefer different temperatures.

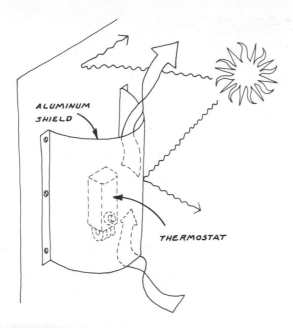

Figure 4-7: A sunshield keeps the direct sun from heating the fan thermostat and making it "think" the greenhouse is hotter than it is. The outside of the shield should be reflective, with the inside painted a dark color.

Photo 4-7: These thermostats, mounted on a west-facing surface, are shaded from direct sunlight by a shelf, a vertical board and a strip of reflective fabric (shown open) that closes with a small piece of Velcro. Air is still free to circulate around the thermostats. One thermostat controls the back-up heater, two control the motorized top vent opener and one controls the heat exchange fan. The boxes above the thermostats are more top vent controls and a relay.

Most fruiting plants such as tomatoes and cucumbers thrive in higher temperatures, while cabbage family plants and other greens require cooler temperatures. Also, different stages of growth require different temperatures. Seed germination is encouraged by very warm temperatures, while seedlings require a narrow temperature range, with care taken to avoid overheating or chilling them. Mature plants have a much broader temperature tolerance. Warm soil will also give plants greater tolerance for colder air temperatures. (Bed design for warmer soil temperatures is discussed later in this chapter.) Some owners have observed that higher than normal temperatures are tolerated by plants with sturdy root systems in deep growing beds. This may be due to the root system's ability to supply water to the leaves as fast as the sun evaporates it. Wilting occurs when evaporation exceeds the supply of moisture to the leaves from the roots.

Temperatures are not always optimum in a passive solar greenhouse. In the compromise between energy conservation and maintaining optimum growing conditions, greenhouse temperatures are allowed to fluctuate or "cycle" up and down in order to take better advantage of the sun's energy. Most mature vegetable crops are not adversely affected by temperature cycling.[3]

Different areas in the greenhouse will have different cycling characteristics, creating zones of temperature. These zones can be used to advantage by matching crops to location. Areas near the south glazing will have the greatest temperature fluctuations, being hottest during the day and coldest at night. They also have the highest light levels. Areas on top of heat-storing water barrels at midheight along the north wall will be relatively even and moderate in temperature, but with fairly low light levels. Areas on the floor next to an aisle will be relatively cool and dark, with cold night temperatures. Tomatoes would be appropriate next to the glazing; seedlings would do well on top of the heat storage, and lettuce would be fine near the aisle and closer to the floor.

A well-designed and well-built greenhouse can always be maintained within the plants' "comfort zone." The exhaust system and the house/greenhouse air exchange system play the major role in keeping the greenhouse from overheating. In warm climates, shading and other cooling methods are required. Passive heat storage in the greenhouse helps to moderate both high and low temperatures by storing some of the surplus solar heat during the day and releasing it at night. Having a back-up heating system ensures that minimum temperatures can always be maintained.

---

[3] Temperature cycling is necessary in any passive solar heated structure. Heat flow is caused by the difference in temperature between objects: The temperature of the greenhouse must fall below that of the heat storage for heat to move from storage to the surroundings.

Back-Up Heating

Just about every attached solar greenhouse needs some type of back-up heating system, whether it is an actual heater in the greenhouse or simply a way to bring in house heat when it's needed. A properly designed and built greenhouse will generally need only small amounts of back-up heat, much less than the solar heat it contributes to the house. Having a back-up system is your best insurance against plants being damaged or killed by a long cold period when the greenhouse heat storage is exhausted. Back-up heat is also useful in elevating the greenhouse temperature for seedling germination.

There are several types of back-up heating systems suitable for attached greenhouses, including portable and permanently installed heaters. It's also possible to create a zone separate from the house's central heating system. A simpler way is to utilize the air exchange between the house and greenhouse for back-up heating as well as for solar heating the house.

Heat Exchange with the House

In most attached solar greenhouses, the same system that puts solar heat into the house can be used to put house heat into the greenhouse. You can think of this as using the house for part of the heat storage for the greenhouse. Solar heat is "stored" by using it to heat the house during the day and "retrieved" by borrowing heat from the house on cold nights to heat the greenhouse. Air exchange systems are usually low in cost. The only costs are for a thermostat, a fan and possibly a back-up heater. If the air exchange is by natural convection, through doors, windows or vents, these can simply be left open during periods of extreme cold, allowing warm house air to mix with cooler greenhouse air.

The air exchange approach is practical if the house heating system has enough capacity to carry the additional heating load of the greenhouse and if the area where the cold air will enter the house will not cause discomfort. The capacity of the central heating system is usually adequate to handle the needs of smaller greenhouses. Central systems are ordinarily oversized by enough to cover the greenhouse heat load, which commonly represents a relatively small portion of the total house-plus-greenhouse load. If the house has been insulated, or if other major heat conservation measures have been taken since the heating system was installed, it almost certainly has the needed excess capacity for a small- or medium-sized greenhouse. But if the system has to struggle to keep the house warm during the coldest periods, adding the greenhouse to the furnace load may not be a good idea. If there is any doubt, the furnace capacity should be compared against a heat load calculation for the house with the greenhouse, for which you may need advice from a heating system professional.

In many attached solar greenhouses natural convection air exchange is used successfully for back-up heating. When the house is heating the greenhouse, the direction of airflow through the vents (including doors and windows) is the reverse of the daytime solar heating flow. During a sunny day, warm greenhouse air rises and flows into the house through the upper vent, drawing cooler house air in through the lower vent. At night, the house air is warmer and enters the greenhouse through the upper vent, drawing cold greenhouse air into the house through the lower vent. This system does require attention to opening vents, windows or doors on cold nights, or on days before cold nights are anticipated. But with a little trial and error, the right amount of opening for various outdoor night conditions can be found. (Guidelines for sizing these vents are in chapter 6.)

Cold air entering the house from the greenhouse on a cold night can cause uncomfortable drafts if the exchange system is not designed carefully. With natural convection systems, these problems are minimized, since convection moves the air rather slowly, with cold air gradually diffusing across the floor of the house, where it mixes with warmer air. The lower vents should not be placed where the air will directly move over people, such as directly by a couch or table. Moving the vent a few feet from where people sit will give enough room for the cold air to mix with warm air before it reaches people. In general, vents should be placed as far as possible from sitting areas while still keeping them in the room to be heated by the greenhouse.

With fan-driven air exchange, the air should be directed away from the thermostat that controls the central heating system so that the thermostat isn't "fooled" into "thinking" that it is colder in the house than it actually is, causing the furnace to run more than it should. If the area of the house in which the exchange fan is located is served by an area heater, such as a floor or wall furnace, a freestanding heater or an individually controlled baseboard heater, the placement of the fan relative to the heater thermostat is less critical.

A simple line-voltage heating thermostat can be used to turn on the fan if the greenhouse gets too cold. Fan-driven air exchange systems need not reverse the direction of airflow to warm the greenhouse at night. (See chapter 6 for a wiring diagram.) There are also commercially available greenhouse air exchange fans complete with thermostats. (See the list of suppliers in Appendix 1.) The prewired fan systems have a higher materials cost but require less labor. If the wiring is to be done by a professional electrician, the prewired fan controllers or complete systems may be economical.

A fan-driven air exchange system has the advantage over natural convection of easy automation. Just as the exhaust fan thermostat provides insurance against overheating, the air exchange fan thermostat provides insurance against freezing temperatures in the greenhouse. Many greenhouse owners who rely on manually controlled air exchange for back-up heating also keep a portable electric heater with a thermostat in the greenhouse for those times when the cold air is not wanted in the house or for cold nights when the vents are inadvertently left closed.

Portable Electric Heaters

Portable electric heaters are inexpensive and simple to install, needing only a GFI-equipped electric outlet in the greenhouse. GFI outlets interrupt the circuit, cutting off the power to it, if the ground is interrupted in any way. These heaters are reliable and easy to control, and usually have their own thermostats. They have the disadvantage of using what is, in many areas, the most expensive fuel, electricity, and therefore shouldn't be used in greenhouses that are anticipated to use a lot of back-up heating.

Electric heaters that incorporate a fan ensure the best heat distribution throughout the greenhouse. Radiant-type heaters are inappropriate, as they can cause hot spots on plants while leaving other areas cold. Baseboard or other convection heaters are not as good as the fan-type heaters, since they do not move as much air around in the greenhouse. Combination fan plus radiant-type heaters are acceptable, since the bulk of the heat will be moved by the fan in the form of warm air.

The thermostats on most electric heaters are not usually marked in degrees, but rather with something vague like "high" and "low," requiring a little experimenting to keep the greenhouse at the desired minimum temperature. In some cases, an additional thermostat may be needed.

Portable electric heaters can be placed almost anywhere on the floor of a small greenhouse (up to 150 square feet), since the fan will distribute the heat. Avoid having the heater fan blow the warm air directly at the glazing, as this will waste heat.

There are a few special considerations for installing electric heaters. If you need an electric heater larger than 1,500 watts, you will need two 120-volt heaters, or one 240-volt unit, since 120-volt units are rarely made larger than 1,500 watts. Each 120-volt heater should have its own electrical circuit, with a 20-amp circuit breaker. Often there will be room for a new circuit on the house breaker box, and a line can be run specifically for the greenhouse heater, lights and additional wall sockets. If the breaker box is filled, you'll have to run a branch off an existing circuit, paying careful attention to the capacity of the existing breaker and the size of the wire connected to it. A 240-volt heater will require installing a new 240-volt circuit and circuit breaker.

Wiring should be run on the surface of all the walls to avoid puncturing the vapor barrier. The wire can be run in regular round conduit, or in a system like Wiremold (TM), which makes surface mounting easier, doesn't require special tools to install and looks neater. Check with local electrical supply houses for this type of system.

Gas Heaters

Thermostatically controlled natural gas or propane heaters have the advantage of the same ease of control as electrical heaters while using (in many locations) a less expensive fuel. The disadvantage is that they require gas lines and flues. In addition, a fan may be required in larger greenhouses to distribute the heat, if the heater itself does not include a fan. Gas heaters are appropriate where a relatively large back-up requirement is anticipated, and, of course, where gas prices are low relative to electricity.

All gas-burning heaters must be properly vented. A chimney or vent pipe to the outdoors is absolutely required. While the carbon dioxide produced by combustion would be useful to plants, combustion bi-products, including carbon monoxide, are toxic to both plants and people.

Gas heaters with thermostats are much easier to use and are more economical to run than heaters with a simple valve that controls the flame size. The temperature in the greenhouse is maintained automatically, with the heater burning fuel only when needed. Manually controlled heaters can be used quite successfully, though, by adjusting the size of the flame according to the outside temperature.

The placement of a gas heater is usually determined by the proximity of the gas supply and the convenience of locating the flue. Care must be taken to leave sufficient space between the heater and any wood or other combustible material. If the heater ends up in a corner of the greenhouse, a small circulating fan may be needed for even heat distribution.

With any gas heater, some thought should be given to air leaks through the flue and to some resulting safety concerns. Most gas heaters take combustion air from the heated space, leaving the flue an open hole for warm air to escape when the heater isn't running. An automatic flue damper will greatly reduce this air leak and also will prevent cold air from being drawn down the flue by an air exchange fan when the heater isn't on. In order to avoid the potentially dangerous situation of the air exchange fan drawing combustion gases down the chimney when the gas heater is running, the gas heater thermostat must *lock out* the air exchange fan whenever the gas heater is on. This is fairly easily done with a relay. Through-the-wall gas heat-

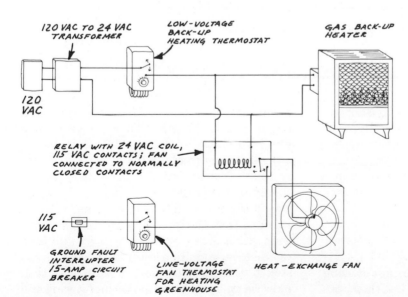

Figure 4-8: The low-voltage (24 VAC) thermostat for a gas heater is connected to a relay (with a 24-VAC coil) that disconnects the heat exchange fan whenever the gas is burning. This eliminates the possibility of the fan drawing combustion gases into the greenhouse or house and keeps the back-up heat in the greenhouse.

TABLE 4-2: BACK-UP HEATING CHOICES

BACK-UP SYSTEM	CONTROLS	WHEN APPROPRIATE
Heat exchange with house	Vents (manual)	For low-cost installation; if automation isn't needed; if house heating system has enough capacity to also heat greenhouse
	Thermostat and fan (automatic)	When automatic operation is needed; if buffer area is available in living space to mix cold and warm air
Portable electric heater	Thermostat (automatic)	When heat exchange from house not possible or desirable; in addition to manual heat exchange as freeze protection "insurance"; if small back-up load determined
Gas heater	Valve (manual)	Where gas is least expensive fuel and moderate to large backup is determined; if hookup is available
	Thermostat (automatic)	Same as manual, but when automatic operation required
Wood stove	Manual	Where wood is inexpensive; if time is available to tend stove; if moderate to large back-up load is determined
Zone of central house hot water system	Thermostat (automatic)	If central boiler has capacity and runs efficiently at low loads; if moderate to large backup is determined

ers, which combine an exterior combustion air intake and an exhaust flue in one wall penetration, offer an alternative. Their sealed combustion chambers prevent warm greenhouse air from escaping up the flue and avoid the problems associated with the air exchange fan.

Wood Stoves

Wood stoves have the advantage of using what is often the cheapest fuel, but they have several disadvantages. They can occupy a large area in the greenhouse, since even a small wood stove must be at least 18 inches away from any combustible material. Masonry, metal shields and/or fire-rated drywall should be used as wall materials in the vicinity of the stove. The plants must also be shielded from the intense heat which radiates from a hot stove or stovepipe. In addition, wood stoves require attention. They must be stoked and checked periodically, and time must be taken for wood gathering, storing and

RELATIVE INSTALLATION COST	ADVANTAGES	DISADVANTAGES
No cost if existing door and window openings are adequate	No hardware cost; cold air moves slowly into living area; uses no greenhouse space; uses house as heat storage for greenhouse	Requires attention; brings cold air into living space
Low	Same as above plus automatic controls	Blows cold air into living space; makes some noise in house
Low if electrical outlet available; low to medium if new circuit must be installed	Ease of installation; uses very little greenhouse space; automatic controls	Expensive fuel in most areas
Medium to high (needs flue and gas line)	Low cost fuel (in many areas)	Installation costs rather high; may require fan; uses some greenhouse space
Same as manual gas heater	Same as manual gas heater plus convenience of automatic controls	Same as manual gas heater
Medium to high (needs shielding and flue)	Low fuel cost (in many rural areas)	Requires shielding of plants; requires flue and shielding of structure; requires attention; uses a lot of greenhouse space
High (skilled labor required)	Automatic controls; uses little greenhouse space; good heat distribution	High installation cost

handling. Wood stoves are also relatively expensive to install, when the cost of a chimney, stovepipe and shielding is included. But when the cost of wood is low relative to other fuels, the labor to install the stove and attend to it is available and a relatively large back-up heating use is anticipated, a wood stove can be quite appropriate.

In general, though, a small stove is all that is required, except in very large greenhouses. The stove should be large enough or tight enough to burn all night, as the coldest hours will be just before dawn, the worst time to have to get out of bed just to stoke a fire.

Adding a Zone from a Central Heating System

If the house has a hot-water heating system, a loop can be added for the greenhouse back-up heating. A new zone would consist of a separate loop of pipe from the boiler, with its own circulating pump or zone valves, a thermostat placed in the greenhouse and a radiator or fan-coil unit. This zone can thus run independently of the rest of the system, with the boiler and circulating pump turning on when the greenhouse thermostat calls for heat.

The central heating system should be the hot water, or boiler type, rather than forced air, since creating the supply air extension for the greenhouse would present too many control complexities, particularly for periods when the house doesn't need heat but the greenhouse does. The first requirement for the zone approach to be practical is that the boiler have some excess capacity. If the boiler does not run continuously during the coldest times of the year, it probably can handle an additional load. You can use table 4-3 to determine the greenhouse load. Add this to the house load and check the boiler rating to see if it can handle the extra load. Check with a heating professional if you have any doubts.

A fan-coil unit is a good choice for the heat distribution within the greenhouse. The hot water from the boiler circulates through a fan-powered water-to-air heat exchanger that works like a car radiator. Warm air from a fan coil is easily directed throughout the greenhouse for even, well-controlled heating. In larger greenhouses, a polyethylene distribution tube can be attached to the fan coil, for precise air distribution. This is simply a polyethylene tube that has the same circumference as the outlet from the fan-coil unit. It is usually suspended from the ceiling with loops of string, hanging limp when the fan is off and inflating when it goes on. Holes are cut along the tube, placed to distribute air where you want it. For best use of the heat the holes should be placed to direct air at the plants, not at the glazing. With the right wiring, the fan can double as the air circulation fan when needed. The fan is wired to a timer that has it running during all daylight hours, for air circulation, and to a thermostat that turns it on whenever the back-up heating thermostat

calls for hot water for the fan coil from the central system. The five options for back-up heating are summarized in table 4-2.

Sizing the Back-Up System

The back-up system must be sized to keep the greenhouse temperature in the plant "comfort zone"—that is, above 50°F—during the coldest times of the year. Since the primary path for heat loss is through the glazing, the heating capacity needed for the back-up heating system can be based on the area of the glazing, as in table 4-3. (Infiltration, usually the second largest component of heat loss, and other heat losses are factored into these guidelines.) Table 4-3 assumes that the greenhouse is built with the levels of energy conservation suggested (in chapter 5) for each climate region. In cold and moderate climates the greenhouse is double glazed and is well built, i.e., all joints are tight, and vents and doors are weather-stripped and fit tightly. The table also assumes that no night insulation is in place on the glazing. Even if night insulation is used, the back-up system should be sized to keep the greenhouse warm if the glazing is left uninsulated.

Gas heaters are most often rated by their Btu per hour (Btu/hr) of fuel *input* rather than heat output. But some of this heat goes up the chimney—up to 50 percent. If output or efficiency ratings are not available, it is safe to assume that the heater is 50 percent efficient. In this case, double the required heat output to determine the required input capacity. Also, remember to include east- and west-facing glazing in totaling the glazed area, and to count any uninsulated exterior doors as glazed area, since 1 inch of wood has about the same insulation value as double glass.

For an example of this calculation take an 8-by-15-foot greenhouse that has 150 square feet of glass on the south, 10 square feet of glazing on each endwall and a 2½-

TABLE 4-3: MINIMUM BACK-UP HEATING CAPACITY*

CLIMATE	PLANT GROWING THROUGHOUT WINTER	SEASON EXTENSION ONLY
Cold	13 watts (44 Btu/hr)	10 watts (34 Btu/hr)
Moderate	10 watts (34 Btu/hr)	6 watts (20 Btu/hr)
Warm	6 watts (20 Btu/hr)	5 watts (17 Btu/hr)

NOTES: *Cold climates, as used here, are those where winters are longer than summers (with more than 6,000 heating degree-days); moderate climates have winters and summers of about equal length (with 4,000 to 6,000 heating degree-days); warm climates have summers that are longer than winters (with less than 4,000 heating degree-days). See the heating degree-day map in figure 5-7.*

This table is based on a 1 Btu/hr/°F heat loss for the whole greenhouse per square foot of greenhouse glazing, and design temperatures of 0, 10 and 25°F in cold, moderate and warm climates, respectively. One watt equals 3.41 Btu/hr.

*Per square foot of south, east and west glazing.

by-7-foot uninsulated door. The total glazed area is:

$$\text{Glazed area} =$$
$$150 + (2 \times 10) + (2.5 \times 7) = 187.5 \text{ ft}^2$$

For growing in the greenhouse all winter in a cold climate, 13 watts are required per square foot of glazing for a total of:

$$\text{Heating capacity} =$$
$$(187.5 \text{ ft}^2) \times (13 \text{ watts/ft}^2) = 2,438 \text{ watts}$$

Thus a 2,500-watt electric heater is adequate.

For season extension (10 watts/ft²), the minimum required size would be:

$$\text{Heating capacity} =$$
$$(187.5 \text{ ft}^2) \times (10 \text{ watts/ft}^2) = 1,875 \text{ watts}$$

For this example, a gas heater of unknown efficiency for all-winter use would require a heat input capacity of:

$$\text{Input capacity} =$$
$$(187.5 \text{ ft}^2) \times (44 \text{ Btu/hr}) \times (2)$$
$$= 16,500 \text{ Btu/hr}$$

Hot water baseboard units deliver about 500 Btu/hr or 150 watts per foot of baseboard. For the above example of the all-winter greenhouse in a cold climate, about 16½ feet of baseboard is required:

$$\text{Feet of baseboard} =$$
$$(2,438 \text{ watts}) \div (150 \text{ watts per foot})$$
$$= 16.3 \text{ feet}$$

Fan-coil sizing is a little more complicated and should be based on manufacturer's data for a particular unit. This can sometimes be done by plumbing supply houses that sell the units. They will need to know from you the boiler water temperature, usually 190°F, and the greenhouse temperature, which we'll call 55°F. (As with the baseboard, heat delivery will increase for colder greenhouse temperatures, so we'll size the unit for 55°F.) They'll also need to know the flow rate of the water from the boiler. If your supplier can't check your calculations for you, have a heating system professional check them before purchasing equipment.

Shading and Cooling

Shading devices aren't always necessary, even in warmer climates, for preventing summer overheating. Thorough ventilation will

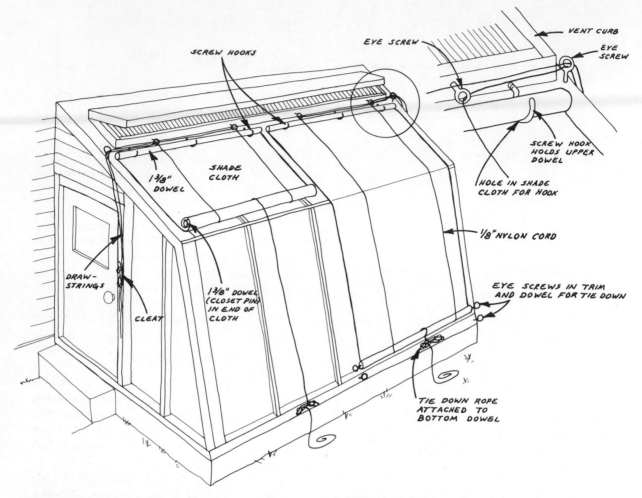

Labels in figure:

SCREW HOOKS

EYE SCREW

VENT CURB

EYE SCREW

SHADE CLOTH

1 3/8" DOWEL

SCREW HOOK HOLDS UPPER DOWEL

HOLE IN SHADE CLOTH FOR HOOK

DRAW-STRINGS

CLEAT

1 3/8" DOWEL (CLOSET PIN) IN END OF CLOTH

1/8" NYLON CORD

EYE SCREWS IN TRIM AND DOWEL FOR TIE DOWN

TIE DOWN ROPE ATTACHED TO BOTTOM DOWEL

Figure 4-9: Summer shade cloth can be mounted on dowels and operated with the same hardware as the inside roll-up curtain, allowing flexibility in the amount of shading. A tie-down rope is used to keep the wind from picking up the shade cloth, and in windy areas, eye screws are added to each end of the bottom dowel and tied to eye screws on the bottom trim.

keep the greenhouse cool enough in many cases. Where shading is needed, there are a variety of approaches, including trees, standard greenhouse shade cloth, external roll-down slat-type blinds or reflective shades inside the greenhouse. Many greenhouses in climates with hot summers are built with partially solid roofs and steeply sloped glazing to discourage summer sun entry. While this design does limit overheating, it can also substantially reduce the available light in the greenhouse, particularly under the solid roof. Thus a balance must be struck between designing for summer cooling and for growing

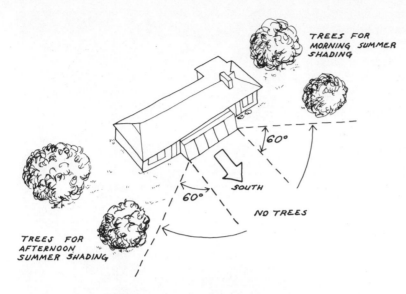

TREES FOR
MORNING SUMMER
SHADING

60°

SOUTH

NO TREES

60°

TREES FOR
AFTERNOON
SUMMER SHADING

Figure 4-10: Shade trees to the southwest and southeast of the greenhouse will greatly cut down on summer heat gain, with almost no shading of the winter sun. When locating trees, try not to block south-facing house windows. Tree height should also be planned: The final height of trees within 60 degrees of true south should be no more than one-third their distance from the greenhouse.

plants. (This balance, which depends on your needs as much as on your climate, is discussed more in chapter 7.) The shading techniques presented in this section will be most needed on moderate and warm-climate horticultural greenhouses. These greenhouses will tend to have broad expanses of sloped glazing, and will therefore be more in need of shading than nonhorticultural greenhouses. Shading devices can also be very useful for reducing the cooling load in fan-ventilated greenhouses.

Trees, Shade Cloth, Slat Shades and Shading Compound

Care must be taken in using trees for greenhouse shading, whether the trees are existing or newly planted, to avoid decreasing light levels and solar heating (see figure 4-10). Trees should not be placed close to the south face of the greenhouse. If they are close enough to shade the greenhouse in the summer, they can drastically cut down the available sun in the winter. A typical bare-branched tree blocks about 50 percent of the sun.

Shade cloth is an outdoor fabric, designed to absorb and reflect from 20 to 70 percent of the incident sunlight, depending on the color and density of the weave. There are several varieties, though it is most commonly made of some plastic material, and has a life span up to about five years. You can find it in commercial greenhouse supply catalogs.

The cloth can be temporarily tacked up on the outside of the greenhouse or installed on a roller for more control of the shading. For easy control the roller can be arranged with ropes and pulleys, in the fashion of a bamboo window shade. If the primary purpose of the shade cloth is light control for shade-loving plants in a small portion of the greenhouse, rather than for temperature control in the greenhouse as a whole, small pieces of shade cloth can be placed inside the greenhouse over the plants. Shade cloth is also available mounted on frames for standard glass sizes. Exterior shades made of wood or aluminum slats (usually more expensive than shade cloth) are also available from commercial greenhouse manufacturers and suppliers.

Shading compound is a light-colored solution, similar to whitewash, which is used by many commercial greenhouses to block and reflect summer sunlight. It is applied on the·outside of the glazing in early summer with rollers, brushes, mops or a spray gun. Some types wear off easily, with the rain removing most of the compound by autumn; others are more permanent. Check with the supplier or manufacturer of any shading compound to see if it is compatible with your greenhouse materials and find out how easily it can be removed. Check too on the toxicity of the compound.

Reflective Shades and Solar Staircases

Reflective shades or insulating shades or shutters that are used to reduce winter heat loss can also be used for summer shading. They do, however, block all the light, rather than just decreasing its intensity, and should not be used directly over growing beds that are used in the summer. If insulating shades or shutters are used for summer shading, it is important that they be reflective on the side facing the glazing—white or preferably silver—in order to reflect as much sunlight as possible. If the shade is tightly sealed around all its edges, the heat easily builds-up to 150 or 200°F, high enough to decrease the life span or damage the greenhouse, the seal on double glass units or shade materials. It is best to leave interior shades or shutters loose enough to allow for a flow of air to carry away excess heat.

For greenhouses that aren't used much for growing plants, sloped glazing can be transformed into the equivalent of a series of small vertical glazings with a system called Solar Staircase (see photo 4-8). Solar Staircase gives all the advantages of summer shading

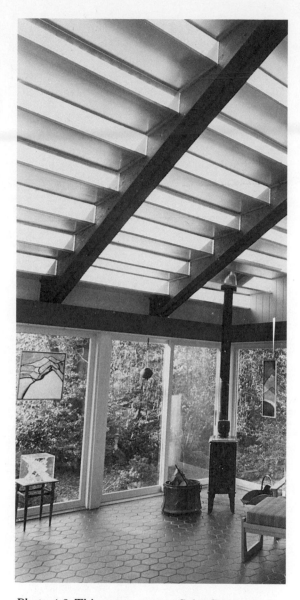

Photo 4-8: This sunspace uses Solar Staircase, a patented system of horizontal aluminum reflectors under sloped glazing to admit low winter sun while reflecting high summer sun. The reflectors, which are made of polished aluminum or glass mirrors, also help keep heat inside. The system can be fitted with one or more layers of glazing inside (underneath) the staircase to further decrease heat loss. *(Photo courtesy of Norman B. Saunders.)*

but with nothing to move or adjust, and it provides excellent overhead illumination to a sunspace. See Appendix 1.

Evaporative Cooling

In areas with hot, dry summers (such as the American southwest), cooling techniques beyond ventilation and shading may be needed if the greenhouse is to be kept within the upper range of the plant comfort zone during the hottest part of summer. Evaporative cooling units—often called "swamp coolers"—incorporate a fan that blows air through porous mats that are kept wet by a small pump drawing water from a reservoir in the bottom of the unit.

Evaporative cooling may be desirable if the greenhouse is used for ornamental plants that need shading and a highly controlled greenhouse environment. If the intention is to grow vegetables, it is simpler, and more energy conserving, simply to move to outdoor gardening in the summer. In areas with high humidity in the summer, evaporative cooling will be of little use.

Where only occasional evaporative cooling is needed, the walkways and interior surfaces of the greenhouse can simply be sprayed with a garden hose. Evaporative cooling pads, with a water reservoir at the bottom and a pump to trickle water over the pads, are used in conjunction with an exhaust fan for more continuous automatic cooling.

Beds and Benches

Even though growing beds and benches are usually built after the greenhouse shell is completed, they should be planned right along with the rest of the structure. This will ensure that the growing areas are in proper relationship to the glazing, vents and solid portions of the greenhouse.

Benches are most useful for plants like ornamentals and seedlings that are grown in

Photo 4-9: Open-grille benches such as these provide good air circulation and drainage around the plant pots.

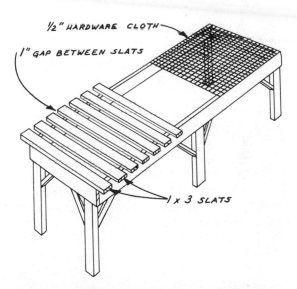

Figure 4-11: Slatted or screened bench tops allow good air circulation around potted plants. They can be mounted on legs or on the wall as shelves, or set on top of heat-storing water containers, so that warm air can circulate up around the plants.

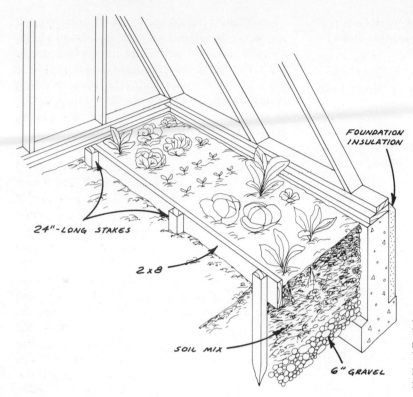

FOUNDATION
INSULATION

24"-LONG STAKES

2 x 8

SOIL MIX

6" GRAVEL

Figure 4-12: In-ground beds are
the cheapest and simplest of all
styles. The foundation wall must
be insulated to help keep the
roots warm, and the earth below
must be well drained.

pots or other small containers. Benches can
also make good use of otherwise unused space
in a greenhouse, such as the space along the
back wall or above heat storage containers.
Beds are more useful for growing vegetables,
particularly where more soil depth is needed
for root crops.

A bench can be as simple as a board on
top of a barrel, or one can be built as a
freestanding table or as a shelf attached to a
wall. The construction should be quite light
and open, for good water drainage and good
air circulation around the plants. Metal
screen, such as ¼-inch hardware cloth, or
narrow slats of wood (1 × 2 or 1 × 3) with an
inch or so of space between, can be used for
the surface of the bench.

Beds can be built completely or partially
above the ground or right in the ground with
the soil surface at ground level. Aboveground

beds have several advantages. Since they are
raised above the ground, they tend to have
warmer soil temperatures, particularly if the
south face of the bed is directly behind south-
facing glazing. In a greenhouse with a glazed
vertical kneewall, heat storage can even be
placed under the growing bed to provide additional heat to the soil. Good drainage is easier
to accomplish in aboveground beds than in-
ground beds, where the subsoil may not readily absorb water.

On the other hand, aboveground beds
take up vertical space in the greenhouse. If
the wall of the house where the greenhouse
will be built (the common wall) is particularly
short, the greenhouse glazing may have to
slope directly to the ground, requiring in-
ground or partially in-ground beds. (Another
solution to the short common wall problem is
to build the greenhouse floor below grade.

This "pit-type" construction will allow a full working height inside the greenhouse, but has a higher construction cost.) In-ground beds are cheaper to build since they require fewer materials. Beds in the earth can also take advantage of the warmth of the earth, keeping the plant roots warmed over prolonged cold spells. This is useful in greenhouses that are allowed to become quite cold at night (as near to freezing as possible without plant damage), but in greenhouses that are kept at temperatures warm enough for faster growth (around 50°F at night) the raised beds will promote warmer soil temperatures. A significant disadvantage of ground level beds is that they place the plants at the lowest level in the greenhouse, where cold air settles.

The following design guidelines for growing beds are aimed at encouraging the best plant growth.

Growing beds should be as deep as possible, 1½ to 3 feet deep. This depth provides a wide range of environments to support the variety of soil organisms needed to break down organic nutrients. Deep growing beds also hold water much longer than shallow beds, allowing less frequent watering. Deep beds also allow more room for good root development.

Growing beds must have good drainage. Beds built above the greenhouse floor must have many holes in the bottom. When the beds are watered, the drain holes will ensure that the bottom of the soil does not get soggy, which can cause root rot. The bottom 4 to 6 inches of the bed should be filled with gravel to assist with drainage. *Do not* line the bottom of the beds with plastic, as this will surely waterlog the plant roots. The sides, however, can be plastic-lined to stop leakage.

Before building a growing bed in the ground, be sure that the earth below the bed has good drainage. During the wettest season of the year, dig a hole to the depth of the planned bed and fill it with water. If the water drains out immediately, the bed probably won't have drainage problems and only a little gravel is needed in the bottom. If the water seeps out slowly, be sure to put 4 to 6 inches of gravel in the bottom and to water the bed sparingly when it is planted. If the water just won't drain, you'll be better off with above-ground beds.

The bed shown in figure 4-13 is built with 4-by-4 legs at the corners, and, if it is over 4 feet long, 2-by-4 legs in the middle. A *tension rod* is used on longer beds to keep the sides from bulging out. The legs are attached inside the bed rather than outside to give more aisle space and a nicer appearance. The bottom planks rest on 2-by-4 stringers that are screwed into the side of the legs. The planks aren't nailed down, since the soil will hold them in place. When you put the planks in, leave ½ inch between them, since they will swell quite a bit as they soak up irrigation water, and drill 1-inch drain holes every 6 inches in the boards. You can also leave the boards an inch apart to create gaps for drainage. If your gravel is small enough to fall through the cracks, line the bottom with plastic insect screen.

Screening is another alternative for the bottom of the beds, which provides even better drainage. A layer of hardware cloth is attached to the bottom with 2-by-2 battens screwed into the bottom edges of the side boards. Every 3 feet or so along the length of the bed, a 2 × 2 is run across the bottom to give the mesh additional support. The hardware cloth is covered on top with plastic insect screen if the gravel in the bottom of the bed is so fine that it would fall through the hardware cloth.

If pressure-treated lumber is used for the bed, and you don't want the soil in contact with it, you can line the walls with 6-mil polyethylene. This can be done by lining the whole bed with polyethylene, folding it into the corners to avoid cutting, and using a small

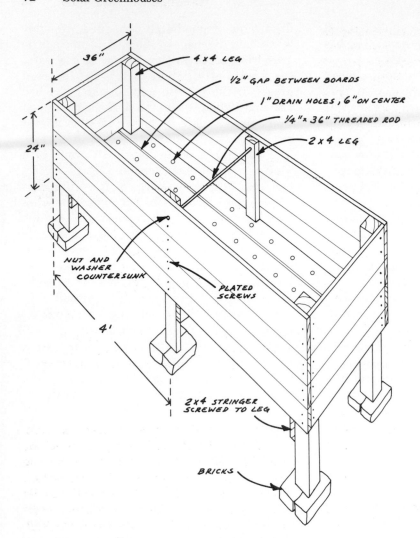

36"

4 x 4 LEG

½" GAP BETWEEN BOARDS

1" DRAIN HOLES, 6" ON CENTER

¼" x 36" THREADED ROD

2 x 4 LEG

24"

NUT AND
WASHER
COUNTERSUNK

PLATED
SCREWS

4'

2 x 4 STRINGER
SCREWED TO LEG

BRICKS

Figure 4-13: Aboveground beds provide an easy working height. Naturally rot-resistant cedar or redwood, or pressure-treated lumber will last the longest.

batten (½ inch by ¾ inch or so) around the inside of the top to hold it in place. Then cut out the plastic in the bottom everywhere the polyethylene is not in contact with wood, which will be everywhere except over the 2-by-2 hardware cloth supports. The only problem with plastic liners is that you have to be careful when you work in the soil with a trowel or other tools to avoid puncturing the liner.

Another alternative for the bottom of growing beds is rigid cementitious corrugated roofing (Ondulite is one brand) screwed to the underside of the walls of the bed.

Keep the growing beds warm. A warm root zone will keep plants growing at air temperatures below their normal minimum growing temperature and also accelerate growth at normal temperatures.

Freestanding aboveground beds can be

placed directly behind the south glazing to directly absorb the sun's heat. The wood wall of the bed between the soil and the sunlight will slow the absorption of the heat somewhat, but will not insulate the soil excessively. The glazed vertical kneewall shape is best suited to this approach, since the bed can be moved very close to the glazing, with little wasted space.

A variation of this is to place the bed on top of some type of heat storage, such as small water barrels or other water containers. If the containers are 12 to 18 inches high, such as 35-gallon drums or 5-gallon honey tins, the bed can be as much as 2 feet deep without making it too high to work on comfortably. Steel drums can provide full support for the bed, but with smaller, weaker containers the bed must be supported on its own legs. When water containers are placed under the beds, the foundation of the kneewall must be as low as possible to minimize shading of the heat storage.

The height of the top of the foundation is set to keep all wood at the required 6 to 8 inches above the highest part of the earth to avoid termite problems. If the earth slopes 1 foot from one side of the greenhouse to the other, that will mean the foundation sticks 18 to 20 inches out of the ground, at its highest point. Since 55-gallon drums are about 24 inches in diameter, they would be mostly shaded when laid on their sides, if the inside floor is level with the ground at the lower end of the slope. The solution is either to level the earth around the greenhouse, so you can have a shorter foundation, or to build up the level of the floor so that no more than one-third of the barrel is shaded.

Beds can also be built directly against the south foundation wall, either aboveground or inground, using the foundation as one of the walls of the bed. In order to keep the soil warm, the foundation wall should be either well insulated or solar heated. If the south

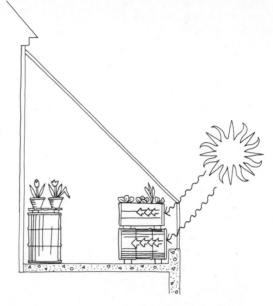

Figure 4-14: Heat storage and planting beds placed just behind the glazing will be heated directly by the sun. The warm root zone will boost winter plant growth.

foundation wall has a good solar exposure, and if your climate and configuration of the house will not completely bury the south side of the greenhouse with snow, the foundation wall can be turned into a solar collector by double glazing its surface. Moderate snow falls will melt away from the warm south wall, but if a large house roof and the greenhouse both dump snow in front and if you are in a snowy climate, the sun-warmed foundation may not be a good idea. Construction details for a solar heated foundation are in chapter 9.

In designing growing areas, avoid creating the potential for "pooling" of cold air on the plants. The greenhouse floor is usually below the level of the house floor, often by as much as 3 feet. If the house door is left open at night to keep the greenhouse warm, air circulation will occur mostly above the house floor

Figure 4-15: In smaller green-houses a continuous front and rear bed will give maximum utilization of the space for growing, while still allowing comfortable aisles and not requiring a reach of more than 3 feet to get to the back of any bed. In the deeper greenhouse, water barrels are shown stacked behind the rear bed. Heat storage can also be incorporated under the beds.

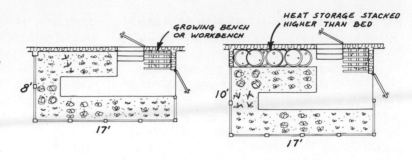

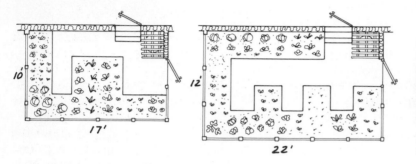

Figure 4-16: With larger floor areas, peninsula beds allow you to make use of as much of the space as possible while still allowing you to reach all parts of the beds. A small space, such as behind the door, is often a good place for a small bench for pots or for a working area.

level, leaving a pool of cold air on the floor of the greenhouse. If at all possible, put the top of the growing bed above the level of the house floor.

Beds should be easy to work in. Above-ground beds are easy to work if they are waist-high and are no wider than a person can comfortably reach, about 3 feet. If a bed is accessible from both sides, it can be twice this wide. Be sure there is enough room between beds for your wheelbarrow.

Remember the light! Place growing beds under and next to glazing and keep the top of the beds above the bottom of the glazing. The north bed in the greenhouse should be at the same height or higher than the south bed to prevent it from being shaded.

Don't use toxic preservatives on wood used in growing beds. Use rot-resistant wood such as cedar, redwood or cypress, or simply replace the boards after a few years. Or you can use copper naphthenate preservatives, which are not toxic to plants and don't leach into the soil or get absorbed by plants. *Do not use preservatives containing pentachlorophenol or creosote, which are most definitely toxic to plants.* Obtain recommendations for proper use and follow the manufacturer's directions when using any preservative.

Growing Bed and Bench Layout

Greenhouses built to maximize plant growth can have more growing area than overall floor area. This is accomplished by using beds, benches, shelves and hanging pots in every possible location. Greenhouses built more for the combination of solar heating, horticulture and living space will often have one built-in bed along part or all of the south side, with the rest of the area devoted to living space or for temporary benches for seedlings or ornamentals.

In greenhouses with a north-south dimension of 10 feet or less, having two beds that run east to west will use the space fairly efficiently, as shown in figure 4-15. In deeper greenhouses, a "peninsula" plan, as shown in figure 4-16, will make for better space utilization. (Heat storage could be placed under the front and/or rear beds or benches, depending on the shape of the greenhouse and the heat storage requirements.) A good rule of thumb for sizing growing beds for vegetables is to allow 20 to 40 square feet of growing bed per person.

In season-extension greenhouses, a bed is often built along the south side of the greenhouse, with the north side devoted to benches and shelves for spring starts and ornamentals or other container plants, such as herbs.

Watering Systems

Watering the greenhouse is one of the tasks most taken for granted in greenhouse operation. But it must be done conscientiously and carefully.

A watering system can be as simple as a watering can for a small greenhouse, or as elaborate as an automated hydroponic system that supplies both nutrients and water. When seedlings or other potted plants in small containers are in the greenhouse, daily watering is often required, so the watering system should make watering an easy, pleasant task.

Watering Cans and Garden Hoses

Water can be put into a large plastic garbage can or other nonrusting container in the greenhouse. This allows the water to warm up a little before it's used. Leave the lid ajar on the garbage can to allow the chlorine to evaporate from chlorinated water supplies.

By elevating the garbage can above the level of the beds you can siphon water from the can directly to the plants using a short length of garden hose. You could also put hose bib (valve) in the bottom of the container to create a gravity-flow system for simple watering. Having a pressurized water sys-

Photo 4-10: Vertical space is used well in this greenhouse, which has flats on the ground and on a shelf, and hanging plants above. (Photo courtesy of Rodale Press Photography Department.)

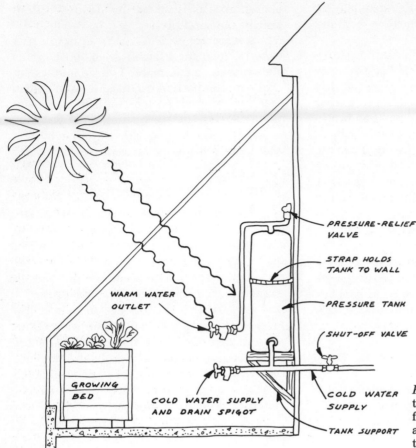

PRESSURE-RELIEF
VALVE

STRAP HOLDS
TANK TO WALL

PRESSURE TANK

SHUT-OFF VALVE

WARM WATER
OUTLET

GROWING
BED

COLD WATER SUPPLY
AND DRAIN SPIGOT

COLD WATER
SUPPLY

TANK SUPPORT

Figure 4-17: A tank placed in
the sun will provide warm water
for irrigation. Be sure to provide
a drain valve if the greenhouse is
to be left to freeze in the winter.

tem—using either city or well-pump water pressure—allows you to use any type of hose nozzle, like a mister or sprayer, but complicates preheating the water and doesn't allow evaporation of dissolved chlorine.

To add solar water warming, a dark-colored tank is "spliced" into the line between the cold water supply and the hose bib. A 30-gallon tank is big enough for most small- to moderate-sized greenhouses. The tank should be placed anywhere it will receive direct sun without blocking light to the plants.

You don't have to paint the tank black. A primary red or primary blue will absorb enough heat while reflecting parts of the visible light spectrum useful to plants. Be sure that the platform for the tank will hold the 300-plus pounds of 30 gallons of water and the tank. You will also have to install a temperature/pressure relief at the top of the tank and a shut-off valve inside the house to allow all pipes and the tank to be drained. This is particularly important if you don't intend to heat the greenhouse in the winter. This system can also be used to preheat hot water for the house.

Drip Systems, Mist Systems and Overhead Irrigation

These watering systems are usually found in large commercial greenhouses, where they are much more economical than the cost of labor for frequent hand watering. They can be run manually, or automated with timers or humidity controls and motorized valves.

Drip systems consist of a series of plastic pipes that branch into small tubes or drippers that drip water on the soil at each plant or pot. This system uses water very efficiently, since there is minimal evaporation. Plant foliage is also kept dry, an important feature for some crops, and the humidity is kept down, since water isn't being sprinkled about. Drip systems can be automated with a simple timer connected to a solenoid valve in the water line. By adjusting the main gate valve that controls the flow rate through the drippers and by setting the amount of time the water runs, the irrigation can be controlled fairly precisely. A typical drip system with a timer, solenoid valve, and pipe and drippers for 30 outlets costs about $100.

Mist systems spray a fine mist of water down on the plants from a special misting nozzle inserted into a plastic plumbing pipe or tube suspended above. They are used for keeping up humidity levels in dry climates and for evaporative cooling as well as for irrigating seedlings or cuttings that need moist air around them. In dry climates, these systems are particularly useful when coupled with an automatic humidity controller, or *humidistat,* which turns on the mister whenever the humidity gets too low. A small automatic system with three or four spray nozzles will cost in the $150 to $200 range, and a manual system could be put together for $25 to $50. Mist systems require that water pressure be at least 40 pounds per square inch and 50 psi is recommended.

Designing for Disease Control

The solar greenhouse environment is as attractive and as nurturing to plant pests as it is to plants. Organisms that live in some parasitic relationship to plants have naturally evolved to thrive under the same conditions as their hosts, and sooner or later these pests will find your greenhouse. If you're not prepared for them, they will compete quite successfully for the food you are growing. Solving pest problems with toxic chemicals is even less acceptable in the greenhouse than in the outdoor garden, since poisons sprayed into the greenhouse are very likely to find their way into the house from an attached greenhouse. Biological pest control, or the use of beneficial insects or other organisms to combat an unwanted one, is even more important in the greenhouse than in the outdoor garden. For example, ladybugs or a small insect called a predatory gall midge can be imported to eat aphids. *Integrated pest management* combines biological controls with benign chemicals, such as a spray made from chili powder and garlic tea or mild soap, for pest control.

Healthy plants are the first line of defense against pests. Supplying a good balance of water, air, nutrients and light in the appropriate temperature regime will give the plants the best possible resistance to diseases and pests.

Listed below are design considerations that can decrease disease and pest problems:

The interior of the greenhouse should be easy to clean. Materials should be chosen for ease of cleaning, within the allowable budget. A smooth wall or growing bed wall surface painted with gloss or semigloss enamel is much easier to clean than rough-cut boards. Tile or smooth concrete floors are the easiest to clean; brick is a little more challenging and gravel and dirt floors are virtually impossible to clean.

Provide for good ventilation and air circulation to avoid humidity buildup. This includes following the guidelines for exhaust ventilation and providing a circulating fan inside the greenhouse. The relative humidity should stay between 50 and 70 percent.

Soil beds must be well drained. This reduces humidity by allowing the beds to be slightly drier in the winter and eliminates stress on the plants due to salt buildups or water-logged roots.

Provide screens on all openings to the house and to the outside. This will help keep greenhouse pests out of the house and will keep in many insects that are imported to prey on pests.

Provide an easy place to hang up the watering hose. Keep the nozzle off the floor to prevent it from spreading disease.

In this chapter we've explored solar greenhouse design mainly from a horticultural point of view, with the goal of ensuring that the plants will thrive, and that you will have a relatively easy job of helping them thrive in a controlled environment. Some of the systems and design features we've seen are complementary to solar heating and energy conservation concerns, including ventilation, exhaust and shading systems. Others, like shallow-sloped overhead glazing or end-wall glazing, are needed for plant growth and compromise energy conservation somewhat. In the next two chapters, we'll explore ways to include features important for energy conservation in the greenhouse itself, and features needed for making best use of the greenhouse solar heat for heating the house.

Chapter 5

DESIGNING FOR ENERGY EFFICIENCY

Designing an energy-efficient greenhouse requires compromising some of the features of the horticulturally "perfect" greenhouse. Light levels are decreased by double glazing and solid wall or roof areas. But it is possible to arrive at a happy medium. Making small compromises in certain horticultural features can yield big savings in back-up energy use, and some energy conservation features will actually assist plant growth. For example, adding heat storage under growing areas not only decreases back-up fuel use but aids plant growth because the roots are kept warmer.

The first part of this chapter will cover energy conservation in the greenhouse, starting with heat loss in the greenhouse and specific energy-conserving features. The second part covers the design issues involved with solar heating the greenhouse.

Minimizing Heat Loss

In order to establish priorities for greenhouse energy conservation it is important to understand the relative significance of the various paths for heat loss from the green-

house. In this section we will examine and compare heat loss in two greenhouses: one that is designed for maximum growing and maximum solar heating (greenhouse A), and the other for minimum growing and moderate solar heating with a greater emphasis on having a living space (greenhouse B). Greenhouse A has a large glazed area that is sloped at a 45-degree angle. Greenhouse B has glazing illuminating only a small portion of the floor area and has a much smaller glazed area at a steeper angle—about 60 degrees.

Figure 5-1 shows the percentages of the total heat loss through the various parts of the greenhouses, along with actual heat loss amounts for each shown in table 5-1. You can see that by far the greatest loss is through the glazing: It is 66 percent of the total in greenhouse A and 48 percent in B. Next highest is infiltration, followed by heat loss through the solid roof and wall areas and foundation.

Glazing

It's obvious that the top priority for energy conservation is the glazing, and fortu-

79

TABLE 5-1: HEAT LOSS

SOURCE OF HEAT LOSS	AREA (A)	R-VAL	U-VAL*	UA†	% OF TOTAL	SOURCE OF HEAT LOSS	AREA (A)	R-VAL	U-VAL*	UA†	% OF TOTAL
GREENHOUSE A:						**GREENHOUSE B:**					
Glazing and door (double glazed)	340 ft²	1.85	0.54	184	66	Glazing and door (double glazed)	150 ft²	1.85	0.54	81	48
Solid walls and roof (3½" fiberglass insulation)	135 ft²	12	0.085	12	4	Solid walls and roof (3½" fiberglass insulation)	268 ft²	12	0.085	23	14
Foundation (with 2" foam insulation)	38 lin ft	(23 Btu/°F-hr-ft)		9	4	Foundation (with 2" foam insulation)	38 lin ft	(23 Btu/°F-hr-ft)		9	5
Infiltration	(Volume = 1,620 ft³; 1 air change/hr)			44	16	Infiltration	(Volume = 1,620 ft³; 1 air change/hr)			44	26
Evaporation/ condensation	(15% of glazing loss)			28	10	Evaporation/ condensation	(15% of glazing loss)			12	7
Total				277	100	Total				169	100

*U = 1/R; R is in hr-°F-ft²/Btu.
†UA = U-val × Area Btu/hr-°F

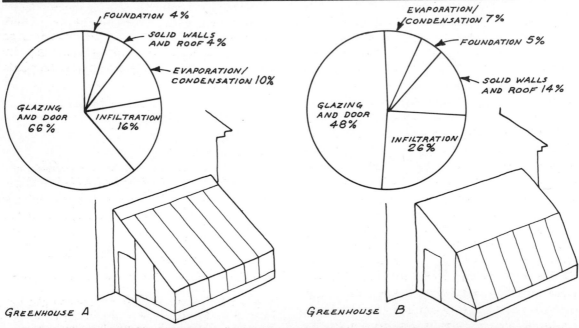

Figure 5-1: The two greenhouses shown are typical of a horticultural/solar heating greenhouse (A) and a living space/solar heating greenhouse (B). The percentage of the total heat loss through each portion of the greenhouse, shown in table 5-1, makes it obvious that most of your energy conservation efforts should be directed at the glazing, with minimizing infiltration being the next most important objective.

nately there are a number of ways to reduce this heat loss. In moderate and cold climates double glazing should always be used. This will cut the loss through the glazing by about half. Triple glazing and "superglazings" (discussed below) can be used in cold climates where the greenhouse is kept heated at night in winter, either for plant growing or for use as a nighttime living space. The extra layer of glazing, though, does decrease light levels inside the greenhouse. Some types of plants, like salad and cooking greens, aren't affected by the lower light levels, so yields for these won't be decreased. But with fruiting and flowering plants, which require high light levels, the decreased light can result in up to a 20 percent decrease in yields. (With fruiting plants growing under triple glazing, it's doubly important to keep the glazing clean, since light levels will already be low and decreasing them any further will further limit growth.)

The newly developed superglazings mentioned above consist of factory-sealed, double-glass units with a heat-retaining film layer in between. These can be used to significantly reduce heat losses through the glazing because of their relatively high R-value. Glazing units that include Heat Mirror (made by the Southwall Corporation, Palo Alto, Calif.) have the R-value of quadruple glazing, but transmit light about as well as triple glass. They are not inexpensive, but their incremental cost over standard double glass compares favorably with the cost of commercially available night insulation, another conservation option. Another product includes two layers of a highly transparent film (Sungain made by 3M) sealed inside two layers of glass. This four-layer assembly, known was Quadpane, performs about the same as Heat Mirror. Glass with heat reflective coatings deposited directly on the inside surface of one of the layers of double glass is also available. Its insulative value, about R-3, is somewhat lower

than the units incorporating films suspended between the sheets of glass, which is R-4 or higher.

All superglazing systems substantially decrease the amount of transmitted solar energy, to about 50 percent from a possible 70 to 80 percent. In terms of solar heating the greenhouse and the house, this results in performance similar to regular double glazing with night insulation used every night. Not as much solar heat gets in, but there is much less heat loss. This strategy can be very effective for sunspace design, simplifying construction and eliminating the daily task of opening and closing shutters or curtains.

Choosing the optimum air gap between double glazing layers will also decrease heat loss. The effect that air gap has on the overall insulation value of double glazing is shown in figure 5-2. A 1-inch gap has the highest R-value but only slightly higher than a ¾-inch gap.

The air gap for off-the-shelf double-glass units is often only ¼ or ½ inch, but many suppliers can provide units with wider gaps for a small additional cost. The air gap for site-built double glazing can usually be what-

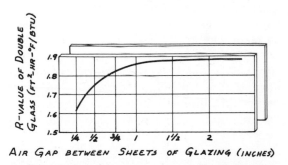

Figure 5-2: The insulation value of double glazing increases as the gap between the glazing layers increases, up to a 1-inch spacing. It is worth choosing the optimum spacing in colder climates.

ever you want, but it is a good idea in cold climates to optimize the spacing, particularly if the greenhouse will be kept heated throughout the heating season. (See chapter 11 for construction details for site-built glazing.)

Using an infrared-opaque glazing material such as glass or certain plastics will save about one-fourth to one-third the heat loss through the glazing, compared with using an infrared-transparent glazing such as polyethylene. However, polyethylene is often used because it is so low in cost. If your initial building budget is limited, you can consider deferring the cost of more expensive glass glazing by initially covering the greenhouse with polyethylene. Later the polyethylene can be replaced with a more heat retaining and longer-lasting glazing.

The choice of a material for the glazing support rafters doesn't affect the heat loss through the glazing, but it does influence the insulation value of the glazed area as a whole. For example, the rapid conduction of heat through aluminum rafters decreases the overall insulation value of a double glazed area by 10 to 15 percent, while for single glazing there is a 10 to 20 percent reduction. In other words, the aluminum framing conducts heat more rapidly than the glazing it supports. However, some manufactured greenhouses have aluminum rafters that incorporate *thermal breaks,* which serve to slow down the flow of heat through the rafter (see figure 5-3). These framing members have an acceptable insulation value, about the same as that of double glazing. Wood, which is a natural insulator, or "thermally broken" aluminum are desirable framing materials for use in cold climates.

Night Insulation

Insulating the glazing at night can significantly reduce overall heat loss and back-up heating use. Keeping the greenhouse warmer

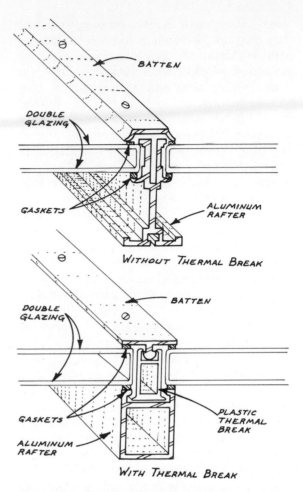

Figure 5-3: Aluminum framing members should have "thermal breaks" (lower cross section), plastic sections that insulate the inside metal from the outside. These can increase the insulative value of the whole glazed area by 10 to 20 percent. In the upper cross section, which has no thermal break, greenhouse heat is conducted directly out between the glazing.

at night also helps in accelerating plant growth. But night insulation is generally expensive to install, with many commercial brands costing at least five dollars per square foot plus installation (though many brands can be owner installed). And like seatbelts, it must be used to be effective. If the greenhouse requires summer shading, the night insulation can double as a cooling device, as long as enough light is still available for whatever summer growing is intended.

In general, night insulation is most useful in cold climates in greenhouses where growing is done in winter, particularly in greenhouses with little heat storage capacity. Night insulation not only saves energy, but keeps the plants and planting beds warmer at night, providing a more beneficial environment for growth.

The following is a summary of the important features of night insulation used for greenhouses.

• It should have an insulation value of at least R-2 in addition to glazing (R-2 is a good compromise between cost and performance)

• There should be tight edge seals or another method for stopping air from getting between the glazing and the insulation

• The insulation material should be moisture and vapor resistant, especially when used in a horticultural greenhouse

• The insulation materials should be reflective on the exterior side, particularly if the system is to be used for summer shading

• The overall system should be easy to use, even when there are beds full of plants between the operator and glazing

• When it's not in use, the insulation shouldn't block glazing or take up otherwise useful space in the greenhouse

Two books, *Movable Insulation* by William Langdon and *Thermal Shutters and Shades* by William Shurcliff (see Further Reading), cover many options for night insulation in detail.

Reflective Films and Fabrics

Night insulation materials for greenhouses can be highly reflective to long-wave infrared heat radiation, or good barriers to

Photo 5-1: Track lighting attached to the rafter is convenient and good looking but might get in the way if you are planning a night curtain.

conduction and convection, or good barriers to all of these modes of heat transfer.

Aluminum foil-faced fabrics or aluminized polyester film (such as Du Pont's Mylar) are both highly reflective *on the aluminum side.* The aluminum is deposited on the film in a very thin layer—only several molecules thick—in a vacuum chamber. Even though it looks like a mirror on both sides, (which tells you it is highly reflective to radiation in the *visible* part of the spectrum on

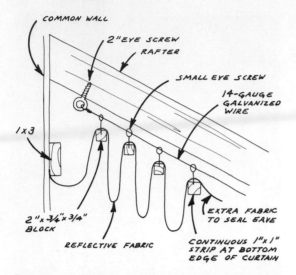

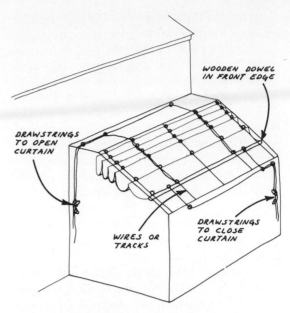

Figure 5-4: Wires are a simple, inexpensive way to hang an overhead curtain. This system suspends the fabric with small eye screws screwed into little blocks of wood under the fabric.

Figure 5-5: Overhead curtain systems can be run on tracks or wires. The top of the curtain can be left open or attached to the common wall with a magnetic seal at the bottom and magnetic or friction side seals. Cords are used to open the curtain and to close it on slopes shallow enough that the weight of the curtain won't pull it down.

both sides) it is about 95 percent reflective to long-wave infrared heat radiation only on the aluminized side. The other side is generally only about 40 to 50 percent reflective. Over time, the aluminum does lose some of its reflectivity, which can drop as low as 60 percent on the aluminized side.

Foil-coated fabric, such as Foylon, has a high reflectivity to infrared radiation on the aluminum side, about 90 to 95 percent when new, degrading to near 60 percent over time. And after three to five years, the aluminum may begin to delaminate from the polyester cloth backing, but Foylon is cheap enough (as low as $0.25 per square foot) to warrant periodic replacement. The back side, which is polyester cloth, absorbs about 80 percent of the infrared energy striking it. The fabric backing makes the material easy to sew if you want to use it as a curtain or roll-up shade.

There is also a new generation of laminated reflective polyester films that have a thin transparent layer covering the aluminum layer to preserve its reflectivity. These are currently beginning to reach the market and are just beginning to be available.

Reflective films or fabric are often mounted on track or cable systems when they're used in large commercial greenhouses, with the material being bunched up when the curtain is open. This same technique can be used in smaller greenhouses and is particularly useful on glazing that is sloped at less than about 60 degrees. A solid roof section at the top of the greenhouse can provide a good out-of-the-way location for the bunched-up fabric when the curtain is open.

One of the difficulties with tracked systems is getting a good seal at the edges.

Photo 5-2: Shown here is a reflective overhead curtain that runs on tracks on the bottom of the rafters and nests up under the solid roof area when it's not in use. It is held onto little wheeled runners on the track with clips, so it can be removed in summer and replaced with a white shade cloth. This allows light for the plants while keeping much of the heat above the curtain, where it is vented out the roof vent.

Photo 5-3: This shade uses a reflective film on a standard shade roller, with magnetic edge seals. A reflective fabric could also be used.

Magnet systems can be used, but it is still difficult to achieve a uniform edge seal. On pitches steeper than 60 degrees and on vertical glazing, standard commercial shade rollers can be used with the thin reflective film or foil-and-fabric laminates in conjunction with magnetic edge seals. The edge is easier to seal with the magnet system, and the material rolls up into a small, neat bundle. That the material can be stored neatly is not only an aesthetic concern but also a practical one: Stored insulation mustn't block any incoming sunlight. A plastic strip magnet like the ones contained in refrigerator door gaskets is adhered to the framing with double-sided tape. An adhesive-backed steel tape is fastened to the edges of the shade material. This tape is thin enough to roll up, yet tempered enough to flatten again when the shade is unrolled. When the shade is pulled it is kept away from the magnet to prevent it from "grabbing" the steel. When the shade is pulled down far enough, it is allowed to contact the magnet along its entire length. It's a simple operation that takes only a little practice to master. This system is relatively inexpensive and is easy to install, but it does require that you be able to stand next to the glazing to operate the shade, which isn't always practical for areas where growing beds are adjacent to glazing. (Sources for materials are listed in Appendix 1.)

Reflective films or fabrics can also be mounted in the same fashion as roll-up bamboo or matchstick blinds for use on vertical glazing. The strings can be run through eye screws or pulleys to a convenient location. The operation of this type of shade allows the magnet to separate from the steel tape incrementally, when it's rolled up, and to contact incrementally when it's rolled down. This makes for relatively easy operation.

Foam Insulation Panels

Rigid foam insulation is well suited for use as night insulation, particularly with irregular glazing shapes such as triangles and trapezoids, which are difficult, if not impossible, to fit with shades or curtains. Pop-in

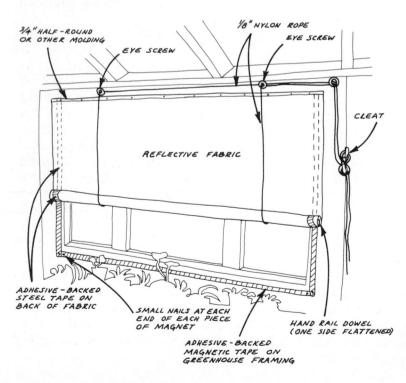

Figure 5-6: This roll-up shade is appropriate for vertical glazing and allows you to operate the curtain from one side of the glazed area, which is important where plants fill up the area next to the glazing. Using simple eye screws, rope and magnetic edge seals, it is effective and easy to build.

panels have the disadvantage of needing storage space, although sliding panels eliminate this problem. Commonly used types include sheets of extruded polystyrene (Styrofoam) and polyisocyanurate with aluminum foil facing (High R, Thermax, R-Max). All of these can provide excellent barriers to heat loss. The foil-faced brands have highly reflective faces on both sides, which add to their insulation value. The outer reflective surface is also quite effective if the panels are used for summer shading. An advantage that the polyisocyanurate foam has over the polystyrene is its higher R-value, about R-8 per inch of thickness compared to R-5 for extruded polystyrene. (This, however, will probably become closer to R-7 over time as the less conductive gas in the foam bubbles is gradually replaced by air.) Some of the isocyanurate brands contain glass fibers in the foam for structural reinforcing. This is a definite advantage as the fibers strengthen the panels quite a bit. The foil skins on both sides also add to the material's strength.

Both expanded and extruded polystyrene foam are less expensive than polyisocyanurate foam, and although they have a lower R-value per inch, they usually offer a high R-value per dollar spent. Avoid buying "beadboard" (expanded polystyrene), which is made of the same tiny expanded foam beads that are pressed into coffee cups. It is too delicate, and it absorbs some water. Extruded polystyrene is stronger and absorbs much less moisture. This type, which is usually blue or pink, has a uniform foam look when it's sliced, rather than the composite of small beads.

Any plastic foam is very susceptible to degradation by ultraviolet light, and it shouldn't be used for summer shading without some type of covering. Foam sheets that are regularly being put up and taken down should have their corners and edges protected

to minimize wear and tear. Duct tape, aluminum or stainless steel tape will give good protection. A light wooden frame will do that and add strength to large panels. (You shouldn't expect foam panels to last forever, but they can give several years of low-cost service with careful handling.)

Even large foam panels are fairly light in weight, but in use they still must be securely fixed with tight edge seals. One method is to put strips of flexible foam around the panel edges to create a snug fit between the glazing supports. The strips can be held in place with the tape used to protect the edges. Two-inch-wide duct tape is often used for this purpose, but it tends to delaminate in a year or two. Metallic tapes (aluminum, stainless steel) are more durable, but susceptible to abrasion from pushing the panels in and out against the framing. Vinyl tape with an acrylic adhesive offers a compromise. (Such tape is available from suppliers of 3M industrial tapes.)

Recently developed are some preweather-stripped plastic extrusions that can be made into lightweight panel frames. (See Appendix 1.) Like the foam strips, the extrusions create a friction fit that requires only that the panel be pressed into place. This requires very accurate measuring and cutting to get the right size. But be sure you don't make the panels so tight that they will be bent when pushed in or pulled out, since this will just hasten their deterioration. And be sure to build in a handle so you can pull the panels out.

Another approach to sealing the panels is to use magnets to hold them so close to the glass that convection is suppressed. This method is effective and doesn't require the precision of the friction fit method. Nightwall brand magnetic clips (see Appendix 1) are made for use with foam panels. One-half of

Photo 5-4: This R-6, push-in panel is made from ¾-inch foil-covered isocyanurate board with soft foam-rubber edges covered with duct tape. Note the little tape handles at the top to aid in getting the panel out.

the clip is a self-adhesive magnet, and the other half is a thin, self-adhesive steel strip. A small aesthetic disadvantage is that these strips are permanently left on the glazing. Pitched glazing will need more strips than vertical glazing to hold the panels.

One solution to the storage problem is to use the panels as sliding shutters. This is particularly useful for insulating overhead glazing when there is enough solid roof area to accommodate the panels when they are opened. The panels can slide on wood or aluminum tracks, and the weight of the foam on the track is usually adequate for the edge seals. If the shutters are used for summer shading, it is best if they have a reflective top surface and an air gap at the top between the shutter and the glazing to let out the hot air that accumulates. (The upper exhaust vents in the greenhouse will allow this heat to escape.) If there is no gap, the resulting high temperatures will hasten the deterioration of the shutter, the glazing sealant and wood-framing materials and can cause the seals to break on factory-sealed double glass.

Other Night Insulation Options

In addition to reflective films and rigid foam panels, there is a variety of quiltlike materials that typically incorporate a layer of fluffy polyester batting, a vapor barrier and fabric covering. These materials are available in a variety of ready-made curtain assemblies.

Moisture can be a problem with these materials when they're used in a humid greenhouse. If the vapor barrier is on the interior side, where common wisdom would place it, vapor migration through the curtain will be stopped. But vapor will still find its way around the tightest seal and will condense on the glazing and the exterior side of the curtain. If the curtain is rolled up while it's moist, water will soak in and reduce its insulation value, and possibly lead to mold or fungus growth. If the vapor barrier is between two layers of batting where it is put in many commercially-made curtains, both sides can get wet.

In a sunspace where humidity isn't a problem, these commercially made curtains can be useful (though you should compare their cost against that of triple glass, Heat Mirror or Quadpane), but in a horticultural greenhouse, you may be better off with a reflective film, push-in panels or a combination of the two.

Another approach to night insulation in greenhouses used primarily for growing is to insulate only the plants, rather than all the glazed areas. The insulation can be a curtain that runs on a frame or on cables over the bed, or it can be a series of rigid foam panels that form little tents over the plants. This strategy is especially effective if the heat storage is under the planting beds, or if the growing beds are deep enough (1 to 2 feet) that they have substantial heat storage capacity in their soil. But if at least some heat storage cannot be included under the insulation with the plants, this type of insulation will not be that effective. This strategy is also inappropriate for greenhouses that might be damaged by freezing if *all* the heat storage is under the insulation with the plants. This would include greenhouses with plumbing in them or with undersized water heat storage in small containers.

External insulating shutters have been built in a variety of designs, including shutters that double as reflectors, bifold shutters that move sideways or up and down, and removable shutters that are put in and taken out. These shutters have the advantage of not taking up any indoor space or being in the way of plants or support posts. Properly positioned shutters can also act as reflectors that increase solar heat gain and light levels in the greenhouse. But all outdoor shutters do share a common problem: They are outdoors where they are subject to wind, snow, rain, sun and freezing water. Another drawback is that you have to go outside to operate them (if there is no indoor operating mechanism). While all of the problems cited here can be solved, the

Photo 5-5: These sliding roof shutters offer night insulation in the winter and shading in the summer.

solutions usually require more effort and expense than would be required for equivalent indoor night insulation.

Infiltration

Infiltration accounts for the second largest portion of greenhouse heat loss. The following guidelines tell what can be done to bring the infiltration rate down to a very acceptable one-half air change per hour. You can consider these guidelines as being essentially minimum construction standards to keep down back-up heating costs:

• All vents and doors to the outside should have weather stripping and tight-closing latches; vent materials should be chosen and vents should be constructed to resist warping

• A continuous vapor barrier (6-mil polyethylene) should be installed on the inside of all insulated walls (above the foundation) and roof sections; all joints and holes in the vapor barrier should be taped or sealed with acoustic sealant (a type of caulking)

• The seam between concrete or concrete block foundations and the sill-plate should be filled with a sill-sealer and thoroughly caulked on the inside

• All glazing seams should be thoroughly caulked or gasketed

• The seam between the house and greenhouse should be totally caulked, inside and outside

• Use expanding foam caulking around all door and window frames, and in any joints where the crack is wider than ¼ inch

• If the greenhouse is in a very windy location with little shielding, additional windbreaks such as fencing or plantings should be added

• If the greenhouse is to be used as an entry to the house during the winter *and* is used for winter growing in moderate or cold climates,

having a vestibule or air-lock entry is advisable; this will not only save heat in the greenhouse, but will also reduce the shock to the plants of cold outside air rushing in.

In very cold climates, where all-year growing will be done, further measures can be taken:

• Use higher quality magnetic weather stripping on doors, and closed cell neoprene foam on vents

• A tight flue damper should be used on any fuel-burning back-up heater in the greenhouse

• Temporarily seal all vents and other openings that are closed during the winter with tape or rope caulking

Minimizing infiltration involves a combination of choosing the right materials and paying close attention to their installation. Care taken with these details will result in higher energy savings as well as better plant growth.

Solid Walls and Roofs

These areas represent a very small fraction, typically about 5 percent, of the overall heat loss in a greenhouse with a lot of glazing (such as greenhouse A in figure 5-1). In greenhouses with glazing over less than half the total surface areas, the percentage is higher—as high as 15 percent with minimally glazed designs (such as greenhouse B in figure 5-1). But since this percentage is so small, extra high levels of insulation are hard to justify in either case. You will be better off spending the extra time and money on cutting infiltration and glazing losses. In greenhouses with either a little or a lot of glazing, 2-by-4 stud wall construction with 3½-inch fiberglass insulation is good for warm and moderate climates, and in cold climates, 2-by-6 stud walls with 6-inch batts are recommended. Roof rafters should also be 2 × 6 or larger in cold climates, and they can be as small as 2 × 4 in moderate and warm climates if that doesn't present any structural problems. The space between rafters should be almost filled with fiberglass insulation, leaving only enough room under the roof sheathing for venting.

In any greenhouse, a good vapor barrier is essential to maintaining the integrity of the insulation. If water vapor from the greenhouse can penetrate the walls during the winter, it will migrate through the insulation. The farther it goes toward the outside the colder it gets, and when the temperature drops to the dew point, the vapor condenses in the fiberglass, which lowers its insulation value. If a lot of water accumulates over successive winters, the wood in the walls can actually begin to rot. Since the relative humidity is always high in a plant-growing greenhouse, vapor barriers are even more important in greenhouses than they are in houses. Although 4-mil polyethylene sheeting is adequate for stopping vapor, many builders prefer 6-mil (1 mil = 0.001 inch) sheeting because it is less susceptible to tearing while it is being installed.

Yet no matter how much care is taken in installing the vapor barrier, there will probably be some holes from nails that miss studs, from sharp corners of interior sheathing bumping the sheeting while it's being installed and from corners where it is difficult to overlap separate sheets of polyethylene. For this reason, the insulation should be vented to allow any moisture that gets into the stud wall to escape. Wall insulation isn't usually vented in common residential building practice, but because the exterior skin of a solid wall is usually permeable to vapor, moisture that gets into the walls can get out. The cracks between exterior sheathing pieces and between sheathing and framing members at the top and bottom of the wall will usually let enough vapor out to provide adequate venting. For this reason, exterior plywood sheathing should *not* be caulked or glued to the framing on a greenhouse. This is often done in house construction, but in a horticultural greenhouse it is important to ensure that the exterior skin isn't absolutely hermetic.

If the outside sheathing is very tight, 2-inch button vents should be installed in each stud cavity, as detailed in chapter 10. If your wall sheathing is fairly loose—boards, for example, instead of plywood—Tyvek, a vapor permeable air barrier, can be installed between the exterior sheathing and siding to cut down the wind's intrusion into the insulation. Since it's vapor permeable, Tyvek won't trap moisture in the wall, and it will increase the insulation value of the wall by keeping the cold outside air from blowing through it. However, this strategy is cost-effective only on fairly large wall expanses on greenhouses with minimal glazing. If you have small pieces of Tyvek lying around as scraps from another job, it takes minimal labor to install, so you may as well do it. But it probably isn't worth the effort if you have to go out and buy a roll of it to cover a small area. Exterior siding such as clapboards or shingles is preferable to a monolithic finish material such as a finished plywood sheathing, since the smaller siding pieces will permit more air circulation. Stains are preferable over paints for exterior sheathing, since stains are more permeable to vapor.

Floors and Foundations

As we saw in table 5-1, the heat loss through the floor (foundation) also represents a small fraction, about 5 percent, of the total in the example greenhouses. This assumes that the floor is either a concrete slab, or brick or gravel that is within a foot above or below the ground level. It is also assumed that the perimeter of the foundation is insulated. The floor itself doesn't usually have to be insulated if the perimeter is insulated because the earth under the greenhouse has sufficient insulation value and is sufficiently warm that the heat loss to the underlying ground is small. (Damp sites may be an exception to this rule and should be evaluated individually.)

Heat loss through the perimeter will be quite high if it is not insulated. Perimeter insulation should always extend below the frostline, or, if the ground doesn't freeze in your area, at least a foot below grade. It should go high enough up the foundation to meet or overlap the insulation in solid walls and to come as close as possible to the bottom of the glazing on glazed walls.

Every effort should be made to ensure that the insulation is *continuous* from the solid walls down into the ground. (In chapter 9 construction details show how this is done.) Insulation can be placed on the interior or the exterior of the foundation. Placing it on the outside of a concrete or masonry foundation encloses this mass inside the envelope of insulation, which adds to the total heat-storing capacity of the greenhouse. However, unless warm air is moved over the interior foundation surface when the sun is shining, the heat storage contributed by the foundation is relatively little because it doesn't usually receive direct sunshine, and the air next to it is usually the coolest air in the greenhouse. A circulating fan can be ducted with polyethylene tubing, such as the type used with the fan-coil back-up heater, to bring warm air to the foundation. Details for placing and protecting foundation insulation from moisture, physical abuse, insects and sunlight deterioration are covered in chapter 9.

Two-inch extruded polystyrene insulation is recommended for foundation insulation. This amount (about R-10) strikes a good balance between energy conservation and ease of construction for all climates. It's not really worth the extra effort to go to 3-inch foam, even in cold climates, because there will be only a minimal decrease in overall heat loss, compared with using 2-inch foam. But if the growing beds are in the ground and in contact with the foundation, thicker insulation is recommended for keeping the beds warm to promote better growth.

Two-inch-thick fiberglass board insulation is a new entry into the foundation insulation field, and it promises to be an effective competitor with polystyrene, helping to drain the foundation, providing cushioning against frost heaving and being less susceptible to attack by insects. (One brand name is Warm-N-Dri by Owens-Corning.) This material can be substituted where extruded polystyrene is indicated in this book.

Solar Heating the Attached Greenhouse

In any structure, solar heating involves three basic processes: solar heat collection, heat storage and heat retrieval. In the greenhouse, solar heat is collected by the south-facing glazing and to a much lesser extent by east- and west-facing glazing. Heat is stored in any of the massive materials in the greenhouse, including water-filled containers, masonry in walls and floors, and the soil in growing beds. When the greenhouse air cools down, heat is retrieved from these masses by convection, conduction and radiation.

This type of solar heating is called *passive* solar heating, since all these processes occur without mechanical aids such as fans. An *active* solar heating system would use a fan to move heat around. There is a gray area in between active and passive, sometimes

TABLE 5-2: RECOMMENDED GREENHOUSE ENERGY CONSERVATION FEATURES

GREENHOUSE COMPONENT	CLIMATE		
	WARM	MODERATE	COLD
Glazing	Single for season-extension greenhouse; double for living space and winter growing	Double for all uses	Double for all uses; triple or superglazing where decreased light levels are acceptable
Night insulation	Not needed	Not needed	Needed for winter growing only; R-2 to R-4
Infiltration control	Continuous vapor barrier; attention to caulking and weather stripping	Same as for warm climate plus vestibule entry if used for winter growing and for house entry; tape vents shut in winter	Same as for moderate climate, plus better weather stripping and caulking, if used for winter growing
Roof insulation	3½″ fiberglass	3½ to 5½″ fiberglass for small solid roof areas; 5½″ for larger roof areas	Same as for moderate climate
Wall insulation	3½″ fiberglass	3½″ fiberglass	3½″ fiberglass for small wall areas; 5½″ for larger wall areas
Floor on grade, foundation perimeter, and below grade foundation	2″ extruded polystyrene around perimeter to below average frost depth	2″ extruded polystyrene around perimeter to below average frost depth	2″ extruded polystyrene around perimeter to below average frost depth; 3″ polystyrene for in-ground growing beds

called *hybrid,* where only some of the functions are fan assisted.

Within the greenhouse passive systems generally make the most sense. Active collection of solar heat with separate external collectors doesn't make much sense, since the greenhouse itself is already an excellent collector. Active heat storage is used in some greenhouses, but equal performance can usually be achieved by simpler and less costly passive heat storage. Passive heat storage, such as water-filled containers, makes good use of the sun shining into the greenhouse and needs no electrical controls. In general, using the natural paths for heat transfer in the greenhouse will be simpler and less costly in construction, operation and maintenance.

An attached greenhouse, though, uses the adjacent house for at least part of its heat storage or back-up heating requirements. As discussed earlier, the greenhouse gives some of its heat to the house on sunny days and takes heat from the house on cold nights or cloudy days. Since this heat transfer often uses a fan, the house/greenhouse combination is often a hybrid system.

Houses that are less than 100 percent solar heated, in the 30 to 80 percent range, usually store enough heat to offset heat losses for somewhere between one and three days, depending on climate. In attached greenhouses, though, much less heat storage gives the same performance, due to heat exchange with the house. A well-sited attached greenhouse can be "over 100 percent" solar heated. That is, it contributes more heat to the house than it uses in backup over the course of the winter. During a sunny month, the greenhouse will give the house much more heat than it takes back, while during a cloudy month the balance shifts. Overall, though, the greenhouse we'll design will be "100 percent plus."

Enough heat storage to carry the greenhouse for one day can usually be put into areas that can't be used for growing, such as under growing beds or benches. Or, the available growing areas can be slightly reduced by putting the heat storage against solid wall areas on the north or back side of the greenhouse. In greenhouses with some solid roof area, the space under the roof can provide a good storage location, since it is somewhat light-deficient for growing plants but still receives good winter sun.

Even attached greenhouses that incorporate no "intentional" heat storage can be completely solar heated in certain situations. The soil in the growing beds, the floor, walls and ceiling of the structure, and any contents of the greenhouse all provide some mass for heat storage, with heat from the house providing back-up heating needs. In this case, almost all the excess solar heat collected in the greenhouse is transferred into the house with an air exchange system. The house uses this heat to warm itself during the day and must have enough intrinsic heat storage to absorb any surplus solar heat. The design requirements for the "no-storage" greenhouse are discussed later in this chapter.

Solar Heating Basics

In most of North America, there is enough sunshine to effectively heat a well-designed solar structure. Recalling a previous rule of thumb, 1 square foot of south-facing glazing provides the heat equivalent of about 1 gallon of fuel oil per year. On a clear day, solar energy reaches the glazing at about the rate of 300 Btu per hour (about 100 watts) on each square foot of glazing. (You could image 100-watt light bulbs suspended over each square foot of glazing as providing the same heat as the sun on a clear day.)

Sunlight striking the glazing is either *direct* or *diffuse*. Direct sunlight is sunshine uninterrupted by clouds and casts definite shadows. Diffuse sunlight is what illuminates the earth on overcast days. It casts a very indefinite shadow, if any. Direct winter sunlight contains about six to eight times the amount of energy as diffuse sunlight. Unlike active space- or water-heating collectors, greenhouses can make good use of diffuse sunlight. For example, the diffuse light admitted through double glazing on a cloudy day will roughly offset the glazing heat loss when it is about 45°F colder outside than inside. If the temperature difference is less than 45°F, the glazing will actually be collecting more heat than it's losing. And when it's colder than this, the heat loss is at least offset, while the plants inside use the diffuse light for photosynthesis.

Climate has a great effect on the amount of available solar energy. The term *percent of possible sun* refers to the fraction of time the sun is above the horizon that it will cast a shadow and is a measure of the relative "sunniness" of a region. Climates referred to in this book as "sunny," are those with at least 60 percent of possible sun. "Cloudy" climates are those with less than 50 percent, with "average" climates from 50 to 60 percent. A map of the United States with annual percent of possible sunshine is shown in figure 5-7. Local conditions, such as fog or haziness due to moisture or air pollution can reduce the available sun further and can be expected to reduce greenhouse solar-heating performance to some extent.

External shading is probably one of the biggest culprits in reducing the solar energy coming into a greenhouse. Shading from nearby buildings, trees or from the house itself (if the orientation of the greenhouse is more than 45 degrees from true south) can greatly reduce solar-heating performance. Choosing as sunny a site as possible, as discussed in chapter 2, is critical.

After considering these external factors, the amount of solar energy actually entering the greenhouse is, of course, going to be greatly affected by the area of south-facing glazing. In a greenhouse with two or more planes of glazing (such as a glazed kneewall plus sloped glazing), the total available sun will be more strongly a function of the size of the *aperture* than of the combined area of the planes of glazing. Aperture is taken to be the

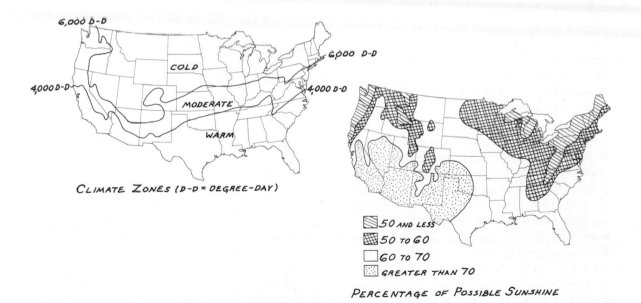

CLIMATE ZONES (D-D = DEGREE-DAY)

PERCENTAGE OF POSSIBLE SUNSHINE

Figure 5-7: The map on the right shows the annual percentage of the hours from sunrise to sunset that the sun is not behind a cloud. We'll consider climates with 50 percent and less of possible sunshine as being cloudy, 50 to 60 percent as being average and greater than 60 percent as being sunny. Throughout this book, climates with less than 4,000 degree-days are considered "warm," from 4,000 to 6,000 "moderate" and above 6,000 "cold." The map on the left divides the United States into those three zones.

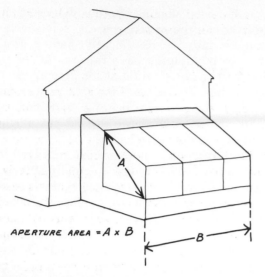

APERTURE AREA = A x B

Figure 5-8: The amount of sun intercepted by the glazing is more nearly proportional to the aperture area than to the total square feet of glazing. The aperture area is the length of the glazed area (B) times the straight-line distance from the lowest point to the highest point (A) of the glazing.

area in the plane made by the top and bottom lines of the glazing, as shown in figure 5-8.

The size of the aperture is usually a function of considerations other than solar heating the greenhouse, including illumination over areas used for growing (discussed in chapter 4), the area needed for solar heating the house (to be discussed in chapter 6) and the budget for the project. In chapter 7 we'll work through a design procedure that meshes all these requirements.

Maximizing the Solar Gain

The amount of available solar energy that is actually transmitted through the glazing is a function of several factors, including the angle at which the sun strikes the glazing,

the glazing material and number of layers, the size and shape of the glazing framing members and, of no small importance, the amount of dirt on the glazing.

The more nearly perpendicular the sun is to the glazing, the more solar energy is transmitted. On a daily basis, the best transmission occurs around noon (for a south-facing greenhouse) since that is when the winter sun is most nearly perpendicular to the glazing. On an annual basis, the slope of the glazing will determine whether the best transmission occurs in winter or summer. A steeper slope favors winter transmission, while a shallower slope favors summer transmission. An intermediate slope can be an appropriate compromise, particularly when other design factors come into play. For example, a house with a low eave favors a shallower slope if the glazing is to run under the eave. Generally, the slope of the glazing is not the most critical factor in optimizing solar heating of the greenhouse, since the greenhouse will collect much more heat than it will use, with the surplus going to the house. Glazing slope is a little more critical when you want to maximize the solar heat available to the house, and this is discussed further in chapter 6.

The orientation of the greenhouse is a somewhat more important factor than the glazing angle. Greenhouses facing within 30 degrees of true south will generally need less back-up heat than greenhouses facing farther away from south. If the site requires a choice between a west-facing or east-facing greenhouse, the east-facing site is a better choice for a horticultural greenhouse because the morning sun is important for providing heat and light for photosynthesis early in the day.

Differences in the transmittances of different glazing materials is less a factor in overall solar gain than might be expected. A single layer of most common glazing materials transmits about 85 to 90 percent of the sunlight striking it at near perpendicular angles; double glazing transmits 70 to 80 percent. Almost all glazing manufacturers specify the transmittance at "normal incidence," which means perpendicular to the glazing. All the glazing materials suggested in this book fall within this range, at least when new. If it is necessary to maximize solar gain, low-iron glass, which has a transmittance of 91 percent per layer (82 percent for double), is worth the extra expense. Otherwise, any of the other glazings are acceptable.

Glass is the only material whose transmission of solar energy will not degrade with time. The transmittance of all plastic glazing materials does go down in time, although the rate of the decrease varies quite a bit from one plastic to the next. Unfortunately, the useful life of a plastic is largely a function of its price: the more expensive the plastic, the longer the life. (An exception to this is polycarbonate, which is somewhat more expensive yet shorter-lived than some other plastics. It is, however, much more impact resistant than other plastics.) It's always a good idea to read manufacturers' warranties and the instructions for the maintenance and care of plastic glazings. Some manufacturers guarantee that the light transmission will not degrade below a specified minimum for a certain number of years (although such warranty claims are difficult to substantiate). Periodic washings can help maintain the clarity of plastics, particularly in urban environments, where the combination of dust and pollution in the presence of sunlight, air and moisture can degrade some plastics more rapidly than normal. Dirt also blocks out sunlight from any glazing by as much as 5 to 10 percent.

The distance that a glazing material can safely span will make a difference in overall light transmission because the more rafters that are needed, the more sunlight will be blocked. Thus, you should always choose the maximum safe distance between glazing supports for any given material.

Heat and Light Distribution

A certain amount of the sunlight passing through the glazing is reflected back out by light-colored interior surfaces. Direct sunlight striking a *diffusing reflector* (such as a white-painted endwall or backwall) is scattered in all directions fairly uniformly. Sunlight striking the side of a white-painted rafter is scattered in the same way, but as much as half of the sunlight striking a rafter is reflected back outside. Reflection to the outside is one of the trade-offs made between solar heating and horticulture. A structure designed only to collect solar energy would be black inside, or at least dark colored, while one meant for plant growing requires a light color to bounce more light onto plants.

Exactly what fraction of the incoming solar energy is converted into warm moisture-laden air and what fraction is stored in the greenhouse depends on what is growing. When plant growth fills much of the volume of the greenhouse and the leaves are intercepting most of the sunlight, there is more air heating and evaporation than heat storing going on. During late winter or early spring, when young, short plants aren't blocking the sun from the soil or any heat storage to the north of the growing beds, a larger proportion of the solar energy will be stored.

The amount of the sun's heat that is converted into warm air also depends on the placement of the heat storage. If the sun shines directly on the heat storage it will absorb as much as three times more heat than storage that is not in direct sun. (Other factors are the physical properties of the heat storage material, including the ability to absorb and conduct heat, which are discussed later in this chapter.) In a greenhouse with at least half the heat storage exposed to direct sunlight during the middle part of the day, anywhere from 15 to 30 percent of the solar heat gain is actually stored.[1]

Plant-filled greenhouses, therefore, can be expected to provide more moisture and warm air to the house than the same greenhouse without plants. But this is not to say the overall fuel savings will be greater, since more heat will be required at night for the plants. In terms of design, it's important to place heat storage where it will be in direct sun as much of the day as possible, even if the greenhouse is full of plants.

Storing Solar Heat

The ability of a material to store heat depends on its *conductivity* and its *heat capacity*. Heat capacity, as used here, refers to how much energy is required to raise 1 cubic foot of the material 1°F. For example, a cubic foot of water requires 62 Btu to raise it 1°F, and a cubic foot of concrete absorbs 32 Btu to become 1°F warmer. This means that water has almost double the heat capacity, per unit of volume, of concrete. Materials with higher heat capacities will thus take up less space in the greenhouse for equal heat storage capacity. The heat capacity of various stone and brick types varies somewhat above or

below that of concrete, depending on the density. The focus here is on water and masonry because they are the most commonly used materials for solar heat storage, although adobe and phase change materials are sometimes used. The other important function of these materials is in preventing overheating in the greenhouse. By storing surplus solar heat, the peak daytime temperature in the greenhouse is lower, meaning less heat loss and therefore more heat put to use.

The *absorptivity* of the surface of a material is also important in passive heat storage. This refers to the percent of the solar energy striking the material that is actually absorbed by it. Black-colored materials absorb about 95 percent of the energy striking them, while shiny metallic materials may absorb only 5 to 10 percent. Darker surfaces, of course, are preferable for heat storage. A red- or blue-colored surface strikes a good compromise between the need for light for photosynthesis and absorption of heat for storage. Red or blue absorbs almost as much heat as does black, while still reflecting parts of the spectrum that are important for plant growth.

Water

Water is probably the most frequently used heat storage material because it is inexpensive and has a high heat capacity per unit of volume—twice that of masonry—and it is easily installed. Water is very effective in storing heat because convection, not conduction, is the primary mechanism of heat transfer in water storage. As the water near the sunlit side of the container warms up, it becomes lighter (just like air) and rises, causing mixing currents to form. As time goes on the water "stratifies" into layers of uniform temperature, with the warmer layers at the top. Having growing beds or benches on top of water containers takes advantage of this heat

---

[1] In measurements taken in the NCAT greenhouse of the temperature of the water in 55-gallon heat storage water barrels placed directly behind glazing, the temperature of the barrels rose about 10°F over the course of a sunny day. These barrels were standing vertically under a bench, with no shading of the front surfaces, which were exposed to the sun. This represented about 30 percent of the energy transmitted through the 3-foot-high portion of the glazing directly in front of the barrels. The barrels against the north wall of the greenhouse did not warm up nearly so much, as they were in shade over half the day, gaining only 3 or 4°F over the day. Together, the front and rear barrels absorbed about 25 percent of the transmitted sunlight, much more than might be expected from the temperature rise of only 3 to 10°F.

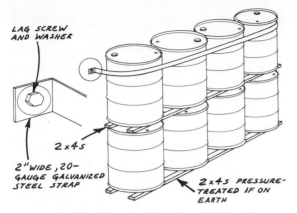

LAG SCREW
AND WASHER

2 x 4 s

2" WIDE, 20-
GAUGE GALVANIZED
STEEL STRAP

2 x 4 s PRESSURE-
TREATED IF ON
EARTH

Figure 5-9: Fifty-five gallon drums (or any steel containers) need to be kept off the ground to keep from rusting. And if they are stacked, any upper barrels should be securely anchored with a steel strap. Arrange the drums on the bottom row so the small bung is where you can reach it in case you ever have to drain a drum. Leave the bung loose and use 2 × 4s between courses of barrels so you can get to the bungs on the lower course.

at the top because soil and plant roots are warmed.

There are many types of containers available for water. One of the most commonly used is the 55-gallon drum. These drums are 3 feet tall and 2 feet in diameter. When full, they weigh about 425 pounds and store quite a bit of heat. Warmed up 10°F, a filled barrel stores over 4,000 Btu. Fifty-five gallon drums can usually be found used for five to ten dollars. They are very strong, and they can be safely stacked on top of each other, or be used to support growing beds or benches. This saves building a separate support structure for beds or benches located over the heat storage.

Since 55-gallon drums are usually made of steel, they are susceptible to rusting. Some steel drums such as those used for food or cosmetics can be found with a plastic coating inside, which greatly increases their life span as water containers. All-plastic, 55-gallon drums are also sometimes available, though occasionally at a higher cost. To counteract steel's susceptibility to rust, a corrosion inhibitor can be mixed with the water and a ⅛-inch film of motor oil poured on top of the water to slow down evaporation of the water (see Appendix 1 for a source for a corrosion inhibitor). The outside of the barrels should be painted if the original paint is cracked or damaged (or if the color is not appropriate) to minimize rusting from the outside in. If properly rustproofed, barrels can last for many years, but they should not be expected to last indefinitely. Between 5 and 20 percent of unlined drums can be expected to leak each year, depending on their initial condition. The leaks are usually slow, though, and the rest of the water can be siphoned out.

Barrels can be painted just about any dark color. Black paint can be used on those that are in direct sun but are not "visible" to the plants—that is, light reflecting off the barrels will not reflect onto the plants. This includes drums underneath benches or beds in the front of the greenhouse, when they are placed directly behind glazing, and barrels under rear beds or benches, as long as the front beds aren't lower than those in the rear.

Drums should be placed securely and accurately before they're filled since they weigh over 450 pounds when full. If they are placed on earth or gravel floors, the floor should be thoroughly compacted beforehand, to avoid later settling of the floor and shifting of the barrels. Barrels stacked two high against a wall should have the top row secured to the wall with strapping or other means.

Smaller water containers can also provide effective heat storage. Thirty-five gallon "grease" drums are shorter and smaller in diameter than the 55-gallon drums, making them easier to place under benches or beds and into otherwise unusable spaces. A great variety of other containers can be used, just

Photo 5-6: Fifty-gallon fiberglass water tubes, made by Solar Components Corporation, are an attractive and compact heat storage. Note the restraining rope at the top to avoid the possibility of toppling.

Photo 5-8: Fifty-five-gallon drums stacked three high make good use of the vertical space in this greenhouse, leaving space for a wide aisle and a sitting area at the end. *(Photo courtesy of the Memphremagog Group.)*

Photo 5-7: A greenhouse can combine various heat storage techniques, each suited to its location: shown here are bricks on the floor, 55-gallon drums under the rear bench and Navy surplus sono-buoy containers filled with water on the shelf on the rear wall.

Photo 5-9: Two-liter bottles support slatted benches (one bench was removed for the photograph) in the front of this greenhouse, storing heat directly under potted plants and flats of seedlings.

Photo 5-10: Water Wall modules, made by One Design, Inc., are designed to fit over studs 24 inches on center. *(Photo courtesy of One Design, Inc.)*

about anything that will hold water (such as honey or cooking oil containers, soda bottles and plastic milk jugs).

Small containers can absorb heat more quickly from the air (by convection) than larger containers, as they have more surface area compared to the volume they contain. For this reason they collect heat better than larger containers in locations that are out of direct sunlight. But for the same reason smaller containers also lose heat more quickly than larger ones. This doesn't have much effect, normally, as long as there is enough total volume of water storage in the greenhouse. It can, however, be a disadvantage for season-extension greenhouses in cold climates when the greenhouse isn't used in the winter. Smaller containers will freeze more quickly than larger ones and are, therefore, more susceptible to damage from the expansion of the freezing water.

It is important to note, however, that water-filled containers don't freeze immediately when the surrounding air temperature drops below 32°F, because the heat in the water is given up fairly slowly. When the water begins to freeze, a good deal of heat is given off as the water changes from a liquid to a solid, which helps to delay the freezing of the whole container for quite a while. This change of state occurs at too low a temperature (32°F) for the heat that is released to be of any use in keeping the air in the greenhouse above freezing, but it is useful in keeping the containers from bursting when the greenhouse is only slightly below freezing.

Color can be a problem with plastic containers. Many plastic containers are opaque white, or very light colored, which is not very good for absorbing radiant energy from the sun, and paint won't adhere to them. These containers are thus more appropriate for places where they aren't in direct sunlight. If the containers are transparent, or translucent like gallon milk jugs, the water inside can be colored with a little ink or dye to increase its absorptivity.

Another problem with small plastic containers is strength: They can't be stacked very high without intervening support shelves. Their big advantage is cost: They can usually be had for the taking.

Large plastic containers made specifically for heat storage are available from a number of sources. The large almost-clear tubes made of fiberglass-reinforced plastic (made by Solar Components Corp., Manchester, N.H.) are good looking, don't take up a lot of space, and they are available in a number of diameters and heights. They require the same care as any large container when they are placed on a dirt or gravel floor, and if the tall tubes are used, they should be leveled carefully and secured from tipping over. There are several other varieties of containers available, some of which are listed in Appendix 1.

Another water container manufactured for heat storage is made by One Design, Inc. (see Appendix 1 for the address) to fit over and attach to wall studs spaced 24 inches on centers. They turn an ordinary stud wall into a translucent, heat-storing "water wall," that shares stored heat between the house and greenhouse. The high-density polyethylene modules are 48 inches square and 7 inches deep. They are molded with a "dent" in the backside to go around the stud that will be in the middle of their 48-inch width. Each unit holds 53 gallons.

Any clear water container will tend to support the growth of algae if it's left uncovered or even loosely covered, unless a little chlorine is put in the water. Periodic dosings of chlorine (one-tenth gram of pool chlorine per gallon of water) may be needed, since the chlorine does evaporate, and algae will continue to grow in the water. Covers will help keep the humidity down, but they should be left a little loose to accommodate the expansion of the water as it warms up.

Masonry

Although it has about half the heat storage capacity of water, masonry has some advantages over water. Masonry doesn't rust; it can be used as a structural element; it doesn't freeze, and, to some eyes, it is nicer to look at. Greenhouses attached to houses with solid masonry walls have a special advantage. The common wall can serve as heat storage for both the house and greenhouse. Greenhouses attached to houses with masonry-clad walls (such as brick veneer) also have a ready-made heat store. If the wall isn't insulated, some of the stored heat will find its way into the house. Adding new masonry, however, may require skilled labor, usually making it more expensive to install than water.

The term "masonry" is meant to include a variety of materials: poured concrete, bricks and concrete blocks, stone and tile. The composition of these materials varies quite a bit, and as a consequence, so does the heat capacity, by up to 25 percent above or below the nominal 30 Btu per cubic foot per degree Fahrenheit. The highest density materials should be chosen whenever possible, to maximize heat storage capacity. *Face brick,* rather than the lighter weight *common brick,* should be used where there is a choice. Stone should be the aggregate in concrete or concrete block, rather than cinders or other less dense materials, and the cores of concrete blocks should be filled with concrete after installation.

The conductivity of masonry ranges from 7 to 10 Btu per square foot per degree Fahrenheit per inch of thickness for concrete, and from 5 to 9 Btu for brick. Conductivity is important when choosing a masonry heat storage material because materials with higher conductivities store more of the heat they absorb. Stored heat is also retrieved more rapidly when the greenhouse cools down.

Because of masonry's relatively slow conductivity, a masonry heat storage wall shouldn't be too thick. For masonry common walls, 8 inches is about the thickness that one day of full sun can effectively heat. Thicker masonry will also release heat a little more slowly than would be desirable, but is acceptable if the greater thickness is needed for structural reasons. Thinner masonry, such as 4-inch-thick bricks, poured concrete or concrete blocks, is recommended for floors or for covering insulated walls. (Recommended quantities are listed in table 5-5, later in this chapter.)

TABLE 5-3: HEAT STORAGE CAPACITY OF SOME COMMONLY USED MATERIALS

MATERIAL	HEAT STORAGE CAPACITY (Btu/ft³-°F)
Water	62
Common brick	23
Face brick	25
Concrete, rock aggregate	30
Concrete, cinder aggregate	25
Adobe	20

Photo 5-11: In this narrow greenhouse masonry columns were built exclusively for heat storage. Their exposure on three sides increases the amount of heat they can absorb and release.

Phase Change Materials

Phase change materials (PCM) store heat by using the relatively large amount of heat needed to melt a material. Water, for example, changes from the solid to the liquid phase at 32°F, absorbing 143 Btu per pound as it melts and releasing 143 Btu as it freezes. A variety of salt compounds have been developed that change from a solid to a liquid at a temperature that is useful for solar heat storage, anywhere from 55 to over 100°F. As the material is heated by the sun to its melting point, the solid crystals of the salts melt, absorbing quite a bit of heat. When the material cools down at night through its phase change point, it freezes (crystallizes) and releases the energy it absorbed during the day.

Phase change materials have two advantages over conventional heat storage materials. They take up less space, having from two to ten times the heat storage capacity of water and therefore 4 to 20 times the capacity of masonry. Since the phase change process absorbs heat without raising the temperature of the material, the greenhouse will stay cooler during sunny days, helping avoid warmer temperatures that may stress the plants and that increase heat loss from the greenhouse. The main drawbacks with PCM are its cost and an as yet uncertain level of reliability for the technology as a whole.

TABLE 5-4: HEAT STORAGE CHOICES

STORAGE SYSTEM	ADVANTAGES
Water	
55-gallon drums	A lot of storage per unit, so few units needed; structurally strong; large size lessens freezing potential; release heat slowly
5- to 35-gallon metal containers	Higher surface area-to-volume ratio, so absorb heat easily by convection as well as radiation; easier to handle even when full; moderate structural strength; compact, fit in otherwise unused spaces
¼- to 10-gallon plastic containers	Higher surface area-to-volume ratio, so absorb heat easily by convection as well as radiation; require no rustproofing or painting; very compact, fit in otherwise unused spaces
Large plastic containers designed for heat storage	Good appearance; variety of sizes available to fit in various spaces; require no painting or rustproofing
Masonry	No freezing problems; can double as a structural element; requires little or no maintenance; solid masonry between house and greenhouse stores heat for both spaces
Phase Change Materials	Take up little space; greenhouse stays cooler than with conventional passive storage; no freezing problems
Active (forced air with rock bin)	If under floor, takes up no floor space; greenhouse stays cooler than with conventional passive storage; good air circulation

If you use PCM, choose one with a melting temperature of 65 to 70°F, unless you intend to keep the greenhouse at indoor house temperatures. Actually, a melting point of 55°F—just above the thermostat set point—would be ideal. Some suppliers of low temperature PCM are listed in Appendix 1.

Heat Storage in the Floor

It's a common misconception that the floor is always an ideal place for passive heat storage. The floor of a horticultural greenhouse that is filled with plants doesn't offer much heat storage since it is rarely in direct sun. It is shaded by plants, beds and benches for most of the day, and it is always covered with the coldest air in the greenhouse. But if the floor is exposed to the sun for most of the day, it can be a very effective location for heat storage. For example, the living space portion of a greenhouse might be open enough to expose the floor to direct sunlight. In such a case, masonry (concrete, tile or brick) is the best choice for floor heat storage material, since it has relatively good heat storage capacity, conductivity and absorption.

A gravel floor is relatively ineffective for heat storage, even if it is in direct sun, since gravel has poor conductivity. Gravel is an inexpensive floor covering that helps to keep the greenhouse floor from getting muddy, but

DISADVANTAGES	RELATIVE COST
Heat easily absorbed only by radiation; steel drums require cleaning, rustproofing and painting; heavy when filled	Low (if recycled)
Cleaning, painting and rustproofing required; more susceptible to freeze damage than larger containers	Low (if recycled)
More susceptible to freeze damage than larger containers; shelves required for stacking more than a few high	Low (if recycled)
Some types not strong enough to support more than their own weight; heavy when full; poor absorber of heat by convection	High
Heat capacity and conductivity lower than water; stores less heat per unit of volume than water; poor absorber of heat by convection	Moderate to high
High cost; new technology; most available materials have melting point too high for greenhouse use	Very high
Requires electrical energy to run; requires skilled design and construction labor	Moderate to high

won't add much or any effective heat storage capacity to the greenhouse. Gravel floors have been used in an active heat storage system by running air distribution ducts under the gravel to blow air up through the gravel. While this is an easy way to build a rock storage system, it isn't recommended because the spaces between the stones will gradually fill up with dirt and other things that drop on the floor. This will gradually clog up the passage of air through the rocks and eventually result in poor heat storage. Earth floors can provide only a little better heat storage than gravel, depending on the characteristics of the earth. (Dense, moist earth will store more heat than drier, lighter earth.)

The No-Storage Greenhouse

Heat storage is an important component in the horticultural greenhouse, but it is possible to effectively operate a plant-growing greenhouse with no added heat storage at all. In a "no-storage" greenhouse, the house simply takes in all the solar heat above the amount required to keep the greenhouse warm while the sun is shining. If the greenhouse needs to be heated at night to protect plants, heat is drawn from the house. This arrangement is practical under certain circumstances.

The house must be able to use all the solar heat that the greenhouse can collect without becoming overheated. (This capability is discussed more fully later in this chapter and in chapter 6.) Such a house would have enough heat storage capacity to store heat from the greenhouse in excess of that required to heat the house during the day. Or the house could be large and have a relatively large heat loss and few south-facing windows to heat it on a sunny winter day, using all the excess greenhouse heat for daytime heating. If there is fairly little solar heat gain coming from the greenhouse because of shading or other site

constraints, or because the greenhouse has a small aperture area, the house may be able to absorb the relatively small output of solar heat, even if the house is tight and well insulated and has relatively little heat storage capacity. The storage sizing procedure in this section gives more guidelines for deciding if a no-storage greenhouse is appropriate for a given house/greenhouse combination.

Having no heat storage is more practical for season-extending than for winter-growing greenhouses, since season-extending greenhouses require no heat during midwinter. Some successful winter-growing greenhouses, however, have been built with no heat storage. These tend to be small, tightly built greenhouses, with low heat loss, attached to fairly large homes where the nighttime heat required from the house makes little difference to the house's overall heat requirements. Back-up heaters in the greenhouse can supplement the heat available from the house.

It must be practical to have cold greenhouse air entering the house frequently at night in the winter if the greenhouse is kept heated all year. Generally, the greenhouse will be attached to a daytime living area, so introducing cold air into this space at night is not a problem. Larger rooms occupied in the evening offer enough volume that cold air introduced will mix with the warmer room air, avoiding cool drafts. If the air exchange is not automatically operated, people must be willing to tend vents or doors as required. If the greenhouse is used for season extension only, nighttime air exchange will only be needed during the part of spring and fall when the greenhouse is kept heated, decreasing these difficulties. Again, a back-up heater in the greenhouse can be used for heat when air exchange isn't wanted. (Nighttime air exchange is also discussed in chapter 4.)

No heat storage is recommended where a very short season extension is desired—perhaps adding a month onto either end of the outdoor growing season—or where the climate is very warm. Such places are those parts of the southern United States along the Gulf of Mexico and the Mexican border where freezing occurs infrequently.

Sizing the Heat Storage

The amount of heat storage needed in a greenhouse depends on a number of factors, including the climate, the overall heat loss of the greenhouse, the area of the glazing for heat collection, whether or not the greenhouse is to be used all winter or just to extend the growing season, how much of the surplus solar heat from the greenhouse can be used and/or stored in the house, and how long the storage is intended to keep the greenhouse warm. Storage sizing information that takes these factors into account is provided in table 5-5.

Having heat storage within the greenhouse has some definite advantages, even if the size of the greenhouse aperture relative to the house heating load does not require it. (This relationship is discussed in the next chapter.) It allows a larger greenhouse aperture to be built, since the extra heat gain can be stored in both the greenhouse and the house. Having storage in the greenhouse also minimizes the amount of air that must be exchanged between the house and the greenhouse, somewhat decreasing the required fan or vent size, since the storage absorbs some of the heat that would otherwise go into the house as warm air. If nighttime air exchange should be minimized—for comfort or noise or any of the other reasons listed in chapter 4—or if the size of the greenhouse aperture will bring in more heat than the house alone can store, storage should be incorporated into the greenhouse. Storage will also help to stabilize the temperature in the greenhouse somewhat if the air exchange fans or vents are inadvertently left closed when they are needed. In general, having storage within the greenhouse makes the greenhouse less dependent on the house for heat distribution and back-up heating.

The Heat Storage Sizing Table

The amount of heat storage material that will be needed is largely a function of the area of the glazing and the overall heat loss of the greenhouse. These are both taken into account in the sizing table (table 5-5 assumes that the greenhouse is built to the conservation standards recommended for each climate zone). It often turns out, however, that the exact amount of storage finally installed is often determined by the amount of available space rather than by the exact calculated requirements. But it's unlikely that this will cause a problem. Since the greenhouse exchanges heat with the house, having a precise amount of heat storage is not necessary. If, however, the greenhouse won't exchange air with the house, the storage requirements increase in order to store more of the solar heat within the greenhouse.

Greenhouses used for growing through winter require substantially more heat storage than season-extension greenhouses in order to maintain growing temperatures without a lot of back-up heat. If the greenhouse is to be used as a season extender, care must be taken during winter to avoid freezing damage to water-filled heat storage containers when the greenhouse isn't kept heated. The containers should be large, at least 50 gallons, to minimize the chances of a hard freeze. Also the total quantity of water storage in a season-extending greenhouse shouldn't be reduced greatly below the amount recommended in table 5-5. If there is only a very small amount of water—for example, 100 gallons when 500 is recommended—it is almost sure to freeze without back-up heating, since such a small amount won't even come close to keeping the greenhouse above freezing. Rather than mini-

TABLE 5-5: RECOMMENDED QUANTITIES FOR HEAT STORAGE MATERIALS (Per Square Foot of South-Facing Glazed Area)

	WINTER GROWING		SEASON EXTENSION	
CLIMATE	WATER (gal)	MASONRY (ft³)	WATER (gal)	MASONRY (ft³)
Cold	4	1⅓	2½	⅚
Moderate	3	1	2	⅔
Warm	2	⅔	1	⅓

NOTE: *This table is based on the following assumptions.*
* *Masonry is to be no more than 8 inches thick; any thickness over 8 inches is not considered as contributing to greenhouse heat storage; masonry is also to be of moderate to high density, such as concrete, solid concrete block or high density brick*
* *The use of energy conservation features in the greenhouse is to be as recommended earlier in this chapter, with tight construction*
* *One-half the surface area of the heat storage is to be exposed to direct sunlight for at least half the day*
* *No night insulation is to be used*
* *Air exchange with the house is assumed to both draw heat from the greenhouse during the day and draw heat from the house at night; if there is no air exchange, recommended quantities should be increased by one-third*
* *Occasional freezing can occur if there is no back-up heating*
* *For phase change heat storage provide 80 Btu of latent heat capacity in place of each gallon of water recommended in this table*
* *Some attached greenhouses won't need any heat storage; if the aperture area is 75 percent or less of the maximum recommended area (see table 6-3 in the following chapter), no heat storage is required as long as there is nighttime air exchange with the house or a heater in the greenhouse*
* *For a greenhouse with aperture that is larger than the maximum recommended in table 6-3, storage quantities should be doubled for the area of glazing above the maximum (discussed in the text)*

mize the amount of water, it may be better to use masonry instead or to have no heat storage at all and depend on a greenhouse heater or air exchange with the house. Table 5-5 assumes that backup will be needed occasionally in the greenhouse to keep the heat-storing water containers from freezing.

Table 5-5 also assumes that no night insulation is used, but if this insulation is added, the greenhouse will need somewhat less back-up heating, increasing the solar-heating performance. You can reduce the amount of storage below the recommended amounts if night insulation is installed, but if the insulation isn't actually used, the back-up heating load will increase.

The heat storage amounts recommended in table 5-5 are designed to provide the amount of heat required to keep the greenhouse warm for an average January night after the storage has been warmed by a sunny day. This amount strikes a balance between meeting the back-up heating needs of the greenhouse, the demands on the greenhouse space for growing, and providing solar heat to the house.

Having more heat storage than the recommended amounts may be necessary in some situations. If nighttime heat exchange with the house isn't practical for back-up heating, back-up fuel use may be excessive if there isn't additional heat storage. In such cases, the recommended heat storage quantities should be increased by one-third. If night temperatures in the greenhouse are to be kept relatively high—in the upper fifties or sixties—either for exotic plants or to use the greenhouse for living space, additional storage should be included, particularly if night insulation isn't used.

A Procedure for Sizing Storage

The following is a step-by-step procedure for sizing masonry and water heat storage for a greenhouse.

First, find the recommended maximum greenhouse aperture from table 6-3 in the following chapter.

Second, if the aperture for the greenhouse you're designing is 75 to 100 percent of the recommended maximum, use the heat storage quantities listed in table 5-5.

Third, if the greenhouse aperture is less than 75 percent of the recommended size, heat storage is not needed in the greenhouse *if* there is nighttime air exchange with the house or there is a greenhouse heater in use during the months the greenhouse will need back-up heat. Relying solely on air exchange is not practical if cold air introduced into the house would be uncomfortable, if the house heating system is not capable of handling the extra heating load, or if manual vents are used for air exchange, and the occupants are unwilling or unable to tend vents as needed.

Fourth, if the aperture is larger than the recommended maximum, add heat storage to the house (discussed in chapter 6) or additional heat storage to the greenhouse, in *double* the quantity recommended per square foot of glazing for the aperture area above the recommended maximum.

Fifth, if there will be no heat exchange with the house at night, the recommended heat storage should be increased by one-third above the quantities recommended in table 5-5.

For example, let's determine the heat storage requirement for a greenhouse with 300 square feet of south-facing glazing. The greenhouse will be in a moderate climate, attached to an insulated 1,100-square-foot home. Air will be exchanged freely with the house during winter, as the house furnace has excess capacity. Air exchange with the living room will be done with an automatic fan. The greenhouse will be used only for season extension.

Look at the aperture sizing table (table 6-3). This house can use solar heat from a greenhouse with as much as 330 square feet of aperture if the greenhouse has adequate heat storage (1,100 ft^2 × 0.30 ft^2 of aperture/ft^2 of floor area), or from 250 square feet of aperture if the greenhouse has no storage (330 × 75%). With a 300-square-foot aperture the greenhouse will need 2 gallons of water or ⅔ cubic foot of masonry heat storage per square foot of glazing, for a total of 600 gallons of water (300 × 2) or 200 cubic feet of masonry (300 × 0.67). This could be done with twelve 55-gallon drums of water, or 300 square feet of 8-inch-thick masonry (see table 5-5).

If in this same example, the greenhouse were to be used for winter growing, the heat storage requirements would be increased by 50 percent as indicated in table 5-5. Eighteen 55-gallon drums of water could provide the necessary 900 gallons of water. The requirement for masonry would climb to 300 cubic feet. If there were no air exchange with the house or no separate greenhouse heater, the requirements are increased by another 33 percent, for a total requirement of 1,200 gallons [(900 × 0.33) + 900 = 1200] or 400 cubic feet of masonry [(300 × 0.33) + 300 = 400]. Clearly, exchanging heat with the house makes sense for minimizing the amount of heat storage.

Placement of Heat Storage

The placement of the heat storage determines its effectiveness in absorbing and storing solar energy. Heat storage that is located in direct sunlight for most of the day can absorb as much as three times the heat as the same amount of shaded storage. The ideal heat storage—from the point of view of heating the greenhouse—would be located directly behind the glazing. This, of course, would block light from the plants, but there are several other locations for heat storage that will receive an acceptable amount of direct sunlight without limiting light to the plants.

The north wall of the greenhouse is one such location. This area receives direct sunlight from the low-angle winter sun, except if tall crops are grown in the south beds in winter, and also receives less daylight relative

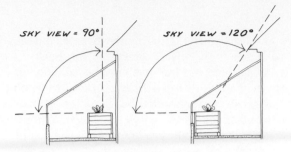

Figure 5-10: Plants in the front of a fully glazed greenhouse get more light than those in the back, since the front has a greater view of the sky. In the winter, the low sun will shine on the back wall, making it a better place for heat storage than for plants.

to the rest of the greenhouse, making it a good place to reduce the growing area. If the north wall is to be used exclusively for heat storage, water containers or masonry can be extended from floor to ceiling, leaving, of course, openings for windows, doors and vents to the house. If this area is needed for plants, the beds or benches can be placed on top of the heat storage.

Photo 5-12: Placing heat storage under a bench lets the plants take best advantage of the stored heat.

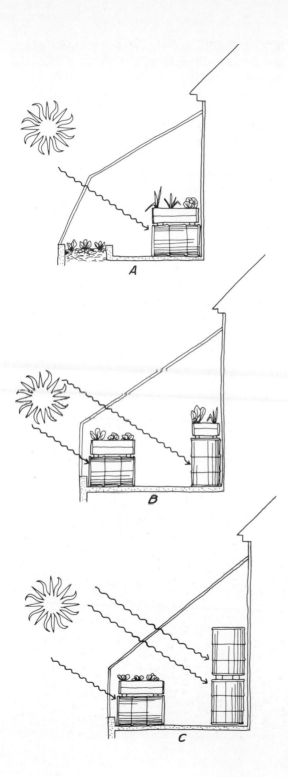

Figure 5-11: Having the heat storage low at the front of the greenhouse and higher in back gives both locations access to direct sunlight and makes good use of the varying vertical space in the greenhouse. In-ground beds (A) will shade the rear storage containers very little, while front beds on top of the heat storage will shade the rear more (B), especially if tall plants like tomatoes are put in front. A double stack of drums (C), or other taller storage, solves this problem.

Storage can likewise be placed against solid portions of east- and west-facing walls. These walls will receive direct sun for only about half the day and have the same decrease in overall illumination (compared to illumination levels at the south glazing) as the north-wall area, making them another good location for heat storage.

There are several approaches to placing water under growing beds. One is simply to put all the beds on top of containers, if there is enough overhead room for plants to grow. Smaller drums or other containers can also be placed in whatever space remains under the beds and benches after the big containers have been placed. Where it is possible to place the water containers in direct sunlight the larger containers are preferable, since they are easier to install and will distribute heat within the container easily, while many small containers can't transfer heat as easily from one to the next.

Another approach is to raise only the northside growing beds on top of heat storage while keeping the south growing areas at ground level to expose the heat storage to more sunlight. A variation of this is to keep the south beds or benches only slightly lower than the north growing area so that the heat storage will receive direct sun.

Placing water containers under the south bed directly behind kneewall glazing puts them in an optimum location for receiving sunlight throughout the day. In order for this strategy to work well, it is important that the greenhouse foundation not block the sun from containers.

Masonry can be used for constructing aboveground growing beds. This adds to the heat storage and provides a sturdy, long-lasting growing bed. Placing a masonry bed directly behind the glazing will not only place the masonry in an ideal location, but will also help to warm the soil. An in-ground bed can use the existing masonry of a continuous foundation as one of its walls. As mentioned earlier, glazing the south-facing portions of the foundation will transform this masonry into a useful heat storage component and also improve heating of the soil.

Chapter 6

DESIGNING THE GREENHOUSE FOR SOLAR HEATING THE HOUSE

In the previous two chapters, the design of the greenhouse has been developed from the points of view of horticulture and of minimizing auxiliary energy use in the greenhouse. In this chapter we'll look at designing the greenhouse to be an effective supplier of solar heat to the adjacent house. To some extent the two goals of horticulture and solar heating the house are mutually supportive: Minimizing obstructions in the glazing aperture, for example, helps light levels for the plants *and* increases solar heat gain. Lowering heat loss in the greenhouse helps plant growth by keeping the plants warmer at night and saves more heat for the house. But compromises have to be made when you want both solar heating and plant growing. Plants need warmth at night. This can be solar heat that is stored in the greenhouse that would have otherwise gone into the house, or it can be heat taken from the house at night, or energy used by a back-up heater. All of these offset solar savings. The humidity generated in the greenhouse also absorbs solar energy that would otherwise be converted to warm air for the house. Some of this latent heat does end up as useful heat in the house and some ends up making the house more comfortable to live in, but some is simply lost when moist air leaks to the outdoors. For these reasons, a sunspace without plants can deliver somewhat more heat to the house than a plant-filled greenhouse, but the difference is not so great that it should lead you to abandon plant growing. Chapter 7 deals with combining the solar and horticultural design requirements into an effective, multipurpose structure.

This chapter concentrates on attaching the greenhouse to an existing house. The information is certainly applicable to new construction, when the house and greenhouse are built at the same time. With new construction you have the opportunity to achieve much higher auxiliary fuel savings since it is so much easier to conserve energy and incorporate additional heat storage in a new house. In designing a retrofit, though, the house is, for the most part, a given, and you must work within existing constraints as you design the greenhouse.

The method presented here for sizing the greenhouse for solar heating represents a moderate approach, in that the amount of south glazing that is used captures only as much heat as can readily be used by the house without requiring the addition of a heat storage component to the house. This can represent a savings of auxiliary fuel ranging from an amount too small to be noticed—10 percent or less—up to 50 percent, depending on the many factors outlined in this chapter. Much greater savings can be realized with solar greenhouses, particularly with new construction. However, obtaining higher solar contributions (greater than about 50 percent) requires careful consideration and analysis of many factors that are particular to each house. If you want your greenhouse to supply 60, 70 or an even higher percentage of your house's heat load, or if it's important that the actual heating fuel displacement be accurately predicted, you will need the services of a professional designer who is experienced in passive solar heating and greenhouse design.

A word of caution is in order here. The solar performance predictions made in this book should be regarded as similar to the Environmental Protection Agency (EPA) mileage ratings for cars: Your actual heating percentage may vary. Every effort has been made to have the predictions fall into the middle of the range of performance that can be expected, but a particular house requires analysis of its situation to accurately predict savings.

Insulation First, Solar Heating Second

If one of the primary purposes of the solar greenhouse is reducing fuel use, the first task should be exploring the potential for energy conservation in the existing house.

Dollars spent to conserve energy will generally yield a higher rate of return than dollars spent for solar heating. This is illustrated later in this chapter by the small fuel savings predicted for even a relatively large greenhouse added to an uninsulated house.

Intrinsic Heat Storage

The fact that adding heat storage to an existing house can be difficult and expensive influences the design process. An active storage component, such as a basement rock bin receiving forced air, is typically expensive. And there is usually not room enough for passive storage (thermal mass) to be easily or attractively added to the living space. Fortunately, however, the heat storage capacity of all the materials (wood, plaster, brick, furniture and everything) already in the house can be used without modification to store a useful quantity of solar heat. This is accomplished by sizing the greenhouse glazing to bring in enough solar energy to make maximum use of that existing heat storage capacity. Heating up the house's structure and its contents— within the limits of comfort—can represent a few hour's storage in a leaky, uninsulated house, or a whole night's storage in an energy-efficient house. Working with the existing heat storage capacity essentially defines the upper limit for the size of a relatively inexpensive greenhouse addition. Adding more glazing means adding expensive heat storage, or dumping (that is, wasting) excess solar heat out the window to avoid overheating.

Choosing the Right Size

There is, then, one basic question that needs to be answered in order to size an add-on greenhouse for heating the house: How many square feet of south-facing glazing can be added to a given house before additional heat storage is required to absorb excess heat? In order to understand this question a bit more, we can look at four different sizes of greenhouses attached to the same model house.

First, a very small greenhouse, perhaps with only 50 square feet of glazing, is attached to a 1,500-square-foot house that is moderately well insulated. All the solar heat that the greenhouse generates is easily used in the house. When it is very cold and sunny, the house furnace will come on during the day to supplement the heat from the greenhouse. The greenhouse never overheats the house. There may be a 5 to 10 percent reduction in fuel use in the house, which is usually too small to be noticed.

Second, a slightly larger greenhouse, perhaps with 150 or 200 square feet of glazing, is attached to the same house. On a sunny day in winter, the greenhouse supplies the total heat load. As soon as the sun goes down, the house furnace comes on. This greenhouse might save 10 to 20 percent of the house's fuel use. The greenhouse occasionally gives more heat than can be used in the house on sunny spring and fall days.

Third, a larger greenhouse, with 300 square feet of glazing, is attached to the house. On a sunny day in midwinter, the greenhouse adds enough heat to the house to raise the temperature to around 80°F. Because of the existing thermal mass the furnace does not come on until perhaps 10:00 or 11:00 P.M. In the spring and fall there is enough heat generated that the house cannot use it all. It could be dumped into the basement, into otherwise unheated or underheated rooms, or outside through an open window. This greenhouse might save 20 to 30 percent of the conventional fuel use.

Fourth, a still larger greenhouse, with perhaps 400 or more square feet of glazing, is added. On even a half-sunny day the greenhouse heats the house entirely. Heat storage is added to the house to take better advantage of the large amount of heat generated on a clear day. Perhaps exterior insulation has been added to the basement walls, and air from the house is circulated by a fan through the basement, storing heat in the masonry. The air circulation makes the house comfortable, even thought the air temperature is over 80°F. This greenhouse could displace 30 to 50 percent of the house's typical fuel use.

These four simple examples serve to illustrate the range of possibilities for the space heating capability of different sizes of greenhouses. Another way to examine the relationship between greenhouse size, cost and fuel savings is to graph greenhouse size against cost and against the decrease it causes in home heating energy use. We'll take as our example the medium-cost greenhouse that was shown in table 3-1 and a 1,500-square-foot, energy-conserving house, as defined in table 6-2, in a moderate climate. Holding the house size constant, we'll vary the size of the greenhouse and see how that affects cost and solar fraction. (We'll assume that the floor area of the greenhouse is equal to its south-facing glazed area.) Line A in figure 6-1 shows that fuel savings increase with greenhouse size, *but not proportionally*. There is a point of diminishing return: As the greenhouse gets larger, the fuel displaced per square foot of greenhouse glazing decreases. The 8-by-10-foot greenhouse saves about 10 percent of the annual home heating energy use. Doubling this size, to a 10-by-16-foot greenhouse, about doubles the savings. However, doubling the size again, to a 10-by-32-foot greenhouse, does not again double the performance: Fuel savings increase only by 50 percent not 100 percent.

The same kind of relationship holds true with cost versus size, shown in line B. As the greenhouse gets larger, the total cost continues to rise, but again the cost doesn't rise proportionally. The cost per square foot

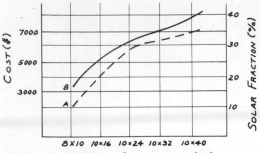

Figure 6-1: The amount of heating fuel saved increases with increasing greenhouse size (line A), but not proportionally: After a certain point, each additional square foot of glass contributes a smaller amount of energy to the house. The same is true for cost (line B). Cost increases with size but slows down for bigger greenhouses, until additional heat storage is needed in the house.

The "Cost" in the graph is for contractor-built greenhouses and is based on medium-cost construction from table 3-1. The "Solar Fraction" (the fraction of heating fuel displaced by solar heat) is based on a 1,500-square-foot, energy-conserving house—level 3 in table 6-2—in a moderate climate with a south-facing glazed aperture equal to the floor area of the greenhouse.

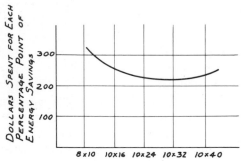

Figure 6-2: The cost per unit of fuel savings decreases as the greenhouse gets larger, reflecting definite economies of scale in construction, until the greenhouse gets so big that additional heat storage is needed in the house. This expense offsets the economies of scale.

decreases as the economies of scale affect construction costs, as discussed in chapter 3. The cost per square foot rises more and more slowly as the greenhouse size increases, until the greenhouse becomes so large, 10 by 40 in our example, that additional heat storage in the house is required to make use of the extra solar energy collected. Having to add this storage raises the construction cost, making this a somewhat less attractive option when adding a greenhouse to an existing house. (In new construction it is usually easier to add this extra storage to achieve higher solar fractions.)

When approaching the greenhouse as an investment in solar heating you're likely to ask How much will it cost, and how much heating energy will it save? And even more to the point, you might ask: At what size greenhouse am I getting the most fuel savings per dollar that I'm spending? This relationship— dollars spent for each percentage of fuel savings versus greenhouse size—is graphed in figure 6-2. An interesting thing happens here: The dollars spent per gallon of fuel saved are high for a small greenhouse, since construction costs are high, and they decrease as the size increases, since construction is cheaper per square foot with the larger sizes. But when the greenhouse gets so big that additional heat storage is required in the house to utilize all the solar heat being collected, the cost per unit of savings starts to rise again.

In other words, the intermediate-size greenhouse which makes as much use as possible of the intrinsic heat storage capacity of the house without requiring additional storage, gives the most solar heat per dollar spent. The 8-by-10-foot size will give some solar contribution, but it will be relatively small. Any fuel savings may be difficult to distingish from other variations in fuel use from year to year. The 10-by-16-foot size is a better investment because it returns more solar heat at a lower cost per gallon of fuel saved. The 10-

by-24 foot and 10-by-32-foot sizes show the lowest cost per unit of fuel saved and represent the best return on investment. When the greenhouse gets to 10 by 40 and additional storage is required to make use of the extra solar heat, the cost per unit of savings starts to rise again, and the investment becomes less attractive. Of course, with the larger greenhouses, there is likely to be more attraction to the benefits of living and plant-growing space, in addition to having more solar heat.

We have explored this relationship between cost, size and fuel savings for a specific example, but the trend would be the same for other levels of construction cost, other levels of insulation in the house and other climates. A very small greenhouse will give a relatively small solar heat contribution that may actually be difficult to distinguish from other yearly variations in fuel use. Increasing the size is an increasingly better investment, until the larger size requires additional heat storage in the house, at which point the increase in expense is not matched by the increase in solar performance.

The guidelines in this chapter are admittedly biased to lead you toward intermediate sizes, which usually represent a good compromise between cost and performance. Remember here that we are only looking at solar heating performance and not at other uses (food production, extra living space, recreational value and the increased resale value of the house) that represent a return on the investment and will influence greenhouse size.

Greenhouse Location and Solar Performance

Locating the greenhouse adjacent to the most-used living areas of the house has a strong effect on fuel savings. A greenhouse that dumps its solar heat directly into the main living area allows that room to be warmed while the rest of the house is left cooler. Thus, even though a moderately sized greenhouse may heat only one or two occupied rooms, the overall energy savings can be significant. Larger greenhouses that heat more than just the adjacent living area also save additional fuel when their heat is directed first to spaces that are occupied by day. As the day progresses and more solar heat is brought in the house, doors can be opened to distribute heat to the rest of the house. The heat from a greenhouse attached to a back bedroom, far from the daytime living area, may contribute as much warm air to the house as one attached to a living area, but unless that heat can be moved into inhabited spaces, back-up heat may be needed even on a sunny day. This of course decreases the fuel savings created by the greenhouse.

In the greenhouse sizing procedure in this section, the size of the aperture is referenced to the number of square feet of floor area to be heated. This can refer to the whole house or to just a portion of it. If a small greenhouse is all that is possible, perhaps for reasons of cost or siting, the sizing procedure may be used to determine how much of the house can usefully receive greenhouse heat.

Variability of Greenhouse Performance

A multipurpose solar greenhouse will naturally be a more variable solar heater than a single purpose passive or active solar space-heating system. The greenhouse heat output varies for a number of reasons. If the greenhouse is used for growing plants, the quantity of foliage in the greenhouse will vary during the heating season. When the greenhouse is bare of plants, the heat storage mass and the soil are fully exposed to the sun, absorbing more solar energy and leaving less to be transferred to the house. As the plants get bigger, they absorb more of the incoming solar radiation. Since the plants are lightweight, they don't store any appreciable amount of energy, which causes more of the solar energy to become hot air. And the plant leaves will convert more solar energy to latent heat, as the leaves transpire and give off water vapor. Thus, the more the heat storage is blocked by leaves, the more hot air and moisture become available to the house.

A season-extension greenhouse will have a different annual cycle than an all-winter greenhouse. In the season extender, the greenhouse is rather bare when plants are first seeded in spring, allowing the heat storage to absorb as much energy as possible, leaving a somewhat smaller amount for the house. By late spring the storage may be much more shaded, particularly if tall, large-leafed summer crops such as cucumber vines or tomatoes are growing. This greatly increases the amount of solar energy that is converted to hot air, increasing the amount of heat that is available to the house, whether or not it's actually needed for space heating. The same situation can exist in the fall, when summer crops are still tall and full of foliage.

In the winter-growing greenhouse the soil may be in shade all the time if a continuous cropping scheme is used. In this scheme, only one or two individual plants are harvested at a time, with a new seedling replacing each one that is harvested, leaving a continuously intact plant canopy over the soil. In the late spring, summer and fall, shading of the storage will increase if tall, leafy summer crops are planted. Again more hot air might be available at a time when the house doesn't need as much heat. Preventing greenhouse or house overheating at these times is done with vents to the outside.

The temperature at which the greenhouse is run can vary with the stage of growth of the crops and the types of crops. Seedlings, for example, require higher temperatures than do mature plants. Tomatoes, cucumbers and other warm-weather crops require substantially warmer temperatures for good yields than do cold-weather crops such as greens. When more heat is required in the greenhouse, more heat will be taken from the house at night or even on cloudy days in colder climates, decreasing the net fuel savings. The cropping pattern may be changed to use less back-up heating energy. Crops requiring minimum night temperatures of 40 or 45°F will, of course, use less energy (solar or backup) than those that need to be kept at 50 or 60°F.

The way a greenhouse is operated will naturally have a substantial effect on the quantity of heat delivered to the house. If the air exchange vents (doors, windows or vents) between house and greenhouse are manually controlled, getting solar heat into the house is directly dependent on paying attention to opening and closing vents at the right times. If you forget to open the vents for just a few hours on a sunny morning, you can lose 50 percent of the solar heat that would have been available. Forgetting to open a vent at night (to maintain a minimum greenhouse air temperature) could mean that an electric back-up heater in the greenhouse will run for several hours. This can be expensive if the house is heated with a fuel that costs less than electricity.

Another heating variable is water vapor. When the greenhouse has much foliage and the air in the greenhouse is quite humid, additional energy is transferred to the house by the water vapor in the warm greenhouse air (latent heat transfer). Some of this extra energy will be useful and some will not. The higher humidity in a residence allows a lower thermostat setting with no loss of comfort (due to decreased evaporation from your skin) and therefore a small decrease in heating fuel use. If you used a humidifier in the house before you had the greenhouse, you'll be able to turn it off when moist greenhouse air comes in. But on the other hand, some of the vapor that comes in simply leaves the house via infiltration, taking its latent energy outdoors. Also, some water vapor condenses on windows, increasing heat loss through them. How much latent heat is useful and how much is lost is difficult to quantify, and the amount changes with the seasons. It depends on many variables, such as how many plants you have and how much you water them, how leaky the house is, and outdoor temperatures and wind-speeds.

Variability in performance is one of the pleasant surprises a greenhouse offers. A greenhouse full of plants is more akin to an organism with cycles and changes, whereas other solar-heating systems are more like machines. While this may be confusing when you're trying to specify the best design, it is also insurance that variations from specific rules of thumb are not usually fatal. A great variety of greenhouse designs can all yield significant energy savings.

Determining the House Heat Load

In order to size the greenhouse for solar heating the house, we must first determine how much heat the house needs, or the "house heat load." Two simple methods for determining the heat load for a house are presented here: You can add up your actual fuel use, relative to weather conditions over a number of years, or you can use a rule of thumb, based on house type, to make an estimate. If you have past fuel records, these will be the most accurate; if not, the rule of thumb will be sufficiently accurate.

In the fuel use method, the quantity of fuel used is translated into actual heat delivered to the house by assuming an overall efficiency for your heating system and by accounting for any fuel used for domestic water heating. The first step is gathering your fuel bills and adding them up for the previous heating season. If your fuel is delivered in bulk, as is fuel oil, the most accurate method is to fill up the tank before and after the heating season. Otherwise, you may have to do some estimating based on how much fuel was delivered during the heating season and how much you have left in the tank afterwards.

If you use the same fuel for heating domestic water as you do for heating the house, you have to take this into account, since most of the heat that goes into the hot water ends up down the drain. To do this, look at your fuel use during the summer months when no heat is used. Average these months' fuel use, and subtract this amount from months when heat is used to get that portion of the fuel used for heating. For example, if you use 12 therms of gas per month during June, July and August, subtract 12 from the total number of therms used per month in the heating season.

Your fuel dealer or serviceman can usually tell you the heat delivery efficiency of your heating system. If not, you can use the efficiencies listed in table 6-1. The heat delivered to your house is equal to the amount of fuel used times the efficiency at which it was used times the heat content of the fuel:

$$\text{Heat delivered} = \\ (\text{quantity of fuel delivered}) \times (\text{efficiency}) \times \\ (\text{heat content of fuel})$$

For example, if you had 350 gallons of oil delivered last heating season and your heating system runs at 70 percent efficiency, you actually used 34,300,000 Btu to heat your house:

$$\text{Heat delivered} = (350 \text{ gallons}) \times (0.70 \text{ efficiency}) \times (140,000 \text{ Btu per gallon}) = 34,300,000 \text{ Btu}$$

After calculating the amount of heat delivered to the house for the year, check with the weather bureau or a local fuel dealer to find out how cold it was. This information is usually available in degree-days (dd), which is the sum of the average difference between 65°F and the outdoor temperature for each day of the heating season. For example, if you lived in a warm climate where the heating season is 100 days long and the average outside temperature is 45°F every day, the heating season would have 2,000 dd:

$$\text{Degree-days} = \left(65 - \frac{\text{average outdoor}}{\text{temperature}} \right) \times$$

$$(100 \text{ days}) = (65 - 45) \times (100) = 2,000 \text{ dd}$$

Since the outside temperature is in reality different every day, degree-days are figured for each day and then added up to get the degree-days for the year. The inside temperature of 65 assumes that you really keep the house at 68 to 70°F, but that the heat from cooking, lights and appliances, and body heat make up the difference. This is a good assumption unless your house is superinsulated, in which case these *internal gains* make more of a difference. Degree-day calculation procedures shouldn't be used for such houses.

Once you know how much energy your house used for the heating season and you know how cold it was, you can figure the house's *heat loss coefficient*, or the number of Btu lost per hour per degree of temperature difference between inside and out:

$$\frac{\text{Heat loss}}{\text{coefficient}} = \frac{\text{heat delivered (Btu)}}{(\text{annual dd}) \times (24 \text{ hr/day})}$$

(The 24 hours per day factor is needed to convert degree-days to hours, to put the coefficient in terms of loss per hour.)

For example, if your house used the 34,300,000 Btu in the earlier example, and the heating season had 3,500 degree-days, your heat loss coefficient would be 408 per Btu per hour per degree Fahrenheit:

$$\text{Heat loss coefficient} =$$

$$\frac{34,300,000 \text{ Btu}}{(3,500 \text{ dd}) \times (24 \text{ hr/day})} = 408 \text{ Btu/hr-}°\text{F}$$

TABLE 6-1: HEAT CONTENT OF FUELS AND TYPICAL HEATING SYSTEM EFFICIENCIES

FUEL	HEAT CONTENT	TYPICAL HEATING SYSTEM EFFICIENCY (%)
Coal	check with supplier	
Electricity	3,413 Btu/kwh	100 for resistance heaters; check with installer for heat pump coefficient of performance, which will be greater than 100

FUEL	HEAT CONTENT	TYPICAL HEATING SYSTEM EFFICIENCY (%)
Fuel oil	140,000 Btu/gal	70
Natural gas	100,000 Btu/ therm 1,000 Btu/MBtu 1,035,000 Btu/ mcf 103,500 Btu/ccf 1,035 Btu/scf	70
Propane	100,000 Btu/ therm 1,000 Btu/MBtu 2,500,000 Btu/ mcf 250,000 Btu/ccf 2,500 Btu/scf 91,500 Btu/gal 21,630 Btu/lb	70
Wood	Seasoned hard- wood: 24,000,000 Btu/cord Nonseasoned hardwood: 16,000,000 Btu/cord Seasoned soft- wood: 16,000,000 Btu/cord	40 for nonair- tight stoves 50 for airtight stoves 60 for airtight furnace

NOTE: *For gas, propane and oil furnaces and boilers, the efficiency is higher for the new generation of energy-efficient units and can be increased on older units with new burners and automatic flue dampers. Check with the person who services your system for an estimate of efficiency.*

Finally, we'll reduce this heat loss coefficient to heat loss per square foot of floor area. This is heated living area in the house, excluding basements that are not intentionally heated but are only kept warm by heat leaking from the furnace or water heater. Include any area kept within 10°F of the temperature maintained in the primary living spaces, like bedrooms or heated storage rooms, but exclude rooms like woodsheds or unheated wings of the house. If the heated area of our example house were 20 by 41, or 820 square feet, it would have a heat loss per square foot of 0.50 Btu per square foot per hour per degree Fahrenheit:

Heat loss coefficient/ft^2 of living area =

$$\frac{408\ \text{Btu/hr-}°\text{F}}{820\ \text{ft}^2} = 0.50\ \text{Btu/ft}^2\text{-hr-}°\text{F}$$

In the absence of fuel bills the rule of thumb method for determining a house's heat loss is sufficiently accurate for sizing a solar greenhouse heating system, particularly in light of the variability of greenhouse heat output that was discussed earlier. It is not intended to be used for calculating the size of a furnace for a house, nor is it intended as an accurate prediction of heating fuel use for a heating season, although it can be used to obtain a rough estimate for both.

The values in table 6-2 apply to single family houses or duplex units that are not larger than 1,800 square feet and not smaller than 800 square feet. (Houses within these limits have the volume to surface area ratio assumed for the table.) Heat loss calculations for houses outside these size limits should be calculated using the fuel bill method. The chart will also lose accuracy when used for houses with window areas less than 12 percent or greater than 30 percent of the heated floor area. The heat loss from row houses should not be estimated using this chart, since they have such large common wall areas. For this type of house you should use the fuel bill method.

The heat loss coefficient that you will determine is based on the level of insulation and other energy conservation features in the house. (The greenhouse you'll be adding is not included as part of the living space.) The various levels of energy conservation are described in table 6-2.

Using the Heat Loss Table

To use table 6-2, find the description that best matches the energy conservation features of your house, and use the accompanying per-square-foot heat loss coefficient.

Heat loss from a portion of a house can also be estimated, to the extent that that part is representative of the house as a whole. For example, if a greenhouse is being designed to heat a corner kitchen and living room of a single story house, the heat loss from that corner is probably representative of the heat loss from the house as a whole.

How Much Solar Heat for the House?

Of all the solar energy that strikes the greenhouse glazing, a small fraction—from 10 to 30 percent—actually ends up as solar-heated air delivered to the house. All of the following factors must be subtracted from the available solar radiation before it becomes house heat.

• Mullions and other framing members in the glazed area can reflect and absorb up to 20 percent of the available energy. Lightweight framing systems can cause less of this interference.

• Reflection off the glazing itself and absorption of solar heat by the glazing will reduce the available radiation passing through double glazing by 25 to 30 percent. Transmission of solar radiation is better with certain glazings, such as low-iron glass, where the reflection and absorption losses may be as low as 18 to 20 percent. Using high-transmission glazing can be an effective strategy for increasing overall solar gain.

• A certain portion of the solar radiation striking surfaces inside the greenhouse is simply reflected right back out through the glazing by light-colored surfaces and plants. In this way, 5 to 10 percent of the available radiation can be lost. (The higher interior light levels needed for plant growth, which white interior surfaces provide, justify these reflection losses, if the greenhouse is intended primarily for growing.)

• Heat loss from the greenhouse to the outside during sunny periods will account for anywhere from 15 to 25 percent of the incoming solar energy, depending on the level of energy conservation in the greenhouse and on the climate (cold, moderate, warm). With interior temperatures rising to 80 or 90°F on sunny winter days, daytime heat losses from the greenhouse are substantial because of the wide indoor-outdoor temperature difference and relatively poor insulation value of glass.

• The soil, the greenhouse structure and added heat storage will pick up from 10 to 25 percent of the incident radiation, depending on the quantities and position of the massive materials and on the level of foliage growth in the greenhouse. Even in greenhouses with no "intentional" thermal mass, as much as 5 percent of the incoming sunlight may be stored as heat in the soil and in the structure of the greenhouse.

• The amount of solar energy that is actually used in the photo-chemical reactions involved in plant growth is very small, less than 1 percent, of the incident energy.

As mentioned above, 10 to 30 percent is left for heat transfer directly to the house. This figure will be somewhat higher for no-storage greenhouses and for greenhouses that

TABLE 6-2: HEAT LOSS COEFFICIENTS FOR VARIOUS HOUSE TYPES

HOUSE TYPE	DESCRIPTION	HEAT LOSS COEFFICIENT*
1. Old and leaky	No insulation in walls or roof; no weather stripping; has storm windows; no basement or perimeter insulation (1 air change per hour, ACH)	1
2. Insulated (10- to 30-yr-old house or older that has been insulated)	5½″ insulation in roof; 3½″ insulation in walls; storm windows or double glazing; no basement or perimeter insulation; weather stripping on all windows and doors (0.75 ACH)	0.5
3. Energy conserving (built or reinsulated to current energy-conserving standards)	7½″ insulation in roof; 5½″ insulation in walls; double glazing or storm windows plus R-2 night insulation or triple glazing; 2″ foam polystyrene, basement wall or slab perimeter insulation; insulated doors; good quality weather stripping on all doors and windows (0.6 ACH)	0.2
4. Superinsulated (built to extremely stringent energy-conserving standards)	12″ insulation in roof; 8″ insulation in walls; double glazed plus R-4 night insulation or triple glazed plus R-2 night insulation; 4″ foam polystyrene basement wall or slab perimeter insulation; insulated doors; high quality weather stripping on all windows and doors; airlock vestibule entry-way; air-to-air heat exchanger (0.3 ACH)†	0.1

*In Btu/hr-°F-ft² of living area.
†Actual ACH is 0.5, but with energy saved by heat exchanger the effective ACH is 0.3.

share a masonry wall with the living space. The amount of any nighttime heat transfer from the house back to the greenhouse depends on how warm the greenhouse is going to be kept, on the size and effectiveness of the heat storage in the greenhouse and on the climate. All the above figures are expressed as ranges to emphasize the variation that is possible from one greenhouse to the next and from season to season.

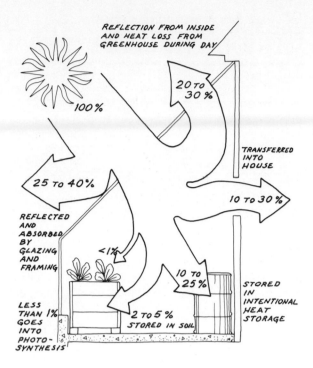

Figure 6-3: This illustration shows heat balance on a sunny day. Of all the sunlight reaching the greenhouse, only 10 to 30 percent is transferred into the house as warm air. This figure can be somewhat higher for greenhouses with no added heat storage.

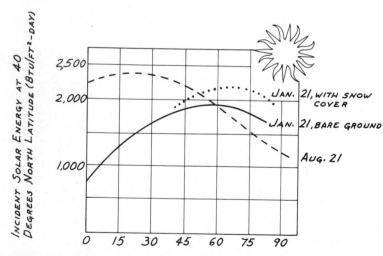

Figure 6-4: As the graph shows, the steeper angles (90 degrees is vertical glazing) are by far the best for admitting winter sun while still excluding summer sun. However, shallower slopes are useful for overhead illumination of growing areas in horticultural greenhouses.

Glazing Angles and Greenhouse Shapes for Optimum Solar Heating Collection

A basic principle of passive solar heating is that vertical, south-facing glazing is the best for both admitting low-angle winter sunlight *and* excluding high-angle summer sunlight. If the sole purpose of a solar greenhouse were to produce heat for the house, it should indeed have vertical glazing. In fact, it wouldn't have to enclose any significant volume, which is like saying it wouldn't have to be a greenhouse. If your only desire is getting heat for your house, you might as well build a flat-plate collector system onto the south wall or simply install more windows for direct gain heating. This is why solar greenhouses should be considered as more than just heat producers. The fact that they *do* enclose floor space means they automatically provide additional benefits of a living space and a place to grow things.

It is true that a slightly tilted surface collects more heat than a vertical one, but the difference in heat collection is generally not worth the extra expense of tilting the glazing. When permanent or frequent snow cover reflects additional sunlight onto vertical glazing, it becomes just about as efficient as sloped glazing for winter heat collection. And in areas with hot summers, the overheating potential of sloped glazing should be avoided if the slope isn't needed for increasing interior light levels.

Figure 6-4 shows the relationship between glazing angle and the amount of available solar energy. In January, glazing angles from 45 to 90 degrees (from horizontal) intercept similar percentages of the available solar energy. Even a glazing angle as shallow as 30 degrees collects only 20 percent less energy than the optimum slope (though this varies somewhat with latitude). In August, however, the shallower angles intercept much more sunlight, making the steeper angles more appropriate on a year-round basis because they will collect less heat in summer.

What all this boils down to is that, while vertical or slightly tilted glazing is optimal for solar heating, having a shallower tilt that increases light levels over growing areas (or improves the architectural design) doesn't result in an unacceptable decrease in solar-heating performance. Additionally, since shallower glazing angles often result in increased overall glazing area, this offsets the decrease in winter solar gain per square foot of glazing. But careful attention must be paid to avoid summer overheating with shallower glazing slopes. The use of some kind of shading system may be needed even in cold climates and will definitely be needed in moderate and warm climates (see chapter 5). Photo 6-1 shows a greenhouse that has house heating as a primary purpose, and photo 6-2 shows one that uses sloped glazing over the growing

Photo 6-1: With its large expanse of steeply pitched glazing this greenhouse is shaped primarily for solar heating. *(Photo courtesy of Mark Ward Greenhouses, Inc.)*

Photo 6-2: This greenhouse addition has a nice combination of tilted glazing for plant growing and vertical glazing for the living space. The sliding glass door provides convenient passage in and out of the living space.

areas and vertical glazing for the living area. When a smaller floor area in the greenhouse is all that is needed to satisfy minimal plant-growing ambitions but when substantial heat collection is wanted, the greenhouse can be stretched out along the width of the house, or it can be stretched vertically, to achieve a large glazed area for solar collection without much floor space.

Sizing the Greenhouse Glazing for Solar Heating the House

To review, the greenhouse aperture is optimally sized when it can capture enough sun to fully heat the house on a sunny winter day. Optimal sizing also relates to making full use of the intrinsic heat storage capacity of the house (framing, drywall, furniture, floors, and so forth). This means that on sunny winter days the house will not overheat. The aperture sizing table (table 6-3) indicates the size of greenhouse aperture that will give this level of performance. These recommendations are based on the size of the house, the level of energy conservation in the house and the climate. As you would expect, houses that are less energy conserving need larger aperture areas to offset their higher heat losses. Houses in colder climates will need more aperture area than would the same house in a warmer climate.

In order to help you design the ultimate size of the greenhouse glazed area recommended in this sizing procedure, the areas presented are *aperture* areas, not actual clear glass areas. The listed areas assume that about 10 percent of the aperture will be blocked by framing members and trim of one sort or another. For example, 1½-inch-wide rafters and battens spaced every 24 inches occupy 6 percent of the width. With 1½-inch blocking between the rafters every 36 inches, another 4 percent is blocked.

TABLE 6-3: MAXIMUM RECOMMENDED SOUTH-FACING APERTURE AREA

CONSERVATION LEVEL OF HOUSE	RECOMMENDED MAXIMUM SQUARE FEET OF SOUTH-FACING GREENHOUSE APERTURE AREA PER SQUARE FOOT OF HEATED FLOOR AREA OF THE HOUSE		
	WARM CLIMATE (less than 4,000 dd)	MODERATE CLIMATE (4,000 to 6,000 dd)	COLD CLIMATE (more than 6,000 dd)
1. Old and leaky*	0.33 (20 to 30)†	0.5 (15 to 25)	0.6 (10 to 20)
2. Insulated	0.18 (25 to 30)	0.30 (20 to 30)	0.47 (15 to 25)
3. Energy conserving	0.09 (25 to 35)	0.17 (20 to 30)	0.28 (15 to 25)
4. Superinsulated	0.04‡	0.07‡	0.14 (20 to 30)

NOTES: *Recommended aperture area should be decreased by 3 times the area of south-facing glass in the house not covered by the greenhouse.*

Maximum recommended aperture should be decreased by 25 percent if there is no heat storage in the greenhouse, by 20 percent if there is one-fifth the recommended storage, by 15 percent if there is two-fifths the recommended storage, by 10 percent if there is three-fifths the recommended storage and 5 percent if there is four-fifths the recommended storage. (For heat storage recommendations, see chapter 5.)

The aperture can be increased by 1 square foot for each 12 square feet of surface area of masonry in the house that will be exposed to the flow of warm air from the greenhouse.

Use higher fuel savings in sunny climates, lower in cloudy climates. See the text for further adjustments to saving predictions. This table assumes recommended greenhouse conservation levels, heat storage placement and siting, house-greenhouse air exchange, insulated common wall, no night insulation, aperture within 30 degrees of due south, 10 percent aperture blockage and winter growing.

The values for leaky houses are presented for use only in estimating the contribution from a greenhouse built for growing plants. If you are building a greenhouse to conserve energy in the house, insulate first!

†*Ranges (in percentages) of the estimated reductions of heating fuel use for the houses are given in parentheses.*

‡*Greenhouses are not required for solar heating.*

The aperture sizing procedure can also be applied to greenhouses that are intended to heat only part of the house, if the portion to be heated has roughly the same heat loss characteristics of the rest of the house. If, for example, a part of the house, the kitchen, living room and dining room, is to be solar heated and these rooms comprise the east half of the house, the floor area of that portion of the house can be used with table 6-3.

The glazing areas recommended in table 6-3 are presented as *maximum* glazing areas that can be added per square foot of house floor space. Houses that already have some south-facing glazing may not be able to use as much of the recommended greenhouse glazing, since the total south glass area may cause overheating. This is because a square foot of south window admits much more solar heat to the house than does a square foot of greenhouse glazing. Windows transfer about three times as much solar energy to the house as an identical area of greenhouse aperture. Therefore, *the size of the greenhouse aperture should be reduced by three times the area of any south-facing windows in the house that aren't going to be covered by the greenhouse.* The reason that the aperture is not reduced for south-facing windows that will be covered by the greenhouse is that these windows won't add any additional heat to the house. They simply admit some of the heat already captured in the greenhouse.

If, for example, table 6-3 calls for up to 300 square feet of greenhouse aperture and there is 50 square feet of south-facing window area that won't be covered by the greenhouse, the greenhouse aperture should be reduced by 150 square feet ($3 \times 50 = 150$). The same procedure is used to reduce aperture area for greenhouses sized for distributing heat to only a portion of the house, by accounting for noncovered windows in the area to be solar heated. Thus, if the portion of the house to be solar heated has 20 square feet of south-facing windows and table 6-3 calls for 150 square feet of aperture, only 90 square feet should be used [$150 - (3 \times 20) = 90$].

The maximum recommended aperture should also be decreased if there is no added heat storage in the greenhouse. With little mass to absorb some of the incoming solar energy, more heat is available for transfer to the house. *The maximum recommended aperture should be decreased by 25 percent for greenhouses without added heat storage, by 20 percent if one-fifth the recommended storage is added, by 15 percent if two-fifths the recommended storage is added, by 10 percent if three-fifths the recommended storage is added and by 5 percent if four-fifths the recommended storage is added.*

For example, in a cold climate, for all winter growing, 4 gallons of water are recommended per square foot of aperture. If the aperture sizing chart calls for up to 200 square

feet of aperture, 800 gallons of water are needed ($4 \times 200 = 800$). But let's say that we want to use 55-gallon drums, which means 15 are needed, but we only have enough space for 9 barrels. This is three-fifths the recommended amount of storage, so the aperture should be reduced by 10 percent, from 200 to 180 square feet. If the aperture were decreased by 25 percent, from 200 to 150 square feet, no storage would be required, as long as the criteria for a no-storage greenhouse are met (see chapter 5).

The aperture can be *increased* if the house incorporates more intrinsic heat storage than is assumed by the aperture sizing guidelines, which are based on the mass contained by wood-frame houses with drywall or plaster walls. Some houses have masonry in the living space. Masonry floors and walls will absorb somewhat more heat than will plastered walls and joist-framed wood floors. But masonry will only be useful for heat storage in areas where solar heated air will actually be in contact with it. If the masonry is isolated it shouldn't be counted as being useful for solar heat storage. (Note: Slab floors covered by rugs are *not* considered as being useful for storage.) The rule of thumb for having masonry in the house is that *the recommended aperture area may be increased by 1 square foot for each 12 square feet of exposed masonry surface where warm air from the greenhouse will be circulated.*

This guideline assumes that the masonry has a median heat storage capacity (about 30 Btu per pound per degree of temperature rise), that it is insulated from the outdoors and that air circulated from the greenhouse is at 80°F.

For example, a masonry house has 650 square feet of concrete floor and 400 square feet of insulated masonry wall in areas where warm air is circulated from the greenhouse. Dividing the total masonry area of 1,050 square feet by 12 gives a maximum allowable increase of aperture area of 87.5 square feet (1,050 ÷ 12 = 87.5).

Performance Predictions: Decrease in Fuel Use

Table 6-3 includes a range of estimated percentages of the house heating fuel that can be displaced by solar energy for different climates and house types. Of course, no individual house can be expected to have the exact savings shown in the table 6-3: A more precise performance prediction for a particular house would need somewhat more extensive analysis and calculation. But what follows are some suggestions for more closely aligning the performance predictions to your situation.

In sunny climates, the performance will be toward the upper end of the given range and toward the lower end in cloudier climates. (Figure 5-7 in chapter 5 shows the percentages of possible sunshine for different regions of the United States.) Local conditions should always be considered when determining how sunny an individual microclimate is, but the map gives a general indication of "sunniness."

Performance can be increased somewhat over the estimates in table 6-3 if the greenhouse is contributing heat to a well-used part of the house and if the rest of the house is allowed to be cooler on sunny days. While the rest of the house is unoccupied, the house thermostat can be set lower to decrease the need for heating fuel.

The heating percentages in the chart assume that the greenhouse is heated to around 50°F at night. If the greenhouse is not kept this warm, or if it is not heated at all at night, the heating percentages will increase by as much as one-third.

The percentages further assume that the greenhouse faces within 30 degrees of true south. The performance of greenhouses that face 45 degrees or more away from south will be significantly poorer. The sidewall of the greenhouse that faces most nearly south should be glazed in these situations, to increase both solar heat and light levels. For example, if the greenhouse faces southwest, the southeast sidewall should be glazed and the northwest sidewall should be opaque, at least where it is not directly adjacent to a growing bed. The solar-heating performance of greenhouses oriented far from true south is impossible to predict with a performance table as simple as the one used here, but experience has shown that greenhouses facing even farther off south than 45 degrees can capture enough solar heat to take care of their own heating requirements, as long as the endwall that faces closest to south is glazed. The greenhouse in photo 7-1, for example, has sloped and vertical glazing that faces 65 degrees west of south and a glazed vertical sidewall facing 25 degrees east of south. A good solar exposure helps this greenhouse perform quite well: It gets full sun from about 11:00 A.M. to 3:00 P.M. It essentially heats itself and delivers about the same amount of solar heat to the house as it takes from the house over the course of the heating season. Since the fuel bills for this house have remained the same after the greenhouse was built, this addition can be thought of as being 100 percent solar heated.

Table 6-3 also assumes that the glazing is mostly unshaded from 9:00 A.M. to 3:00 P.M., when about 90 percent of the day's solar energy is available. If the aperture is shaded during the midday hours, the performance prediction should be reduced to the extent that the aperture is shaded during these hours. (See the discussion of site surveys in chapter 2.) If your site survey shows that the sun is obstructed for half or more of the midday period, don't count on much or any decrease in fuel use for the house, although the greenhouse may be able to heat itself.

You'll get solar heat into the house on sunny days, but over the course of the year the amount of backup needed will balance this gain. If the greenhouse is shaded for one-third of the midday period, you can cut the predicted percentages in half. For example, if the greenhouse is mostly shaded between 9:00 and 11:00 A.M., it is shaded for 33 percent of the 9 A.M. to 3 P.M. period. If table 6-3 predicts a 40 percent reduction in fuel use for an unshaded greenhouse, this savings should be cut in half, leaving a 20 percent net fuel savings.

If the glazing areas are decreased from the recommended maximum areas, percentages of heating fuel displaced by solar can be decreased proportionally. For example, if table 6-3 predicts a 20 percent heating fuel reduction for a 200-square-foot aperture, 10 percent will be predicted for 100 square feet. However, if the glazing area is increased above the recommended amount, the fuel savings won't necessarily increase proportionally (due to the diminishing return of increased glazing area), as was explained in the first section of this chapter.

The energy savings predicted by table 6-3 should also be reduced to account for existing south-facing windows that are covered by the greenhouse. Those windows were already giving solar heat to the house before the greenhouse was built. Once they are covered, they only contribute heat already captured by the greenhouse. Therefore, the predicted fuel savings should be based on the greenhouse aperture minus three times the area of any existing windows to be covered by the greenhouse. Thus, if you had 100 square feet of south-facing window covered by 300 square feet of greenhouse aperture, the net result would be no decrease in fuel use. More often, however, a much smaller window area is covered relative to the size of the greenhouse. For example, if the greenhouse aperture is sized to be 0.28 times the floor area (shown in

table 6-3 for an energy-conserving house in a cold climate) and the house has 1,000 square feet of heated living space, the maximum recommended aperture would be 280 square feet ($1,000 \times 0.28 = 280$). But there is also 30 square feet of south windows not covered by the greenhouse and 25 square feet that are covered, so the maximum aperture should be $280 - (3 \times 30) = 190$ square feet. The prediction of fuel savings, however, should be based on 115 square feet, which is this size minus three times the area of the covered windows $[190 - (3 \times 25) = 115]$.

Table 6-3 predicts a 25 percent savings for the full 280-square-foot aperture (assuming the situation fits into the guidelines for choosing the upper end of the 15 to 25 percent range). The effective added aperture is 115 square feet, 41 percent of 280, so we could expect 41 percent of 25 percent, or about a 10 percent fuel savings from just the greenhouse ($0.41 \times 0.25 = 0.10$).

Whether the wall between the greenhouse is of wood-frame or masonry construction will also affect the solar-heating performance of the greenhouse. Table 6-3 assumes an insulated frame wall. If the wall is 8-to-12-inch-thick solid masonry and is unshaded for most of the day, the heating fuel reduction for the house may be increased somewhat over that predicted by the chart, perhaps by as much as one-third in an ideal situation where the masonry is unshaded for most of the day. Also, the timing of the heat delivery to the house will be changed, with the heat stored in the masonry delivered to the house in the evening, because of the slow movement of heat through masonry.

In very cold climates, with over 6,000 degree-days, the sizing recommendations for cold climates can be used. However, the solar-heating percentages will be decreased somewhat due to the increased heat loads of both the house and greenhouse. The amount will depend on how warm the greenhouse is kept at night. Performance of sunspaces that are unheated at night will be affected very little, but all greenhouses used for winter growing in very cold areas may end up with no net heat savings for the house (but perhaps with a 100 percent solar heated greenhouse).

Table 6-3 assumes that no night insulation is used, but if it is used, the solar-heating performance will increase by as much as 20 percent, since considerably less back-up heat will be needed at night.

In superinsulated homes, the percentage of fuel actually displaced by the greenhouse may be smaller than predicted, since the internal gains—lights, appliances and body heat—account for such a large portion of the heating requirements. Note also that the recommended aperture for greenhouses added to superinsulated homes is very small. In warm and moderate climates, a greenhouse is rarely needed for solar heating a superinsulated house. In cold and very cold climates only a superinsulated house with very few south-facing windows can use a greenhouse for solar heating. The greenhouse is still useful for its other attributes, though not for solar heating.

Some Sample Sizing Calculations

Example 1: What is the maximum aperture that can be added to an insulated (type 2 in table 6-2), 1,500-square-foot house in a cold climate? The house already has 85 square feet of south-facing glazing (actual glazed area of the windows, not overall window size), and the greenhouse will face due south at a site that is unshaded from 9:00 A.M. to 3:00 P.M. From table 6-3 we see that 0.47 square feet of aperture can be added per square foot of house floor area for a total of 705 square feet (0.47 × 1,500 = 705). Next we have to subtract three times the existing south window area that isn't covered by the greenhouse, which will be 20 square feet, giving a maximum recommended aperture of 645 square feet [705 − (3 × 20) = 645].

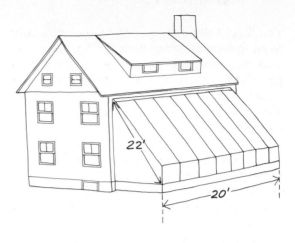

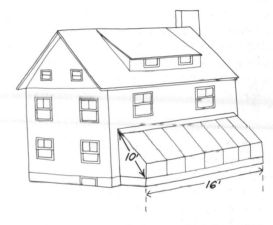

Figure 6-5: This example house, which has 1,500 square feet of floor space, is moderately insulated and is in a cold climate, can effectively use a greenhouse aperture up to 645 square feet, without requiring additional heat storage in the house. If the house were more energy conserving, only 270 square feet of aperture can be added. Interestingly enough, both greenhouses give a similar percent reduction in fuel use, which emphasizes the impact that a house's energy efficiency has on the required greenhouse size for solar heating.

Figure 6-5 shows one possible greenhouse shape. If the energy conservation level of the house were increased to make it a type 3 in table 6-3 (energy conserving), only 0.28

square feet of glazing would be recommended per square foot of house floor area. Since the upstairs windows wouldn't be covered, there would be 50 square feet of uncovered windows leaving a recommended aperture area of 270 square feet [(0.28 × 1,500) − (3 × 50) = 270]. Figure 6-5 also shows a possible greenhouse shape for the energy-conserving house.

Example 2: A small greenhouse is to be added to the living room of a single-story 1,000-square-foot insulated (type 2 in table 6-2) house in a moderate climate. The greenhouse heat is going to be used only in the living room/dining room area and kitchen on the east end of the house. The area of these rooms is 200 square feet, and their heat loss is representative of the loss from the house as a whole. There are 20 square feet of existing south-facing windows but these would be covered by the greenhouse. From the table, 0.30 square feet of aperture are recommended per square foot of living area, for a total of 60 square feet (0.30 × 200 = 60).

Figure 6-6 shows a possible greenhouse design for this example. If a larger greenhouse were desired, the heat from it could be distributed to other rooms of the house. It's interesting to note that if this were a superinsulated house in a cold climate, this same aperture area would be recommended for the *whole* house.

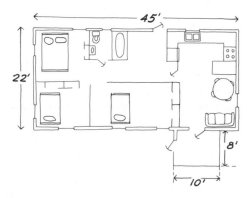

Figure 6-6: In this example, a 1,000-square-foot house, moderately insulated and in a moderate climate, needs only 60 square feet of aperture to heat just the living room. Up to 300 square feet of aperture could be used if the heat were to be distributed throughout the house.

Larger Greenhouses and Increased Heat Storage

Solar greenhouses can be sized to provide as much solar heat as needed by a house, even up to 100 percent solar heating, as long as enough heat storage is added in the house. This additional storage can be incorporated in a number of ways.

In new construction, water containers or masonry can be built into the common wall between the house and the greenhouse. Masonry can be incorporated in the house

itself in areas near the air exchange vents from the greenhouse in walls or in floor slabs. Remember that in order to be useful as heat storage, this masonry must be put in the areas where greenhouse air will be circulated.

In existing houses, the options for adding storage are naturally more limited unless you're ready and willing to make major changes. Heat storage is simply large and heavy, and therefore hard to retrofit to existing houses. Masonry or water storage that is added near the greenhouse warm air outlets is likely to be awkward looking in most houses and would require basic structural modifications in some situations. Phase change materials are more compact but not as useful inside the house because they are out of direct sunlight. Slab floors that have perimeter insulation will provide much more heat storage capacity than wood floors, but it isn't usually practical to add a slab to a joist-supported floor.

If your basement is a heated living space and if there is insulation on the exterior of the masonry walls, all this mass can function as heat storage. If the basement gets warmer than the upstairs, some of the heat will gradually work its way up through the floor, although more often only enough heat can be stored in the basement to offset basement heat losses. If heat from the greenhouse isn't wanted in the house during the day because of solar gain from other south-facing windows, greenhouse air can be circulated directly into the basement with a fan.

The guideline of 1 square foot increase in recommended maximum aperture size per 12 square feet of exposed masonry in the main living space can be applied to basement masonry, as long as you only count masonry that is in direct contact with moving warm air. If a fan, for example, blows only across the middle third of an 800-square-foot basement floor, only that area, 266 square feet, is useful storage. This would allow 22 additional square feet of aperture ($266 \div 12 = 22$). In most cases, partition walls and piles of stored things restrict airflow to a small fraction of the total exposed masonry. You will have to assess your basement to see how much masonry can actually be exposed to the airflow. In general, at least a 10-foot-wide path between natural convection airflow inlets and outlets can be considered useful, including masonry walls in that area.

Air circulation between the greenhouse and the basement will usually require a fan, to bring the hot air down, but circulation through the house, into the basement and then into the greenhouse can sometimes be accomplished with natural convection, depending on the house layout. (The specifics of airflow paths and associated vents and fans are covered below.) If the basement isn't insulated, and you don't plan to insulate it, it is better to decrease the size of the aperture than to direct solar heat to an uninsulated area. If, however, the greenhouse is oversized for more growing or living space, though, it's better to dump excess heat into the basement than directly outdoors, since at least some of the heat will be useful.

Heat Exchange Basics

Most of the heat moved from the greenhouse to the house travels by the exchange of warm greenhouse air with cooler house air, either by natural or forced (fan powered) convection. The warm air tends to spread out across the ceiling, warming the ceiling, which then radiates heat downward to all the objects and surfaces (and people) in the room. As the warm air near the ceiling cools, it mixes with other air of equal temperature. If a fan is used to bring air into the house, the greenhouse air will mix more rapidly with the room air, warming the various room surfaces more equally. In either case, cooler room air returns to the greenhouse through return vents.

The speed at which warm air moves through a room does affect your sense of comfort. Because of the evaporative cooling effect it produces, moving air feels cooler than still air at the same temperature. If greenhouse air at 60 or even 70°F were blown into a room, it would feel cool and drafty. For this reason, thermostats for fans are usually set to go on at 80°F or higher. At this temperature, slight air movement won't be uncomfortable. And ideally the airstream should be directed up across the ceiling away from the areas where people will be sitting.

The cooling effect of moving air can also be utilized to increase the effective heat storage of the living space by allowing the room to reach a higher temperature before overheating discomfort is sensed. The moving air feels cooler, but with its higher temperature more heat is stored. Moving air temperatures as much as 5 or 10°F above normal comfort levels will still feel quite comfortable, which means that more heat can be stored in the house.

The Heat Capacity of Air

As you would expect, air has a very low heat capacity relative to any of the common building materials and heat storage materials discussed so far. It holds only 0.018 Btu per cubic foot per degree Fahrenheit temperature rise.[1] A cubic foot of water, for example, stores 62 Btu for the same 1°F temperature rise. Another way to look at this is that when a kitchen match is fully burned (1 Btu), it will raise a cubic foot of air 56°F, but it will raise a cubic foot of water less than 0.02°F. This rather low heat capacity is the reason that large volumes of solar heated air need to be moved into the house in order to make the best use of the available solar energy and to prevent overheating the greenhouse.

Airborne water vapor in horticultural greenhouses can contribute substantially to the amount of heat available for transfer to the house. This additional heat capacity is almost entirely due to latent energy, which is the energy required to evaporate the water. Virtually all the water used in the greenhouse evaporates sooner or later—from the plants, the soil and even a wet floor—absorbing quite a bit of energy. At 1,054 Btu per pound, each gallon of evaporated water takes about 8,800 Btu, about the equivalent of the solar energy transmitted by 8 square feet of aperture during a sunny day.

The extent to which water vapor increases the heat capacity of the air depends largely on the amount of plant growth and how much they are watered. Greenhouses with few plants will generate little humidity, but a plant-filled greenhouse that is watered frequently will put a great deal of vapor into the air. It is not uncommon that a greenhouse with a moderate number of plants will maintain a relative humidity of 90 to 95 percent when it's closed to the outside or to the house. (This humidity is too high for the plants, but such conditions are easily avoided by venting into the house in the winter.)

When solar heated greenhouse air is circulated into the house, the heat in the water vapor is transferred to the cooler house air and surfaces. When some of the vapor condenses on cooler surfaces in the house, the latent heat is released. Air returning to the greenhouse is both cooler and drier, with a relative humidity of perhaps 40 percent. The mixing of this air reduces the greenhouse relative humidity to around 80 percent. The end result is that the heat transferred in a cubic foot of moist air is up to three times the amount of energy transferred in a cubic foot of dry air.[2]

---

[1] The heat capacity of air is 0.018 Btu per cubic foot per degree Fahrenheit at sea level. At higher elevations, the air is less dense and consequently has a smaller heat capacity. At an elevation of 2,000 feet the heat capacity is about 0.017, at 5,000 it is 0.015 and at 7,000 it is 0.014. Throughout the discussions, 0.018 is used for calculations. At higher elevations recommended air volumes should be adjusted upward in proportion to the decrease in heat capacity. The size of air vents should also be increased proportionally.

[2] The greenhouse air at 80 percent relative humidity (rh) and 80°F contains 0.0011 pounds of water per cubic foot of air. The return air, at 60°F, 40 percent rh contains 0.00037 pounds of water. Each cubic foot of air that goes into the house, under these circumstances, leaves 0.0011 minus 0.00037, or 0.00074 pounds of water, in the house, as increased relative humidity in the house and condensed water, either invisibly in the dry house contents or visibly on cold window surfaces. Some of this moisture

In terms of designing an air exchange system, this means that vents and fans could be smaller for greenhouses where plants are grown through the winter. But it is better to design the air exchange system for dry air and have the capability to move more air when required. Natural convection systems will automatically handle the variations; fans should have slower speeds for times when the energy transferred by the air is greater.

Moisture in the House: Will It Be a Problem?

A greenhouse full of plants can move as much as 2 to 3 gallons of water vapor into the house over the course of a sunny day. Whether or not this will cause a problem depends on many factors. The most common problem caused by excess moisture in the house is excessive condensation on the windows. A small amount of condensation usually isn't a problem, but when there is so much that water runs down the window and onto the window sill there can be some damage to wood or paint.

If a house falls into either the "uninsulated" or "insulated" categories previously discussed in table 6-2, the infiltration through the house will remove water vapor fast enough to prevent excess condensation. But if the house has single glazing, condensation may occur fairly frequently on the cold windows. (If the house has a single glazing, condensation on the windows is probably common even without the greenhouse, so it doesn't really create a new problem.) The inner surface of double glazed windows will generally be above the dew point except in the coldest weather, so there isn't going to very much condensation.

In energy-conserving houses (type 3 in table 6-2), the relative humidity will get higher than in less efficient houses, since more of the greenhouse moisture is retained. Houses with as few as 0.5 air changes per hour may have problems with excessive condensation on double-glazed windows in very cold weather. If, for example, the indoor relative humidity is 40 percent (quite high for a cold winter day) and the indoor temperature is 70°F, the dew point will be 45°F. The inside surface temperature of the window will get this low when the outside temperature goes below 10°F, and condensation will occur. Higher relative humidity in a frame house also means that there should be an effective vapor barrier in insulated walls and ceilings to minimize vapor transmission to the insulation. Houses that were insulated when they were built are likely to have an adequate vapor barrier, but when insulation has been blown into existing stud or joist cavities, there may be a need to add a barrier. This can be done with special latex paints made for this purpose or with a couple coats of oil-base paint.

If the house has fewer than 0.5 air changes per hour, the interior relative humidity will be higher still and condensation will occur at a lower relative humidity and/or a higher outdoor temperature. In these cases, an *air-to-air heat exchanger* may be needed to keep the relative humidity low enough to minimize condensation. Superinsulated (type 4 in table 6-2) houses are almost sure to need this heat exchanger to avoid excessive condensation.

Air-to-air heat exchangers are becoming relatively common in superinsulated houses. These devices are used to exhaust stale air

---

escapes outdoors via infiltration through cracks in the house. The energy required to evaporate this water in the greenhouse—1,054 Btu per pound times 0.00074 pounds, or 0.77 Btu—was also left in the house (except for the infiltration losses).

The air itself—excluding vapor—cooled 20°F during its journey through the house, releasing 0.018 Btu per degree Fahrenheit times 20°F, or 0.36 Btu. The cooling of the water vapor in the air is a small amount of energy—about 0.01 Btu.

from the house whenever a humidistat senses that the humidity is above the level set on the humidistat. Heat exchangers are much more effective than simple exhaust fans because they transfer most of the available heat from outgoing air to an incoming stream of fresh air. Moisture from the outgoing air condenses in the exchanger in cold weather and is piped to a drain. Air-to-air heat exchangers used for humidity reduction should not be the type with heat exchange cores that are permeable to water vapor. This type would allow the humidity in the outgoing air to be transferred into the incoming air, defeating the goal of dehumidification. In very cold weather, this moisture will actually freeze in the exchanger, so it is important that the unit incorporate an automatic defrost cycle. Some manufacturers are listed in Appendix 1.

Airflow Options: Natural and Forced Convection

Natural convection, or thermosiphon air-flow, was discussed earlier in connection with infiltration and exhaust venting. To review, it is a flow of air created by a temperature difference: warmer, lighter air rises, and cool-er, heavier air falls.

One nice effect of using the temperature difference between the house and the green-house to power the air exchange is the auto-matic control of the rate of airflow. When the greenhouse is a little warmer than the house, just a little air flows. As the greenhouse warms up further, the flow rate increases.[3] At night,

when the greenhouse becomes cooler than the house, the flow reverses, following the same pattern of increasing flow with increasing temperature difference. This reversal can be used for back-up heating of the greenhouse, or it can be stopped with simple *backdraft dampers,* which allow air to flow in only one direction (see chapter 12 for details about these dampers).

Using Fans

Fans offer a relatively simple way to move air (forced convection) from the green-house into the house through vents that are smaller than those used for natural convec-tion airflow. This can be an advantage if there are no existing windows or doors in the house-greenhouse common wall and if making large openings would be impractical.

Fans also offer a greater degree of control over how the flow of air is directed through the house. With a fan it's much easier to move solar heated air into rooms that aren't adja-cent to the greenhouse, either on the same floor or an upper or lower floor.

The amount of air that a fan will move is usually described in cubic feet per minute, or cfm. This air movement is usually tied to a certain *static pressure.* This refers to the amount of pressure or resistance that the fan can overcome and still deliver the rated cfm. A high static pressure reduces the flow rate a fan can produce. For example, a fan that must push air through a long, narrow passageway will be working against a much greater static pressure and will deliver less air than the same fan simply sitting out in the middle of a room with no restrictions. A restricted fan will also use more power and make more noise. Static pressure is usually measured in *inches of water* in fan applications. This refers to the difference in the height of water in a U-shaped tube (an instrument called a *U-tube*

---

[3] The air velocity through a natural circulation vent sys-tem is proportional to the square root of the temperature difference. As the temperature difference doubles, the flow rate increases by a factor of 1.4, the square root of 2. For example, airflow through a set of vents when the greenhouse is at 80°F and the house is at 60°F will be 1.4 times the flow when the greenhouse is at 80°F and the house is at 70°F.

manometer) that has one end open to the pressurized (outlet) side of the fan and the other end open to the ambient air (see figure 6-7). The greater the height difference, the greater the static pressure. A condition of no pressure against the fan is referred to as "free air."

Fans used for house-greenhouse air exchange are designed for very low static pressure, lower than 0.1 inch of water. (By contrast, the blower for a forced air furnace may run at a static pressure as high as 1 inch of water. This high pressure capability isn't usually needed for greenhouse air exchange systems.) If ducting is used, the static pressure may reach as high as 0.1 inch, but proper design will minimize this, decreasing the potential for increased noise and power consumption.

It is important that the fan be as energy efficient as possible. Larger, slower-moving fans will use less power, make less noise and last longer than smaller high-speed fans. The slower-moving air will also make the living area more comfortable. So it is worth the effort to cut a larger hole and install a larger diameter fan, particularly if the fan is going to exhaust air into a much-used living area.

Airflow Paths through the House

There are a great variety of ways to move greenhouse-heated air through the house. The path can include only one room or most of the house, one, two or three floors. You can literally make heat go where you want, though some paths are more easily accomplished than others. Natural convection within the house will tend to distribute warm air throughout open areas unblocked by walls and closed doors. Fan-forced airflow uses a little electricity to get around these barriers.

One-Room Airflow

The simplest arrangement is to circulate air from the greenhouse only to the room directly adjoining it. This arrangement works well with natural convection (see figure 6-8). Natural convection will also circulate air into any rooms adjoining this space if the doors to

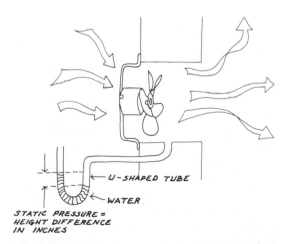

Figure 6-7: A U-tube manometer is an instrument that shows the static pressure on a fan as the difference in height of the water in the two sides of the U-tube.

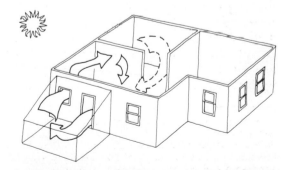

Figure 6-8: A one-room path for the air loop is the simplest and most direct. Some heat will also go to other parts of the house.

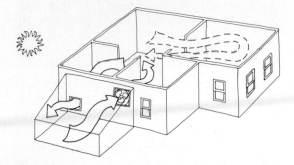

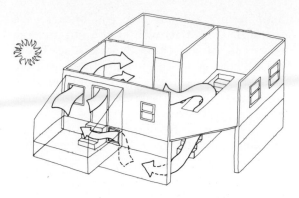

Figure 6-9: A two-room airflow path can be driven by convection but is more effective with a fan as shown here. Heat is transferred from the greenhouse into a well-used area, with cooler air taken from less-used rooms. Some heat will find its way into adjacent rooms via natural convection.

Figure 6-10: A loop into the main floor, through the basement and back into the greenhouse can be convection driven. An insulated basement can also store some heat for use in the greenhouse at night.

those rooms are left open. These rooms won't be heated as much as the directly adjoining room but they will still receive substantial amounts of warm air. This flow will be decreased by such things as small or low doorways or long hallways.

Two Rooms on One Floor

This path is usually appropriate where the greenhouse "straddles" two adjacent rooms of the house. Heated air is brought into the house near the ceiling of one of the rooms and is returned to the greenhouse via the floor of another room, creating a longer circulation and heat distribution path (see figure 6-9). This airflow path can make use of the fan to circulate air first to more occupied living spaces and second to less used areas.

If this flow were done by natural convection, there would have to be upper and lower vents in both rooms, with the relative size of the vents in each room based on how much of the greenhouse heat was desired for each room.

Main Floor to Basement Airflow

If the house has an insulated basement living space and the greenhouse covers an opening into the basement, air can be directed into the main floor from the greenhouse, down a stairway into the basement and back out to the greenhouse through a basement window or door (see figure 6-10). If the house foundation is insulated on the outside, this circulation pattern can make use of the heat storage capacity of the masonry foundation. The flow can be natural or fan driven, depending on how direct or convoluted the path is.

In very cold climates, if the greenhouse is not heated in the winter, cold air from the greenhouse will circulate into the basement at night, unless the opening to the basement is closed, causing unnecessary heat loss from the basement, and (at worst) a frozen water pipe. If the greenhouse is to be used only for season extension and left to freeze during winter, the basement can be used as a "warm" air source only when there are plants in the greenhouse. Cold air will not "pool" in the lower areas of

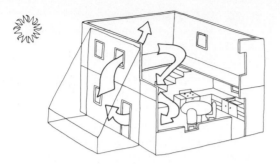

Figure 6-11: A two-story loop will tend to keep the upstairs somewhat warmer than the downstairs, unless a fan is used to bring the warm air down.

the greenhouse, but will flow into the basement and be replaced with warmer basement air.

Upper Floor to Lower Floor Airflow

If the greenhouse is tall enough to cover rooms on both the first and second floors, air can be brought into the house on the second floor, drawn down the stairwell and returned to the greenhouse from the first floor. As with the basement scheme, doors need to be left open to complete the loop. This scheme is often used with natural convection, because with a "taller" path the flow rate can be considerably greater than with a single-story air path. The cooler upstairs air near the floor of the second story will fall down to the first floor while the warmer upstairs air will stay near the ceiling. This will delay the delivery of warmth to the first floor, which can be a problem if the first floor is the main living area and if it tends to be cool in the morning. If there are enough south- and east-facing windows in the lower floor to warm that area early, the delay will not be a problem. The

basement can even be added into this loop, giving a greater height and a more powerful flow (if the greenhouse aperture is large enough to warrant adding the basement heat load).

If the heat from a two-story greenhouse is needed mostly on the first floor, a single-story loop can be created. But if the stairway to the second floor cannot be closed off, warm air will find its way up there anyway. If there is a way to close off the stairs, solar heat can be kept downstairs as long as needed and then allowed to go upstairs when the first floor is warm enough.

Designing Vents for Natural Convection

With its noiseless, sunpowered flow, natural convection is truly an elegant way of moving heat around. The main challenge of a natural convection system is in creating simple, automatic controls for vents that must not only admit warm air to the house, but also allow house air into the greenhouse for back-up heating. A backdraft damper is the right solution for moving air in one direction only—usually from greenhouse to house—but if reverse airflow is occasionally needed to keep the greenhouse warm, the backdraft dampers must then be propped open. However, if windows and doors are used as vents, automatic control for airflow in *either* direction is difficult (unless you want to build a giant backdraft damper for a window opening). This is not a fatal disadvantage, since the doors or windows can be left open much of the time that the greenhouse has plants in it. One solution is to have a separate, thermostatically controlled heater to provide back-up heat for the greenhouse. The vents with their backdraft dampers are thus automatic for solar heating the house, and the heater is automatic for heating the greenhouse, so you can just about let the greenhouse run itself. (The only drawback here is if your backup is electric and electric rates are high in your area.) If the common wall has no existing penetrations, the labor cost associated with installing vents may be as high or higher than the cost of installing a fan. Adding a door and windows, or perhaps one sliding glass door, is often done to allow for natural convection as well as to gain access and a view. These are advantages that can't be had with a fan.

Vent Placement

Air exchange vents should be placed to take the best advantage of the effects of natural circulation: The upper vent should be as close as is convenient to the ceiling of the room receiving the warm air. If this is not at the very peak of the greenhouse, this is all right as long as the vent is at least in the upper quarter of the greenhouse. The lower vent should be as near the floor of that room as possible. Since the rate of airflow through the vents depends in part on the difference in the height between the upper and lower vents, you should maximize this distance.

If possible, vents should be distributed across the common wall to promote even circulation and avoid hot or cold spots. It is generally not worth the effort to move existing doors or windows, but if new vents are installed they should be located to spread out the airflow as much as possible.

Vent Sizing

Natural convection vents must be large enough to transfer all the surplus solar heat from the greenhouse into the house. If the vents are larger than necessary, no harm is done, but if they are too small they won't be able to move enough volume to prevent over-

heating in the greenhouse. This not only increases heat losses from the greenhouse, but may damage plants.

The following rules of thumb should be followed in designing vents. *Vent area should be 10 percent of the aperture area.* This assumes that there is an 8-foot vertical separation between the centers of the top and bottom vents, that the minimum dimension of the vents is at least 1 square foot and that the vents are not screened.

The area of vents with insect screening should be doubled to equal 20 percent of the aperture. For example, a greenhouse with a 150-square-foot aperture is to be built onto a house with no existing doors or windows in the common wall. If only vents (no doors or windows) are to be added for air exchange, 10 percent of 150, or 15 square feet of unscreened vent are needed. If the vents are screened, 30 square feet would be needed. The unscreened

TABLE 6-4: FACTORS FOR ADJUSTING VENT AREA FOR VARIOUS VENT SPACINGS

DISTANCE IN FEET FROM CENTER OF LOWER VENT TO CENTER OF UPPER VENT	MULTIPLY THE REQUIRED VENT AREA BY:
20	0.63
15	0.74
10	0.89
8	0
6	1.15
4	1.41
3	1.60

vent plan could include two upper and two lower vents, each being less than 4 square feet. The dimensions might be 1⅓ feet high by 3 feet wide. If the centers of the upper and lower vents are more or less than 8 feet apart, you must adjust the vent area by the factors listed in table 6-4. Referring to the above example, if the vents can only be placed 6 feet apart, the required vent area is multiplied by 1.15, giving a required (unscreened) vent area of 17.25 square feet.

If a single opening such as a door is used for venting, a portion of the upper half of the opening becomes upper vent area, and a portion of the lower half becomes lower vent area, with a stagnant area in the middle of the opening. The total area will have to be increased to account for this stagnant zone. Table 6-5 gives the factors for determining the effective vent area of single openings.

TABLE 6-5: FACTORS FOR ADJUSTING VENT AREA FOR SINGLE OPENINGS

Height of Single Opening (ft)	Divide the Area of Single Openings by These Numbers to Find the Effective Area
1	4
2	2.8
3	2.3
4	2
6	1.6
8	1.4
10	1.2

If the common wall has vents on two floors of the house, and the stairway between floors is left open, the full areas of all openings on the lower floor will generally act as lower vents, and all openings on the upper floor as upper vents. Mixtures of doors and windows at various heights in a single floor common wall require a certain amount of judgment to determine which are high and which low. In general, all openings above the midpoint of the common wall can be considered high; all below, low. If a door is in the lower part, with windows above, for example, the whole door opening would probably act as lower vent area, with all the window openings as upper vent area. However, the airflow patterns of some arrangements of windows and doors at different heights are difficult to predict. You may have to experiment with which openings are opened and which are closed to direct warm air where you want it.

Backdraft Dampers and Other Vent Controls

For small vents that are less than 2 feet in height backdraft dampers are effective and easy to build, and they provide some degree of automation. They consist of a very light-weight flap that hangs over the vent opening. Sun heats the air in the greenhouse, making it lighter. This heated air leaves the greenhouse through the upper vent, and cooler, heavier house air flows into the greenhouse through the lower vent, pushing the damper flaps open. When the sun goes down and the house air is warmer and lighter, the flaps close, stopping the flow of cool air back into the house.

The damper flap is usually made of a thin plastic such as the very thin polyethylene covers that come from the dry cleaner. This flap is supported by a slightly tilted piece of screening when there is no air flowing, because the thin (1 mil) film is so limp. The tilt of the support screen ensures that the flap will thoroughly seal the opening against cold air. (On a vertical surface, the flap can tend to hang away from the screen slightly, admitting cool air to the house.) Usually a ½-inch mesh support screen (hardware cloth) is used, to minimize the obstruction to the airflow. (See chapter 12 for construction detailing.)

Backdraft dampers are an ideal control for moving air in one direction, but if the vents are used to move air in both directions, for solar heating the house and for back-up heating in the greenhouse, the backdraft dampers will have to be propped open at night to achieve the reverse airflow. If the greenhouse is only used for season extension, this may be a minor problem. The vents could be left propped open for the spring and fall when the weather is cold enough that the greenhouse needs some backup. During winter, when the greenhouse isn't heated at night, the backdraft dampers are an effective control. If the greenhouse is used throughout the winter and requires back-up heat on most nights, it may be more appropriate to simply leave the vents partially open all the time, to admit enough heat to keep the greenhouse warm, while not increasing heat loss from the house more than necessary. If the common wall has vents with backdraft dampers and a door or window, the vents can be used when solar heat is taken from the greenhouse but no heat from the house is needed in the greenhouse. When the greenhouse needs heat, the door or windows can be left open to provide enough heat to maintain the desired temperature.

In cold climates, rigid foam plugs or insulated shutters are recommended for the wall vents. When it is very cold and the greenhouse isn't using back-up heat from the house, the heat conducted through the backdraft dampers and the cold air leaked around them will result in unnecessary heat loss and cold drafts on the floor of the house. (See chapter 12 for construction details.)

Fan-Powered Heat Exchange Systems

Fans have the advantage of automation and therefore ease of operation, and they usually require less installation labor than natural convection vents. The system itself consists of a fan, a return air vent and one or two thermostats, or a more sophisticated thermostatic controller. Some type of flap or shutter is usually used over the fan and return vents to both minimize the movement of air when the fan is not running and to direct the flow of air when it is running. Operation is quite simple, the same as a natural convection flow with the addition of the fan: Warm air is blown into the house and cooler air is pulled into the greenhouse through the return vent. When the greenhouse is too cool, the fan moves air from the greenhouse into the house, and warm house air is pulled into the greenhouse. The fan need not be the reversible type, although some costlier fans and controllers incorporate this option. As with the natural convection approach, insulated vent shutters or foam plugs for the fan and return vents may be desirable in cold climates, for use on cold nights when the greenhouse isn't getting heat from the house.

Using a fan system has a few distinct advantages over natural convection, the primary one being complete automation. With a pair of thermostats, a fan can automatically bring solar heat to the house and bring house air to the greenhouse for back-up heat at night.

Another advantage of a fan is its size. Since it needs a much smaller opening than a natural convection system, it is easier to install. There is also more flexibility in placement since fan system openings aren't located strictly by the rules of natural convection.

The main disadvantage of a fan is its use of electricity, although this consumption is not great. Poorly designed fan systems (usually too small and too high speed) can also be noisy.

Fan and Return Vent Locations

The fan and return vents are placed to take advantage of natural convection when solar heat is being collected. The fan vent is placed as high as is convenient in the common wall, and the return vent is as low as possible. This reduces the power consumption of the fan because of the boost it gets from natural convection. It also keeps the fan away from small children and from splashing water. It isn't critical that the fan be at the very peak of the greenhouse or that the return be at the very lowest point, as long as the fan is in the upper third of the wall and the return is in the lower third.

Some care must be taken in directing the air inside the house. If possible, direct the air along the ceiling or along the junction of the wall and ceiling with a grille or a simple piece of hanging cloth, to an unoccupied part of the room. It is also important to select a fan that is large enough to move sufficient volume at low velocity to avoid drafts (see the section on fan selection below). Blowing air directly on the house thermostat should also be avoided, as this would make the thermostat "think" it is either warmer or colder in the house than it really is.

The fan and return vents should be placed as far apart in the common wall as is convenient to increase the scope of the air circulation as much as possible. For example, if the fan vent is at the upper east end of the common wall, the return vent should be at the lower west end. But if the situation doesn't

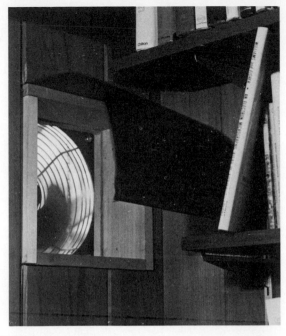

Photo 6-3: This cloth flap directs the air from the fan along a wall in the living room to prevent draftiness in the sitting area. It has weights in the bottom hem to control airflow direction and to prevent it from flapping.

permit a wide separation of the vents there will still be adequate warm air distribution without any "short circuiting" of the air from the fan directly to the return vent, since the warm air will tend to spread out across the ceiling, and cool air will come from near the floor.

Fan Sizing and Selection

With a little care, you can choose a fan with enough capacity to keep the greenhouse cool and transfer as much heat as possible to the house, yet quiet enough to be easy to live with.

The heat exchange fan should be sized to deliver 5 cfm for each square foot of green-

house aperture. This flow rate assumes that the aperture is completely unshaded for at least part of the 9:00 A.M. to 3:00 P.M. period and that there is the recommended quantity of heat storage in the greenhouse. *If there is no heat storage, the fan should be sized to deliver 7 cfm per square foot of aperture.* Both flow rates will also be adequate for providing back-up heat to the greenhouse. For example, a greenhouse with heat storage and 150 square feet of aperture should have a fan that can deliver 750 cfm (150 ft^2 × 5 cfm/ft^2).

To minimize draftiness the diameter of the fan should be large enough to obtain a relatively slow air velocity. The larger the fan diameter, the slower the velocity, which means less noise, less power consumption and longer fan life. A velocity of less than 300 feet per minute (fpm) is acceptable when the air is to be blown across the ceiling of an occupied room. If the fan is blowing air into an unoccupied room, a faster air velocity of up to 450 fpm is acceptable. For example, a 2-foot-diameter fan has an area of 3.14 square feet (3.14 × 1^2). If the fan moves 600 cfm the velocity is 600 divided by 3.14, or 191 fpm.

The return vent should be the same size or larger than the fan opening to ensure unrestricted air movement. Any oversizing of the return vent relative to the fan also reduces the velocity of the air at the return vent and minimizes draftiness in the immediate vicinity.

An easy way to select a fan is to choose a multispeed unit whose lowest speed has the desired output. In the above example, a three-speed fan rated at 2,000, 1,000 and 700 cfm would be adequate when run on the lowest speed. Fans can also be custom built, if you like to tinker with such things, by selecting fan blades, motors, and housings, and assembling the pieces. This requires familiarity with fans and motors, but is not out of the realm of most fan suppliers. When looking for

a low-velocity fan you may have to mount a determined search, since most fans are designed to deliver much higher velocities. A velocity of 1,200 to 1,800 fpm is quite common for a 24-inch fan.

Another important feature for a fan is *thermal protection.* A thermally protected motor has a heat-sensitive switch inside it that turns off the motor if its temperature gets too high. This will save a motor from being damaged or even burning out if, for example, the fan turns on but the opening is blocked.

In some cases it is necessary to move the greenhouse heat from one side of the house to a room or rooms on the other side without heating the spaces in between. Perhaps the main living areas are on the north side of the house or the greenhouse is too small to heat both a distant living space and the intervening rooms. To make such a "jump," you can couple the greenhouse fan with ducts to put heat where it's needed. The design of the fan and duct system should be done by someone such as an HVAC contractor (heating, ventilation and air conditioning) or engineer familiar with air systems, since ducts introduce additional static pressure on the fan. However, the same general rules for fan selection apply to duct design: Use ducts with a large cross-sectional area to maintain slow velocity and to minimize static pressure. Warm air ducts should always be run through heated space in the house whenever it's possible. If a duct has to be run through an unheated attic or basement, it should be heavily insulated with at least 5½-inch (R-19) fiberglass insulation. In most cases, the return airflow can flow through the house, so it won't have to be ducted. Distribution ducts aren't always needed to deliver warm air to distant rooms. If the greenhouse is large enough to heat a north-side living space and the intervening rooms, greenhouse air can be moved from room to room with small circulating fans using doorways between rooms as return vents.

Fan Thermostats and Controllers

The piece of equipment that really makes the fan useful is the thermostat. If the air exchange fan is used only for bringing heat into the house, only a single *cooling thermostat* is needed. This device turns the fan on when the greenhouse gets above the set point, usually 80 to 85°F. If the fan is also used for back-up heating, a *heating thermostat* is needed to turn on the fan below the set point, around 50°F for many plants. A schematic for wiring the thermostats is shown in figure 6-12.

Another type of controller, a *differential thermostat,* turns on the fan based on temperature difference. If the differential is set at 10°F, the fan is activated whenever the greenhouse is 10°F warmer than the house.

Some controllers have a fixed differential, while others can be adjusted. Some also incorporate a heating set point for the greenhouse that turns on the fan when the greenhouse gets colder than a certain temperature, regardless of the house temperature, to provide back-up heating.

Some differential thermostats can change the speed of the fan in proportion to the temperature difference between the house

and greenhouse. If the house temperature is a certain number of degrees (5 to 10°F or more) below that of the greenhouse, the fan is run at full speed. As the house temperature rises, and the differential decreases, the fan is slowed down and finally stopped when the house is almost as warm as the greenhouse. These *proportional differential controllers* adjust the airflow to the available solar heat in the greenhouse. (If you want to use one of these controllers, be sure that the speed control is compatible with the fan motor.)

If the greenhouse is to be used for growing plants as well as for solar heating, a differential thermostat may not be well matched to the control requirements. The plants have a certain range of temperatures in which they will grow well, their own "comfort zone." But a differential thermostat responds to the heat requirements of the house. A simple thermostat more closely serves the needs of the plants for temperature control and performs almost as well as a differential thermostat in delivering solar heat to the house. For solar-heating *and* plant-growing greenhouses, this thermostat is preferable; for the solar-heating and living space greenhouse, a differential thermostat will deliver slightly more solar heat to the house, but may not be worth the extra cost.

Some controllers can reverse the fan

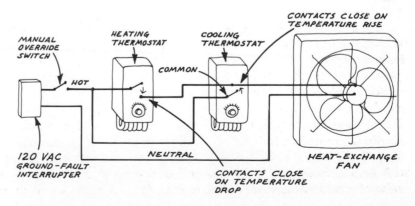

Figure 6-12: In this schematic for a dual-purpose fan system, the two line-voltage thermostats turn on the fan if the greenhouse is too hot (solar heat available for the house) or too cold (greenhouse needs heat from the house).

when the greenhouse needs back-up heat. These require the right sort of fan and wiring to make the reversal work. The reversing feature isn't really needed for back-up heating: Air drawn from the house will be warm enough for the greenhouse whether it comes from the floor or the ceiling. Actually, air that does come in low through the return vent will be distributed in the greenhouse more effectively. But warm air that is brought in nearer the top of the greenhouse will tend to stay there, leaving cooler air near the plants.

Combination fan and controller units are available from several sources. Some brands include differential thermostats, while others use simple thermostats. Most of these combination units have small fans, for ease of installation. They are usually small enough to fit in between framing members that are on 16-inch centers. Before purchasing a combined unit, listen to it run and decide if the noise level is acceptable.

One possible drawback of some combined units is that it is not possible to use the

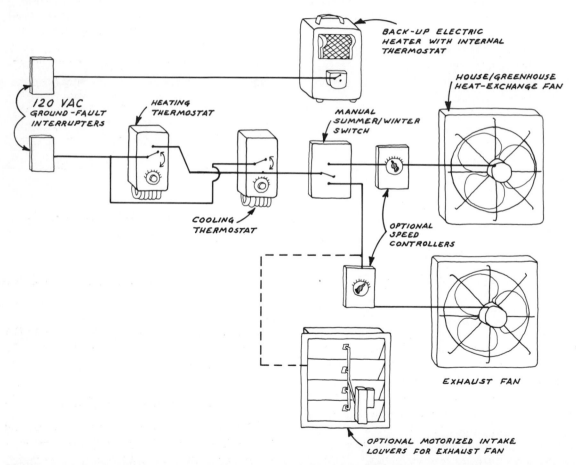

Figure 6-13: In this schematic for controlling an exhaust fan and a heat exchange fan with the same thermostats, the "summer-winter" switch is used to select which fan is used. The speed controller allows you to adjust the rate of airflow.

TABLE 6-6: GREENHOUSE TEMPERATURE CONTROL STRATEGIES

Temperature Zone	When House Needs Heat	When House Doesn't Need Heat
Too hot for plants	Turn on heat exchange fans or open heat exchange vents	Turn on exhaust fan or open exhaust vents
Cooling thermostat set point: 75 to 85°F		
Plant comfort zone	Vents to house open or closed; fans off	Exhaust vents open if outside near plant comfort zone temperature; fans off
Heating thermostat set point: 45 to 55°F		
Too cold for plants	Turn on heat exchange fans or open heat exchange vents*	Turn on heat exchange fans or open heat exchange vents* (Close exhaust vents if open)
Back-up heater set point: 35 to 40°F		
Plants freeze	Back-up heater goes on	(Not likely when house doesn't need heat)

If there is no air exchange with the house at night, turn on the back-up heat.

controller to operate a separate exhaust fan in the summer, which can be done in a system you assemble yourself (see figure 6-13). With this sort of "summer-winter" system you choose which fan is controlled by the thermostat. Having the optional speed controller allows you to change the airflow rates of either fan for changing seasons and to control noise levels. The back-up heater in figure 6-13 is shown as an electric heater. It has its own thermostat, and its set point is lower than that of the heat exchange fan, so it isn't tied into the fan thermostats. Table 6-6 shows the overall control strategy for a system like the one in figure 6-13.

Fan Louvers, Flaps, and Plugs

When the fan isn't running it is usually desirable to close off the fan and return vents to prevent natural convection from exchanging air. Flaps or louvers over the fan vent are opened by air pressure from the fan, and closed by gravity when the fan turns off.

TABLE 6-7: HEAT EXCHANGE SYSTEM CHOICES

HEAT EXCHANGE SYSTEM	CONTROL	ADVANTAGES
Vents with backdraft dampers	Automatic backdraft dampers for solar heating; manual operation for back-up heating	Quiet; no electricity needed: solar-powered air movement; slow air movement through house
Manual vents, including doors and windows	Manual operation for solar and back-up heating	Same as vents with backdraft dampers; may not require creating additional wall penetrations
Fan-powered system	All automatic with thermostatic control	Thermostatic control can be used to control exhaust fan; requires only small vent holes in common wall; more control over airflow paths through house
Fan system plus manual vents	Automatic and manual operation	Advantages of both fan and vent systems: quiet and no power when vents used; automation when needed

Aluminum louvers are usually used with higher velocity fans, but the slower-moving fans recommended here may not generate enough pressure to fully open them so a cloth flap can be used. Louvers are not a good choice for the return vent because it is subject to even less pressure, since there is inevitably some air leakage in the greenhouse and the house. A lightweight cloth or plastic flap (such as would be used in a backdraft damper) that will respond to lower air pressure is more effective. The flap can be weighted, if it is too light, to prevent it from flapping in the breeze of the fan and to direct the air stream downward or, by shifting the weights, to one side.

In cold climates, insulated hatches or push-in rigid foam plugs are useful for periods when the greenhouse is left unheated and the fans are turned off. Insulating the fan and return vents will avoid excess heat loss from the house. It is, of course, important that the fan isn't turned on when the vent is closed, since the fan could overheat and even burn out if it isn't thermally protected.

Combining Natural Convection and Fan Power

When properly designed and built, natural or forced convection are effective heat exchange systems for greenhouses. In some situations, however, the two can be conveniently combined to provide the best features of both options. For example, the common wall may have windows and doors that aren't big enough for the vent area needed for natural convection, so a small fan system is added. Fan systems are often added even where win-

DISADVANTAGES	COMMENTS	RELATIVE COST
Relatively large holes in common wall required; no automatic back-up air exchange	Use electric heater in green-house as extra backup if vents are closed on cold nights	Low for materials; moderate to high for labor depending on house
All manual operation	Same as vents with backdraft dampers	No cost if adequate existing vent area; moderate to high if there are no existing doors or windows
Uses some electricity; creates some noise and possibly drafts if system isn't properly designed and built	In cold climates additional backup usually needed; use slow rpm, larger fans for quieter operation	Higher materials; low to moderate for labor; higher costs if bringing power to fan is difficult
If doors or windows don't already exist, duplication expensive	Often consists of adding fan system to existing doors and windows	Same as fan plus return if windows or doors exist; materials and labor high if no openings exist

dows and doors would provide sufficient air exchange on their own, to provide automatic operation when the windows and doors are closed. Table 6-7 outlines the possibilities and summarizes the heat exchange system options.

Preventing Summer Overheating

It is important that the savings in heating fuel and the increased comfort provided by a solar greenhouse aren't offset by an increased summertime cooling load and overheating. In addition to ventilation and shading options, steeper glazing slopes can be used to fend off more of the high angle summer sunlight while admitting more winter sunlight. Part of the roof area of the greenhouse can also be made solid to keep the common

wall in shade during the hottest part of the summer. Since both of these techniques limit prime space for plant growing, they should be used selectively if horticuluture is an important part of your plan. Steeper glazing pitches and solid roofs can also decrease the overall aperture, reducing winter heat collection. In warmer climates, where there is greater risk of summer overheating, this may be justified, but if other methods can be used that don't sacrifice winter collection area, these are preferable for both heating and horticulture.

In cold climates, adequate convection and/or fan-powered ventilation is usually all that is required to keep the greenhouse cool enough in the summer to prevent overheating the house. Shading may be needed in some cases, but that can be done after the greenhouse is built if it proves necessary.

In moderate climates, a steeper glazing pitch or solid roof section may be needed only if summers are very hot, but thorough shading of the glazing would be a simpler solution. If maximizing the light for the growing area is important, or if the maximum aperture is needed for solar heating, shading techniques are usually preferable over the inclusion of design changes that would compromise cold weather performance.

In warm climates, a partially solid roof area is recommended for reducing summer heating of the house, if lighting for the growing area can be compromised. To determine the proper overhang length you can start by making a cross-sectional drawing of your greenhouse as shown in figure 6-14.

In moderate climates, the overhang should shade the common wall completely from 10:00 A.M. to 2:00 P.M. on June 21 (sum-

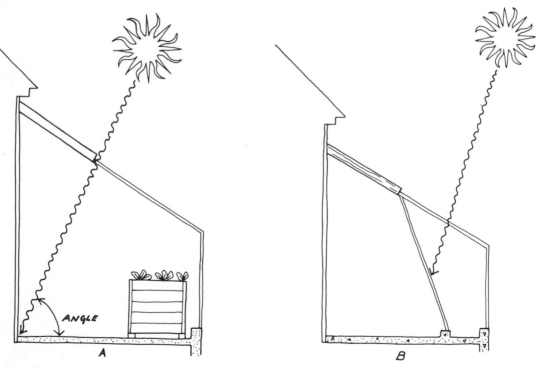

Figure 6-14: The steeper glazing angle in A reflects away more high-angle summer sunlight (compared to a shallow angle), but tends to shorten the depth of the greenhouse, unless a larger solid roof section is added. In warm climates, a solid roof section helps keep the greenhouse and house cooler in the summer. The size of the overhang is calculated to keep direct sunlight off the house from 10:00 A.M. to 2:00 P.M. on the summer solstice in moderate climates, and sun off the house from May through August in warm climates. In cold climates overhangs are not required. To determine the length of overhang, take 90 minus your latitude in warm climates and 90 minus latitude plus 13 in moderate climates. You can draw this angle as shown above in B on a cross section of the greenhouse to define the outer edge of the overhang. For example, in a moderate climate at 35 degrees latitude, the resulting angle would be 68 degrees (90 − 35 + 13 = 68).

mer solstice), the day the sun is highest in the sky. In warm climates, it should shade the common wall during the same hours from May 1 through August. This will be adequate for minimizing overheating in spring, but it is likely to be deficient in late summer and early fall. But an overhang that is shaded against all possible overheating at this time would excessively limit solar heat gain in the spring. This is why movable shading solutions are preferable for more precise control in different seasons.

Greenhouses that face more to the east or west will require special attention to prevent overheating. Trees are the best solution for east and west summer shading. They can be placed to admit winter sun while excluding early morning and late afternoon summer sun (see figure 4-10 in chapter 4). In some cases, solid roof areas can be useful, but steeper glazing angles will not help, because the early morning and late afternoon sun is low in the sky and would strike steeply angled glazing more directly. Again, movable shading techniques are very useful for such greenhouses, and, in conjunction with trees, often provide the best and the easiest solution.

Chapter 7

DESIGN INTEGRATION

In the previous three chapters greenhouse design has been developed from three points of emphasis—horticulture, energy conservation and solar heating—in order to develop the greenhouse features appropriate for each of these needs. As we have seen, these functions conflict in some cases, while in others they complement each other.

In this chapter, the various design issues are integrated into an overall design, taking into account all the functional requirements for the greenhouses as well as architectural and structural considerations. The process of bringing all these variables together into an overall design isn't a linear progression. It's more a matter of putting all the pieces on the table and seeing how they fit together, trimming some requirements to accommodate others. A design that feels right and works well may not emerge the first time, so keep at it and put the pieces together more than once.

Remember that once you have a complete design in hand, you still need to have the design checked by your local building inspector and by someone familiar with structural

design, to be sure circumstances particular to your house, your site and your climate are adequately addressed. If you are unsure of the solar heating design, due either to unfamiliarity with solar heating or to unusual circumstances with your house or site, you might also have this aspect of the design checked by a solar heating specialist. You can think of having your design checked by professionals as an insurance policy that you only have to pay for once.

It's likely you'll find that many design solutions will work for you. This is one of the nice things about solar greenhouses: There isn't just one right way to design them, and there is no one greenhouse design that is right for all houses.

Architectural Considerations

In addition to the strictly functional aspects of a greenhouse, integrating the appearance with that of the house as well as considering the movement of people in and out of the greenhouse will make the new addition more satisfying and easier to live with. Having easy access to the greenhouse from the house is important not only to be able to enjoy sitting in the sun, but to simplify the routine maintenance tasks like watering. And having easy access from the greenhouse to the outside makes spring and summer operations like transplanting or hauling soil and fertilizer much easier, and it avoids tracking any mess into the house. If the greenhouse will cover the main entry to the house, the flow of traffic through the greenhouse into the house should be carefully considered.

The ease of providing access from the house to the greenhouse depends largely on the layout of the house. In houses where the main living area faces the common wall, the greenhouse may cover an existing entry door. If there is no door, one can be added. A good choice is a sliding glass door or a pair of French doors, which give not only access and an opening for natural convection air exchange, but also a wide view into the greenhouse. A standard hinged single door can be cheaper to install, particularly where an existing window opening can be extended down to the floor. This avoids a potentially expensive alteration of the wall structure, since there is already a structural beam over a window. The door need not be insulated, since the greenhouse will provide some insulation, even when it isn't heated, but it should be weatherstripped to seal as tightly as an exterior door, to minimize infiltration. In cold climates, glass doors should be double glazed, unless the greenhouse is kept heated to 50°F all winter.

Where there are bedrooms or other less-used rooms on the south side of the house, the access solutions aren't as easy, and the result isn't always an optimum one because the greenhouse is more removed from the main living areas of the house. Nevertheless, a door should still be installed in the common wall. If the greenhouse is attached to the bedroom, a sliding glass door will provide a wonderful morning view of greenery that will be brightly lit if the greenhouse has any east-facing glazing.

Any greenhouse that is intended for growing more than just a few plants should have an outside door. The best alternative is a ground level door with no steps up or down. In many situations, there may be a height difference between the greenhouse floor and the ground outside, so stairs will be needed. They should be arranged in a straight line whenever possible so that a plank can be laid over them for rolling a wheelbarrow into the greenhouse.

If the greenhouse covers the main entry door of the house, traffic through the greenhouse must be considered. If the greenhouse is used for growing plants in winter, a vestibule between the greenhouse and the outside should be considered in cold climates to minimize thermal shock to the plants by the cold air that comes in when the outside door is opened. If the greenhouse isn't used for winter growing, the greenhouse itself will act as a vestibule for the house, providing a buffer for the house when doors are opened. In greenhouses that do serve as the main entry to the house, the floor should be an easy-to-clean material such as tile, brick, slate or concrete, rather than earth or gravel.

It is also important to be able to close off the greenhouse from the rest of the house, in order to avoid involving the house in the wide temperature cycling that the greenhouse experiences. Having a greenhouse that can be closed off is going to seem like a very good idea when the greenhouse is colder or hotter than the house. Many unseparated "integral" greenhouses do exist, with many satisfied owners, but these people are either tolerant of the temperature cycling that is caused within the living space, or they have taken special measures, like Solar Staircase, summer shades, extra vents or night insulation to reduce unwanted heat gain and loss through the glazing.

If it's important to preserve the view from the house windows that will be enveloped by the greenhouse, you should use glass for the glazing, rather than a translucent or ribbed plastic. And some care should also be taken to avoid placing the eave of the greenhouse or a structural post in a place that blocks the view out the window.

In city and suburban areas maintaining privacy in the greenhouse or in the rooms adjoining the greenhouse must be considered. Translucent glazing is one solution, either for the whole glazed area or just for those areas that provide a view in from the outside. Another consideration in the choice of a glazing material is the way it will look from the outside. Clear glass will make the greenhouse more transparent and perhaps lighter looking than translucent glazing. And glass will continue to look good for many years, while plastics will tend to get scratched and aged looking.

Another consideration in covering windows with a greenhouse is the effect on daylighting in the house. If a solid roof area of the greenhouse projects out 3 or 4 feet over a window in the common wall, the daylight coming in through that window will be drastically reduced. The overhanging roof blocks direct sun and shields the window from most of the diffuse sunlight on cloudy days. If the solid roof can be placed several feet above the window, the shading is minimized. Painting the underside of the roof white will also help, but if the window is an important light source for the room, you may want to decrease the size of the overhang, if your climate permits, or install a skylight in the solid roof just over

the window. An opening skylight also doubles as an exhaust vent.

Matching the Greenhouse to the House

Matching the design detailing of the greenhouse to that of the house will make the greenhouse fit in and blend better with the house. Design detailing includes such things as the style and color of trim, siding, doors and roofing materials and window size and shape. The quality and type of materials in the greenhouse should also match the house, if possible, not only for appearance reasons but so the house and greenhouse maintenance can be done at the same time. If it's possible, matching the angle of one of the planes of the greenhouse with the angle of the roof of the

Photo 7-1: In designing this greenhouse, the owners wanted the height, style and placement of the windows, and the type and color of siding material to match the look of the house and its neighbors. It is interesting to note that despite facing 65 degrees west of south and being shaded by the row of houses until 11:00 A.M., the greenhouse collects enough heat to contribute about the same amount of heat to the house that it requires to keep it growing ornamental plants all year.

Photo 7-2: The nook of this L-shaped house offered a perfect place for a diagonal, south-facing greenhouse addition. A deck is incorporated on the side, and photovoltaic panels inside the greenhouse are used to charge batteries, which are also charged by a wind system. *(Photo courtesy of Rodale Press Photography Department.)*

house helps the greenhouse blend in. There is usually enough flexibility in the design to adjust the angle of at least part of the greenhouse roof or glazing to that of the house roof, resulting in a pleasing visual echo of the house roofing.

Sometimes the shape of a house will present a good niche in which to place the greenhouse. L-shaped or U-shaped houses present a natural spot, as long as the niche is on the south side of the house. This offers increased protection for the greenhouse from cold winds, although the house will shade the greenhouse more in such a location. The diagonal greenhouse shown in photo 7-2 takes advantage of the south-facing niche provided by the L-shaped house.

Making a Place for People

Many prospective greenhouse owners plan for part of the greenhouse to be used exclusively as a solarium, devoting enough area for a table and a couple of chairs or a bench. The amount of space you need

Photo 7-3: This greenhouse made use of the existing porch roof for the solid roof area of the greenhouse and the masonry porch railing and steps for heat storage. A new front entry door was incorporated into the south face of the greenhouse addition.

depends on what kind of furniture you plan to use. For example, a 5-by-8-foot space will give you ample room for a small table and two

Photo 7-4: Having a place to simply enjoy the fresh greenhouse air is often the favorite aspect of the greenhouse.

chairs. When you are choosing the final shape of the floor plan, you can cut out a scaled top view of your planned furniture, to arrange it in the floor plan and make whatever adjustments are needed. Even in greenhouses where plants virtually fill the space, a chair always seems to find its way into a sunny corner, for enjoyment of sunny winter days.

Structural Considerations

Building a greenhouse whose structural members are thin enough to avoid unnecessary shading must be balanced with the need for strength and durability. The forces of the wind and snow buildup, as well as the weight of the greenhouse materials themselves, must be considered. In many manufactured greenhouses this is accomplished by using metal framing that is at once thin and strong. In the older commercial greenhouses thin wood

"glazing bars" or rafters were supported by purlins made of angle iron. (Many builders have used recycled parts from old greenhouses, making use of their lightness and strength to achieve a strong skin with little shading. One of these is shown in photo 4-1.) Most site-built greenhouses use conventional framing techniques, however, which require more attention to sizing framing members to minimize shading. The forces, or "loads," that act on the greenhouse, and the ways to counteract them are discussed here, and specific design details are covered in chapter 10, including such things as the required thickness of rafters and designs for diagonal bracing.

Live Loads and Dead Loads

Dead loads include the weight of the building materials that make up the roof—the rafter, the glazing, and, if the roof has a solid section, wood or plywood sheathing and roofing materials. The total dead load on a rafter is simply the sum of its own weight plus the weight of the materials it supports. For example, a 2 × 6 weighs about 3 pounds per lineal foot; a square foot of ³⁄₁₆-inch-thick glass weighs about 1¾ pounds. A typical dead load on a rafter with double glass glazing is from 12 to 15 pounds per foot of rafter. If the rafters are spaced 3 feet on centers, this translates into a dead load of 4 or 5 pounds per square foot.

Live loads include the force of the wind and the weight of snow piling up on the roof. Even though snow will usually slide off the greenhouse glazing, it will sometimes stick,

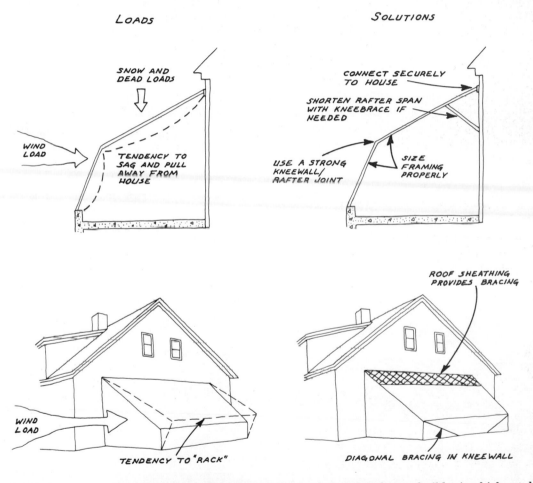

Figure 7-1: The cross sections above show the effects of live loads (wind and snow buildup), which act directly on the face or on the roof, and dead loads (the weight of the materials themselves), as well as the solutions for counteracting them. Wind loads from the side area are resisted by diagonal bracing. Solid areas sheathed with plywood offer excellent diagonal bracing. Specific detailing of structural joints and sizing guidelines for framing members are included in "Section III: Construction Detailing."

even on 45-degree slopes, so its weight has to be counted when sizing the rafters. Live loads are much greater than the dead loads, ranging from 40 to 65 pounds or more per square foot, depending on the climate, exposure to the wind and snow buildup.

Snow loads, dead loads and wind that blows at the glazing exert downward forces on the structure, as shown in figure 7-1. Correct rafter sizing is needed to counteract these forces, and the rafters must also be firmly attached to the common wall to eliminate the tendency to pull away from the house. A rigid joint at the kneewall also helps counteract the tendency for vertical kneewalls to "kick out." A support from the rafter back to the house (called a *kneebrace*) that is well tied to both the house and the rafter not only works to counteract kicking out, but allows the use of a thinner rafter, since the rafter span is decreased.

Winds that come at the side of the greenhouse tend to deform it slightly, also shown in figure 7-1. If the greenhouse is tucked into an "L" on the house, either diagonally as shown in photo 7-2 or square to the house, the house

will counteract this "racking" force. If the greenhouse is attached only at the common wall, though, its own structure must be strong enough to resist this force. Diagonal bracing is the most effective approach. A diagonal across a square framing opening changes the opening from a "squooshable" square to two rigid triangles. This can be done with a cable arrangement to minimize shading (see chapter 11). If there is a solid roof section, plywood roof sheathing provides excellent bracing, adding stability to the whole structure. In minimally glazed greenhouses (such as the example greenhouse B in chapter 5), the solid roof provides all the bracing that would be needed. But in a greenhouse where most of the surface is glazed (example A in chapter 5), roof sheathing alone may not be sufficient. Diagonal bracing in the kneewall will usually provide enough rigidity for the whole structure whether or not there is roof sheathing. Having tight joints in the framing also provides some diagonal bracing. (Specific structural recommendations are given in chapter 10.) In general, larger greenhouses with maximum glazing that do not have one endwall

Photo 7-5: These diagonal cables provide stiffening of the structure in this windy, hilltop location.

supported by the house need some type of diagonal bracing, particularly when the site is exposed and windy.

Defining Your Purposes and Design Constraints

In order to complete your greenhouse design, it is important to examine the constraints placed on the design by your needs and your intentions for the greenhouse as well as those imposed by the house, site, climate and budget. Is growing plants your main interest? Will the greenhouse be used for winter growing, for extending the growing season or for growing in the summer? Is the use of the greenhouse as a living space a priority? Is solar heating your house the major purpose? Now is the time to work in all of your current ideas, before you have to cast the design in stone and begin building. In this design process, you can try out different ideas in areas you are unsure of, running through the design procedure in this chapter as many

times as it takes to finalize your ideas and arrive at a blend of purpose and design that you're comfortable with.

If the solar survey for the house (chapter 2) showed that some of the available locations have more sun than others during the middle part of the day, always try to put the greenhouse where it will receive the best sun. If the choice is between the best sun and attaching the greenhouse to a more-often-used part of the house, the sunnier spot is usually the better choice. At some sites, there will be no perfect or even good location for a greenhouse. Such a site shouldn't be ruled out completely, as it may be quite good for plant growing or for having a solarium for part of the day.

House Height and Greenhouse Height

The shape of the greenhouse is often restricted by the height of a single-story house. (Two story houses don't usually present a height limitation.) If the design emphasizes solar heating, the glazing angle might be steep, coming from just under the eave of the

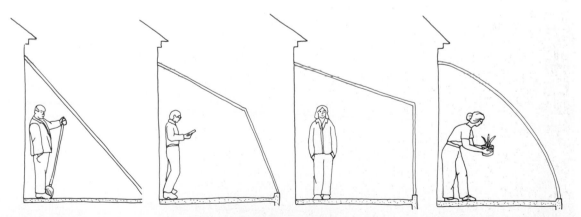

Figure 7-2: These shorter cross sections are needed for single-story houses with relatively low eaves. Some solid roof area (not shown) will be required if you don't need all the overhead glazing for plant lighting, particularly in warm or moderate climates. If you do need the overhead light in these climates, movable summer shading can be used.

house directly down to the ground, or the angle can be shallower for more growing space as shown in figure 7-2.

If you need still more standing room than the shape can provide with the floor on ground level, the floor can be dug down below grade to provide more headroom. Known as a *pit greenhouse*, this is a common solution to the problem of a low eave coupled with the need for more headroom.

Terrain Constraints

If the ground where the greenhouse is to be located is relatively level, a greenhouse floor directly on grade—such as a concrete slab, bricks or gravel—is the most straightforward and usually the least expensive. If the ground slopes away from the house, setting the floor into the ground on a leveled pad will give more height between the greenhouse floor and the house eave. If the ground slopes toward the east or west, the foundation can be

Photo 7-6: This greenhouse takes advantage of an existing deck, which had a foundation and framing strong enough to support the greenhouse. Since the yard is small and the house is close to the lot line, using the existing deck avoided the need for a variance by the zoning board from the setback requirement. *(Photo courtesy of Mark Ward Greenhouses, Concord, Mass.)*

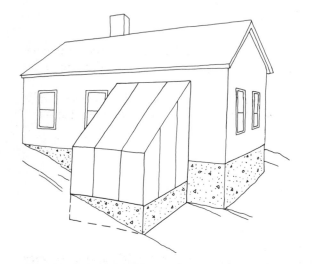
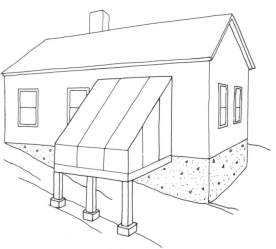

Figure 7-3: If the earth on the south side of the house slopes very much, either the foundation will have to be dug into the ground on one end or the greenhouse floor raised up, or a little of both. The dug-in foundation lends itself better to greenhouses where a tall aperture is needed. A platform or somewhat elevated foundation can raise the greenhouse floor up to the house's main floor level, although the raised platform shortens the length of the aperture.

cut into the ground as shown in figure 7-3. Another approach to hilly sites is to put the greenhouse on a platform (see figure 7-3), usually supported by piers, as long as the decrease in available height for the green-house is acceptable.

Climate and Design

The effect of climate on the design of a greenhouse cannot be overemphasized. If the greenhouse is not well matched to its climate, it simply won't perform as well as it could. The following summarizes special design considerations for the more extreme climates, hot or cold, cloudy or sunny, as previously defined.

Hot climates:
• Include shading—by a solid roof section, movable shading or both
• Include good ventilation
• Steeply sloped glazing minimizes summer overheating but decreases growing area
• Vertical glazing with minimal overhead glazing reduces summer heating and provides light for a few plants
• Overhead glazing can be increased to maximize growing area but will require summer shading
• Removable glazing is an excellent solution to overheating

Cold climates:
• Sufficient venting precludes summer overheating
• For best solar performances, the glazing angle should be as steep as possible (at least 40 degrees)
• A glazing angle shallower than 50 degrees won't benefit from the reflection of sunlight off snow
• Design must prevent snow buildup from shading the glazing or snow must be removed
• If the greenhouse is used for growing plants through the winter, the shape should be able to accommodate night insulation for all glazing
• If the house roof dumps snow on the greenhouse, design for the impact and the extra snow load

Cloudy climates:
• Design must allow the plants to take advantage of available light levels
• Double glazing gains more heat than it loses from a cloudy sky when the temperature is above freezing

Sunny climates:
• Overhead glazing can be reduced with less effect on plant growth under the solid roof areas
• Light-colored (preferably white) walls are doubly important next to growing areas

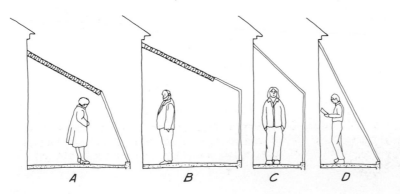

Figure 7-4: These cross sections are appropriate for relatively small growing areas in addition to solar heating, with A and B providing some living space in addition.

Budget

In the end, the budget for a greenhouse project often ends up as the final judge of design issues. Floor area, aperture area and the quality of materials used are all affected by the amount of money that is available for the project. Even if increasing the size of the aperture offers a good return on the investment in solar energy, the larger area can't be built if the money just isn't there. But there are a couple of arguments you can use to influence "the judge."

Matching the quality and detailing of the house can help justify increases in the cost of higher quality materials because of the resulting increase in the resale value of the house. The choice between higher- and lower-cost materials may also boil down to a choice between more and less durability. Increasing the initial investment in materials can thus be thought of as deferring future maintenance costs.

If there isn't enough money to build the greenhouse with both the quality and size you want, your choices are between a larger greenhouse of lesser-quality materials and a smaller greenhouse of top-quality materials. The larger greenhouse will give you more solar heat, more space and more growing area, and therefore a higher ongoing return on the investment. The smaller greenhouse built of higher-quality materials, on the other hand, may create a higher increase in the resale value of the house.

Working with standard sizes of building materials can help to keep costs down. Tempered glass, for example, is made in various standard sizes for sliding glass doors. Since the production volume of these units is so high, the unit cost is relatively low. The cost of these standard size single or sealed double glass units is often less than half the cost of custom sizes of tempered glass.

Another tactic in reaching compromises with the budget is *staged construction*. For example, if the design calls for a sliding glass door between the house and the greenhouse to replace an existing door, this part of the job could be delayed until the money is available. Or, the greenhouse framing could be built to accept standard tempered glass, but it could be glazed at first with lower-cost plastic glazing and reglazed a few years later with glass.

Greenhouse Shapes and Floor Plans

In this section, a variety of greenhouse shapes is discussed in relation to such issues as height, glazing angle and the number of glazing planes, the choice between flat and curved glazing, determining the extent of solid roof and wall areas, determining the greenhouse floor level (above-, below- or on-grade) and greenhouse shapes for sites that face somewhat away from south. A review of the definitions of height, length and depth is given in figure 7-6.

Tall or Short?

In general, taller greenhouses allow for a steeper glazing angle without reducing floor area. The steeper glazing angle both reduces summer heat gain and increases winter heat gain. Taller greenhouses also achieve better natural convection ventilation because of the greater height (chimney effect) difference between the top and bottom vents. On two-story houses, or houses where part of the basement wall is exposed, a taller design allows for a two-story airflow path, if you want the warm air to go to the upper floor. A tall greenhouse also accommodates more aperture area for a given length, which can be important for narrow sites or where there is a need for maximum solar heating. Wanting solar heat in an upper floor shouldn't necessarily be the only reason for building a two-story greenhouse. Simply opening up the indoor stairway for warm air to rise upstairs, or installing a fan system are lower-cost ways to deliver heat upstairs. The increased solar heat collection area, or perhaps the potential for an upper level deck or balcony may figure more strongly in a decision to build a two-story structure.

Shorter greenhouses, on the other hand, keep the construction closer to the ground, which can be a help to a less experienced builder. Shorter shapes often make a better match to the scale of the house, giving the combination a nicer look. Many manufactured greenhouses are relatively short, since their shapes are developed to fit onto the greatest possible number of houses, including short houses. But some manufacturers can custom modify a unit to make it as tall or deep as you want.

Glazing Angles

Steep glazing has all the advantages previously discussed. In short, the angle should simply be as steep as other constraints permit. On the other hand, greenhouses can function quite well with relatively shallow glazing pitches, if the house isn't tall or wide enough. The greenhouse depth can be increased as needed for additional floor area. The glazing angle will be decreased if the sloped glazing is taken directly down to the ground as was shown in figure 7-5, and so will headroom. But by including a vertical or near-vertical knee-wall, adequate headroom can be created. Minimizing the height of the kneewall and attaching the top of the glazing aperture to the highest possible connection point on the house will yield the steepest slope possible while still keeping a relatively simple-to-build framing. If this leaves the overhead glazing at a shallow slope, the solar heat collected through this area will be compromised by the shallow pitch. The kneewall will be the more effective collector, with the overhead glazing supplementing the heat collected in the winter to a lesser degree. In snowy climates, sloped glazing should not be flatter than 45 degrees to avoid snow building up on the surface. At steeper pitches, snow will tend to slide off the glazing, which eliminates the task of shoveling snow off the glazing. A shallow-pitched roof section can be inserted between the top of the glazing and the house to "push" the glazing to a steeper pitch.

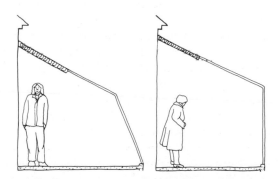

Figure 7-5: To increase the growing area the overhead glazing must be extended. These cross sections are appropriate for moderate-size growing areas. In hot climates the overhead glazing will usually need shading in the summer.

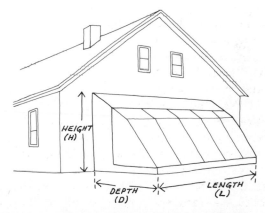

Figure 7-6: The terms depth, length and height shown here are used in discussing greenhouse shapes.

How Many Planes of Glazing?

A greenhouse with a single plane of glazing is naturally much simpler to build than one with two or three angles. There are fewer tricky corners, like the joint between the kneewall and the pitched glazing, to frame and to seal against water. Structural problems are decreased because the house and foundation triangulate with the structure to make it rigid, eliminating the need for diagonal bracing. Glazing can be simpler, too. By using one of the plastic double glazings that are available in long enough pieces (up to 20 feet), the rafters can be glazed with single, full-length pieces, eliminating any horizontal seams. If you want to add a large glazed area to your house, a single-plane design can be very inexpensive.

The disadvantage of having a single plane of glazing is the lack of vertical height in the southern part of the greenhouse, particularly if the glazing angle is shallow. If aboveground beds or benches are to be used next to the south side of the greenhouse, some floor space is wasted. This can be avoided by sinking the foundation into the ground, but the increased costs associated with a pit-type foundation will usually offset any savings in the aboveground parts of the greenhouse. An alternative is to grow plants at ground level in the front part of the greenhouse.

Another disadvantage of a single plane of glazing in a horticultural greenhouse is that it is difficult to include a continuous intake vent. If the greenhouse is relatively small, adequate ventilation can be achieved with vents in the endwalls, perhaps coupled with exhaust vents in the ridge. Wider single-plane greenhouses, though, may need a fan to ensure adequate ventilation, especially if the plane is fully glazed and has no solid roof overhang.

Designing the glazing for two planes allows all the flexibility of shape discussed in the previous sections. The additional complexity of two planes, though, does require more labor for framing and glazing. But two-plane designs can be kept simple. Such designs have been used, for example, to add a small-scale commercial greenhouse to the side of a barn, using low-cost 2 × 4 framing, minimal foundations and lightweight polyethylene glazing. And with care and attention to detail, the added plane doesn't present any insurmountable problems. Details for framing and glazing such places as corners where overhead glazing meets kneewall glazing are all covered in "Section III: Construction Detailing." If the simpler, single-plane shapes don't meet your requirements, the double-plane aperture is certainly worth the extra effort.

The glazing can also be designed for three planes, with a glazed vertical kneewall, a steeply sloped overhead glazing and then a shallow-pitched roof glazing meeting the house. This can represent unnecessary complexity (and extra cost) and usually can be avoided with a little planning. A more practical and common cross section has three planes of *framing,* with a vertical kneewall, which may or may not be glazed, a steeply sloped glazing section and a shallow-pitched solid roof section. The kneewall gives more headroom inside, the sloped glazing gives some overhead illumination and the solid roof increases depth and allows the whole arrangement to fit under a relatively low eave. This shape is detailed in chapter 10.

Flat or Curved Glazing?

For most site-built greenhouses, flat glazing planes are much easier to build. They accept all types of glazing, flexible or rigid, and are better adapted to using standard materials and standard building practices. Curved glazing is found at the eave of several manufactured greenhouses, though primarily

Photo 7-7: This curved frame, fiberglass glazed greenhouse offers a functional, low-cost approach. *(Photo courtesy of Gothic Arch Greenhouses, Mobile, Ala.)*

as a visual amenity. While the curve does present a pleasing line, it increases both initial and replacement costs.

Greenhouses that imitate the shape of the low-cost commercial greenhouses use an overall curved shape to decrease construction costs (see photo 7-7). The frame can be made with curved metal pipe, or an arch can be made of wood laminations. The glazing is either double polyethylene or a flexible plastic such as a fiber-reinforced plastic. Both wood- and metal-frame curved greenhouses are available from manufacturers at remarkably low prices. Components such as the arches and plastic extrusions that hold down the polyethylene are also available (see Appendix 1 for a list of kit manufacturers). While these greenhouses may not look as elegant and the glazing may not last as long as glass glazed greenhouses, they can perform just as well for a lot less money. The shape of the curves of various manufactured units varies somewhat, but usually tends to be a good compromise between providing sufficient interior space and a steep enough angle for

good solar-heating performance. If you plan to build your own in this style, design for the steepest possible glazing slope, as discussed previously. And compare prices with the manufactured units because this is one type of greenhouse where the kit may be just as cheap as one you could build yourself.

Unglazed Area: How Much?

Solid roof sections have been discussed previously in various contexts, including the amount needed for summer shading and the extent to which it decreases both light levels for plant growth and solar gain for heating. Your purposes for the greenhouse, along with the other design constraints, will determine the amount of solid roof area you finally choose. Basically you want enough of a solid roof extension to provide sufficient shading in the summer and enough to provide the depth you need, but you don't want so much that your growing areas are in the shade. A sometimes overlooked factor in solid roof design is light levels inside the house.

Solid endwalls are recommended only where growing areas are not adjacent to the wall. If the greenhouse were to be used only for solar heating, there would be no need for endwall glazing. If part of the roof is solid and part is glazed, the endwall glazing could extend as far back to the house as the overhead glazing. This not only gives side illumination to growing areas that are under the overhead glazing, but gives the greenhouse a clean visual line between solid and glazed areas (see figure 7-6).

Having a solid kneewall below the top of the growing bed or bench is appropriate if the sun is already blocked from shining on this area in the winter. If the solar survey shows that the sun barely makes it over the top of an obstruction during the winter months, the lower kneewall may not have enough solar exposure to be worth the effort and cost of

(continued on page 172)

TABLE 7-1: COMPARING GREENHOUSE SHAPES

Shape:	A	B
Horticultural characteristics	Rather small area directly under glazing gives limited prime growing area; low headroom in front requires ground level front beds or a pit foundation	Midsize well-lit growing area directly under glazing; low headroom in front requires ground level front beds or a pit foundation
Solar heating characteristics	Optimum glazing angle for winter solar collection	Lower glazing at optimum winter angle, upper glazing at flatter angle than optimum
Summer cooling characteristics	Steep glazing angle rejects most summer sun, minimizing need for additional shading in hot climates	Upper glazing may require shading in areas with hot summers
Architectural comments	Easily accommodated where little height available at common wall; use with pit foundation if more headroom needed; decreases daylighting of house through common-wall windows	Easily accommodated where little height available at common wall; use with pit foundation if more headroom needed
Construction comments	Short rafter spans in roof and aperture don't require large framing members; plans and kits available for this shape (see Appendix 1)	Short rafter spans don't require large framing members or supports; plans and kits available for this shape (see Appendix 1)
Climate, latitude and general comments	Good shape for solar heating and solarium use in all climates and latitudes; set glazing angle at (90 − latitude) − 23 degrees for optimum winter solar heating	Good shape for solar heating, growing and solarium use for all climates; solid roof area helps with summer cooling in climates with hot summers

	C	D
	Midsize well-lit growing area under glazing; headroom in front for stand-up beds/benches; allows full-width eave vent for good airflow over plants	Entire greenhouse well lit for growing; shape creates midsize growing area; ample headroom in front for stand-up beds/benches; allows full-width eave vent for good airflow over plants
	Sloped glazing at near-optimum angle, vertical knee-wall picks up ground/snow reflection; headroom allows heat storage under front growing area	Sloped glazing at near-optimum angle, large vertical glazing picks up ground/snow reflection; headroom allows heat storage under front growing area
	Solid roof area blocks some summer sun; sloped glazing may require shading in hot climates; tall shape increases natural convection through upper/lower vents	Large vertical glazing blocks summer sun; sloped glazing may require shading in hot climates; tall shape increases natural convection through upper/lower vents
	Requires tall common wall; steep slope can match pitch of house roof; good shape for 2-story airflow; spacious interior for solarium	Shallow depth good for limited sites; tall vertical glazing accommodates sliding glass doors
	Long rafter spans require thicker rafters or intermediate support	Short rafter spans require only small rafters; some kits available for this shape; tall vertical area easily accepts commercially built windows and doors
	Good shape for solar heating, growing and solarium use for all climates; sloped glazing should be as steep as house permits to favor winter over summer solar gain	Good shape for solar heating and growing for all climates; good for snowy climates, since vertical glazing picks up reflection from snow; not recommended for climates with hot summers unless shading is installed on sloped glazing.

(continued)

TABLE 7-1: COMPARING GREENHOUSE SHAPES (Continued)

SHAPE:	E	F
Horticultural characteristics	Entire greenhouse well lit for growing; good shape for large growing area; good headroom in front for stand-up beds/benches; allows full-width eave vent for good airflow over plants	Midsize well-lit growing area directly under glazing; headroom in front for stand-up beds/benches; allows full-width eave vent for good airflow over plants
Solar heating characteristics	Large aperture area for maximum solar heating; sloped glazing at near-optimum angle, vertical glazing picks up ground/snow reflection; headroom allows heat storage under front growing area	Sloped glazing at flatter-than-optimum angle for winter solar collection, but large vertical glazing picks up ground/snow reflection; headroom allows heat storage under front growing area
Summer cooling characteristics	Sloped glazing will require summer shading in all but cold climates; tall shape increases natural convection through upper/lower vents	Sloped glazing will require summer shading in all but cold climates
Architectural comments	Requires tall common wall; steep slope can match pitch of house roof; good shape for 2-story airflow; spacious interior for solarium	Allows relatively spacious interior with a shorter common wall; standing headroom throughout greenhouse; tall vertical glazing accommodates sliding glass doors
Construction comments	Long rafter spans require thicker rafters or intermediate support	Long rafter spans require thicker rafters or intermediate support; tall vertical area accepts commercially built windows and doors
Climate, latitude and general comments	Good shape for solar heating, growing and solarium use in moderate and cold climates; good light for plants in cloudy climates; can be used in hot climates with shading of sloped area	Good shape for moderate solar heating and moderate growing with ample solarium space for cold and moderate climates; can be used in hot climates with shading of sloped area

G   H

Entire greenhouse well lit for growing; good shape for large growing area; good headroom in front for stand-up beds/benches; allows full-width eave vent for good airflow over plants

Entire greenhouse well lit for growing; good shape for moderate to large growing areas; headroom in front for stand-up beds/benches, depending on shape of curve

Sloped glazing at flatter-than-optimum angle for winter solar collection, but large vertical glazing picks up ground/snow reflection; headroom allows heat storage under front growing area

Near-optimum aperture, depending on the shape of curve, near-vertical lower glazing picks up ground/snow reflection, depending on shape; allows heat storage under front growing area

Sloped glazing will require summer shading in all but cold climates

Entire structure may require summer shading in all but cold climates

Easily accommodated where little height available at common wall; standing headroom throughout greenhouse; tall vertical glazing may accommodate sliding glass doors

Easily accommodated where little height available at common wall; plastic glazing not aesthetically compatible with all houses or owners; can be configured as relatively narrow or moderately wide

Many kits available, mostly with aluminum frames and curved eaves; tall vertical area easily accepts commercially built windows and doors

Low-cost kits available

Good shape for solar heating, growing and solarium use for moderate and cold climates; favors growing; can be used in moderate and hot climates with shading

Good shape for solar heating and growing in moderate and cold climates; some solarium space; can be used in hot climates with shading

(continued)

TABLE 7-1: COMPARING GREENHOUSE SHAPES(Continued)

Shape:	I	J
Horticultural characteristics	Entire midsize greenhouse well lit for growing; low headroom in front requires ground level front beds or a pit foundation	Entire small-size greenhouse well lit for growing; low headroom in front requires ground level front beds or a pit foundation
Solar heating characteristics	Near-optimum glazing angle for winter solar heat collection	Optimum glazing for winter solar heat collection
Summer cooling characteristics	Entire structure will require summer shading in all but cold climates	Entire structure may require summer shading in all but cold climates
Architectural comments	Use with pit foundation if much standing room needed; steep slope can match pitch of house roof; can cover 1 or 2 stories, for large aperture and/or 2-story airflow	Use with pit foundation if much standing room needed; can cover 1 or 2 stories for large aperture and/or 2-story airflow
Construction comments	Long rafter span requires thicker rafters or intermediate support; single glazing plane relatively easy to build	Single glazing plane relatively easy to build
Climate, latitude and general comments	Good shape for solar heating and moderate growing for cold and moderate climates; set glazing angle as steep as greenhouse interior space requirements and house permit	Good shape for solar heating and limited growing for all climates; favors solar heating; adjust glazing angle as greenhouse interior space requirements and house permit, to (90 − latitude) − 23 degrees for optimum winter solar heating

K	L
Low-light levels; growing possible next to glazing; plants will be phototropic	Generally low-light levels, but skylight can be placed to illuminate selected areas
Vertical glazing good for admitting winter sun (particularly when ground is snow covered) and for blocking summer sun	Vertical glazing good for admitting winter sun (particularly when ground is snow covered) and for blocking summer sun
Vertical glazing admits little summer sun, decreasing ventilation requirements	Vertical glazing admits little summer sun, decreasing ventilation requirements; skylight may require summer shading in warm climates
Roomlike shape integrates easily with house; good for adding glazing to south-facing porch; decreases daylighting of house through common-wall windows	Roomlike shape integrates easily with house; daylighting of house through common-wall windows can be retained by placing skylight over window
Relatively easy to build, since construction is the same as conventional house building; tall vertical area easily accepts commercially built windows and doors	Relatively easy to build, since construction is the same as conventional house building; tall vertical area easily accepts commercially built windows and doors
Good shape for solar heating and solarium use in all climates	Good shape for solar heating and solarium use in all climates; skylight can illuminate small area for houseplants

glazing it. A way to check this is to sit on the ground at the spot where the kneewall would be built and do another survey. This will show when the kneewall would be shaded. If it doesn't meet the criteria set forth earlier—that the glazing have direct sun for at least half of the 9:00 A.M. to 3:00 P.M. period—the kneewall should be solid. A kneewall should never be solid if it extends above the height of the growing area, as was discussed in chapter 4.

Avoiding excess aperture area is another reason for a partly or completely solid knee-wall area. If the aperture is larger than needed for solar heating and overhead glazing is needed for plant growth, there is no point in glazing the kneewall below the top of the planting bed or bench, unless there will be heat storage underneath that will be directly heated by the sun. Solid kneewalls can also give a greater sense of privacy and coziness, particularly if the greenhouse is somewhat exposed to public view.

Floor Level: Above-, Below- or On-Grade?

Determining the best floor level depends on several factors—solar access, the terrain around the house, access between house and greenhouse, the height of the house and the budget. When the ground around the house is flat and there are no obstructions to the sun, placing the floor on-grade is usually the simplest and least expensive option. In some cases the solar access will be much better higher up on the house. This is where a second-floor greenhouse can be appropriate, as long as there can be access to the greenhouse from the second floor and the extra cost is acceptable. The Morrison greenhouse (photo 7-1) is a case where all of these conditions were met. The main living areas of the house are on the second floor, the second-floor

level is much sunnier, and there was a need for an additional room on the ground floor underneath the greenhouse.

When the house is fairly short, and the site doesn't permit a long greenhouse but having a rather deep greenhouse for adequate growing space is desired, a pit foundation may be the answer. The glazing can be brought to the ground in one plane, as steeply as the depth of the greenhouse permits, with the necessary headroom obtained by digging into the earth. (The Baerg greenhouse, shown in the example section at the end of this chapter, uses this strategy; see photo 7-13). Good drainage is critical to the smooth functioning of a pit greenhouse. Groundwater is not only a nuisance when it gets the floor wet, but it greatly increases the conductivity of the earth, stripping heat away from the greenhouse foundation. Pit foundations shouldn't be used where the drainage is poor or where the house has a history of cellar flooding unless adequate drainage is installed.

Shapes for Off-South Greenhouses

If the greenhouse faces significantly off south—more than 45 degrees—the shape should be determined by its uses as a solarium and for growing plants, since it will not be a very efficient solar heater. Solar heating, though, should not be ignored: south-facing endwalls should be glazed as much as possible. But the other uses will dominate the demands on the shape. If your site is way off south, use the horticultural and architectural considerations in table 7-1 for selecting a shape. Shading will probably be required either with trees, shade cloth or blinds, or shading compound. Good ventilation, following the guidelines for south-facing apertures, is also important. Table 7-1 summarizes the important characteristics of several greenhouse cross sections to help in choosing a shape appropriate for your situation.

Floor Plan Options

The cross sections described in table 7-1 were not tied to an actual size, since each could be essentially any depth or length and still retain the characteristics of that shape. The shapes were generally indicated as being appropriate for tall or short common walls, but the heights are also quite flexible, mainly limited by the height of the house. When a certain cross section is coupled with a floor plan of a particular depth and length, the greenhouse becomes a three-dimensional form. The interior layout is strongly influenced by shape and floor area, although it can be changed even after the greenhouse is built.

The shape of the floor plan is influenced by several factors: the house, the site, the solar access and the intended uses of the greenhouse. In this section, the options for the depth and length of the floor plan are explored first, and then four general floor

Photo 7-8: The shallow depth of this greenhouse avoids dominating the small front yard. The inward sloping wall below the floor gives an interesting architectural line to the outside and allows room for a flower bed underneath.

plan shapes are presented in table 7-2 to summarize the range of possibilities and appropriate uses for each. In the following section, a process for matching the greenhouse cross section to a floor plan is described, completing the design of the greenhouse shell.

Floor Plan Depth and Length

If your house needs a fairly large aperture and the site is uniformly sunny across the south face of the house, a long floor can be quite appropriate. If you don't require any living space and only want minimal room for plants, the depth can be quite small, as little as 4 to 6 feet, like plan number 1 in table 7-2. If the south face is not uniformly sunny and the house has sufficient height to allow a taller greenhouse, it may be appropriate to "squeeze" the greenhouse onto the sunny end of the house and make it tall enough to incorporate sufficient aperture, with a floor plan like number 2 in table 7-2. Or, the location of the main living area on one end of a two-story house might dictate that the greenhouse be placed on that end, with sufficient height to allow a two-story airflow loop that involves the the second floor. The floor plan then might be relatively short but with enough depth to accommodate a tall shape, like number 3 in the table. Or where both height and length must be large for an aperture both long and tall, and for a large living area, the floor plan might be as large as number 4.

The size of the site is often a limiting factor on the size and shape of the floor. A small house lot where the greenhouse must be set back from the property line, for example, might limit the ultimate depth. Or the yard space behind a city row house might limit the length of the floor plan but allow for much more depth. Table 7-2 reviews some of the characteristics of some typical floor shapes.

TABLE 7-2: FLOOR PLANS

FLOOR PLAN SKETCH:	1 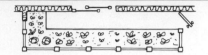	2 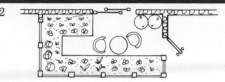
Depth:	4 to 6 ft	6 to 12 ft
Length:	10 ft and up	12 to 25 ft
Solar heating characteristics*	Aperture can be wide, but not very tall, unless it is vertical; minimal room for heat storage, unless under growing area	Sloped aperture can be moderately wide and moderately tall, up to 1½ stories; some room for heat storage in addition to placing it under growing area
Horticultural characteristics	Accommodates 1 bed/bench across front for relatively small growing area	Accommodates 1 front and 1 rear bed/bench for moderate growing area
Architectural comments	Almost no room for living space; good for shallow sites or for covering long south wall of house	Moderate-size living space possible; good for average site

*The comments relating aperture height to floor area apply to sloped glazing. Vertical glazing, of course, can go as high as desired on as shallow a depth as interior space requirements dictate.

Combining the Cross Section and the Floor Plan

In this section, a procedure is outlined for combining a floor plan with a cross section. It involves a series of steps, though the process of arriving at a final design isn't really so formal or cut-and-dried. If you go through the steps several times, you could come up with a different solution each time. Materials choices will also influence the outcome: The use of standard sizes of glazing materials will affect the ultimate size and shape of the aperture. But don't be discouraged if the shape changes many times. Design changes on paper are always easier and much less expensive than those that happen after construction begins.

If at all possible, allow some time for the design to "rest" before you plunge into construction. It is best to sit on the design for a few days once it's complete. A month is better.

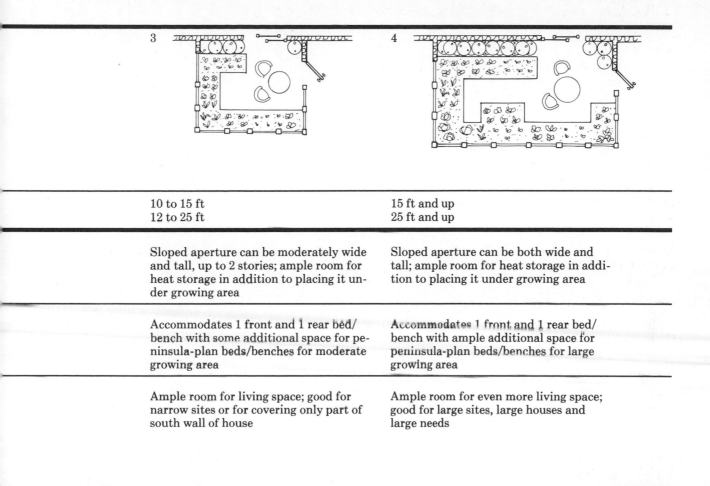

10 to 15 ft 12 to 25 ft	15 ft and up 25 ft and up
Sloped aperture can be moderately wide and tall, up to 2 stories; ample room for heat storage in addition to placing it under growing area	Sloped aperture can be both wide and tall; ample room for heat storage in addition to placing it under growing area
Accommodates 1 front and 1 rear bed/bench with some additional space for peninsula-plan beds/benches for moderate growing area	Accommodates 1 front and 1 rear bed/bench with ample additional space for peninsula-plan beds/benches for large growing area
Ample room for living space; good for narrow sites or for covering only part of south wall of house	Ample room for even more living space; good for large sites, large houses and large needs

This will give you a chance to discuss the design with others, as well as to just put it away for a while and come back to it with a fresh perspective.

As you go through the design process, you'll need to make sketches—of floor plans, cross sections and your house in relation to the greenhouse. These will help resolve many of the questions that come up. Working on graph paper with a ¼-inch grid will help in making scale drawings. Using a scale of ¼ inch to 1 foot will make the sketches easily readable for determining actual areas for growing, heat storage and living space, as well as for laying out aisles and leaving room for doors to swing. The scale drawings of the cross section will allow you to determine the actual size needed for glazing and other materials, and, conversely, to fit the cross section to standard material sizes, particularly the glazing, and to the house.

Perspective sketches are also useful for

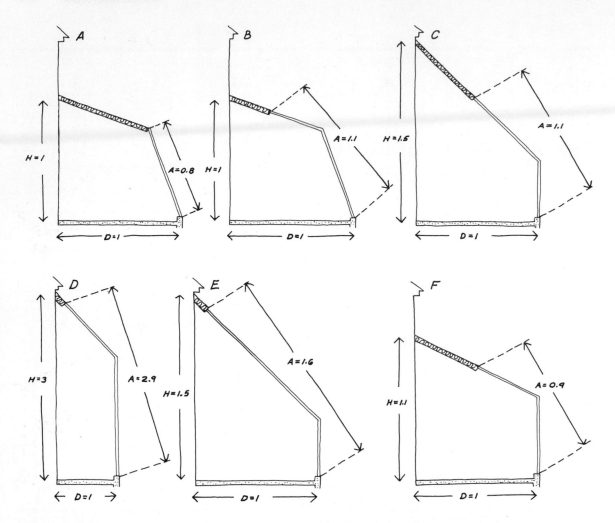

Figure 7-7 (above and to the right): The relative proportions of the various greenhouse cross sections discussed in table 7-1 are shown here, for help in matching the available height (h) on the common wall to the required depth (d) and aperture area. The aperture (a) is shown as a fraction of the depth (which always

gaining a sense of what the greenhouse will look like on the house. An easy technique is to use photographs as a base for sketches. You can take some pictures of the outside of the house where the greenhouse will be attached, and then draw in the outlines of the greenhouse. Another technique is to draw on tracing paper over the photos.

A full-size "string-and-stick" mock-up is invaluable for getting a feel for what the greenhouse will look like from the outside, how its shape will relate to the shape of the house, how the interior space will feel and what the view from inside the house will be (see the photo that opens "Section II: Designing the Greenhouse"). This can be made

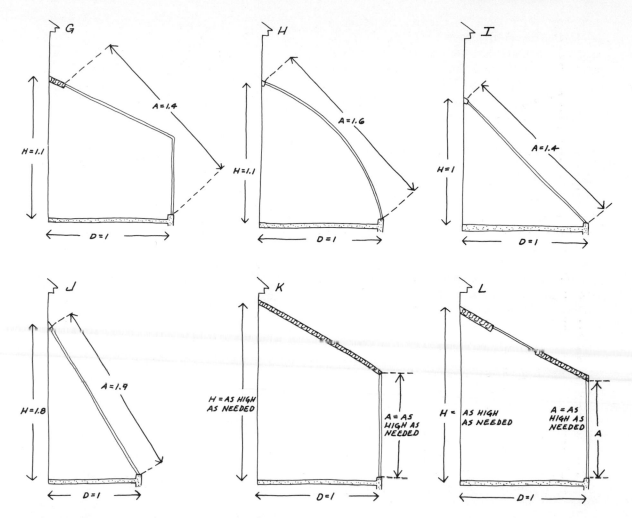

equals 1). The aperture in greenhouses K and L can be adjusted to whatever dimension is needed, since the glazing is vertical.

simply by using scrap boards or poles for uprights, connecting them with string for the horizontal and sloping lines. The edges of solid parts of the roof and walls can be represented with strings or boards to get a better feeling for visibility from within the greenhouse and from within the house. If you build the mock-up carefully, it can also be used to verify the dimensions arrived at with scale drawings. You can check that standard glazing sizes, for example, will actually fit where you plan to put them.

Choosing a Final Shape

1. Growing bed and bench area: Determine the area needed for growing beds and benches (refer back to chapter 4). Make a tentative decision about how much area is needed for beds and how much for benches, and if the beds are to be above or in ground. Decide also if the greenhouse will be used for winter growing or season extension.

2. Living space: Determine the open floor area you want to have for living space. If you have a particular size table and chair group in mind, cut out a ¼-inch-to-the-foot scale top view of it for your ¼-inch graph paper. This will allow you to "move" the furniture around to see if and where it fits best.

3. Aperture area and heat storage: Based on the information in chapter 6, determine the required aperture size to achieve the desired amount of solar heating. From the heat storage information in chapter 5, determine the amount and type of heat storage you will use.

4. Height and length of the common wall: Measure the height and width of the common wall that is going to be covered by the greenhouse. Make a sketch of the common wall to show doors and windows, and any other openings, such as a kitchen exhaust vent. On the sketch, mark the maximum allowable greenhouse height, considering aesthetics as well as solar access. If part of the common wall is partly shaded, note these areas on the sketch. Figure 7-9 shows an example sketch.

5. Sketching a floor plan: Choose a general shape for the floor. (Refer to the sample bed layouts in figure 4-15 as well as table 7-2.) Make a sketch that incorporates the growing beds, whatever living space you want, walkways, and space for any doors that swing into the greenhouse. Allow room for heat storage if it isn't planned to be underneath the growing areas. Show the common wall in the sketch, including the relative positions of any doors and windows (see figure 7-9).

6. Matching a cross section to the floor plan: Use table 7-1 to choose one or more basic cross sections that meet your require-

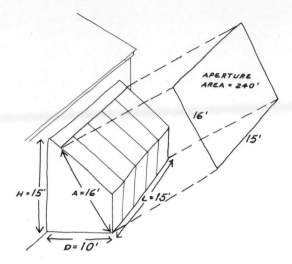

Figure 7-8: Using the proportions given in figure 7-7, greenhouse cross section E, with a depth (d) of 10 feet, would have a height (h) of 15 feet (1.5 times depth) and a 16-foot-long aperture (a) (1.6 times depth). If the length (l) were 15 feet, the aperture would have an area of 240 square feet ($15 \times 16 = 240$).

ments and are appropriate for your climate. The cross sections shown in the table are shown again in figure 7-7 with their proportions. The overall height of the cross section and the aperture are shown as fractions of the depth. For example, cross section E has a height that's 1.5 times the depth and an aperture that is 1.6 times the depth. Thus a 10-foot-deep greenhouse would be 15 feet high with a 16-foot aperture. If this shape is coupled with a floor that's 15 feet long, the floor area would be 150 square feet ($15 \times 10 = 150$), and the aperture area would be 240 square feet ($15 \times 16 = 240$), as shown in figure 7-8.

Choose one or more of the cross sections that give you close to the right height and aperture, and make a scaled sketch (or sketches) of them.

7. Adjusting the shape: Both cross section and floor size may need some adjusting to accommodate the needed aperture area, interior space, the overall size of the common wall and the size and placement of existing windows and doors. Adjust your sketch as needed and show where the greenhouse attaches to the house on the sketch you made of the common wall. Heights, lengths, depths and angles may need juggling to accommodate all the requirements.

If at this point you have a fairly good idea of the type of glazing materials you will be using, check the standard sizes against the sizes of the various glazed areas in your sketches. This can help you avoid having to use expensive custom sizes, if you are using tempered glass, or excessive waste of material, if you are using plastics. Often, adjusting the glazed areas to standard material sizes involves only minor adjustments to angles, heights and lengths. If there is a solid area in the roof, it can be adjusted to accommodate standard glazing materials.

Add in the important details as you adjust the shape, including the doors, vent or fan openings and the location of a back-up

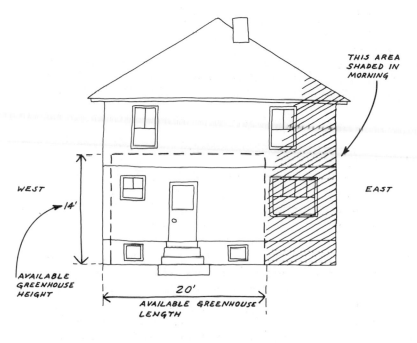

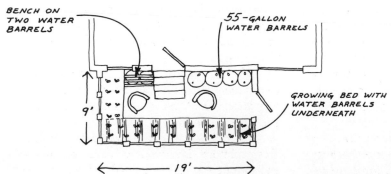

Figure 7-9: This sample sketch shows the part of the common wall that is shaded in the morning and the dimensions of the available space for the greenhouse, both necessary elements of a planning sketch. A floor plan sketch should show growing areas, living space, heat storage locations and other elements such as house windows and doors.

heater (if you plan on having one). Note the locations of any existing electrical outlets and hose bibs or where you will add them. The size and location of exhaust vents, in particular, can affect the overall cross section. The location of the exterior door will also be affected by the shape and height of the endwall.

8. Mock-up: Try out the design by using perspective sketches, the photograph technique, and the stick-and-string mock-up. The full-size mock-up will give you the best sense of what the space will look like inside and how the greenhouse shape will interact with the house shape.

A Sample Design

In this example the design procedure is followed step by step, with the steps numbered as in the previous discussion.

1. Growing bed and bench area: The greenhouse is to be used for growing fruits and vegetables through the winter and a few house plants year-round. The growing bed is sized to provide 30 square feet per person based on the rule of thumb of 20 to 40 square feet per person. There are two adults and one child, which calls for a total bed area of 2½ times 30 square feet per person, or 75 square feet. Approximately 10 square feet of bench area is to be used for houseplants. (All the beds are to be at about waist height for ease of working and to accommodate heat storage underneath.)

2. Living space: Only a small area is desired for living space. The existing stairs from the house will provide a sunny place to sit, but it would be nice to also fit in two chairs, if possible, each requiring a 9-square-foot area.

3. Aperture area and heat storage: The 1,400-square-foot house is in a moderate climate. It is old, but insulated and tightened up enough to be in the type 2 category of energy conservation (see table 6-2). There are no massive masonry elements that would increase the allowable amount of aperture, though there is 55 square feet of window area on the south side of the house that won't be covered by the greenhouse. Based on the aperture sizing table (see table 6-3), the maximum aperture area is 420 square feet. Subtracting three times the existing noncovered window area gives a maximum aperture of 255 square feet for solar heating the house.

The heat storage will be water, for compactness and low cost. Based on the heat storage sizing guidelines in chapter 5, 3 gallons are needed per square foot of glazing, for a total of 765 gallons of water, or 15 or 16 55-gallon drums.

4. Height and length of the common wall: The common wall is 14 feet high. Using the entire height would bring the top of the greenhouse to just below the second story windows. The eastern part of the south wall is in shade until about noon, leaving about 20 lineal feet of south wall on the western side that gets full sun. (A sketch of the south wall is shown in figure 7-9.) A door to the kitchen is also on this side, making it a good site for easy heat exchange with, and access to, the house.

5. Sketching a floor plan: The floor plan shown in figure 7-9 uses the whole width of the sunnier area of the south wall. Keeping the west endwall of the greenhouse slightly in from the west wall of the house is usually better for appearance and avoids disturbing the corner trim of the house. A 3-foot-wide growing bed is planned for the south and west sides of the greenhouse. The south wall actually faces a little east of south, so glazing the west endwall is a better choice over glazing the east endwall. It is to be glazed from just above bed height to the peak of the greenhouse.

The floor plan is 9 feet deep and easily accommodates the 3 feet of existing stairs from the kitchen door, the 3 feet of aisle between the stairs and the south bed, and the

3-foot-wide bed. The bench is next to the house, where the slightly diminished light level will be appropriate for the house plants. The aisles could be compressed a little, to reduce the depth of the greenhouse, but this size allows ample space for the water barrels that won't fit under the beds, for a sitting area and for the 10-square-foot bench for house-plants. Several 55-gallon drums can be fit into the northeast corner.

6. Matching a cross section to the floor plan: The floor plan is 9 feet deep and 19 feet long, and 255 square feet of aperture is needed for solar heating. Since the aperture will be 19 feet wide, it will have to be about 13½ feet high (255 ÷ 19 = 13½). This is about 1.5 times the depth of the floor plan. Both the E and G cross sections give the needed aperture height and floor-plan depth. They both have enough kneewall height to accommodate the growing beds with storage underneath.

7. Adjusting the shape: A glazing angle somewhere between those of E and G gives

the right aperture and the right overall height, as shown in figure 7-10. While the full over-head glazing may cause summer overheating problems, it is needed to achieve the desired aperture area for solar heating and provides excellent lighting for plant growing. Particular attention must be paid to sizing the exhaust vents, and some type of shading may be needed for the glazing.

Intake and exhaust vents will be continuous at the eave and ridge. Based on the rule of thumb that the vents should be one-quarter the aperture area for greenhouses that are over 8 feet high, these vents should be one-quarter the height of the aperture. (Since the vents are the same width as the greenhouse, making them one-quarter of the aperture results in their area being one-quarter the aperture area.) The aperture is 14 feet so the total vent height needs to be 3½ feet. A 1½-foot-high vent at the bottom plus a 2-foot opening at the top gives the necessary vent area.

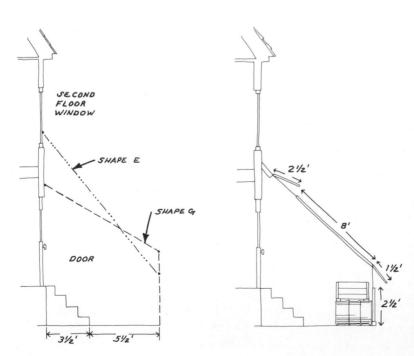

Figure 7-10: In the design example, when cross sections E and G are sketched onto the common wall, it's clear that a little adjusting is needed. The final shape on the right has an in-between overall height to put it under the second-story windows, and it has an in-between kneewall height to allow for an eave (intake) vent and the growing bed over the heat storage. Once the shape is at least tentatively established, the locations of vents and doors can be added.

The height of the kneewall should also be somewhere between those of E and G. The kneewall should be as short as possible to keep the sloped glazing at as steep an angle as possible, while still allowing enough room for the 55-gallon drums to be placed on their sides underneath the south growing bed. The beds will be 18 inches deep on top of the 24-inch-diameter barrels, and there must be 18 inches of space above the top of the bed to avoid restricting airflow through the lower vent. This gives a total height to the kneewall of 5 feet.

The glazing for the greenhouse will be glass. Since the greenhouse is in a moderate climate and it will be used for winter growing, the glazing should be double layer. The sloped part of the aperture is about 8½ feet from the eave to the bottom of the vent, and the vent is 2 feet from top to bottom. (These dimensions are taken from the scale drawing of the adjusted cross section.) If standard 76-inch-long tempered double-glass units were used on the slope, that would still leave about 2 feet above this glass to the bottom of the exhaust vent (8½ − 6½ = 2). Filling this area in with a small custom-sized double-glass unit would be expensive, since overhead glass should be tempered. And the 2-foot vent would also require custom-sized tempered units. There are several approaches to this sort of problem. First, check around for other stock sizes of tempered glass. Ninety-two inches by 28, 34 and 46 inches can often be found. This would allow you to use one length of fixed glass between the eave and the exhaust vent (nicely avoiding potentially troublesome horizontal joints in the sloped glazing), though it would require making the vent a little longer, 2½ instead of 2 feet. The vent then, would still require custom tempered units, unless you could find a glass supplier that had smaller pieces of tempered glass. Sometimes 34-by-24-inch glass (or thereabouts) can be found (often used in storm doors, which are required to use either tempered glass or plastic). This glass could be used for both the top and bottom vents, although the vertical glass in the kneewall need not be tempered. If you do end up needing custom tempered glass for only a small area, check the price and compare this increase in cost to the cost of the project as a whole. Often the increase won't be that great when looked at in this context, and it can be worth the extra expense, especially if custom glazing this one area results in all the glazing in the greenhouse being glass. Another approach is to use a mix of plastic and glass since the plastic can be cut to fit an odd-sized opening.

The glass could be placed in the lower area of the slope for a view out. A 4-foot-wide, double-layer plastic could be cut in half, with half used for the area between the glass and the vent. The same material could be used for the kneewall. The size of the intake vent and the glazing below it can be adjusted to just split 4-foot-wide material, about 1½ feet for the vent and 2½ for the kneewall.

The width of the tempered glass will determine the exact length of the greenhouse, which will be a multiple of the width of the

Figure 7-11: A perspective sketch is very useful in visualizing the design. This sketch was made by tracing a photo of the house and its neighbors and then drawing in the greenhouse shape.

glass, plus whatever gap there is between each sealed unit, plus the width of the edge detail at each end of the glazed area. Until the glazing is actually designed, the final length of the greenhouse can only be estimated. With 34-inch-wide glass it will probably be close to a multiple of 3 feet, which means the greenhouse can be about 18 or 21 feet long, rather than the 19 feet that is planned now. Forty-six-inch glass ends up with something close to a multiple of 4 feet. Once the glazing details are worked out (described in chapter 11), the design will have to be slightly adjusted for the final dimensions.

 8. *Mock-up:* Figure 7-11 shows a perspective sketch of the greenhouse, and the photo that opens "Section II: Designing the Greenhouse" shows a stick-and-string mock-up of an 18-foot-wide version of this shape.

Some Case Studies

 It is always useful to see how others have approached and solved their design problems. This section describes several built examples of attached solar greenhouses, showing a variety of designs that serve a variety of purposes and situations. Some of the examples won't have any features useful in your design, while others may be close to what you want.

The Kemble/Flannigan Greenhouse: Low Cost for Season Extension

 The primary purpose of this greenhouse is producing seedlings for the garden and to extend the very short growing season in western Montana. At an elevation of about 7,000 feet, frosts occur every month of the year, and a snow flurry in July isn't so unusual. Tomatoes, cucumbers and peppers are grown in the greenhouse during the summer, with seedlings and greens grown in the spring and just greens in the fall. This is a typical use-pattern

Photo 7-9: The Kemble/Flannigan greenhouse is a low-cost unit made with recycled lumber, glazed with polyethylene and is used as a season extender. Built for a materials cost of $375, it shows that a greenhouse need not be expensive to be effective.

for season extension in northern climates. Thirty-inch-deep growing beds almost fill the entire greenhouse, leaving just enough space for an aisle (see photo 1-1). There is no heat storage, aside from the soil. Heat is vented into the house only when the greenhouse is in danger of overheating during the winter. No back-up heat is used, either. When the weather gets cold enough to freeze the plants inside, the greenhouse is abandoned for the winter.

 The 9-by-11-foot structure was built of recycled lumber and glazed with ultraviolet-resistant polyethylene, to keep the materials cost low, at around $375. Recycling the lumber created lots of labor, i.e., pulling nails, puttying holes, trying to square boards. . . . All told, it took about 200 hours to build the greenhouse, including the time spent recycling the lumber and making some repairs to the house foundation. The greenhouse replaces a part of the front porch (which needed renovation anyway) and uses the porch roof for the solid roof of the greenhouse. The effort taken to carefully apply the polyethylene shows in the greenhouse's neat appearance. There are very few wrinkles. The vents are an interesting feature of this greenhouse. They used hardware originally made for keeping old-fashioned wooden storm windows propped open, similar to the hardware used on folding table legs.

From April until the greenhouse froze in mid-September, Keith Kemble and Dan Flannigan grew about 51 pounds of greens, including salad and cooking greens, about 42 pounds of fruits including tomatoes, squash and cucumbers, and about 10 pounds of beets, for a total yield of 103 pounds. The beds have a total growing area of about 54 square feet. This data shows that a greenhouse need not be expensive to be an effective environment for food production. Keith comments, "What a thrill to have fresh vegetable sandwiches right here in Meadow Gulch. It's a good thing the vegetables in the greenhouse are doing well because the garden has just about been demolished by grasshoppers. . . ." She also comments, however, that "just figuring roughly that we have produced 100 pounds of food, at $0.50 per pound, would be a return of $50, ignoring seed, supplies and time involved. If you put a calculator to it, it's a pretty small return. But what we have found, that we can't put a price on, is that the greenhouse, especially with the hammock, has become our favorite space. We've spent many hours reading, playing with the baby, thinking and sleeping in the greenhouse—and it is just wonderful! We intend to tighten it up more this fall so it will be even warmer on sunny winter days."

The Badeau Greenhouse: Solar Heat, Sun-Room and Winter Salads

The Badeaus' greenhouse is a multipurpose structure: It is used for growing food and ornamental plants, for solar heating the house and for a sunny place to sit in the winter.

Growing beds are in the ground, covering an area within about 4 feet of the glazing. More in-ground growing area is on the north side of the aisle, along with heat-storing water containers and benches for potted plants. The aisle opens up into a small living space that has a table and chairs next to a sliding glass door that leads into the kitchen. This is a favorite wintertime breakfast spot. The detailing, choice of materials and the angle of the upper glazing and solid roof section all complement the house very nicely.

There is 250 square feet of double glass, providing quite a bit of solar heat to this relatively small, 800-square-foot house. The house is located in Rhode Island, which has a moderate but relatively cloudy climate. Since the greenhouse was built, the Badeaus have switched from oil to wood for heating, and the occupancy of the house has changed, so it is not possible to compare fuel use before and after the greenhouse was built. The greenhouse does provide a lot of solar heat, however, eliminating the need to maintain a fire whenever the sun is out and for some time after the sun goes down, probably representing a 25 percent decrease in wood use. During the summer, shade cloth is used on the overhead glazing partly because of the rather

Photos 7-10 and 7-11 (to the right and left): The Badeaus' greenhouse provides all three of the primary attached greenhouse functions: There is sufficient aperture for significant solar heating, enough growing space to provide salads all winter and enough living space for a table and chairs. The angles and detailing integrate nicely with the house.

small area of the exhaust vents, consisting only of a window (3 feet by 5 feet) on the west endwall and a door (3 feet by 6 feet 8 inches) on the east endwall. (This is only 15 percent of the aperture area, rather than the 25 to 33 percent recommended.)

The greenhouse provides a place to grow enough greens for salads every day throughout the winter and tomatoes and cucumbers for much of the winter. The space is also used for growing seedlings in the spring for the outdoor garden. Between having fresh salad greens from the greenhouse and frozen vegetables from the garden, the Badeaus supply all their own vegetables through the winter. For the owners, the rewards of having moist, sweet-smelling air from the greenhouse and a view from the kitchen into a bright space filled with flowers and greenery add a very nice aspect to the house.

The Del Porto Greenhouse: Heating Help for a Large House

The major reason the Del Portos built their greenhouse was to cut their high heating bills. The year before the greenhouse was built in 1982, their heating bill was $1,000 in natural gas plus five cords of wood, which can cost $150 to $200 each in this Boston suburb. But with the solar heat from the greenhouse they needed only 3 cords of wood and no gas. Located near Boston, where the climate is moderate with relatively cloudy winters, the greenhouse adds 750 square feet of south glazing to this 5,000-square-foot house. The house is old, but it has insulation in the walls and roof and has been tightened up with "cases of silicone," bringing it up to the level 2 "insulated" category (see table 6-2). On sunny days, the airflow loop goes into the house through upstairs windows, down the stairs to the first floor and down another flight of stairs to the basement. Air returns to the greenhouse through what used to be an outdoor entrance to the basement. When the sun is shining, the air moving through this doorway will literally "blow out a match." The upstairs tends to reach 78 to 80°F, with the first floor running around 68°F. A wood stove is used to heat only an occupied area of the house in the evening. This avoids heating the

Photo 7-12: This large aperture greenhouse, with 750 square feet of glazing, provides substantial solar heating to the 5,000-square-foot house. The Del Porto greenhouse combines standard glass sizes in the kneewall with long extruded acrylic plastic double glazing (Exolite) for the slope, with recycled window sashes used for the ridge vents.

The structure itself incorporates several interesting features. The kneewall was made tall enough to accommodate standard-size sealed tempered glass units (46 by 76 inches) for the fixed glass and a sliding glass door for venting and access. The sloped glazing is 16-foot-long Exolite (a double-wall extruded plastic glazing). Using a full-length piece decreased labor costs and eliminated horizontal seams. The framing accommodates vertical upper vents, which were made of recycled windows. Placing these vents under the house eave simplified waterproofing by eliminating most of the flashing that would otherwise be needed on a sloped vent. A recycled geared vent operator from an old commercial greenhouse allows operation of the vent from the floor of the greenhouse. Mr. Del Porto also saved on cost by supervising construction. The total cost was $9,000, with $1,500 of this in the insulated concrete foundation and insulated slab. Of the rest, two-thirds was labor ($5,000) and one-third was materials ($2,500).

whole house, which saves a great deal of energy in addition to that supplied by the greenhouse. When back-up heat is needed in the greenhouse, the basement door is opened.

The greenhouse is also used as a solarium—its 12-by-28-foot floor area has lots of open floor space—and for growing vegetables. There are several small planting beds totaling less than 40 square feet but the Del Portos have plans for more. Storage is provided by the concrete slab floor, by the exposed masonry foundation of the house and by the stucco covering on the common wall, which was painted a dark color for increased absorption. This represents about 125 cubic feet of concrete in the foundation and about 30 cubic feet of somewhat lower density stucco masonry.

The Baerg Greenhouse: High Output for a Small House

In David Baerg's greenhouse, the emphasis is on total food production and solar heating. Its 500 square feet of glazing contributes much solar heat to his 700-square-foot house. In order not to waste the large amount of surplus solar heat collected by the greenhouse, there is an active heat storage system consisting of 11 tons of rock and about 300 gallons of water. Direct air exchange between the house and greenhouse is by natural convection through windows and doors between the basement and first floor of the house and the greenhouse. The air exchange also provides back-up heat to the greenhouse. The house, which has been retrofitted with enough

Photo 7-13: By using a pit foundation, a large glazed area and a relatively large growing area have been tucked under a low eave on the small Baerg house. The full glazing promotes both maximum plant growth and solar heating in this somewhat shady location.

insulation and tightened up enough to be a level "2 plus" house (somewhere between level 2 "insulated" and level 3 "energy conserving"), uses about 200 gallons of oil and less than 1 cord of wood in a winter, probably representing about 50 percent solar heating. It is located near Boston (a moderate, cloudy climate).

The greenhouse is completely glazed to provide maximum light levels. Overheating in summer is minimized by continuous eave and ridge vents and by shading from the many trees around the yard. The vents are usually sealed shut in midwinter, and push-in foam panels are used in the endwalls and ridge vents.

There is 100 square feet of growing bed and 60 square feet of bench area in a total floor area of about 270 square feet. Since there is only one person living in the house, the produce yields tend to be lower than might be

expected for this size growing area, but the greenhouse provides most of David's produce needs and supplies seedlings for his outdoor summer garden. The yields in 1979 were about 70 pounds of fruits and vegetables and 340 seedlings. A greywater irrigation system is used, incorporating an automatic filter and pump connected to a subsurface irrigation pipe in the growing bed. In this system, water from the sinks and the washing machine is filtered and pumped into the growing beds. Care must be taken to use strictly biodegradable detergents, but the result is great savings in manual watering time, and warming of the soil beds whenever hot water is used in the house. Questions exist about the spread of certain bacteria and viruses through such irrigation systems, but neither conclusive proof of a hazard nor lack of hazard has been made. David received a building permit for the system based on the condition that he be the sole consumer of the food that was grown.

The greenhouse was built on a pit foundation, with the floor about 4 feet below grade. This was done to allow the use of the maximum amount of glazing under the rather low eave of this small house. The glazing, framing and the vent operators were all recycled from an old commercial greenhouse. A polyethylene inner glazing is put up in the winter to decrease heat loss. The cost of this 300-square-foot greenhouse was about $5,000, in 1978.

The Pea Greenhouse: A Moderate-Cost Structure

Mary Pea's greenhouse is an inexpensive but fully functional structure that is used for solar heating and growing plants. The 10-by-24-foot greenhouse was built in 1977 for a materials cost of $1,200 plus about 60 hours of labor from Ms. Pea and her neighbors. The

Photo 7-14: Mary Pea's inexpensive but highly functional greenhouse is always full of a variety of plants, including over 1,000 seedlings each spring, and it reduces heating bills by approximately 15 percent.

greenhouse contributes a good deal of heat to the house on sunny days, decreasing heating bills by about 15 percent in Rhode Island's moderate climate. The greenhouse aperture is about 200 square feet, and the house is a level 2, (insulated) 1,400-square-foot ranch house. Due to the orientation of the house, the greenhouse was attached to the two back bedrooms. One of these rooms has been changed into a study, so that on sunny days this solar heated room can be occupied, and the house furnace can be turned off.

The space inside the greenhouse is well utilized, with 135 square feet of bench area. Water containers occupy almost every space that isn't occupied by a plant, totaling over 400 gallons of water for heat storage. The front benches are supported by water bottles, there are shelves of bottles on the north wall, and there are 55-gallon drums under some of the rear benches. All types of recycled containers have been used, including soda bottles, gallon jugs of all sorts and sealed plastic buckets. Air is exchanged with the house through windows, both for solar heating the

house and for back-up heating of the greenhouse. A portable window fan is used to increase the airflow when needed. There is a thermostated electric heater as additional backup, which is used occasionally on very cold nights, adding a negligible amount to the electric bill.

The greenhouse provides a place to grow all the lettuce Ms. Pea uses in the winter and a few additional vegetables, but the main use is for ornamental plants and seedling production. Experiments are always under way to grow new kinds of plants, and over 1,000 seedlings are produced every spring, providing for Ms. Pea's extensive outdoor garden and those of several of her neighbors.

The Russell Greenhouse: An Elegant Sun-Room

The Russells built their greenhouse primarily to add an elegant, sunny living space to their house. The growing space that is incorporated and the considerable solar heat collected by the rather large structure were secondary concerns. The greenhouse was added onto a wing of the house, wrapping around the end and extending the wing. It encloses three somewhat separate areas: a raised dining area, a raised living area and a lower plant-growing area. (The front cover photo of this book shows the interior.) While the living and dining areas are all integral with the greenhouse itself and are therefore subject to temperature fluctuations, the whole wing can be closed off from the rest of the house. The tile and brick floors, curving staircase through white stucco walls, natural redwood framing and finish work, all accented with ornamental plants, give the addition an elegant, luxurious feeling. The greenhouse, located in Pennsylvania, was designed and built by Mr. Russell, who is an experienced builder.

The greenhouse has 625 square feet of

floor space, 170 feet of this in the lower growing area, which includes 75 square feet of growing beds and benches. The bricks in this area are set in sand for easy drainage. There is 150 square feet of vertical double glass and 325 square feet of tempered sloped double glass. The vertical kneewall is taller in the dining area than in the growing area, to give adequate headroom, making the sloped glazing shallower in this area, about 25 degrees, and matching the pitch of the existing kitchen roof. Over other areas, the roof pitch is about 42 degrees, closer to an optimum pitch for the latitude and climate. The greenhouse faces 10 degrees east of south. The insulated concrete slab, the tile and brick floor, the stucco, and the retaining wall between the lower growing area and the upper living areas all add about 200 cubic feet of masonry thermal mass.

A fan is used to transfer solar heat to the house, along with natural convection through the door to the house and through two windows. A Casablanca-type fan suspended over the living area circulates heat around the greenhouse on sunny days. One of the kitchen windows was custom made to have a 4-by-5-foot unobstructed opening for good air circulation as well as a clear view out. A gas heater will be used for back-up heating. The main cooling in summer is provided by a 14-inch-diameter fan in a cupola added onto the top of the wing with the greenhouse. In winter, rigid foam blocks are inserted behind the louvers to cut infiltration.

Awning windows all along the bottom of the vertical kneewall and the door in the endwall provide natural ventilation when it's cool enough outside for these to provide adequate ventilation on their own and provide an inlet for the fan in hotter months. Exterior bamboo shades may be used for shading next summer, to make it a little cooler inside. Construction cost was $25,000, or about $40 per square foot, for the basic greenhouse, with about another $10,000 spent on amenities, including the stucco, fancy interior trim, tile floor, a small patio outside the door, tile around the sink in the growing area and custom windows.

Photo 7-15: The Russell greenhouse incorporates a dining area under the shallower sloping roof glazing, a plant area under the steeper slope, and a living area above and behind the growing area. The greenhouse expanded an existing wing of the house, adding elegant living area and a substantial solar collection area. *(Photo courtesy of Rodale Press Photography Department.)*

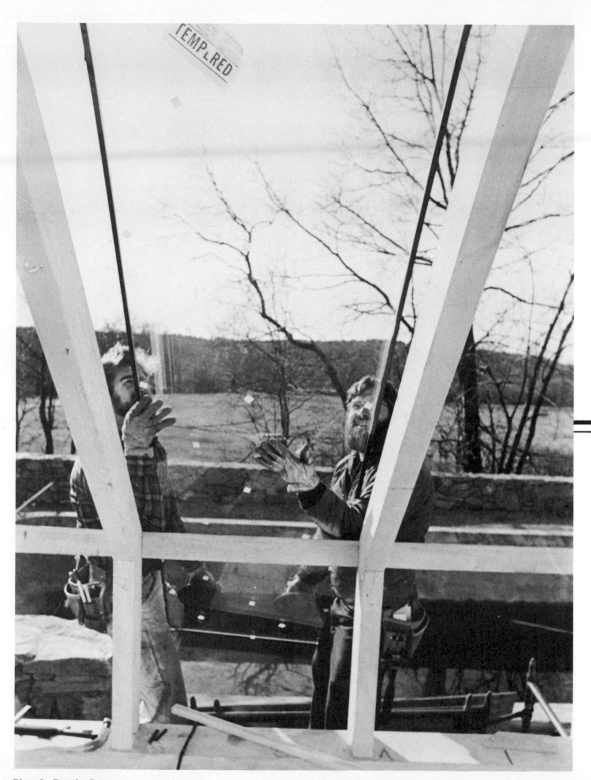

Photo by Douglas Prince

Section III:

CONSTRUCTION DETAILING

In this final section of the book, a variety of construction methods are presented for each part of the greenhouse. From the almost infinite number of ways to build a greenhouse, an array of representative methods has been chosen for each element, covering a range of materials costs and a range of building skills, providing at least one appropriate method for most situations. It is assumed that you have basic building skills, at least from simple foundations to simple finish work, or that you'll be working with someone who does. Therefore, procedural instructions are included only where techniques or materials differ from standard construction. Tips are included here and there for easing construction, but they aren't repeated for every method, so even after you decide which method you'll use, you might check through the rest of the chapter for applicable tips. The cross section illustrations in this section have all been drawn to scale, to allow you to see exactly how things fit together. In addition, sources for various specialized materials are listed in Appendix 1. By paying attention to purpose and detail while you are building, you will build a greenhouse that is sturdy and long-lasting, and a pleasure to live with.

Chapter 8

APPROACHES TO SOLAR GREENHOUSE CONSTRUCTION

In this chapter we'll cover some basic information that applies to several aspects of greenhouse construction. First we'll look at a couple basic rules of solar greenhouse construction and at some general information on construction types and then dive right into a few specific details of caulking, weather stripping and a particular concern of horticultural greenhouses, rot-proofing. This last aspect involves construction techniques as well as proper materials selection, including preservatives, paints and stains. These specifics apply to several areas of construction, so they are covered here in the beginning.

The first rule of greenhouse construction is so simple it is very often overlooked: Remember the *purpose* of the structure as you are building it. Carrying this attention to purpose, which was emphasized in "Section II: Designing the Greenhouse," through to the construction stage will result in a more energy-conserving greenhouse that is better suited to your needs. For solar heating or plant growing, remember to *minimize* the glazing framing as much as possible to let in the maximum amount of light and solar heat. This is not only a matter of choosing a glazing and support framing system that lets a lot of light through, but a matter of precision and attention during construction. Make maximum use of the strength of the glazing support materials: Don't use a 2×6 where a 2×4 will do and don't space the framing members closer together than is necessary. Use exterior battens that are wide enough to cover just the part of the glazing that sits on top of the rafter, rather than covering any part of the opening. Attention to details like these can give you an aperture that is 90 percent clear instead of 80 percent, increasing solar heat gain and overall performance.

It's important for you to know the locations and names of the various parts of the greenhouse as used in this book. Figure 8-1 shows them. The parts and terms not shown in the illustration are the following:

On center: a measurement taken from the center of one to the center of another of two

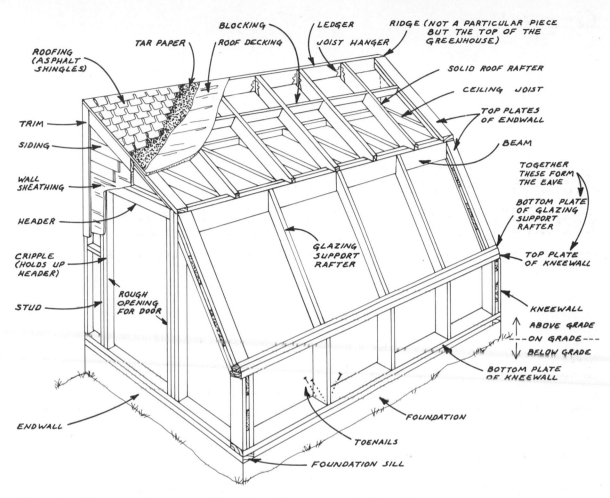

Figure 8-1: These are the names and locations of common parts of greenhouses.

parts. For example, rafters that are 16 inches on centers are spaced with their centers 16 inches apart.

Rebar: steel reinforcing rod used to strengthen concrete

Subfloor: rough flooring that goes on top of floor joists but below the finished floor

Cant strip: a beveled piece of wood

Lag screw: like a wood screw, but usually larger and with a hex head so you can use a socket wrench for installing it

One-by: boards that are nominally 1 inch thick, actually ¾ inch thick. A "1 by 4," written as "1 × 4," is usually ¾ inch by 3½ inches. Nominal dimensions are written in the text with no inch marks.

Mill finish aluminum: plain aluminum, without any finish, as it comes from the mill

SYMBOLS USED IN SECTIONS

FOAM INSULATION

FIBERGLASS INSULATION

END GRAIN OR CUT THROUGH A PIECE OF WOOD

ALUMINUM

CONCRETE

CAULKING

PLYWOOD

GLASS

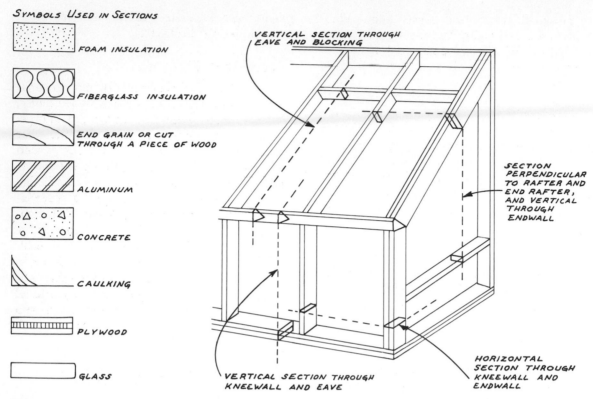

VERTICAL SECTION THROUGH EAVE AND BLOCKING

SECTION PERPENDICULAR TO RAFTER AND END RAFTER, AND VERTICAL THROUGH ENDWALL

VERTICAL SECTION THROUGH KNEEWALL AND EAVE

HORIZONTAL SECTION THROUGH KNEEWALL AND ENDWALL

Figure 8-2: Horizontal and vertical section: If you took a knife and sliced a greenhouse to see how it is built, you would have a *section* or *cross section.* If you sliced it vertically, you would have a *vertical section,* good for examining eave details, for example. A *horizontal section* (horizontal "slice") is good for looking at things like corner posts and how glazing or sheathing wraps around a post. A section perpendicular to a rafter is used to see how glazing fits onto the rafter and is often combined with a section through endwall glazing to show the details where these two glazed areas meet. The symbols used in the sections are also shown.

Stud-Wall versus Post-and-Beam Construction

The glazing support framing can be built as if you were building a standard frame house that uses studs, plates and rafters. For most carpenters this is the most familiar style of construction. In this style the rafters are sized to be large (and therefore strong) enough for the distance they span, usually without any intermediate support. The old commercial wood-raftered greenhouses were built a different way. To admit as much light as possible, they used very small rafters, sometimes measuring only 1½ inches by 1 inch. These rafters were supported fairly frequently with *purlins* made of strong but thin galvanized steel angle iron or pipe, so that they too wouldn't block much light. The purlins were in turn supported by metal trusses or ribs in the larger greenhouses, or metal posts in smaller ones. This style can easily be adapted to attached greenhouse construction. We'll call it *post and beam,* but this doesn't mean using 8-by-8-inch oak posts and beams; it means thin posts and beams supporting thin rafters.

Post-and-beam framing very naturally combines with a lower-cost pier foundation instead of a continuous foundation. Since the weight of the roof is carried from the rafters to purlins to posts, foundation is only needed under the posts. Stud framing can also be built on a pier foundation, using a beam across the piers to support the studs. Pier foundations cut costs, but they also limit you to either a ground-level floor or a platform floor on top of the piers. If you need to go more than a little below grade, a continuous foundation is required to hold back the earth.

If the glazing area is small and the rafter span fairly short, there isn't much difference between the two framing systems. But when the greenhouse is more than 8 to 10 feet deep, a 2 × 6 or 2 × 8 may be needed to span the whole distance without a support, and this begins to block more sunlight than is desirable. The choice between stud-wall framing and post-and-beam framing will depend on the following:

• *The need to maximize interior light levels.* The smaller rafters of post-and-beam construction allow more light into the greenhouse, which is important for horticultural greenhouses.

• *Your preference as a builder.* You may prefer to stick with familiar techniques, although post-and-beam framing is not really very different.

• *How you want the greenhouse to look.* You may want the look of heavier wood rafters, perhaps with a natural finish, rather than the "lighter" look afforded by post-and-beam construction.

As you go through the next chapters, your choice of a framing system will become clearer as the various framing and foundation techniques are discussed.

Building It Tight

Sealing out air leaks is just commonsense energy conservation in any part of the house, but it's doubly important in the greenhouse. Leaks in the greenhouse lose valuable solar heat before it even gets into the house, and they make back-up heating more expensive. The plants' need for fresh air shouldn't fool you into building a leaky structure. Ventilation for the plants should be controlled, coming as much as possible from the house in the winter, rather than from uncontrolled infiltration. Making the greenhouse tight involves taking the extra time to make all the pieces fit together, as well as using the proper grades of wood, caulks, sealants, weather stripping and other materials.

Caulking and Weather Stripping

There is a bewildering variety of caulking materials on the market. Your choice depends partly on the job you are doing and partly on your budget. In general, cracks between the various pieces of the greenhouse open up when the materials cool and shrink and close up when they warm and expand. This means that the caulking must be able to stretch without losing its bond to the surfaces of the materials. In general, materials that expand and contract a lot with temperature change will require more elastic caulking. Metals and plastics change dimension the most, glass is intermediate, and wood and masonry have the least dimensional change. You should avoid using greenwood in a greenhouse: it simply shrinks too much, opening up cracks as it dries.

TABLE 8-1: COMPARISON OF VARIOUS CAULKINGS

Caulking	Adhesion and Flexibility	Tack-free Time*	Cure Time (days)*	Life Expectancy (yrs)
Silicone	Very high	5 mins to 2 hrs †	2 to 10	10 to 30
Acrylic polymer	High	24 to 72 hrs	14	5 to 20
Poly-urethane	High	12 to 48 hrs	5 to 14	10 to 20
Butyl	High adhesion, moderate flexibility	1 to 24 hrs	7 to 14	5 to 20

*Tack-free time is when the caulk "skins over," allowing painting if you are really in a hurry, although waiting for the caulk to cure is preferable. Life expectancy is widely variable and depends on the installation. Cure time is when the caulk develops full strength and adhesion. Tack-free and cure times are rated at 70°F or higher and are longer at lower temperatures. All specifications will vary with specific brands.
†Most silicones lose tackiness quite quickly, but some slower skin-over time formulas are available.

All the caulkings listed in Table 8-1 are suitable for general sealing around the greenhouse. Some exceptions are the sill and the glazing. *Sill sealer,* which is a strip of fiberglass or closed-cell plastic foam material laid between the top of the foundation and the wood sill is easier and cheaper for sealing this seam than tube-type caulks. Sill sealer can be supplemented with caulking or with aerosol expanding foam, if the top of the foundation is too irregular. *Silicone* caulk is the best for sealing glazing, since it can stretch about twice as much as any of the others and has the best resistance to degradation from sunlight.

It's not difficult to caulk a joint in a way that takes best advantage of the properties of the caulk. The trick is to allow the caulk enough contact area for good adhesion while making the bead thin enough that the force required to stretch it isn't greater than the adhesion of the caulk to the materials. The crack should be no wider than ½ inch, and the depth of the caulk should be at least ⅛ inch, but not more than ⅜ inch, to ensure that the bead is thick enough for strength, yet thin enough to be able to stretch when the materials shrink and move apart. The depth of the sealant should be about equal to the expected movement of the joint. You can reduce the depth of oversized cracks with a flexible "backing rod" (a foam rod available from caulking suppliers) that you stuff into the crack with a putty knife. As a general guideline, joints between pieces of wood should be

Toxic Fumes	Paintable	Approx cost/ Tube ($)	Comments
No‡	No§	5 to 7	Clear, white, black, bronze are common colors Clean up with alcohol Good for cold-weather application Best for glazing Most types set up quickly, so don't work too far ahead
Yes	Yes‖	3 to 5	Available in a variety of colors Clean up with xylol or MEK
Yes‖	Yes	5	Many colors available Clean up with xylol or toluol
No	Yes	3 to 4	Good for general crack sealing White, brown, black are common colors Clean up with paint thinner

‡*Acetic acid fumes are released as silicone cures. This is the same acid that is in vinegar, which is irritating but not toxic.*
§*Some paintable formulas are beginning to be available, but most silicones are not paintable.*
‖*Fumes dissipate in about a week, depending on temperature and specific brand. Ventilation required during curing period.*

about ⅛ inch wide (with the caulk therefore about ⅛ inch deep); between 8-foot-wide sheets of polystyrene foam, they should be ¼ to ½ inch. (Polystyrene foam foundation insulation is described in chapter 9.) If the crack is too narrow, it should be widened, either by refitting the piece, or cutting the crack wider. If you recut the crack, cut it deep enough to accommodate a backing rod, since caulk that bonds to the back of the crack won't be able to expand and contract properly. Cracks over ¼ inch deep will generally need a backing rod, not only to keep the bead the right size and shape but also to save on caulking. It's surprising how much caulk you can waste in a wide crack without a backing rod. The extra effort in using the backing rod will also pay off

in reduced maintenance later, as you will be much more likely to get the rated life span out of the caulk.

Although some caulks will adhere to unpainted wood, all of them will stick better to painted, stained or otherwise finished wood. For caulks that can be painted, prime the surfaces and apply the caulk after the primer is dry. Then paint or stain with the final coats. For most silicones and other unpaintable caulks, complete the paint job before caulking. And remember to clean surfaces before caulking. Blow or brush dust out of cracks and wipe down smooth surfaces such as glass or metal with a paper towel or clean rag moistened with a little alcohol to remove any dust, oily residue or moisture. Lightly sand aluminum surfaces with a very fine emery paper to get good adhesion, then wipe with the alcohol-moistened rag. Tool the joint before the caulking gets tacky, to force the caulk against the surfaces for good adhesion, as well as to make a neater-looking joint.

Weather stripping is made for either a compression fit, as in a door closing against a stop, or for a sliding fit, as in the sides of a sash window. In a greenhouse, the weather stripping will mostly be the compression type, unless you use sliding doors or sash windows, but these usually come with their own weather stripping. Vents you build and doors you hang yourself will need a compressible material for a tight seal. Important properties of weather stripping for greenhouse use are its resistance to degradation from sunlight, resistance to absorbing moisture and of course its ability to make a tight seal. Closed-cell foams, including foamed neoprene, vinyl, EPDM (ethylene-propylene-diene-monomer, a very durable synthetic rubber) and tubular vinyl can all be used successfully. They are flexible enough to seal over small surface imperfec-

tions and irregularities, and they're durable enough to last several years. If you are willing to pay more and sacrifice some tightness in the seal in exchange for a long lifetime, you can use spring metal weather stripping. It lasts practically forever, but doesn't fill in irregularities quite as well as the more flexible plastics.

When installing plastic foam or tubular weather stripping, try to avoid placing it where it will be exposed to direct sunlight. This won't always be possible, but keeping it out of the sun will greatly increase its life span. For example, on a vent, the foam should be stuck to the underside of the vent, where it will be in the shade when the vent is open, rather than on the frame of the greenhouse where it would be in the sun. Weather stripping with an adhesive backing should be used only on a smooth surface. If it is on wood, the wood should have all its coats of paint, stain or other sealer before the weather stripping goes on. Clean the surface well before applying. After getting off the dirt and letting the surface dry, wipe the surface down with a

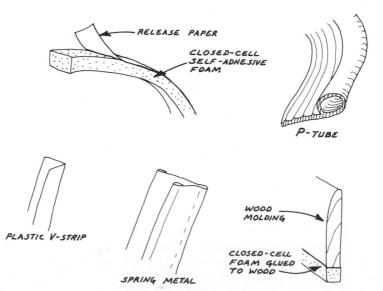

Figure 8-3: Closed-cell foam and tubular vinyl weather stripping seal the best, won't absorb moisture and have a reasonable life span. The spring metal lasts almost forever, but doesn't seal as well. The plastic V-strip seals about as well as the metal and is less costly.

clean rag or paper towel with alcohol on it to remove any oily residue or moisture. Avoid cold weather, if possible, since the adhesives don't stick very well in the cold. Also avoid stretching foams when applying, since they will come unstuck when the foam manages to shrink back to its normal length. The adhesives will not last forever, even under the best circumstances, and the weather stripping may require some tacking up or replacing after a few years. When nailing on tubular vinyl, or refastening foam, use galvanized nails for better durability. Staples will rust.

Building for Durability

Greenhouses present some special aging problems. The exposure of the glazing speeds up the aging of plastic glazing, caulking, trim, fasteners and paint or stain. The high humidity inside a plant-filled greenhouse can warp wood and make a great environment for all sorts of organisms that rot wood and mildew paint. Condensation is frequent enough that the inside of a plant-growing greenhouse will probably be wet more often than the outside. All this requires some extra effort to build a structure that will not only survive, but will require a minimum of maintenance. Parts that will need replacing, such as plastic glazings or foam weather stripping should be designed and built to be easy to change. Replacing plastic glazing, for example, should only require taking off a minimum of the outside trim. Replacing one broken piece of glass shouldn't require removing four other pieces. In general, the details shown in this section of the book are designed with this in mind.

Rot-proofing is one of the big concerns in greenhouse construction. The old wood greenhouses used rot-resistant woods, such as cypress and redwood, and heavily galvanized steel hardward to minimize rust. They were also very well drained. Condensation would be channeled from the glazing to the rafters, from the rafters to gutters in the sill and then to drains. This was intended as much to avoid drips, which would cause spots on expensive flower crops, as to protect wood from rot. Modern commercial greenhouses have gone to all-aluminum materials, avoiding both the repainting that wood requires and potential rot problems. Many solar greenhouse manufacturers produce all-aluminum units.

In your greenhouse, the best overall solution is to keep water from leaking in from the outside and to keep it from sitting anywhere, inside or and outside, by sloping surfaces enough that water always runs off. Higher surfaces should be "shingled" over lower surfaces, rather than butted against them, so that water always runs out and never sits in cracks. Caulking should be used to back up shingling, not substitute for it. Second, make the surfaces resistant enough to water (with sealer, flashing, pressure-treated or rot-resistant wood) so that whatever water does stay in contact with the wood won't harm it. And third, have a way for any moisture that does get in to get out. For example, insulation should be well vented to get rid of water vapor, and floors should be drained to carry off water that is spilled or that drains out of the bottom of pots and growing beds. The construction details in this section incorporate provisions for water to run off and for moisture to escape, and they indicate where rot-resistant wood should be used.

There are several ways to slow down the deterioration of wood. Using rot-resistant woods such as redwood, cedar or cypress is a good solution, particularly where they are exposed, so you can take advantage of their good looks. The heartwood (from the center of the tree) is much more rot-resistant than the sapwood (outer) and should be used if you can afford it. Not painting the wood does decrease light levels inside, but many owners accept that to retain the beauty of the natural wood. But even these woods aren't invulnerable: Water that is left to sit will eventually soften them, so attention should still be paid to slopes and drainage. Putting metal flashing over surfaces that are exposed to a lot of water, such as the sill below the glazing, is another approach. Preservative treatment of the wood, either at the building site or at a pressure-treating plant, and painting the wood are two more weapons against rot. We'll deal with these last two here, as the other strategies are covered in later chapters.

There are certain places where using preservative-treated or rot-proof lumber is a must, including anywhere that wood is in contact with the earth or with concrete or other masonry. Pressure-treated lumber is best for these places. In other locations, it is a matter of judgment and of how the greenhouse will be used. If the greenhouse is not going to be used extensively for plant growing, additional treatment beyond painting isn't

needed. For horticultural greenhouses, there are several choices. Some people build the whole greenhouse out of pressure-treated lumber that is treated for soil contact; others apply a preservative over the whole greenhouse frame before proceeding with insulation, painting and glazing; others have had satisfactory results with a good paint job on just the exposed wood. There is no question that using all pressure-treated lumber gives the best resistance to rot, but not everyone believes it is necessary. Those who do cite stories of framing literally rotting out inside insulated walls. This has happened, but it isn't clear whether this was due to inadequate vapor barriers, vapor barriers damaged during construction or insufficient venting of wall cavities to the outside. If you decide not to treat the wood inside the insulated walls, be very certain that the vapor barrier is continuous and that the outside sheathing has some ventilation, as discussed in chapter 10.

Applying preservative to the frame prior to insulating or painting is a relatively easy

Photo 8-1: This glazing support framing was painted *before* the glazing went on. This is much easier and neater than trying to paint up to the glazing after it is installed. It also gets a protective coat on the wood under the glazing and provides a better bonding surface for caulk.

task that involves minor expense and just a little time. This strategy requires a little advance planning, since the preservative must dry before paint can be applied. Copper naphthenate preservative for site-treated wood is safe for plants, but it must dry for at least a few weeks before plants can be brought into the greenhouse, since the fumes given off while drying are toxic to plants and soil organisms. It is also acceptable to paint only the exposed interior wood if a vapor barrier is used over the insulation in solid walls. The paint must of course be maintained. There are greenhouses built of pine that have lasted 20 years with little degradation, with just occasional repainting. An on-site preservative treatment, though, before painting or staining is easy to do and is recommended for horticultural greenhouses.

Pressure-treated wood is available with a number of kinds of preservatives. Most of them are toxic to plants and therefore can't be used in greenhouses. *Pentachlorophenol* compounds and *creosote* are both deadly to plants. *Chromated copper arsenate* is the best, since it is suitable for in-ground use and doesn't leach into the surrounding soil and usually won't bleed through paint that is applied over it. Pressure-treated wood is available with varying amounts of preservative, depending on the application. Wood used for structural foundations, designated FDN, has 0.6 pounds of preservative per cubic foot of wood. Wood treated for soil and water contact, designated LP22, has 0.4 pounds, and wood used aboveground, designated DP2, has 0.25 pounds. Be sure to get the proper wood for the application: FDN is for structural wood foundations; LP22 is for wood next to concrete or earth and LP2 is for pressure-treated framing used above grade. (Some suppliers refer to these by the pounds of preservative per cubic foot, rather than the American Wood Preservers Bureau—AWPB—designations shown here.) If you are using it for

glazing framing, where you want to be sure it won't warp, get wood that is pressure treated first and then kiln dried, if possible, rather than the other way around, since it is less prone to warping and splitting. This may not be available from some suppliers, or in some areas, so you may have to use wood that was dried first.

Be careful when using preservatives or preservative-treated lumber: they work because they are poisonous to fungus, bacteria and insects. But if they're not handled properly, they can also be poisonous to people. Make sure that the wood you get has been seasoned outdoors for at least 60 days or is kiln dried after treating. Conscientious pressure-treating factories even steam clean the wood after it is treated to remove excess preservative. Wear protective clothing and gloves when handling the wood and be sure to use a dust respirator and goggles when cutting it. Keep the wood and scrap away from pets and children and *don't* burn the scraps, since the fumes are extremely toxic and can result in serious poisoning.

Treating wooden growing beds is another issue. The above-mentioned treatments are supposed to be acceptable when in contact with growing soil, since they don't leach into the soil once they have cured. But if you are concerned with organic food production, you are going to a lot of effort to build a greenhouse where you can grow food free of any pesticides or herbicides, and it seems a shame to risk getting any preservative into the soil. To some this worry seems overly conservative. But you may prefer to build the beds out of plain untreated lumber or out of redwood, being content to replace the wood occasionally rather than worry about it. Another approach is to build a bed with pressure-treated wood sides, with heavy (8 to 10 mil) polyethylene between the wood and the soil, to keep the soil from contact with the preservatives. The bottom of the bed can be galvanized hardware cloth for good drainage, with plastic insect screening laid on top to keep the soil from falling through the hardware cloth. Masonry and in-ground beds, of course, avoid the whole issue.

Paint for the interior is another area where you will have to choose the level of protection you want. No matter what type of paint you use, prepare the surfaces well. You should plane the edges and sand the corners of any boards that you rip to size so that you can get a smooth coat of paint. Set the heads of nails and fasteners below the surface and fill the holes. Seal knots in the wood with shellac or other sealer to prevent sap from bleeding throught the paint. Dust off all surfaces before painting, and paint *both* sides of trim before you install it. This keeps the wood from warping due to moisture being absorbed on the back side. The choices of paint range from exterior latex or enamel to epoxy. Gloss white should be used for best light reflection inside the greenhouse. Latex paint is generally less durable than you would like and isn't as easy to clean as enamel. Enamel is more durable, and with a glossy surface it cleans fairly easily. With a primer and two coats, enamel also acts as a pretty effective vapor barrier, supplementing the polyethylene vapor barrier over the insulation. With enamel or latex paint, an alkyd-resin-based primer should be used for best adhesion to both wood and to the paint on top of it. The purpose of primer is *adhesion,* while the purpose of the paint is weather resistance. Two-part epoxy paint is the ultimate coating. It is virtually indestructible, easy to clean and quite impermeable to water vapor. It is also very expensive and can be difficult to apply. Its fumes are toxic while drying, so use it only with good ventilation. And be sure to use a compatible primer. Some people avoid paint altogether, and use white stain inside, in order to eliminate the possibility of having to scrape flaking paint at some time in the future.

For the outside of the greenhouse, a stain is best, not only for siding but for trim and glazing battens. This not only avoids scraping when you have to recoat, but it allows any moisture that finds its way into the wood from inside the greenhouse to escape. Enamel epoxy, latex, or any other coating that forms a skin, tends to trap moisture and peel from the moisture working its way out through the skin.

Chapter 9

FOUNDATIONS

Foundations perform the dual function of supporting and anchoring the greenhouse. The weight of the structure tends to sink into the ground, while the surface area it presents to the wind gives it a tendency to rack or push over and even lift. The wind can actually exert as much lift as push, so the greenhouse must be securely tied to a well-anchored foundation. Three basic types of foundations are presented in this chapter: the continuous foundation, which is similar to that used in most house construction, the pier foundation, such as that used to support an outdoor deck, and the wood-post foundation, which is like a concrete pier except that it is made of wood.

The type that is best for you depends on several factors, including the soil type and its drainage characteristics, the type of glazing support framing you will be using, local building codes, and, of course, your budget. We'll discuss pros and cons and appropriate applications for each type along with construction details, including foundation insulation. Here and there you'll find special construction tips for procedures that differ from ordinary construction practices.

When building the foundation, it is well worth the time it takes to get it square and level and parallel to the house. Extra effort at the beginning will eliminate some awful headaches later. This is particularly important if you choose glass or plastic panel glazing that requires precise framing. It's a good idea to lay out the location of the ledger, the plate bolted to the house to carry the rafters, when laying out the foundation. The ledger must be horizontal and straight, and the south wall of the greenhouse must be parallel to it. If the common wall is bowed where the ledger will be, you will want to shim the ledger out enough to get it straight. (Otherwise all your rafters would have to be different lengths.) A couple of nails driven into the siding where the ends of the ledger will be, with a string stretched between them, will tell you if the house is bowed. Dropping a plumb bob from each nail will tell you if the house wall is vertical and if the ledger is parallel to the house foundation. If it is parallel, you can simply square the greenhouse foundation to the house foundation. If it isn't, you will want to mark a line that is plumb below the ledger and square the greenhouse foundation to that line.

None of the foundations discussed includes a floor, except for the pier-and-platform foundation (discussed shortly). Standard concrete slabs can be poured inside a continuous foundation, with an expansion joint between the slab and the foundation wall. A floor drain is useful in getting rid of excess water from irrigating and from periodic flushing of growing beds with water. If you have a perimeter drain, you can plumb the floor drain into that, or you can make a small "dry well," filling a hole beneath the drain with gravel. Gravel floors are more or less one big drain, as long as the earth beneath is a little porous. Bricks can be set over gravel or sand to provide drainage plus a more finished look. Platform floors are a little more difficult. If you pour a thin slab on top of the platform, it can be sloped to a drain that connects to the house sewer or septic line, but you must then be careful to keep dirt out to avoid clogging it, and you must run the drainpipe inside the floor insulation to prevent it from freezing. The trap can be put inside the house to allow you to slope the drain while still keeping it above the top of the insulation.

Foundation Insulation

Unless the greenhouse floor is built on an insulated platform, the foundation itself should be insulated. Since the insulation is in contact with the earth, it is particularly important to choose an insulation material that will not absorb moisture. Extruded polystyrene (Styrofoam and Foamula II, for example) is suitable for underground use. The white "beadboard," otherwise known as expanded polystyrene, is not suitable, since it will absorb moisture and thus lose most of its insulation value. The foil-covered polyiso-

cyanurate foams, such as R-Max and High-R, or polyurethane foam are also not suitable, since they too will absorb moisture.

Another relatively new foundation insulation material is rigid fiberglass boards. These are manufactured in such a way that subsurface water drains down the outside ⅛ inch of the fiberglass, leaving the rest of the material dry, retaining its insulation value. This outer layer conducts water down to a perimeter drain, aiding soil drainage. Further, fiberglass board is not attractive to pests (this is discussed later), and it will absorb some expansion of the surrounding earth in areas prone to frost heaves. The fibrous surface also accepts stuccolike surface coating easily (also discussed later). This type of fiberglass board can be substituted for polystyrene foam on continuous foundations. One brand of this material is Warm-N-Dri, made by Owens-Corning.

Insulation can be placed on either the inside or the outside of the foundation. Since the insulation needs to be covered whether it is inside or outside the foundation, it may as well go on the outside to make the foundation part of the interior heat storage mass. The insulation should extend down to the top of the foundation footing, which is usually at the frost line.

Where the insulation goes above grade, it must be protected from physical abuse, such as people and things bumping into it, and from the sun, whose ultraviolet rays will quickly deteriorate it. There are a number of strategies for covering foam, including wet coatings, such as stucco or stuccolike materials that incorporate glass fibers or plastic resins for extra strength and resilience, and dry materials, such as rigid vinyl, fiberglass or metal sheets. The wet coatings have a neat finished appearance and can add structural strength to the foam when applied over a reinforcing mesh. This is helpful where the foam spans between foundation posts above grade. Wet materials are more difficult to apply than rigid ones, however, requiring more careful workmanship to achieve a good-looking, long-lasting result. In the following sections of this chapter, we'll show a particular insulation technique for each type of foundation, but you can use any of the types of covering with any of the foundation types.

Rodents and insects, particularly termites or carpenter ants, are problems that must be dealt with in some areas. The insects can use foam as a passageway to the wood of the greenhouse, and rodents can gnaw at the material, removing precious insulation. Termite shields are appropriate in some areas and so is having only pressure-treated wood or concrete in contact with the insulation. Some builders use poisons in the soil to avoid the possibility of termites bridging the shields with mud tunnels. Others completely encase below-grade insulation in a stucco mixture to absolutely exclude pests. Check with local

Photos 9-1 a and b: Putting the foam insulation between the inner and outer walls of a brick foundation adds the inside half of the foundation to the heat storage capacity of the greenhouse as well as protecting the insulation. *(Photos courtesy of R. W. Chew and Co., Barrington, R.I.)*

builders or building inspectors on these matters.

Continuous Foundations

A continuous foundation is simply a short wall of some type under the entire perimeter of the greenhouse. It can be masonry—poured concrete as shown in figure 9-1, concrete block as shown in figure 9-2, brick or stone—or it can be made with pressure-treated wood. A foundation includes a footing or base support that is large enough to stabilize the foundation in the surrounding earth. In sandy, loose soils a larger footing is needed,

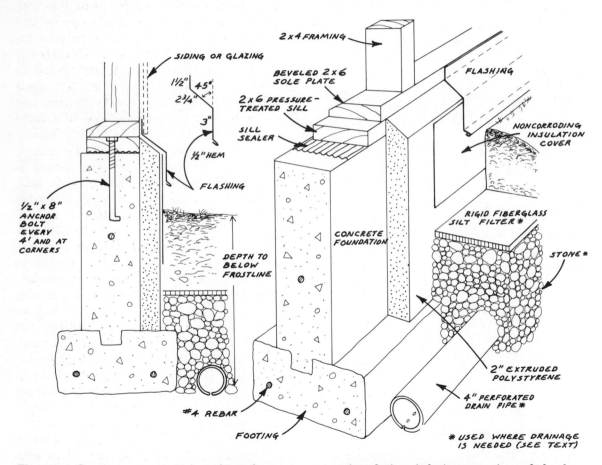

Figure 9-1: Continuous concrete is perhaps the most common foundation. A drain system is needed only where soil drainage is poor. Foundation depth varies with the depth of frost penetration, and the size of the footing depends on the stability of the soil. Some very dense and stable soils can support a footing the width of the foundation wall; sandy, loose soils may require larger footings than shown here. (The notch in the top of the footing helps attach the foundation wall to the footing when the wall is poured after the footing, rather than at the same time.)

while in very dense, stable soils a minimum footing is all you need. The footing must be deep enough to extend below the line of maximum frost penetration, so that freezing earth doesn't lift the foundation and the green-house. The footings shown in figure 9-1 are for average soils. Check with a local structural engineer or builder if you have any doubt about the right footing size for your particular conditions.

Continuous masonry foundations are the most common foundations for attached greenhouses. Builders are most familiar with it; insulating it is a very straightforward proposition. It is practical for all types of soils, and it meets all building codes. It can be used with all types of framing and is compatible with either an earth-level floor, a below-grade floor or a raised joist floor. Continuous foundations are required for pit greenhouses, where the floor is below grade. Continuous foundations generally cost more than the other types because they require more excavation and more masonry. This is particularly true where the climate is cold enough to require foundations that extend several feet below grade.

In moist soils, a drainage system is needed to keep the area next to the foundation dry enough so that freezing of this earth won't push in on the foundation. If the soil adjacent to the foundation is soaked because of poor drainage, freezing will cause expansion that can exert a force strong enough to crack concrete or even shift the foundation. Drainage is particularly important in clay soils, which tend to retain water, and in situations where the slope of the land tends to put a lot of water near the greenhouse. Pit greenhouses should always have a drainage system unless you are positive that the earth is dry. Sloping the earth away from the greenhouse when you backfill the foundation is helpful but it may not be enough for clay or other poorly drained soil. If you are unsure whether or not you need a drain system, check with local builders.

If you do need a drainage system, a conventional system of perforated drainpipe bedded in crushed stone is usually adequate. The pipes are set, holes down, in the stone at the

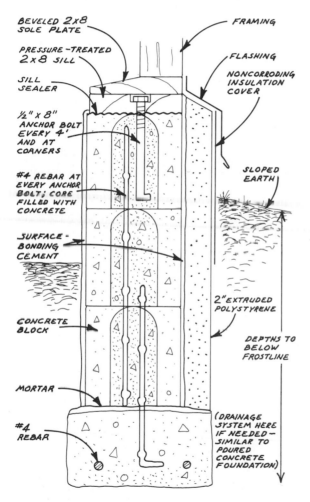

Figure 9-2: Concrete block foundations can be easy for first-time masons with the use of surface-bonding mortar, a mixture of cement, glass fibers and other reinforcing agents, which is troweled on the outside of dry-stacked blocks. For extra strength, cores are filled every 4 feet and at corners with concrete.

level of the bottom of the footing. The pipe should also be as far away horizontally from the footing as your digging permits. Water is drawn toward the drainpipe, so keeping the pipe away from the foundation will keep water away as well. This minimizes heat loss from the foundation, since soil or gravel are better insulators when they're dry. The pipes are all sloped toward a nonperforated drainpipe, which extends as far away as necessary to dump the water either above the surface of the ground or into a dry well (gravel-filled pit). The gravel fill can go up to around 18 inches below grade, with the soil filling the rest of the excavation (slope it away from the foundation). In heavily clay soil, gravel (crushed stone mixed with sand and other small particles) can be used to back fill above the stone to keep the clay away from the foundation. In order to minimize clogging of the gravel with silt from the overlaying soil, a filter of rigid fiberglass insulation board (without the foil facing) can be laid on top of the gravel before adding the soil.

Instructions for building continuous masonry foundations can be found in many construction handbooks and thus aren't included here. Instructions for laying out and building a continuous concrete foundation specifically for a greenhouse can be found in Ecotope Group's *Solar Greenhouse Guide for the Pacific Northwest* and for a continuous concrete block foundation in the New Mexico Solar Energy Association's *Building Your Solar Greenhouse,* and in Rodale's *Gardener's Solar Greenhouse.* Whether you use poured concrete or concrete block usually depends on your skills and your budget. Concrete is usually more expensive, though this varies with location and soil conditions. If you dig the trench yourself and the earth is stable enough to act as the form, a concrete foundation can be inexpensive and relatively easy. If you have to build a lot of forms, the labor can be extensive. You might want to consider contracting out this part of the job: A professional contractor can get it done quickly, with prebuilt modular forms.

If you are unfamiliar with masonry work, *surface-bonding cement* can make a concrete block foundation much easier than poured concrete. The footing can sometimes be poured directly into an accurately dug, squared-off trench, minimizing the need for form building. With surface-bonding cement, the first row of blocks is leveled on the footing with regular masonry mortar underneath, not between, the blocks. Subsequent rows are stacked dry, using scraps of aluminum flashing for shims to level the rows as you go. Once all the block is in place, the surface-bonding cement is troweled to a specific thickness on both sides. It is very important that the cement be the thickness specified (which will vary from one manufacturer to the next), to achieve full strength. A coat that is too thin will result in a weak bond and eventual cracks in the foundation. The mortar contains glass fibers that act as reinforcing, and it has other ingredients to strengthen the mix. The cores of the blocks are then filled with regular concrete at the corners and at 4-foot intervals. The concrete is poured around a continuous rebar going down to the footing, and then an anchor bolt is set into the concrete for later use in fastening the sill plates. Most building supply outlets carry surface-bonding cement.

The sill plate must be of pressure-treated lumber, redwood or other rot-resistant wood. Use a sill-sealer between the concrete and the sill, and use caulking if you can see any daylight between them after the anchor bolts have been tightened down. If the crack is still large, you can use the aerosol-type of expanding foam or conventional caulking with a foam backing rod.

Pressure-treated wood can also be used to build a complete continuous foundation. These foundations resemble little stud walls, except that they are built with wood and fasteners treated to withstand underground conditions. (Note that not all pressure-treated wood is intended for underground use: Use wood specifically treated for this purpose.) The references listed in Further Reading will give you complete how-to information on the design and construction of these foundations.

Insulating Continuous Foundations

Insulation can be placed on the foundation any time after the concrete is set or the block mortar is dry. It's a good idea to bevel the top of the insulation to prevent water from sitting on top. (Another option—not shown here—is to extend the sill plate out over the top of the insulation.) Before installation, cut it on a table saw or with a circular saw and a straight edge guide to get a neat, even cut. Cutting a bevel after the insulation is in place is difficult and usually results in an uneven line. The insulation is held against the foundation with construction mastic, a thick glue that comes in tubes for a caulking gun. Be sure to get a type that is compatible with the insulation. Polystyrene insulation is dissolved by some mastics, so use a compatible variety (one brand is PL200). Foundation waterproofing compound is often used as a mastic with the rigid fiberglass board. Having blobs of mastic every 12 inches is usually enough to hold the foam. You can prop the foam against the foundation with scrap lumber until the mastic cures.

Once the foam is in place, the rigid, sheet-type protective cover can be put on the outside, using the same mastic. As mentioned, there are a few different materials that can be used. The flashing itself can be extended down below grade, eliminating the separate cover, but many soils will corrode the flashing in a couple of years, necessitating a difficult replacement job. Plastic that has been treated

Photo 9-2: Two-inch extruded polystyrene foundation insulation, rigid, noncorroding insulation cover and flashing are all shown here.

to withstand sunlight is a good material since it won't corrode. Several types are available that are made specifically for this purpose, including the Insulgard brand made by Trend Products (see Appendix 1), which costs about $1.50 per square foot. Mobile home skirting material, made for enclosing the space under trailers, and vinyl siding can also be used. You can look around at local building supply dealers for these or other low-cost rigid outdoor plastic sheeting. The cover should be tall enough to extend about 6 inches below grade. (Remember that the earth will settle some after it compacts.) Better a little long than a little short.

The other commonly used covers for foundation insulation are the stuccolike materials made especially for this purpose. These incorporate glass fibers and acrylic resins or other modifiers for better adhesion to and expansion with the foam. This decreases the chances of the coating cracking with wide temperature changes. For this reason, these specialized mixes should be used rather than a normal stucco mix. Some brands come with a fiberglass cloth that covers the foam styrene insulation to act as a reinforcing mesh. The mesh is held in place with a troweled-on mastic. When this is dry, the stucco mixture is applied. Some brands only come with enough of this cloth for the joints of the foam, but covering all the foam with the cloth will produce a stronger result, which is important if more than a foot or two of the foundation sticks out of the ground. Instructions for application vary from one product to the next, depending on the exact makeup of the material. If you don't get enough fiberglass for the whole surface, it's a good idea to scar the surface of the foam for better adhesion of the stucco. (Follow the manufacturer's instructions rather closely to get the best results.)

If the foundation is more than 10 feet long, having a vertical expansion joint in foam styrene is advisable to minimize the chances of the stucco cracking. Cracks admit water which will freeze and eventually force the stucco off the foam. To make an expansion joint, leave ¼ to ⅜ inch between the foam sheets at the center of the foundation if it's less than 20 feet, or every 10 feet if it's longer. Leave a break in the fiberglass mesh at the same spot. Before you apply the coating, put a scrap of plywood or other material of the right thickness in the crack while you are stuccoing. Take it out before the stucco sets up, and smooth the corners on either side of the crack. When the coating is completely dry, put a backing rod in the crack and apply a bead of silicone caulking. (If the stucco doesn't cover the foam inside the crack, be sure not to use a solvent-based caulk such as acrylic polymer or urethane that will dissolve the foam. Test the caulk on a scrap of foam before using. Butyl doesn't stretch enough for this application.)

Reinforcing mesh is not needed when

Photo 9-3: Carefully bent flashing gives the whole job a neat appearance. Shop-bent galvanized flashing is shown here.

applying the stucco coatings to rigid fiberglass board foundation insulation, since the glass fibers provide a good rough surface for the stucco mixture to adhere to. Since glass expands and contracts much less with temperature fluctuations than the foam styrene, expansion joints are not required. Both of these characteristics simplify installation of the fiberglass, but the material does require more careful handling. The glass fibers are extremely irritating, requiring protective clothing, including gloves, respirators and goggles.

Unless the sill plate has enough of an overhang to cover the top of the foundation insulation, flashing will be needed to keep water from getting behind the insulation covering. Flashing can be galvanized steel, aluminum that has been painted, or plain, *mill finish* (unpainted) aluminum. Galvanized flashing has recently shown very fast deterioration in areas that receive acid rain, and so should probably be avoided in the northeastern United States and other afflicted areas. Using galvanized usually means having a sheet-metal shop bend it for you because it's somewhat harder than aluminum. You can do it yourself, but it's difficult and can end up looking messy. Take careful measurements, add a little to the total length you need to account for installation errors, make clear sketches and take them to a local sheet-metal shop for prices. (Typical flashing measurements are shown with some of the illustrated foundation details.) Galvanized steel is sturdy and long-lasting except in acid rain areas, and, if the house has galvanized flashing, you may want to use it to match. But it is harder to work with, even just cutting and fitting the bent pieces. Factory-painted aluminum, which is easier to work with, can also be bent for you at a sheet-metal shop. You can sometimes find the color you want, but if you can't, it can be painted fairly easily, requiring only a light roughening with a fine sandpaper before painting. Galvanized steel and mill finish aluminum, on the other hand, require special procedures and special primers. Mill finish aluminum, though, is cheaper than pre-painted, so you may wish to go this route. Check your paint store for materials, usually including a wash of TSP (trisodium phosphate), a rinse with mild muriatic acid solution, and special primers and paints. Aluminum fasteners should be used with aluminum where it is exposed to the weather, to avoid *galvanic corrosion* (chemical disintegration of metals due to the contact between dissimilar metals in the presence of water). This can be done with aluminum pop rivets or aluminum screws.

The least-expensive aluminum flashing is the kind you buy in a roll, typically 16 mil in thickness (0.016 inches) or 19 mil. Twenty-five mil can usually be had—or ordered through a sheet-metal shop. The extra strength is worthwhile if you can get the thicker material. You can bend it yourself with the technique shown in figure 9-3, and

with a little practice you can make a neat job of it. It won't be as sturdy as the thicker shop-bent flashing, but the creases you give it do add some strength.

Figure 9-3 shows the four steps involved in bending aluminum flashing. (A) The flashing can be cut with a mat knife. Watch out for the razor-sharp edges that will spring up, particularly when the roll is curled-up on the table. (B) Mark the bends with a pencil, and then score them with a butter knife. A sharper knife may lead to a break at the line when you bend it. Bending is easier if you score on what will be the outside of the bend, but this isn't critical. (C) Clamp the aluminum under a straight 2 × 4 or other rigid board to the straight edge of a table that has a square edge. Your pieces of aluminum can be as long as you can tightly clamp down without the middle of the 2 × 4 bending up as you bend the flashing. (D) Gradually bend down the aluminum with a block of wood such as a 12-inch piece of 2 × 4. Start at one end, bending the aluminum down just a little, 15 degrees or so, working your way long the piece. Then go back and bend it more at each pass. (Bending too far at one pass will make wrinkles.) To hem an edge, bend as far as you can under the clamp, remove the piece and turn it upside down on the table, working the hem down until it is flat. For bending angles make a cardboard template of the angle to compare with the aluminum as you go. (It's hard to eyeball angles.) With a little practice you will be able to make neat bends for complex pieces. If you are having trouble with wrinkling, try shorter pieces of flashing.

It is possible to rent a lightweight *break,* a sheet-metal bending rig, from a rental yard, for a day or two to bend all your flashing. You'll be able to use heavier flashing and bend it very neatly. If you use thin aluminum flashing over foundation insulation where it might get bumped or stepped on, such as

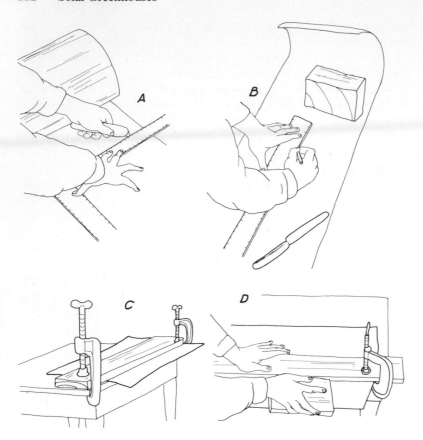

Figure 9-3: This illustration shows how to bend your own aluminum flashing.

under a door, you can replace the beveled top of the foam with a strip of beveled wood nailed to the sill to better support the flashing.

When measuring for flashing, allow 4 to 6 inches overlap from piece to piece, and allow for a folded lower edge, or hem, which gives the bottom edge more strength and conceals a very sharp metal edge. This is a little tough when home-bending 25-mil aluminum without a break, but isn't too hard with the thinner material. On galvanized steel, the hem also hides the cut edge, which will rust. Plan on spending extra time at the corners to fold, trim and join pieces together. Seams can be sealed with silicone caulk. Rigid insulation

covering can also be joined to the flashing with pop-rivets. This avoids relying solely on the mastic to hold the cover in place.

The Sun-Warmed Foundation

As discussed in chapter 4, the south side of the foundation can be turned into a soil-heating collector, as long as it is a couple of feet above grade and it has good solar exposure. One of many possible details is shown in illustration 9-4. In this version, the foundation wall is glazed with a shiplap-pattern corrugated FRP (fiber-reinforced polyester, commonly known as fiberglass) outer glazing and an ultraviolet-resistant polyethylene or flat FRP inner glazing. The FRP can be fas-

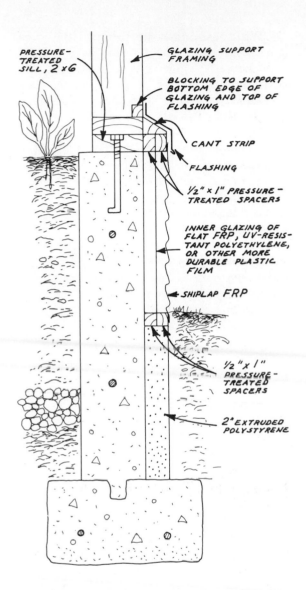

PRESSURE-
TREATED
SILL, 2×6

GLAZING SUPPORT
FRAMING

BLOCKING TO SUPPORT
BOTTOM EDGE OF
GLAZING AND TOP OF
FLASHING

CANT STRIP

FLASHING

½" × I" PRESSURE-
TREATED SPACERS

INNER GLAZING OF
FLAT FRP, UV-RESIS-
TANT POLYETHYLENE,
OR OTHER MORE
DURABLE PLASTIC
FILM

SHIPLAP FRP

½" × I"
PRESSURE-
TREATED
SPACERS

2" EXTRUDED
POLYSTYRENE

Figure 9-4: The sun-warmed foundation turns a continuous masonry foundation into a solar soil heater. The construction detail shown uses pressure-treated lumber (the kind suitable for direct burial) to support low-cost film or plastic sheet glazing. The supports are attached to the concrete with screws and anchors or a masonry nail gun. The glazing material laps over the edge of a rigid insulation covering. Another method could be to continue the kneewall glazing right down over the foundation.

tened with gasketed screws or nails. (These glazing materials are discussed in detail in chapter 11.) Pressure-treated wood (LP22 grade) is used for the spacers that hold the glazing apart, since they are in contact with the foundation and since condensation may form between the glazings due to the contact with the earth. The upper spacers are simply nailed into the sill plate, but the inner of the lower spacers must be fastened to the concrete with lead or plastic shields in the concrete and screws. Silicone is used to seal between all the spacers and the glazing, and between the inner spacers and the concrete. Before glazing, the concrete should be stained any dark color or black for best absorption of heat. A concrete stain is better than masonry paint, since it won't peel. The outer glazing continues below grade to act as a flashing over the foundation insulation.

Pier Foundations

Piers offer an easy way around a good bit of the digging involved with continuous foundations. Holes can be dug by hand much more easily than can a continuous trench, often eliminating the need for a backhoe. This not only saves money but also minimizes the damage to a finished planted yard area. A backhoe makes a big mess. A post hole digger, whether hand- or machine-powered, is helpful for making the holes, and so is a narrow trenching shovel for the insulation. A backhoe, however, can make very short work of the whole job, particularly if insulaton is buried to any depth between the piers. Piers require less concrete and less labor than making forms for poured walls or building up blocks, so the pier foundation is usually cheaper. The holes dug for the piers are also the forms for the footings, and premade cardboard tube-forms can be used to simplify forming the piers. Piers can directly support the posts in post-and-beam framing or a ground-level beam can support stud-wall framing. Piers are also commonly used under a platform-type greenhouse floor.

Special care must be taken when insulating a pier foundation. Since the insulation sits in the ground without the backing of a continuous foundation, you must be careful not to break it when backfilling the earth. And if it extends above grade very far, it needs a protective covering that also gives it some extra rigidity. (Both of these issues are discussed shortly.) If the earth tends to hold moisture or isn't well drained, it may be prone to excessive frost heaving in climates where the ground freezes more than a few inches. If this is the case, don't use a pier foundation along with buried insulation, since the heaving may destroy the insulation.

With post-and-beam framing, the piers can directly support the sill beam on the south side, if the glazing is sloped all the way to the foundation, or, if there is a vertical kneewell, the piers can support posts that support the eave. If the rafters are long enough or thin enough to require a support midway, piers and posts can be used in the endwalls to support a crossbeam. A post resting on a pier inside the greenhouse can also support the crossbeam midway to minimize its size. (See chapter 10, for details.) Solid walls (also covered in chapter 10) can span piers relatively easily. Building codes may not include this type of construction, but it is not inherently more difficult or less structurally sound—it's just different. Some codes simply don't permit it, so check with your inspector

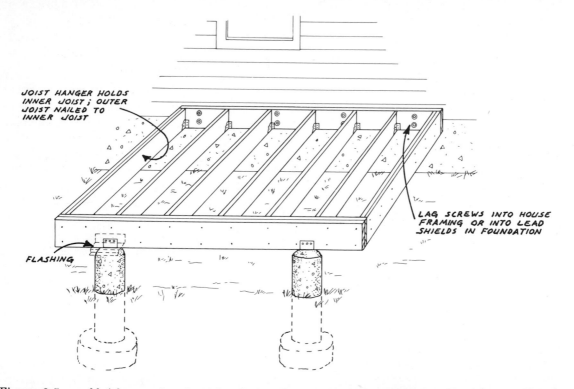

JOIST HANGER HOLDS INNER JOIST; OUTER JOIST NAILED TO INNER JOIST

LAG SCREWS INTO HOUSE FRAMING OR INTO LEAD SHIELDS IN FOUNDATION

FLASHING

Figures 9-5 a and b (above and to the right): Piers with a platform on top require minimal earth work and use standard construction techniques. Be sure the floor is well waterproofed and the insulation underneath well vented.

before getting too far along. In areas where unstable earth or earthquake codes do not permit stand-alone piers, *grade beams* may be an acceptable solution. These are poured reinforced concrete beams that are as wide as the piers and often 12 inches deep. They run between the piers and are connected to them by reinforcing bars cast into the concrete. (The concrete for the grade beams and the piers is poured at the same time.) The finished result, which is quite strong, looks like a continuous foundation above grade and can be treated as one, in terms of insulation and framing.

Piers with a Platform

This is a very straightforward, common construction method, with the exception of extra attention given to keeping water and vapor out of the floor and to venting out moisture that gets in (see figure 9-5). If you are going to grow more than a few houseplants, be certain the floor is waterproof. Use

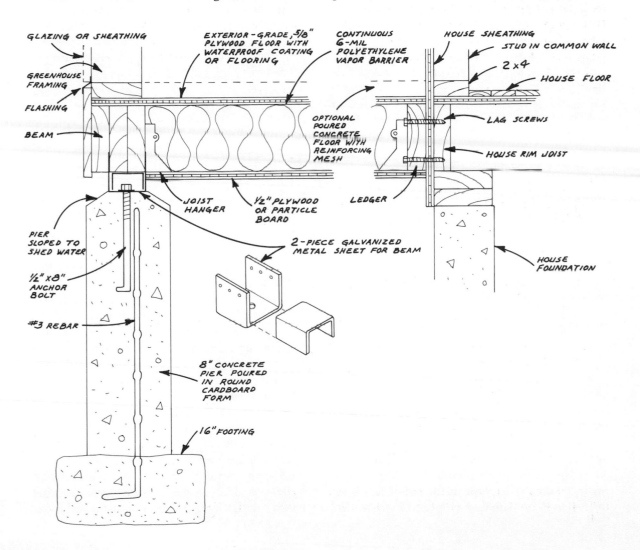

TABLE 9-1: BEAM SIZING FOR PLATFORM CONSTRUCTION

PIER SPACING (on centers)		4 FT	6 FT	8 FT	10 FT
Greenhouse (8 ft wide; 2 × 6 floor joists 16″ on centers)	For Douglas fir #2	double 2 × 6	triple 2 × 8	triple 2 × 10	triple 2 × 12
	For hemlock fir #2	triple 2 × 6	triple 2 × 10	triple 2 × 12	quadruple 2 × 12
Greenhouse (10 ft. wide; 2 × 8 floor joists 16″ on centers)	For Douglas fir #2	double 2 × 8	double 2 × 10	triple 2 × 12	quadruple 2 × 12
	For hemlock fir #2	double 2 × 8	double 2 × 12	quadruple 2 × 10	quadruple 2 × 12

NOTES: *This table assumes stud-wall construction is used, so that the load of the greenhouse is more or less equally distributed across the beam and that the endwalls don't carry the load of the roof. If your framing is different from this, you should refigure the beam size. It is also assumed that the first and last piers are no more than 1 foot in from the endwalls.*

For Douglas fir #2, Fb = 1,261; for hemlock fir #2, Fb = 957. The values for nonrepetitive use are from Design Values for Wood Construction *by the National Forest Products Association. Fb (extreme fiber stress in bending) is a measure of the resistance to bending of a particular species and grade of wood.*

a continuous 6-mil polyethylene vapor barrier, exterior-grade plywood subflooring and a waterproof floor covering, such as ceramic tile, single-piece vinyl, or epoxy paint or resin. The floor insulation underneath should be vented with a standard 1-inch screened *button vent* at both ends of each joist cavity. (A button vent is a circular, louvered aluminum vent with an insect-screen backing. It is glued into a 1-inch-diameter hole with caulk.) Having a rigid covering beneath the insulation is necessary for discouraging mice and other animals from using the fiberglass for nesting. After the joists are up, install the cover underneath, then the insulation (paper or foil side up), then the vapor barrier and then the plywood, being careful not to puncture the polyethylene.

One way to both waterproof the floor and add some heat storage mass is to pour a concrete slab on top. The slab offers the best surface for adhesion of tile or vinyl floor in a greenhouse with more than a few plants growing. Plywood directly under tiles or vinyl will absorb moisture that works its way through cracks in and around the flooring in these humid environments. The moist wood then expands and can let go of the mastic that holds the flooring. If you do use tiles or vinyl without a slab underneath, seal the plywood with a sealer compatible with the flooring mastic, and, if you use ceramic tiles, seal them

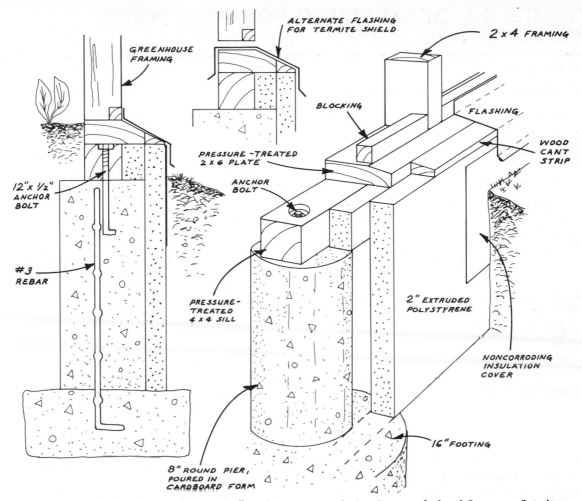

Figure 9-6: Piers with a sill at grade level offer a low-cost foundation for a grade-level floor on a flat site. The amount of wood that should be pressure treated for burial depends on your grade level and local termite conditions. If the earth is up to the plate, or you are in a heavy termite area, all of it should be pressure treated. Note that the framing sits on top of the 2 × 6 plate.

after they are in place to minimize the moisture penetrating the grout (mortar between the tiles). And pay particular attention to sealing between the floor drain and the surrounding tiles. Another approach to finishing the concrete is to simply color the slab with a concrete stain, or, for a smoother, more cleanable surface, paint it with an epoxy paint or resin.

Joist and beam sizing for a platform is shown in table 9-1, which assumes no heavy heat storage beyond a 4-inch slab is to be added to the floor but does account for some growing beds adjacent to the south wall. If you

TABLE 9-2: BEAM SIZING FOR PIER FOUNDATION WITH GRADE LEVEL SILL AND FLOOR ON GRADE

PIER SPACING (on centers)		4 FT	6 FT	8 FT	10 FT
Greenhouse (8 ft wide)	For Douglas fir #2	single 2 × 6	double 2 × 8	double 2 × 10	triple 2 × 10 or double 2 × 12
	For hemlock fir #2	single 2 × 8	double 2 × 8	double 2 × 10	triple 2 × 12
Greenhouse (10 ft wide)	For Douglas fir #2	single 2 × 8	double 2 × 8	double 2 × 10	triple 2 × 12
	For hemlock fir #2	single 2 × 8	triple 2 × 8	triple 2 × 10	triple 2 × 12

NOTES: *This table assumes stud-wall construction is used, so that the load of the greenhouse is more or less equally distributed across the beam and that the endwalls don't carry the load of the roof. If your framing is different from this, you should refigure the beam size. (Notice that these beams are smaller than those in table 9-1, since these don't carry a floor.)*

For Douglas fir #2, Fb = 1,261; for hemlock fir #2, Fb = 957. The values for nonrepetitive use are from Design Values for Wood Construction *by the National Forest Products Association. Fb (extreme fiber stress in bending) is a measure of the resistance to bending of a particular species and grade of wood.*

are going to add water containers, check with a structural engineer to size the joists, beams, piers and footings, and to check the house foundation where the platform attaches to it, so the structure will support the additional weight.

Pier Foundation with Ground-Level Sill

If the site is fairly flat, piers can be used with a sill directly on top, as shown in figure 9-6. The sill supports post-and-beam framing, with posts on top of the piers supporting load-bearing framing. The 4 × 4 sill is strong enough to support a vertical kneewall, as long as the load of the roof is carried by posts directly on top of the piers. If the sill is strengthened enough to act as a beam, it can support stud-wall-type framing. (Use table 9-2 to size the sill for use with stud-wall framing.) The insulation is attached to the outside of the sill, covering the concrete piers, and is supported mostly by the earth. This foundation type is not suitable for a site with much frost heaving, such as poorly drained clay soils in cold climates, since earth movement could crack the insulation.

Figure 9-6 shows the pier foundation with a pressure-treated wood sill at grade level. The sill should be pressure treated for direct burial, as should the bottom plate of the framing if ground-level growing beds have soil directly against the sill. With the 4-by-4 sill centered on the pier, a strip of foam insulation will fill the gap between the sill and the foam on the outside of the piers. A 2-by-6 plate on top of the sill covers the sill and the foam strip, and a cant strip (a beveled strip of wood) covers the top of the outer foam and supports the flashing. The cant strip can be replaced by extending the insulation higher and cutting it at an angle, but if thin flashing is used, the wood strip will make the whole assembly more durable. The blocking between the wall-framing studs gives a place to attach the flashing, as well as to nail on wall sheathing or attach the bottom of glazing. In areas where heavy termite infestation is common, the soil inside the greenhouse should be kept below the top of the sill, and the flashing can be extended to form a termite shield, as shown in figure 9-6.

If the site has much of a slope to the east or west, this type of foundation is awkward because too much of the pier and unsupported insulation is left above grade on the downhill side. It can be done with an insulation covering that lends some strength to the insulation, but piers with metal pipes may be more appropriate.

Pier Foundation with Pipe Supports

Galvanized metal pipes can be cast right into concrete piers, giving a thin yet strong support for a kneewall or sill. If the south glazing slopes directly down to the sill, the pipe ends in a flange underneath the sill, as shown in figure 9-7 and photo 9-5. If the glazing slopes down to a vertical kneewall, the

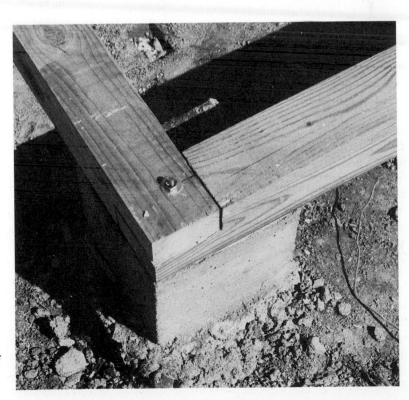

Photo 9-4: A pressure-treated wood beam spanning piers at ground level offers an effective, low-cost foundation, where soil conditions and local building codes permit. *(Photo courtesy of Rodale Press Photography Department.)*

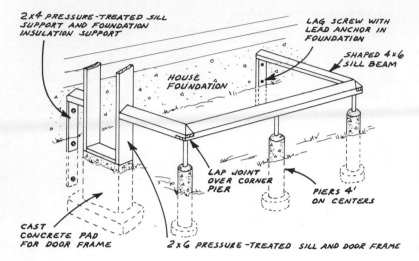

2x4 PRESSURE-TREATED SILL SUPPORT AND FOUNDATION INSULATION SUPPORT

LAG SCREW WITH LEAD ANCHOR IN FOUNDATION

SHAPED 4x6 SILL BEAM

HOUSE FOUNDATION

LAP JOINT OVER CORNER PIER

PIERS 4' ON CENTERS

CAST CONCRETE PAD FOR DOOR FRAME

2x6 PRESSURE-TREATED SILL AND DOOR FRAME

Figures 9-7 a and b (to the left and to the right): In the pier and pipe foundation, the foundation insulation runs between piers and is strong enough to retain a foot or so of depth of growing-bed soil inside above grade.

pipe can continue up through the sill to a flange under the eave, with the sill bolted onto the pipe. Extending the pipe this far not only minimizes the size of the kneewall framing members but also has a structural benefit. It gives the greenhouse the equivalent of diagonal bracing, with the pipe taking care of sideways forces. Where the sill hits the house, it bears on top of a pressure-treated 2×4 that is attached to the house foundation, with its outside edge even with the outside of the piers (see figure 9-7). This 2×4 supports the sill and provides an attachment point for the foundation insulation.

This illustration shows the piers with a stuccolike coating and metal lath covering the foam insulation. This gives enough rigidity to the foam to retain lightweight growing soil inside, a foot or so higher than the outside grade. The insulation is held against the metal pipes, rather than against the concrete piers, in order to fit underneath a 4-by-6 sill. The foam could be moved to the outside of the pier, but this would require flashing or a wider sill and wouldn't look as neat. Since the insulation doesn't cover the piers, they are a source of heat loss, unless pieces of foam are

placed below grade outside the piers, as shown in figure 9-7. In order to be able to insulate the piers in this way, the top of the piers should be below the outside grade level.

The construction sequence for these piers is as follows: Dig a trench for the insulation and dig holes for the footings in the bottom of the trench. Then pour footings for the piers. When the footings are dry, place the cardboard concrete forms in place, backfilling around them just enough to support them and/or brace them with scrap lumber. Then cut the pipes to length and drill a hole through them near the bottom, large enough for a ½-inch-diameter, 4-inch-long steel rod or bolt or rebar. This will keep the pipe from turning once the concrete is set. Put the rod through, screw the galvanized flanges (such as shown in photo 9-6) to the sill, put the pipes in the forms and attach the pipes to the flanges with the set screws. To assure the correct spacing and heights of the pipes, shim the pipes in the forms with rocks at the bottom as needed. The sills can be cut and installed to ensure their proper placement, as well as to set the distance of the south sill from the house. Make *sure* all is level and parallel to the house

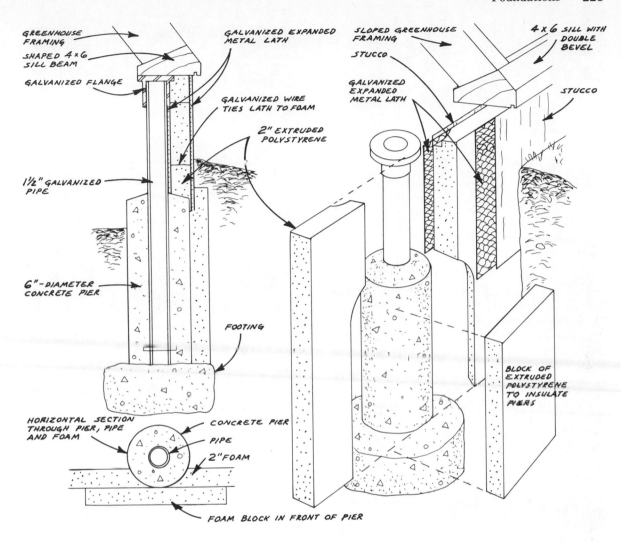

GREENHOUSE FRAMING

SHAPED 4 × 6 SILL BEAM

GALVANIZED FLANGE

GALVANIZED EXPANDED METAL LATH

SLOPED GREENHOUSE FRAMING

STUCCO

4 × 6 SILL WITH DOUBLE BEVEL

GALVANIZED EXPANDED METAL LATH

STUCCO

GALVANIZED WIRE TIES LATH TO FOAM

2" EXTRUDED POLYSTYRENE

1½" GALVANIZED PIPE

6"-DIAMETER CONCRETE PIER

FOOTING

BLOCK OF EXTRUDED POLYSTYRENE TO INSULATE PIERS

HORIZONTAL SECTION THROUGH PIER, PIPE AND FOAM

CONCRETE PIER

PIPE

2" FOAM

FOAM BLOCK IN FRONT OF PIER

and the rafter ledger, bracing the sill and pipes as needed. Then pour concrete, sloping the top of the piers away from the pipe to keep water from sitting there. The whole greenhouse can be built before the foundation is insulated, although this will require digging out dirt that falls into the trenches. When the piers are dry, soak the cardboard forms with water and tear them off before insulating. Another construction method is to cast the pipes into the piers *before* attaching the sills,

cutting them to length after the concrete is dry.

The insulation is cut to fit outside the pipes and set in place. Galvanized expanded metal lath is tied to both sides of the foam with galvanized wire, which is simply poked through the foam, twisted and laid flat. The outside lath is attached to the outside edge of the pressure-treated 2 × 4 that is bolted to the house foundation. It is important to use galvanized lath and wire, to avoid rusting, which

Photo 9-6: With a vertical kneewall, metal pipes (one is shown here) cast into piers can run right up under the eave, providing support as well as resistance to lateral movement with minimum blockage of light. *(Photo courtesy of Mark Ward.)*

Photo 9-5: The galvanized pipes cast into the piers support the sill beam, making an elegant, minimal foundation. The greenhouse was almost finished before the builder went back and insulated the foundation.

can weaken the stucco. Using a premixed stucco material (several are listed in Appendix 1), follow the manufacturer's instructions carefully. (It isn't worth the trouble and potential problems later to mix your own.) Some manufacturers recommend using their stucco directly on the foam, without reinforc-

ing mesh, scarring the surface of the foam for better adhesion. This may be adequate over foam that is glued to a continuous foundation, but reinforcing lath should be used when the insulation goes between piers. The lath will require a thicker application of stucco to cover it, to be sure the metal isn't left exposed anywhere. Any exposed areas will let water in, which will eventually freeze and break up the stucco. Another option is the fiberglass cloth reinforcing, discussed earlier, for continuous foundations, rather than galvanized metal. This avoids any possibility of eventual rusting of metal lath.

Since the foam expands and contracts more than the stucco coating, expansion joints should be installed at least every 10 feet along the foundation and where the foam meets the house foundation, to prevent the stucco from cracking. If the greenhouse is longer than 10 feet, put one expansion joint in the middle, over the pipe that is cast into the pier. When the foam is installed, leave ¼-inch to ⅜-inch gap between the sheets where the expansion joints will be and where the foam runs into the house. The lath should also have a gap at the same point. Mark where the joint is on the sill above the insulation and trowel the stucco over the joint. Then go back before the stucco is dry and open it up at that point. Alternatively, you can put a spacer of ¼- to ⅜-inch-thick material into the joint, and trowel up to it. Remove the spacer before the stucco is dry and neaten up the crack. When it's dry, put a foam backing rod in the crack and caulk it with silicone. Backfill gently, after the stucco has cured, to avoid damage.

Wood-Post Foundations

Wood posts offer an even simpler and less costly foundation than piers. Posts that have been pressure treated for burial are sunk into the ground, and the greenhouse is framed around them. While wood doesn't last forever, foundation-grade pressure-treated lumber is guaranteed for 20 years and is likely to last much longer. This foundation is best suited to a greenhouse with a vertical kneewall since the posts can simply be continued up through the kneewall, to support the eave. The posts can be cut off near the ground, if the sloped glazing will run right down to sill. Likewise, post-and-beam framing is naturally suggested, using the posts to support beams that carry the rafters and walls. However, stud-wall-type construction can be used by attach-

ing beams to the posts near grade level. (Use table 9-2 for sizing such beams, or table 9-1 if the beam will support a platform floor.) Since the posts run from below grade up to the eave, they resist the lateral forces of the wind, eliminating the need for diagonal bracing in shapes with a vertical kneewall. The insulation is only supported by the earth between the posts, so this system shouldn't be used where heavy frost heaves are encountered. Some local building codes won't permit this type of construction without a variance, but it is structurally sound. Pressure-treated wood continuous foundations, for example, are now approved by most codes.

The posts sit on a large rock or a cast concrete footing on the bottom, as shown in figure 9-8. In areas with frost heaving, a 12-inch steel rod or rebar can be put through the bottom of the post, with the post set into a concrete footing, to be sure the post won't pull up, as shown in figure 9-8. Sill support beams are bolted to the posts. Their sizes depend on the spacing between the posts; 2 × 4s would be used to span up to 4 feet, 2 × 6s would be used for spans of 4 to 6 feet; 2 × 8s for up to 8 feet, where the wall above only carries its own weight. For walls carrying the load of the roof, use table 9-2 for beam sizing. A double-beveled 2-by-6 sill is fastened to the top of the support beam. (The sill is notched to fit around the posts.) A 1 × 4 is nailed through the foam insulation to the backside of the beam to hold the foam in place. While the post must be pressure treated for foundation use (designated FDN), the sill, the sill support beam and the 1 × 4 can be standard lumber, unless they are in contact with the earth or if your location is prone to infestation by termites or carpenter ants. These pieces can be LP22 grade pressure treated if they are in contact with the soil, or LP2 if they are above grade but you want to protect against insects. If your budget is tight, but you want to protect against insects, you can treat the above-

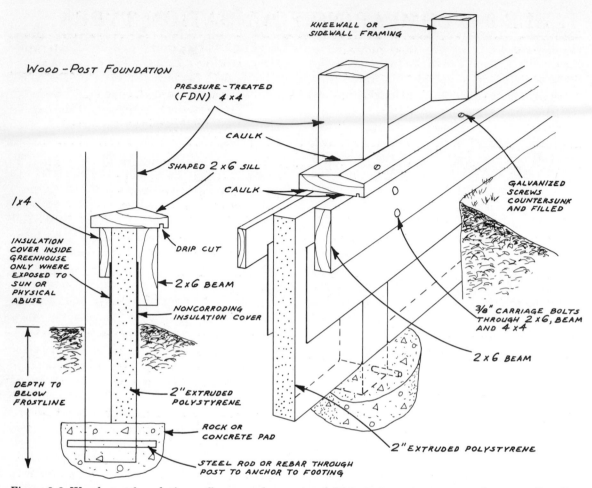

WOOD-POST FOUNDATION

KNEEWALL OR SIDEWALL FRAMING

PRESSURE-TREATED (FDN) 4 x 4

CAULK

SHAPED 2 x 6 SILL

CAULK

GALVANIZED SCREWS COUNTERSUNK AND FILLED

1 x 4

INSULATION COVER INSIDE GREENHOUSE ONLY WHERE EXPOSED TO SUN OR PHYSICAL ABUSE

DRIP CUT

2 x 6 BEAM

NONCORRODING INSULATION COVER

⅜" CARRIAGE BOLTS THROUGH 2 x 6, BEAM AND 4 x 4

2 x 6 BEAM

DEPTH TO BELOW FROSTLINE

2" EXTRUDED POLYSTYRENE

2" EXTRUDED POLYSTYRENE

ROCK OR CONCRETE PAD

STEEL ROD OR REBAR THROUGH POST TO ANCHOR TO FOOTING

Figure 9-8: Wood-post foundations offer a very low cost and fairly fast way to get a greenhouse up. Lumber that is pressure treated for burial in the ground (designated FDN) is guaranteed for 20 years and has been known to hold up for 30 years with no signs of degradation.

grade wood yourself with one of the treatments described in chapter 8. A rigid insulation covering, outside and on the inside where the insulation is exposed, is shown in figure 9-7, but the stucco like materials discussed earlier may also be used. If your site is fairly flat and you use lumber treated for burial below the sill, you can completely bury the insulation, eliminating the need for a covering material.

The construction sequence for this foundation is as follows: Dig post holes and a trench for the insulation. Put in a large rock with a flat side up, or, if the post will not be cast into the footing, pour a concrete pad in the bottom of the holes for a footing, and let it

TABLE 9-3: COMPARING FOUNDATION TYPES

FOUNDATION TYPE	APPLICATIONS*	ADVANTAGES/ DISADVANTAGES	RELATIVE COST
Continuous concrete	All soil types; all framing types	Strongest; meets all building codes; common construction technique; supports insulation	High
Continuous concrete block	All soil types; all framing types	Strong; meets all building codes; easy construction with surface bonding cement; supports insulation	High
Pier with platform	All soil types; stud-wall framing; good for hilly sites	Minimal earth work; floor needs good waterproofing	Medium
Pier with grade-level sill	Avoid soil with frost heaving; all framing types	Minimal concrete; moderate earth work; easy construction technique	Medium
Pier with pipe supports	Avoid soil with frost heaving; post-and-beam framing	Minimal concrete; moderate earth work; requires stucco foundation cover	Medium
Wood posts	Avoid soil with frost heaving; post-and-beam framing	No concrete work; moderate earth work; easy construction technique	Low

*The framing types shown for each foundation type are not hard and fast rules but are the types suggested by the structure of the foundation. Styles can be mixed, as indicated in the text.

cure before you proceed. Set the posts in the holes, with the uncut end of the posts down (if you had to cut them). Leave the posts long at the top, and trim them to their exact length when you are ready to frame the eave. Temporarily brace the posts with diagonal braces going to stakes in the ground, making sure they are plumb and that the spacing between them is correct. If you have some big clamps, clamp the sill support beam to the outside faces of all the posts. Without clamps you can tack the beams on with nails (don't use galvanized—they're too hard to remove). Fasten a joist or beam hanger to the house foundation where the beams meet the house and set these beams in place. With lag screws fasten the endwall beams to the joist hangers. Check the posts again to make sure they're plumb and level before drilling any holes. Check again. Then bolt all the sill support beams to the posts, using galvanized carriage bolts. If the posts are cast into the footings (as shown in figure 9-8) the footings are now poured around the posts and the assembly is left until the concrete is cured. Then bevel the sill and notch it to fit around the posts. Attach it to the sill support beam with galvanized wood-screws, or exterior glue (such as Resorcinol or epoxy) and galvanized finish nails. Counter-sink and fill the holes for either fastener, since this is an outside surface that will shed much rain. Depending on the strength of the wood you are using, supports may be needed for the places where the sill has been notched to go around the posts. A galvanized sheet-metal angle brace, such as is used in house framing, can be used. (These are available from build-ing supply dealers.)

Once this is done, you are ready to insu-late. Slightly loosen the bolts that hold the sill supports to the posts and slip the outer insu-lation cover in place. Tack it to the inside face of the sill support, and then retighten the bolts. Cut the foam and place it between the posts, tacking it in place if necessary. Where the insulation is exposed inside, tack up more insulation covering by simply pinning to the foam. Then nail the 1×4 in place to hold the top of the insulation and inside cover in place permanently. Backfill around the foam gently and backfill around the posts as forcefully as possible without damaging the insulation. Setting posts in the ground so they are firm is something of an art. Use the earth that came out of the hole, avoiding concentrations of gravel or sand, and any organic material such as sod or wood scraps that will rot and eventu-ally loosen up the post. Throw in one shovel-ful at a time, tamping each one *thoroughly* before adding the next. A small stick, like a 2×2, or an old cut-off shovel handle is best for tamping, since your force is spread over only a small area to better compact the earth. Be patient, since this takes a little while to do it right, but you will be satisfied with a sturdy post and a solid foundation.

From the various foundation possibili-ties, you have probably selected one or two that look good for your greenhouse, matching your design requirements as well as your con-struction skills and your budget. Foundations are one area where local knowledge is particu-larly useful, since soil composition and drain-age vary so much from place to place. So, if you are inexperienced in foundation work, check with a local builder, foundation con-tractor or your building inspector for advice before you finally settle on your design and begin to dig holes. In the next chapter, we'll take the next step up in the structure and look at various framing systems.

Chapter 10

FRAMING SYSTEMS

This chapter covers the framing of both the solid and glazed areas of the walls and roof. You'll find that some of the construction details and methods are similar to those used in standard house construction, while others are more specifically adapted to the need for maximum light and moisture protection in a greenhouse. If the structure is going to be used primarily as a nonhorticultural sunspace, with little or no plant growing, moisture protection may still be important, because what starts out as a sunspace sometimes turns into a plant-filled greenhouse. Several framing styles for glazed areas are also presented, along with guidelines for rafter sizing and bracing the structure for rigidity.

The solid portions of a greenhouse can be treated similarly to the solid walls of a house, with the exception that moisture control must be dealt with more carefully. Greater care must be taken to keep moisture out of wall and roof cavities, and greater attention has to be paid to venting out the moisture that inevitably gets in. Ignoring the problem can quickly result in soaking wet insulation, which loses its insulative value and can cause

rotting of the framing wood. There are several approaches you can take to prevent moisture problems. The first and easiest, for most builders, is to install a continuous vapor barrier and provide for exterior venting of the insulation. A second approach is to use a nonabsorbent insulation, such as extruded polystyrene, but a vapor barrier and venting are still required to ensure that the framing wood is kept relatively dry.

A third approach is to use prefabricated foam-core or *stress-skin* panels, made by actually pouring liquid foam between the outer skins and letting it foam up in place or by laminating the skins onto foam boards. These panels provide both insulation and structure. A vapor-barrier interior paint should be used with these panels to keep moisture from penetrating into the foam, particularly if the foam is a type that absorbs water. Stress-skin panels are usually splined together with 2 × 4s, which can represent a moisture problem. Since the 2 × 4 is used like a stud, it presents a pathway for heat loss because it acts as a thermal bridge from the inside to the outside. In cold climates, the inside surface of the panels just over the spline can be cold enough to be below the dew point, causing condensation to form. Standard framing can also be a thermal bridge but the condensation problem is taken care of by the polyethylene vapor barrier. With the panels there is no vapor barrier, and condensation can soak into the 2-by-4 spline, where there is a potential for wood rot. Using a pressure-treated spline will prevent rotting, but the panel joint itself should also be sealed. If the inner skin of the panel is drywall, this isn't possible, since the joint will have to be taped and spackled, and joint compound is very porous. But if the inside is *oriented-strand* plywood or other rigid sheet material, the seam can be caulked. In either case, you should also use a vapor-resistant primer and paint to further resist the vapor migration. It's also possible to use a polyethylene vapor barrier over the inside surface of the panels, and then cover this with drywall.

Some greenhouse manufacturers use the foam panel approach to solid walls, since these panels are well adapted to factory production. They also eliminate the job of installing a vapor barrier when the greenhouse is erected.

Prefab panels represent a rather different style of construction. When formed with a structural skin, such as particle board or oriented-strand board, on both sides, they are quite strong and can take the place of much of the solid wall and roof framing and can even be used for platform floors. Their use substitutes factory labor for site labor, decreasing construction labor while increasing material costs. If your labor costs are high and you want to investigate this type of construction, check around for local panel manufacturers. They will probably be able to assist you with construction tips.

We will deal with the first approach, standard wall construction with extra attention to vapor barriers and venting. The use of rigid foam insulation instead of fiberglass between the studs or rafters doesn't really change the construction process, since the foam can be substituted where fiberglass is indicated.

Whatever style you use, be sure that the interior sheathing is moisture resistant. It should be as moisture resistant as outside sheathing, to withstand the high humidity you'll have if you grow many plants. If you use plywood, use an exterior grade or MDO board (*medium-density-overlay* plywood). MDO has a paper-covered surface that looks like drywall but is actually much more durable than exterior plywood. If you use drywall, use the moisture-resistant type that is used in bathrooms. After the sheathing is up, paint on a vapor-resistant primer, such as alkyd resin primer or latex vapor-barrier primer. The resin primer is preferred for wood sheathings, since it has greater adhesion. Pay attention to painting any exposed edges of sheathings, since they are particularly susceptible to water. All caulking should be done after the sheathing is primed. Caulk all joints and edges, let the caulk cure and then put on the finish coats of paint. Use only galvanized nails or screws.

There is also a variety of inexpensive prefinished paneling materials available that are more or less water resistant, such as Masonite with a glossy enamel-type finish that is sometimes used in refinishing bathrooms. These can be used for interior sheathing and are even available with joint and corner moldings, but you should expect to replace or paint them after a few years. Normal interior wood plywood paneling can be expected to delaminate quickly in a plant-growing environment and shouldn't be used.

Solid Walls

The sequence for putting up the endwalls depends on how you frame for the glazing. If the glazing rafters are supported on a beam that rests on the endwalls, the endwalls are usually built first, either on the ground and then titled up or built in place. The beam is then put in place and the glazing framing built onto that. If the glazing is supported by preformed trusses or post-and-beam framing (described later in this chapter), the rafters are usually put up first, and then the endwalls are built.

The best way to avoid moisture problems in solid walls depends on the exterior sheathing you use. If you are going to use plywood for rough sheathing covered with siding or prefinished textured plywood sheathing, some extra attention needs to be paid to ventilation, since these sheathings are rather impermeable to water vapor and can trap

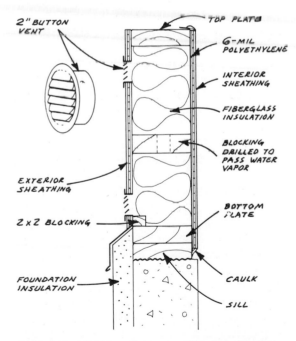

Figure 10-1: Stud-wall construction is quite similar to house wall construction, with extra attention paid to vapor barriers and venting. If the exterior sheathing is plywood or other impermeable material, button vents are needed.

moisture that works its way through the wall, causing the vapor to condense on the inside of the sheathing. With these sheathings, the easiest way to ventilate the stud-wall cavity to the outside is with 2-inch-diameter button vents. They may look a little odd, but they look a lot better than a rotten wall several years later. They are glued in place with a little silicone or butyl caulking. If the top of the stud wall is below an insulated roof area, holes can be drilled in the top plate of the wall to allow moisture to vent into the roof insulation and out through the roof insulation vents. Be sure passageways are continuous, with holes drilled in any stud-wall blocking. Since the button vents admit outside air into the insulation, the insulation value of the wall is degraded somewhat, though not enough to seriously affect performance if the wall insulation is well fitted to each stud cavity and the interior vapor barrier is continuous.

If the exterior sheathing is separate boards, rather than plywood, the cracks in between the boards provide enough ventilation. A porous finish siding, such as wood shingles, boards and battens or clapboards that are stained rather than painted, should be used on top of the sheathing. Tyvek, a vapor-permeable, air-infiltration barrier, can be used between the sheathing and the siding to cut down infiltration while still allowing vapor to escape. This type of exterior wall (wood-board sheathing, Tyvek, and permeable, solid wood siding) is recommended over plywood sheathing and siding, but the plywood is acceptable as long as it is properly vented.

Putting the insulation in the walls and roof has to wait until the structure is closed in, with glazing, wall sheathing and roof in place, to avoid getting the insulation wet. Cut and place the insulation carefully to completely fill each cavity. One square foot of uninsulated area in a 20-square-foot wall that is everywhere else R-20 has the effect of reducing the insulation value of the whole wall to R-14.

Make every effort to be sure the vapor barrier on the inside is continuous. Use a 6-mil rather than a 4-mil polyethylene so that it will resist the inevitable bumps and pokes it will get. Wait to put it up until most of the moving of big pieces of material is over and you're ready to sheath over the barrier right away. When you put it up, use pieces that are much larger than needed, so you can overlap any seams over a solid piece of framing, and trim it later. Leave the vapor barrier loose in the corners, to avoid a situation where there isn't enough room to get the sheathing into the corner without tearing the poly. Run the barrier over window or door openings, cut an "X" from the corners of the opening, fold the polyethylene around all four sides and staple it to the rough framing. Patch the gaps that are left with poly, taping or caulking where the patches overlap. And patch any joints or holes in the rest of the poly with 2-inch-wide polyethylene tape made for this purpose. (3M is one manufacturer.) Also, use spray-in-place foam around window and door frames in solid walls to minimize infiltration. You should also run the poly long over the sill on the foundation and trim it back after the interior sheathing is in place. It is best to avoid electrical wiring inside any wall except the common wall, since the switches or outlets are almost a sure leak in the vapor barrier. Wiring should be run on the surface, with either conduit or a better-looking raceway system, such as Wiremold. These systems are available from local electrical supply houses.

Solid Roofs

Solid roof areas need the same attention to moisture control as do the walls. If the insulation goes between the roof rafters, as shown in figure 10-2, a modified ridge vent

can be used to provide both flashing and venting for the insulation where the roof meets the house. The sheathing is held back a little from the house to provide the air passage. ("Half-ridge" vents are now being produced for this purpose—check your building supply dealer.) Two-inch button vents can be used at the top of the endwalls to serve as inlet vents to the lower end of the solid roof. Several 1-inch holes drilled in each rafter allow air to move between them. Both the button vents and the rafter holes should be located just under the roof sheathing, rather than down near the interior sheathing. If the size of the rafters allows a gap between the top of the roof insulation and the sheathing, this will improve air movement for ventilation, and the holes should be in this area. For small roofs, putting button vents at both the top and bottom ends of the solid roof area will be sufficient as long as you have no holes in your vapor barrier.

Another approach to venting the roof insulation is to drop the ceiling inside to make it horizontal and insulate this ceiling rather than the roof. This gives a triangular area in the endwalls above the insulation where a vent can be placed. This approach is preferred in areas where snow cover sits on roofs all winter and would cover a half-ridge vent.

Connecting to the House

Where the endwalls connect to the house, the house siding must be cut away to get a weathertight connection, as shown in figure 10-3 and photo 10-1. This is fairly easy to do, marking with a chalk line and cutting with a circular saw set to the depth of the siding. (Use an old blade, since you're bound to run into at least one nail.) The gap should be wide enough for the last stud of the endwall, the sheathing and an exterior corner trim board.

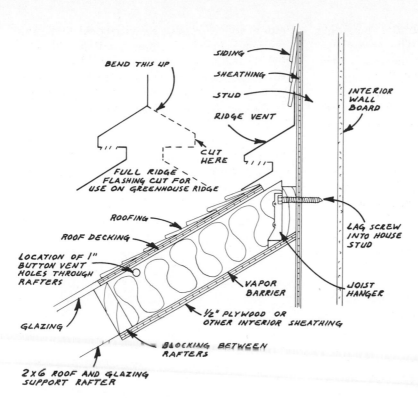

BEND THIS UP

SIDING

SHEATHING

STUD

RIDGE VENT

INTERIOR WALL BOARD

CUT HERE

FULL RIDGE FLASHING CUT FOR USE ON GREENHOUSE RIDGE

ROOFING

ROOF DECKING

LOCATION OF 1" BUTTON VENT HOLES THROUGH RAFTERS

LAG SCREW INTO HOUSE STUD

VAPOR BARRIER

JOIST HANGER

GLAZING

½" PLYWOOD OR OTHER INTERIOR SHEATHING

BLOCKING BETWEEN RAFTERS

2 X 6 ROOF AND GLAZING SUPPORT RAFTER

Figure 10-2: A commercially available ridge vent can be cut in half to be a suitable roof vent at the ridge, along with button vents in the top of the endwall at the lower end of the solid roof. Half-ridge vents are also commercially available.

It can be done without the trim board, but it's a little difficult to get some kinds of siding, like clapboards, to seal very tightly at an inside corner. The stud is fastened to the house with either lag screws or toggle bolts, depending on what the wall is made of. If the wall is masonry, a lead shield is used to anchor a lag screw in the masonry. Remember to use pressure-treated wood for any pieces that contact masonry. If the wall is wood frame, you'll be lucky if the endwall stud is over a wall stud (chances are it won't be) because you can simply lag the endwall stud to the house's stud. If the endwall attaches between house studs, you can use toggle bolts above the house sill and use a lag screw into the sill.

The roof hangs on a ledger that is lag screwed into the studs of the house. The siding is cut away above the ledger to get the

Photo 10-1: The siding has been cut away and two ledgers installed. The top one will carry the rafters and the lower one will support kneebraces. The home-made scaffolding, while a bit heavy to move, made the high up work much easier and safer.

greenhouse roof flashing up under the siding and just enough below for the greenhouse ceiling sheathing. Using joist hangers for the rafters allows the ledger to be concealed inside the greenhouse roof. Attention should be paid to making the connection between the house and the ledger strong, since it will carry half the roof load. In most situations, the ledger can be lag screwed to the studs in the common wall, using two lag screws into each stud to ensure a strong connection. In some older houses, though, with post-and-beam framing, the ledger may not line up with a beam, or in houses with insufficient framing, such as those built as vacation homes, there may not be any studs for attaching the ledger. In these cases, some other approach is necessary. The ledger can be designed as a beam, carrying the roof load to existing posts in the common wall or to posts in the greenhouse endwalls. Consult a structural engineer in such situations.

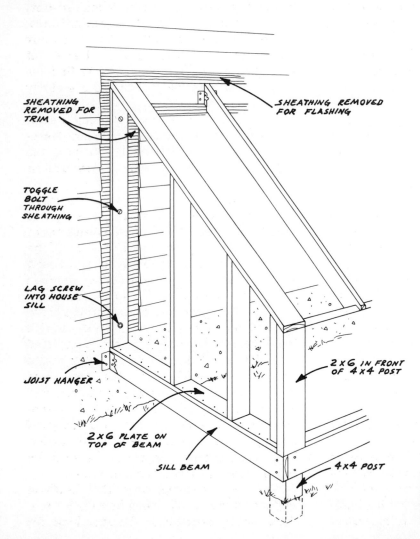

SHEATHING REMOVED FOR TRIM

SHEATHING REMOVED FOR FLASHING

TOGGLE BOLT THROUGH SHEATHING

LAG SCREW INTO HOUSE SILL

JOIST HANGER

2x6 PLATE ON TOP OF BEAM

SILL BEAM

2x6 IN FRONT OF 4x4 POST

4x4 POST

Figure 10-3: Stud walls on a post foundation span the distance between the posts, or between posts and the house, resting on a beam between the posts.

Building the Frame

In this section we'll explore several types of framing systems with drawings of the complete greenhouse frame, construction details of the connecting points and descriptions of the construction process. You'll be able to compare stud-wall framing with post-and-beam framing with preformed truss framing to see which best meets your requirements and preferences. Rafter sizing is also discussed, with a table (10-1) that shows the maximum distance different rafter sizes can span. But before going into the specifics of these framing systems, a few general comments are needed about the illustrations of the various systems and about beam supports, tying the whole structure down and diagonal bracing.

The illustrations of the framing styles (figures 10-6 through 10-9) are not drawn to scale or to represent a particular size, since the appropriate size is something you will determine. Each framing system can be used for a large or small greenhouse. The dimensions of the rafters are a function of the distance they span and the glazing material you use. The type of glazing will also determine how much and what size blocking is needed. The various framing techniques shown are, of course, not restricted to the greenhouse cross sections they depict. Any of the framing styles can be used with any of the shapes (with the exception of the curved laminated arches). The descriptions of how each framing system goes up contain tips to make the process easier. Some of these tips are applicable to all the framing systems, so it's a good idea to read about the others even after you've chosen a system you'll use.

If you need a supporting crossbeam to go across the middle of the rafters, as is shown in the post-and-beam framing (figure 10-8), supporting that beam in the center (with a kneebrace) will greatly reduce the required size of the beam. The kneebrace runs back to the common wall and thus leaves the floor space free of posts. A post to the floor would mean splitting a night insulation curtain, making it more difficult to build and seal tightly. If the greenhouse roof is only partially glazed, placing the support under the junction of the glazed and solid areas leaves the glazed area free of obstructions, even if the support runs down to the floor.

Rafters that are securely tied to the house and the greenhouse eave are important for making a sturdy structure. Wind can exert even more upward lift than downward pressure on a roof, so the rafters should not only bear down on the ledger plate and eave, but they should be *fastened* down. Nailing the rafters into joist hangers that are securely fastened to the ledger with screws gives the necessary strength. Toenails are usually sufficient to fasten the rafters at the eave. Kneebraces should also be fastened to hold the rafters down as well as support them against downward loads.

As was previously discussed, bracing is required to support the structure against wind from the sides. If the house forms one of the endwalls, it will fulfill this function. If the kneewall or part of the roof is solid, plywood sheathing on these areas generally provides sufficient bracing. If a post-type foundation is used, the posts provide sufficient resistance to side forces, as long as the posts are buried fairly deep and the soil is well compacted around them. If the greenhouse has only a single plane extending from the house down to the foundation, no bracing is required. But if both endwalls are exposed and the greenhouse has little or no solid area, diagonal bracing will give needed strength and rigidity. By bracing only the kneewall, there will be enough rigidity for the whole structure.

In house framing, when the sheathing isn't structural, a solid wood brace is cut into the framing, underneath the sheathing, for

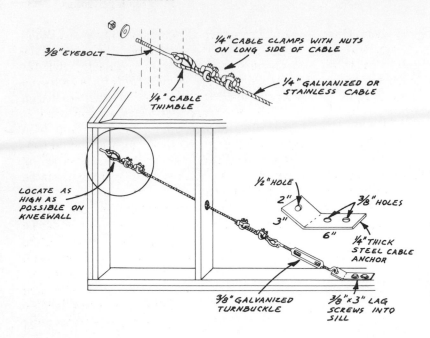

Figure 10-4: A cable makes a very strong yet very "transparent" diagonal brace. The turnbuckle allows you to square and tighten up the frame before the sheathing or glazing go on. Galvanized or stainless cable and fittings are used.

diagonal bracing. This could be done under greenhouse glazing, but it would commit the sin of cutting out sunlight. A pair of cable braces is a fairly easy and much more "transparent" way to brace a kneewall. Figure 10-4 shows an installed cable brace on a vertical kneewall. The same technique can be used with sloped areas, where needed. The cable and fittings should be galvanized steel or treated with some other nonrusting finish. The steel cable anchors can be fabricated from scrap steel, which may as well be uncoated steel, since you will have to paint the anchors anyway after you bend them and drill the holes. Use a good quality rustproofing primer and two coats of enamel on the anchors, and use washers under the lag screws and bolts to keep from tearing up the paint. There are new water-based, acrylic, rustproofing paints, such as Rustocrylic by Rustoleum, that are strong and easy to use.

After the framing is up, the upper anchor is bolted through the end of the kneewall, as high as possible, and the lower anchor is lag

screwed into the sole plate and the sill, at about an equal distance from the corner as the upper anchor. Large washers are used on the outside of the through bolts to distribute the stress over a larger area of the wood. Countersink the washers and nuts into the wood and cut off any excess bolt that sticks out so the trim can cover it. Install the anchors and assemble the cables, thimbles, turnbuckle and clamps, with the turnbuckle extended as far as possible. The thimbles are an absolute necessity, since they keep the cable from making too sharp a turn, which would unevenly stress the wire strands and weaken the cable. Once everything is in place, take up the slack on both braces, but don't tighten them yet. Finish any details on the framing, especially any blocking for the glazing, square the glazing openings and check the endwalls to see if they are plumb. Then the turnbuckles can be used to help square up the whole frame, by tightening one brace or the other. This will allow you to square up the frame as much as possible and let you know if some of your rafter blocking is too long or too short. Once the frame is as square as you can make it tighten both turnbuckles equally a small amount, about one full turn, to finally tighten everything and make the frame quite rigid.

Rafter Sizing

There are a number of factors that affect the sizing of your rafters: the amount of snow loading, the highest wind speeds, the slope and weight of the roofing and glazing materials, the distance that the rafters will span and the type of wood you use. Building codes prescribe the size of rafters that must be used for various situations, taking local climate conditions into consideration, so it's a good idea to check with your local building inspector before picking a size from the guide-lines presented here.

As was previously discussed, the loads on the roof are divided into live and dead loads, a live load being primarily wind and snow, and a dead load being the weight of the rafter and whatever lies on it, whether this is glazing or roofing plus insulation and sheathing. Insulated, sheathed roofs with asphalt shingles have a constant dead load of about 10 pounds per square foot (including the weight of the rafters); roofs glazed with two layers of $\frac{3}{16}$-inch glass weigh about 4 pounds per square foot, and plastic-glazed roofs are from 1 to 3 pounds per square foot. Live loads vary quite a bit. The maximum amount of snow that piles up on the roof of the greenhouse depends on climate and the slope of the roof. (Snow will usually slide off glazing with a slope greater than 30 degrees but can stick to considerably steeper shingled roofs.) Wind speed depends somewhat on climate but more on the exposure of your location. Sheltering trees can cut the wind loads considerably, whereas fully exposed surfaces can experience very high wind loads. Maximum snow and wind

loads very rarely occur simultaneously: When it's very windy, the snow usually blows off the roof. Structural engineers, though, plan for the worst, so if your climate is snowy and you have a shallow-sloped roof, it is wise to design for the combined loads of snow and wind. If your house roof dumps snow on top of a low-sloping greenhouse roof, you should consult a structural engineer before proceeding with rafter sizing, since the extra load can be quite significant.

In general, the following total loads, which include both live and dead loads, can be used for preliminary sizing of rafters. But be sure to check with a structural engineer, architect, or your local building inspector before using the loads indicated here for final sizing. (Note that these loads don't include the weight of any large plants or shelves hung from the rafters.)

• Glazed areas very sheltered from the wind with no snow load, either because the climate is too warm for snow or the roof is too steep for snow to accumulate: 35 pounds per square foot

• Areas of normal winds and normal snow loads, including glazed and solid roof areas: 45 pounds per square foot

• Areas of high winds *or* heavy snow load on a shallow slope, including solid and glazed roof areas: 60 pounds per square foot

• High winds *and* heavy snow, or where the house can dump snow on the greenhouse: loads can be quite high; consult a structural engineer

Table 10-1 shows the maximum recommended span for rafters of different sizes and different materials at different spacings. *Span* is defined as the horizontal distance that a rafter covers, from the center of the support on one side to the center of the support on the other, as shown in figure 10-5. The spacings are on center measurements, that is, the distance from the center of one rafter edge to the center of the next. Allow-

TABLE 10-1: RECOMMENDED SPANS FOR RAFTERS

RAFTER SPACING (on centers)	TOTAL LOAD (psf*)	2 × 3 (actual size: 1½" by 2½")	2 × 4 (actual size: 1½" by 3½")	2 × 6 (actual size: 1½" by 5½")	DOUBLE 2 × 6 (actual size: 3" by 5½")	4 × 6 (actual size: 3½" by 5½")	4 × 8 (actual size: 3½" by 7½")
24"	35	4' 7"	6' 6"	9' 6"	13' 5"		
	45	4' 1"	5' 8"	8' 4"	11' 10"		
	60	3' 6"	4' 11"	7' 3"	10' 3"		
36"	35	3' 9"	5' 4"	7' 9"	10' 11"	11' 10"	16' 1"
	45	3' 4"	4' 8"	7' 0"	9' 8"	10' 5"	14' 2"
	60	2' 7"	3' 8"	5' 11"	8' 4"	9' 0"	12' 3"
48"	35		4' 7"	6' 8"	9' 5"	10' 2"	13' 11"
	45		3' 8"	5' 11"	8' 4"	9' 0"	12' 4"
	60		2' 9"	4' 4"	7' 3"	7' 10"	10' 8"

NOTES: *The maximum allowable spans shown apply to Douglas fir or larch #2. (1) The table may be used for other species and grades of wood by adjusting the spans as follows:*

For the following grades and species the span may be increased by the following percentages:

Douglas fir or larch, select structural: increase 20% (2)
Douglas fir or larch, #1: increase 10% (3)
Southern pine, select structural: increase 18% (4)
Southern pine, #1: increase 7% (5)
California redwood, clear select structural: increase 36% (6)
California redwood, select structural: increase 18% (7)
California redwood, #1: increase 9% (8)
Western cedar, select structural: increase 2% (9)

For the following grades and species the span may be decreased by the following percentages:

Southern pine, #2: decrease 2% (10)
California redwood, #2: decrease 2% (11)
Western cedar, #1: decrease 6% (12)
Western cedar, #2: decrease 14% (13)
Hemlock or fir, #1: decrease 2% (14)
Hemlock or fir, #2: decrease 11% (15)
Spruce, #1: decrease 9% (16)
Spruce, #2: decrease 16% (17)

The numbers that follow in parentheses refer to the numbers above in this note. (1) Based on Fb (extreme fiber stress in bending) of 1,250 psi and E (modulus of elasticity, which is a measure of how springy or how brittle a piece of wood is) of 1,700,000 for 2 × 6 and up; Fb = 1,450 for 2 × 4 and 2 × 3. (2) Fb = 1,800. (3) Fb = 1,500. (4) Fb = 1,750. (5) Fb = 1,450. (6) Fb = 2,300. (7) Fb = 1,750. (8) Fb = 1,500. (9) Fb = 1,300. (10) Fb = 1,200. (11) Fb = 1,200. (12) Fb = 1,100. (13) Fb = 925. (14) Fb = 1,200. (15) Fb = 1,000. (16) Fb = 1,050. (17) Fb = 875. Fb and E values are based on Design Values for Wood Construction *by the National Forest Products Association.*

*Pounds per square foot.

able span depends on the inherent strength of the species of wood (Douglas fir #2 is stronger than redwood #2) and the quality of the pieces of wood that you are working with (big knots weaken wood considerably). Various types of wood are included in table 10-1, with gradings that are standard in the lumber industry. Be sure you are using the grade specified, or you should adjust the allowable span accordingly. Note that if you want to span a distance a little longer than the one listed for the size of lumber you want to use, which allows a 20 percent longer span, which just covers 10 feet. Or you could use a knee-brace, as shown later in figure 10-9, to effectively shorten the span. On 36-inch centers, only a 7-foot span is allowed for the 2 × 6 Douglas fir #2. Going to select structural grade of the same wood allows a span of 8 feet 5 inches, requiring a kneebrace to span the desired 10 feet. Another option would be to use double 2 × 6s of Douglas fir #2, which would allow a 9-foot-8-inch span.

Another way to use table 10-1 is to decide on the size rafter you want, and then find the lumber type and size that will work. For example, if you want to use 2-by-3 rafters on 24-inch centers, with a maximum load of 45 psf, a 4-foot-1-inch span is the maximum allowed with Douglas fir #2, and 4 feet 9 inches is allowed with select structural. Using the rafters with a central pipe beam to break the span in half, as shown in figure 10-8, the 2 × 3s could cover 8 feet with the #2 grade, or 10 feet 6 inches with the select structural grade.

Glazing support rafters at slopes of 45 degrees and steeper, up to vertical, are treated a little differently, since the strongest force on them is the wind. The *vertical height* (see figure 10-5) of the rafter, rather than the horizontal span, is used with the sizing table, as long as the rafters don't support the roof. Since maximum wind load is usually 40 psf, use the 45 psf listings, unless your greenhouse is exposed to extremely high winds, in which case use the 60 psf figures, or the 35 psf load if the site is well sheltered. For example, Douglas fir #2 medium grade 2 × 6s on 36-inch centers can have a maximum height of 7 feet in a location with average shielding from the wind.

If the vertical or near-vertical glazing supports also carry the roof, as shown in figure 10-6, the situation is again different. This is because the glazing supports act as columns as well as working against a wind

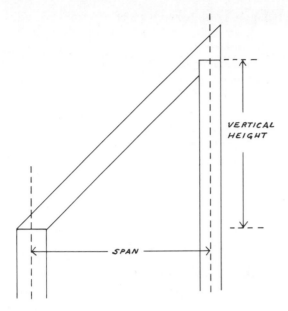

Figure 10-5: The *span* of a rafter is the horizontal distance between the midpoints of the rafter's supports. This is the measurement that is used in sizing rafters. *Vertical height* is used in sizing vertical and near-vertical glazing supports.

you can go to a higher grade lumber rather than a larger dimension. Tighter, straighter grain and fewer knots are what make higher-grade wood stronger, and using a better grade may not amount to a significant increase in the total cost of the greenhouse. It's also more satisfying to work with better wood, and it's easier to paint. (Table 10-1 shows the percent increase in span that the higher grades allow.) The higher grades, "select" and "clear select," are often difficult to find, and you may have to look in larger lumber yards or specialty yards that deal in high-quality wood.

For example, 2 × 6 Douglas fir #2 on 24-inch centers can span a distance of 8 feet 4 inches under a 45 pounds per square foot (psf) maximum load. If your design calls for a span of 10 feet you could use stronger lumber, such as select structural grade 2 × 6 Douglas fir, load. When framing a stud-wall system, as in figure 10-6, Douglas fir #2, (or equivalent) 2 × 4s on 24-inch centers with blocking in the middle can be used, as long as the length is not more than 8 feet. The blocking keeps the 2 × 4s from bending sideways under the load of the roof and helps distribute wind loads to all the vertical supports. Many plastic glazings require this blocking for support anyway, but with glass, it's better to strengthen the framing to avoid blocking behind the glass.

Greenhouse builders sometimes stretch the structural limits of lumber, in order to decrease shading inside the greenhouse. The span limits in table 10-1 are designed to limit "deflection," or bowing, of the wood under the maximum loads. If you are using fiberglass or polyethylene glazings, which aren't adversely affected by some bowing of the framing, you can stretch the spans somewhat. The greenhouse shown in figure 10-6 can be built with 2 × 4s on 47-inch or 48-inch centers on a steep slope when it is glazed with fiberglass or polyethylene. It isn't a good idea, though, to stretch the limits on shallower slopes, where snow buildup can create heavy loads, or for rafters that support double glass, whose seal can be broken by too much deflection. Before building, check the grade, size and spacing of your rafters with your local building inspector, who can help design for local conditions or can refer you to a structural engineer.

Stud-Wall Framing

Stud-wall framing is probably the easiest and most straightforward construction style.

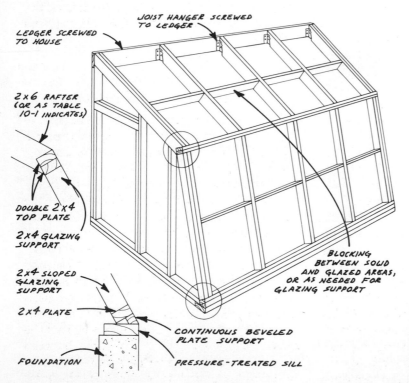

LEDGER SCREWED TO HOUSE

JOIST HANGER SCREWED TO LEDGER

2 x 6 RAFTER (OR AS TABLE 10-1 INDICATES)

DOUBLE 2 x 4 TOP PLATE

2 x 4 GLAZING SUPPORT

2 x 4 SLOPED GLAZING SUPPORT

2 x 4 PLATE

FOUNDATION

CONTINUOUS BEVELED PLATE SUPPORT

PRESSURE-TREATED SILL

BLOCKING BETWEEN SOLID AND GLAZED AREAS, OR AS NEEDED FOR GLAZING SUPPORT

Figure 10-6: Stud-wall framing is one of the simplest and easiest ways to put up a greenhouse. The technique is identical to standard house framing, except that, as shown here, the front wall is often tilted. The simplicity and familiarity of the technique make it a favorite for greenhouse "barn raisings."

A stud-wall frame doesn't require a high degree of carpentry skill, and it can go up quickly. The shape in figure 10-6 was developed and popularized by the Solar Sustenance Project, created by Bill and Susan Yanda and the New Mexico Solar Energy Association (NMSEA), which held barn-raising workshops to build many greenhouses around the United States. (The NMSEA publishes a set of plans for building this greenhouse design, with step-by-step instructions intended to help the novice builder. See Appendix 2.)

The sloped south face of the greenhouse is made of 2 × 4s (as long as they are under 8 feet long), and the roof is usually framed with 2 × 4s or 2 × 6s, again depending on the span. The rafters bear directly on the front glazing supports, eliminating the need for a strong horizontal member at the eave. The greenhouse is built on a continuous foundation, and if the front glazing supports are made to be vertical, the framing is identical to standard house framing. Both the rafters and the glazing supports are often spaced 24 inches on centers to accept 48-inch-wide plastic glazings, but the spacing can be varied to accept other glazing widths. If the rafters need to be closer together than the front supports to support the load of the roof, the double 2-by-4 top plate (which forms the eave) on the front wall (as shown in figure 10-6) will be sufficient to carry the load as long as the glazing supports aren't more than 24 inches apart. If the glazing supports are spaced wider than this, the modified stud-wall-type framing should be used (figure 10-7).

The actual framing is quite straightforward. After the foundation is finished, the sill is installed, the house wall (common wall) is prepared to receive the endwalls and the ledger is put in place. You can save yourself some work up on a ladder by putting the joist hangers on the ledger on the ground, but be careful to mark the ledger with the locations

for the lag screws that will hold the ledger to the house. If a hanger and a lag screw are both at the same place, you can leave off that hanger until the lag screw is installed. To make the ledger parallel to the sill on the south foundation wall, it may need shimming out from the house. You can also achieve this by slightly skewing the sill on the foundation. The front glazing wall is built on the ground and then tilted up in place, on top of a beveled plate support that rests on the sill (see figure 10-6). The wall is then braced in place with temporary supports. The roof rafters are then cut and put in place, and the blocking installed. Rather than mass-producing all your blocking, cut each one individually to help square up the glazing openings. Solid roof areas are a good place to make up for small errors because roofing materials can be cut to size. Glazing that comes in fixed sizes is, of course, less forgiving. Framing the endwalls is a matter of filling in the holes left on the ends, framing openings for doors, glazing, fans and vents as needed.

Modified Stud-Wall Framing

In order to reduce the size and number of the glazing supports, a roof support beam can be put in. The beam carries part of the roof load as well as part of the load from the lower glazing supports. The example shown in figure 10-7 is intended for a solid roof above the beam and a glazed vertical kneewall below the sloped glazing, but the same framing system can be adapted to a variety of cross sections.

The horizontal ceiling under the solid roof provides an easy place to install an insulation vent in the endwall. This doesn't allow for roof vents for the greenhouse, so provisions for greenhouse exhaust venting must be made in the endwalls. (The cavity between the ceiling and the roof also provides a nice location for a batch-type solar water heater if

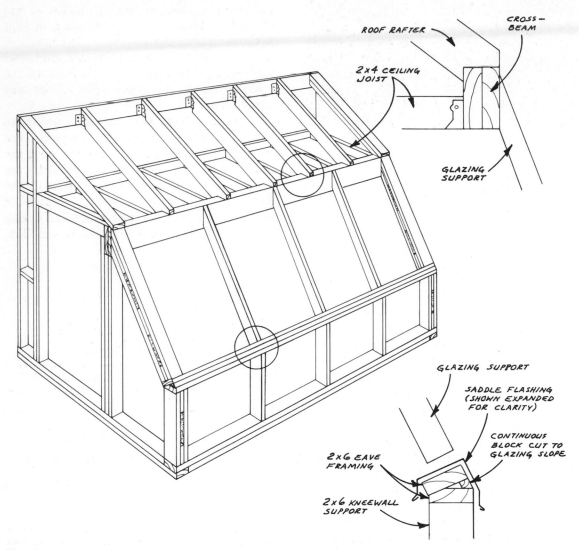

ROOF RAFTER

CROSS—
BEAM

2x4 CEILING
JOIST

GLAZING
SUPPORT

GLAZING SUPPORT

SADDLE FLASHING
(SHOWN EXPANDED
FOR CLARITY)

CONTINUOUS
BLOCK CUT TO
GLAZING SLOPE

2x6 EAVE
FRAMING

2x6 KNEEWALL
SUPPORT

Figure 10-7: This modified stud-wall framing uses a crossbeam to carry the solid roof rafters and to pick up the glazing supports, allowing these members to be smaller and/or farther apart than if they were the only support for the roof. This framing technique is easily adaptable to other cross sections and combinations of glazed and solid areas. The horizontal 2×4s running from the beam to the house are used to carry ceiling insulation. An insulation vent can then be located in the upper part of an endwall. With this design the roof can't be used for greenhouse vents. The example shown is after the style used by Jeremy Coleman in numerous greenhouses, and complete plans for a greenhouse using this framing system are available from him (see Appendix 2).

Photo 10-2: The solid roof area is used for a batch solar water heater, adding hot water to the food and solar heat provided by the greenhouse. *(Photo courtesy of Mark Rosenbaum.)*

the roof slope is steep enough, as in photo 10-2.) The glazing supports at the endwalls are shown as two 2 × 4s laid flat, with blocking in between. This is for making solid endwalls in the trapezoidal areas just next to the south glazing, providing the same 3½-inch thickness as the rest of the endwall. If this area were to be glazed, a single or double rafter like all the rest can be used. The glazing support rafters rest on the beam at the top and on a kneewall at the bottom. The top of the kneewall is covered with flashing before the rafters are put in place, as shown in the detail in figure 10-7, in order to keep moisture off the top of the kneewall. The square-cut bottom ends of the rafters are toenailed through the flashing. The bottom edge of the glazing laps over the kneewall flashing, providing excellent waterproofing. (The blocking needed to support the top edge of the glazing and the bottom edge of the roof sheathing are not shown.)

The construction sequence for this modified stud-wall frame proceeds from framing the kneewall to framing the endwalls enough to get the rafter support beam in place. Then the roof rafters and glazing supports are put in, and the endwall framing is completed. The 2-by-4 ceiling joists can rest in joist hangers or sit on top of a second ledger on the common wall. On the other end they can be nailed into the sides of the roof rafters or sit in joist hangers. Setting the bottom of the joists flush with the bottom of the beam allows you to end the ceiling sheathing on the bottom of the beam, sealing this edge of vapor barrier very effectively.

The crossbeam that supports the rafters and the glazing supports has to carry half the snow and wind loads from the roof and the glazed wall (the other half is carried by the ledger above and the kneewall below). The beam sizes in table 10-2 can be used for preliminary sizing of the beam, using Douglas fir-larch #2 for the shape shown in the illus-

TABLE 10-2: SIZING THE CROSSBEAM

Span (ft)*	Size Required
6	3 × 6
8	3 × 8 or 4 × 6
10	3 × 10 or 4 × 8
12	3 × 12 or 4 × 10

Note: The actual thickness of a 3 by is 2½ inches and a 4 by is 3½ inches. A 4 by can be built up with two 2 bys with a strip of ½-inch plywood sandwiched between with plenty of nails. These spans, for Douglas fir or larch #2, can be adjusted for different wood species and grades using the same adjustments as for rafters in table 10-1. All sizing should be checked by a structural engineer.

*This table applies only to modified stud-wall framing (as in figure 10-7) with 8-foot-span roof rafters.

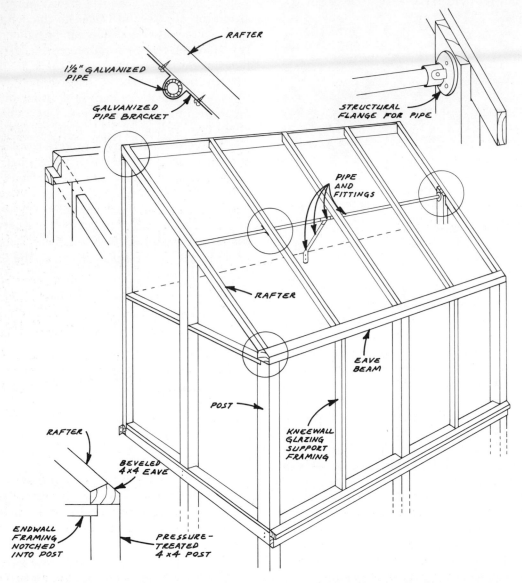

RAFTER

1½" GALVANIZED PIPE

GALVANIZED PIPE BRACKET

STRUCTURAL FLANGE FOR PIPE

PIPE AND FITTINGS

RAFTER

EAVE BEAM

POST

KNEEWALL GLAZING SUPPORT FRAMING

RAFTER

BEVELED 4×4 EAVE

ENDWALL FRAMING NOTCHED INTO POST

PRESSURE-TREATED 4×4 POST

Figure 10-8: Post-and-beam framing allows the smallest glazing support rafters of any of the systems shown and is therefore best suited for greenhouses when maximum interior light is important. Since all the weight is carried by the posts, a continuous foundation isn't needed. Pipe beams support the rafters midway, which allows for rafters that are quite small, shown here as 2 × 3s. Since the posts are buried, they provide lateral bracing and eliminate the need for diagonal bracing. The example shown follows Mark Ward's style.

tration, using 8-foot-long roof rafters and using 6-foot-long glazing supports that are spaced on 3-foot centers.

Post-and-Beam Framing

This is the most light transmitting of all the glazing framing systems presented. The eave, the sill and beams under the rafters are used to support lightweight glazing rafters and vertical glazing supports. The beams can bear on preservative-treated wood posts that go directly into the ground, as shown in figure 10-8, or on metal pipes with concrete piers. A continuous foundation can be used but isn't required. Galvanized pipes, as shown in the example, or galvanized steel angle iron, make strong yet thin supporting beams under the midpoints of the roof rafters. Another pipe (kneebrace) supports this beam pipe midway, running back and attaching to a stud on the common wall, as shown in figure 10-8, or running straight down to a concrete footing in the floor. The latter method is sometimes easier, but it splits up the space a little, which is particularly undesirable for small greenhouses or if you are thinking of using night insulation. The final result is well adapted to greenhouses designed for maximum interior light levels because of the ample roof glazing and the minimal light blocking by the framing members.

Figure 10-8 shows 2-by-3 rafters, but old greenhouses used even smaller rafters, as small as 1 inch by 1½ inches. This was possible because very high quality wood was used (clear heart, tight grain cypress from old trees that are now mostly gone), because they were spaced as closely as 20 inches on centers, and because they were supported every 4 or 5 feet with a purlin. (If you find one of these old greenhouses, it may be worth it to dismantle it and recycle its parts. The rot-resistant

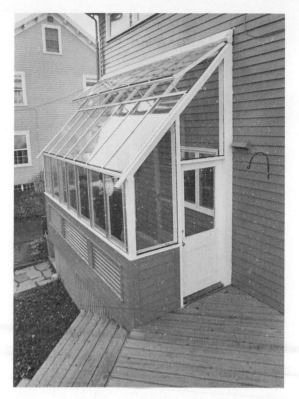

Photo 10-3: Post-and-beam framing allows for the very light framing in a greenhouse that is intended for plant growing. This greenhouse sits on part of a deck and uses the existing deck framing for support and the existing railing as framing for the solid lower part of the kneewall.

cypress will usually be as tight and strong as when it was milled, underneath years of peeling paint.) Buying high-quality wood for this framing isn't very expensive because the rafters are so small.

The pipe used to support the rafters is usually at least 1½ inches in diameter. One-and-one-half-inch *schedule 40* pipe ("schedule 40" refers to a particular thickness of the pipe wall) can span up to 7 feet 6 inches for 35 psf loads, 6 feet 6 inches for 45 psf loads and 5 feet 6 inches for 60 psf, when supporting the

Photo 10-4: Structural pipe fittings with set screws make working with pipe supports very easy. *(Photos courtesy of KeeKlamp, Inc.)*

middle of an 8-foot span roof, with rafters 24 inches on centers or closer. You can use kneebrace supports as necessary to shorten the effective span of the pipe. The kneebrace can be run horizontally back to the house if it is supported from above with a tension member tied securely into the house under the greenhouse ridge. This connection will be under a lot of tension when the rafters are loaded by wind or snow, so be sure to use at least two ⅜-inch lag screws that are long enough to penetrate 3 inches into a solid framing member. The overall framing sequence essentially follows the structure, with the posts going up first, followed by beams and then by rafters. First the house siding is cut away in prepara-

tion for the endwall connections and the ledger, and the ledger is installed as described earlier. The posts are then installed, whether they are pressure-treated wood, as shown in figure 10-8 or concrete piers (with or without galvanized pipes), followed by the endwall stud that is fastened to the house. The foundation insulation is installed next along with the sill beam at the top of the insulation, as described in chapter 9.

Wood posts should be left a little longer than needed so that you can cut them off exactly where you want them once they are in place. (If you cut them before setting them, any differences in the depths of the holes would make the tops of the posts uneven.) Once the posts are up, take careful measurements for the eave beam, and stretch a string across the posts to mark where you want to cut them. Check that this line is parallel to both the ledger and the sill beam and then mark and cut the posts. The horizontal blocking between posts on the endwalls should be installed before the eave beam, if you are going to notch the beam into the posts, as shown in the detail in figure 10-8. Or these horizontals can be attached with galvanized steel angle braces, such as those sold at building supply houses for strengthening framing. The eave beam is then installed on top of the posts.

The pipe cross beam and kneebraces are installed next, using fittings like the one shown in photo 10-4. Where the pipe crossbeam attaches to vertical posts in the endwalls, as shown in figure 10-8, a fitting similar to that shown for the top of pipes in the pipe-and-pier foundation can be used. Often, though, one of the endwall posts will have to be moved slightly out from under the crossbeam to accommodate a door in one endwall. In this case, the same pipe bracket used for attaching the pipe crossbeam to the rafters can be used to attach the beam to the underside of the end rafter. In order to help the crossbeam support the endwall against sideways wind loads, the pipe bracket and pipe should be drilled and pinned together with a (galvanized) 1/4-inch nut and bolt under the end rafter. (This isn't necessary under any other rafters.)

Finally, the rafters are installed. If they are small, the ledger can be notched to accept them, as shown in figure 10-8, or joist hangers can be used. The rafters are toenailed into the eave beam and attached to the pipe beam with galvanized pipe brackets. The kneewall glazing support framing members are toenailed into the sill beam and the underside of the eave beam, and the endwall framing is filled in as needed for doors, windows, fans and vents. With the sill beam at or near grade level, the doorway can go above the beam, with the threshold set on the beam.

Standard threaded plumbing fittings can be used with the pipe, but the threads will rust if they're not painted, and the fittings aren't as structurally strong as are various brands of structural pipe connectors that attach to unthreaded pipe with set screws. These are not only stronger and easier to work with than threaded fittings, but they hide the ungalvanized cut end of the pipe.

Preformed Trusses and Laminated Arches

Preformed trusses make a strong, aesthetically pleasing frame. A truss can consist of just a rafter and a kneewall post, as shown in figure 10-9, or they also can incorporate a floor joist and north wall stud, making a complete wall-floor-roof truss called a *rib truss,* as shown in figure 10-10. The basic truss shown in figure 10-9 includes a vertical kneewall and sloped rafter, with doubled kneewall supports "rabbeted," or cut out, to receive the rafter. The rafter is glued and

bolted, with a permanent waterproof glue, like Resorcinol or epoxy, and carriage bolts, making a joint that is stronger than the wood itself. This strength makes trusses a good choice for very windy locations. They don't require a structural eave, so a very thin member can be used there, making a pleasing visual connection between the sloped and vertical glazing. The crosspiece that forms the eave attaches to the outside of the kneewall, serving to space the trusses and carry the bottom of the sloped glazing. It also makes a convenient place to hinge a continuous eave vent. The kneebraces shown in figure 10-9 are not critical parts of this kind of construction. They can be used with any type of framing to effectively shorten the span of the rafter, allowing a smaller piece or a lower grade to be used.

Preformed trusses can give you some construction headaches if the foundation isn't parallel to the ledger. It is a common mistake to make the foundation and sill parallel to the house foundation without checking to see if the house foundation is indeed parallel to the wall 10 feet above it where the ledger is attached. If you end up with this situation, you'll have to shim the ledger plate, adjust the sill or adjust each arch as you put it up. So before you frame it's always best to double-check the foundation layout to be sure it is going to be parallel to the ledger.

Once the foundation is done, and the sills, bottom plate and ledger (including joist hangers) are in place, the trusses can be constructed to fit the space. If you have a large flat floor, or an even, paved driveway to work on, the job will be much easier. Take careful measurements of the distance between the topmost point of the rafter (generally the top of the ledger) and where the bottom outside edge of the kneewall supports will be, which is the top outside edge of the sole plate. This measurement is labeled c in figure 10-11.

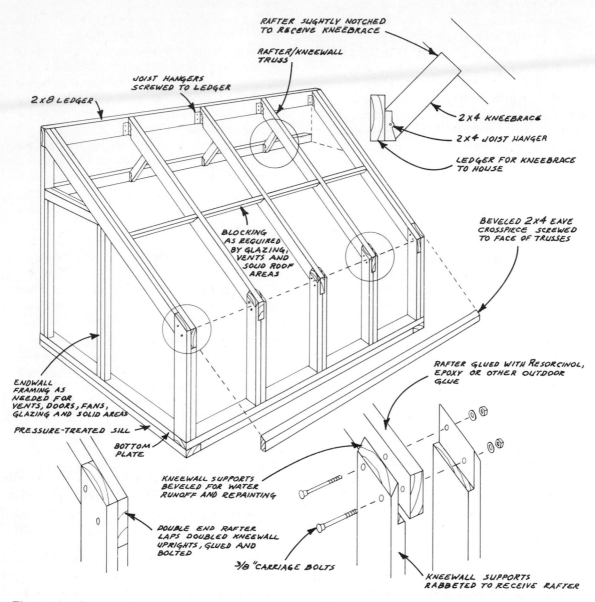

RAFTER SLIGHTLY NOTCHED
TO RECEIVE KNEEBRACE

RAFTER/KNEEWALL
TRUSS

JOIST HANGERS
SCREWED TO LEDGER

2×8 LEDGER

2×4 KNEEBRACE

2×4 JOIST HANGER

LEDGER FOR KNEEBRACE
TO HOUSE

BLOCKING
AS REQUIRED
BY GLAZING,
VENTS AND
SOLID ROOF
AREAS

BEVELED 2×4 EAVE
CROSSPIECE SCREWED
TO FACE OF TRUSSES

RAFTER GLUED WITH RESORCINOL,
EPOXY OR OTHER OUTDOOR
GLUE

ENDWALL
FRAMING AS
NEEDED FOR
VENTS, DOORS, FANS,
GLAZING AND SOLID AREAS

PRESSURE-TREATED SILL

BOTTOM
PLATE

KNEEWALL SUPPORTS
BEVELED FOR WATER
RUNOFF AND REPAINTING

DOUBLE END RAFTER
LAPS DOUBLED KNEEWALL
UPRIGHTS, GLUED AND
BOLTED

3/8" CARRIAGE BOLTS

KNEEWALL SUPPORTS
RABBETED TO RECEIVE RAFTER

Figure 10-9: Preformed trusses make a very strong frame. The crosspiece at the eave can be minimal, making for a nice visual continuity between upper and lower glazing, or it can be used as a place to hang a continuous eave vent. The kneebraces shown here aren't required for this type of framing, but they are an easy way to effectively decrease the rafter span, allowing you to span more distance with a smaller rafter. The kneewall and the rafters are shown here as 2 × 6s, but you should consult table 10-1 for sizes, depending on your greenhouse width and the intended rafter spacing.

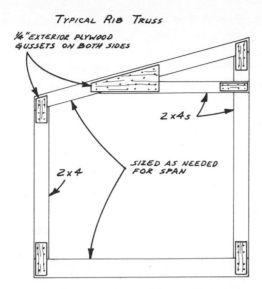

TYPICAL RIB TRUSS

¼" EXTERIOR PLYWOOD GUSSETS ON BOTH SIDES

2 x 4s

2 x 4

SIZED AS NEEDED FOR SPAN

Figure 10-10: Rib trusses include framing members for a kneewall, roof, north wall and floor, allowing the greenhouse to support itself, rather than relying on the house for support. Marine plywood is the best material for the reinforcing gussets for plant-filled greenhouses, but ordinary exterior plywood can be used if it is kept painted.

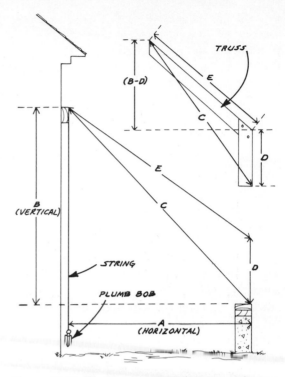

TRUSS

(B−D)

E

C

D

B (VERTICAL)

E

C

D

STRING

PLUMB BOB

A (HORIZONTAL)

Figure 10-11: Final measurements for prefab trusses are best made after the soleplate and the ledger are in place. Check your vertical and horizontal measurements with the rule $a^2 + b^2 = c^2$. Then use b minus the height of your kneewall, d, and a to find e, the length of your rafter in the truss: $(b − d)^2 + a^2 = e^2$.

Hang a plumb bob (or any weight on a string) from the outside of the ledger and measure the horizontal distance (a) between the outside of the plate and the string. Then measure the vertical distance (b) from the point where the horizontal intersects the string to the top of the ledger. If your horizontal and vertical lines are true, you have measured a right triangle, and you can use the following equation, $a^2 + b^2 = c^2$, to check your measurements. If your numbers don't satisfy this rule of geometry, measure again. The next step is to find the exact length of your rafter. The height of your kneewall is a dimension you have determined in developing the final shape of the cross section. Subtract this distance from measurement b. Using the rule for right

triangles, you can now calculate the outside dimension of the rafter (e) with this equation:

$$e^2 = (b − d)^2 + a^2$$

Now the truss can be laid out using the dimensions c, d and e. As a check (or as an alternative to calculation), nail a scrap of wood vertically to the outside face of the soleplate, so that the inside of it simulates the outside face of the kneewall portion of the truss. Measure up the height of the outside of the kneewall and stretch a string where the top of the rafter will be. Check that the vertical is indeed vertical, with a level or plumb bob, and measure dimension e. Make a full-sized drawing on your driveway, basement floor or other large surface or make a jig of long boards. This will help ensure that all the trusses will be the same. Rabbet the kneewall supports as shown in figure 10-9, cut the rafter to the right length and angle, and temporarily clamp the pieces together. Check measurements, adjust the cuts or clamps as necessary and drill for the carriage bolts. Take off the clamps, mix and spread the glue and reassemble, using the bolts and clamps to hold everything until the glue is dry.

Once the glue is dry, the trusses can be installed. If you haven't already, cut the seat where the rafter sits on the joist hanger and mark where each truss goes on the soleplate. Set all the trusses in place, tacking them temporarily into the sill and into the joist hanger. Use some temporary diagonals to keep the trusses from falling like dominoes and to hold them at the right spacing. Eyeball along the top of all the trusses and use a string to see if any are high or low.

You can check along the corners of the trusses at the eave to see if any need shimming up or trimming off at the bottom, or pushing in or pulling out, and if the kneewall is vertical.

Adjusting the trusses is a matter of playing it by ear. Sometimes, trimming the seat at the top or shortening the rafter will bring a high one into line. This will also tilt the kneewall support in a little. Planing the rafter off a little will lower the height of the top surface without changing the location of the eave corner. The final alignments are the most critical if you are using sealed double glass, in which case the openings should all be within ⅛ inch of the designed size and within ⅛ inch of square. All the top surfaces should be within ⅛ inch, and preferably closer, to

make a flat plane. If you use a diagonal bracing cable, install this now, and you can use it to help square up the frame.

Once you have the trusses where you want them, nail them into the joist hangers and toenail them well into the soleplates. Check the spacing between them again, and adjust the temporary diagonals if necessary. Then the blocking and the eave can go on, as well as any kneebraces, if your design calls for them. The kneebraces sit in joist hangers on their own ledger and can be slightly notched into the bottom of the rafter, then toenailed or screwed into place. The endwalls are filled in after everything else is up.

Laminated Arches

Curved laminated arches can be made by bending strips of wood around a form and gluing them together. Once the glue is dry, the arches retain the curve. The arches are used with a flexible plastic glazing such as FRP, a double-walled extruded acrylic or polycarbonate that is thin enough to bend, or polyethylene. (See chapter 11.) With its pleasant curvature and simple fabrication of the arches, this construction style can be both good looking and low in cost.

A bending jig is used for making the arches. The greenhouse shown in photo 10-5 uses only two 1 × 4s for each arch, but more strips of wood could be used if greater strength is needed. The inner strip is bent over the form, glue is applied, and the outer strip bent over the inner one and clamped until the glue is dry. Another method, detailed in the NMSEA's plans book (see Appendix 2) uses blocks of wood between the inner and outer strips. Each arch can be attached to a pier, as was done with the greenhouse in photos 10-5, and 10-6, or the arches can be attached to a continuous foundation or a platform. This type of greenhouse is also available as a kit, either complete or

Photos 10-5, 10-6 and 10-7: For glazing supports, Domenic Bucci's greenhouse uses a laminated, glued arch made of two bent 1 × 4s. The glazing is a double-walled polycarbonate that is thin enough to be bent to the curve of the arches. The foil-covered paper on the top (photo 10-5) is a temporary summer shade. Each arch is attached to a pier at the bottom and is screwed onto the ledger at the top. Diagonal braces were added to the inside corners after some windy-day groans from the greenhouse frame indicated they were needed. The brick south wall of the house, the slab floor and the concrete step that were enclosed when the greenhouse was built all provide some heat storage (photo 10-6). The arches were built by bending 1 × 4s over the bending and clamping jig shown in photo 10-7. A single 1 × 4 is bent over the frame, Resorcinol glue applied and then the other is clamped to it and the two screwed together. Plans for this greenhouse are available from Domenic Bucci (see Appendix 2).

10-5

10-6

10-7

TABLE 10-3: FRAMING SYSTEM SUMMARY

FRAMING STYLE	FOUNDATION TYPE	ADVANTAGES	RELATIVE SKILL NEEDED
Stud wall	Continuous, platform or beam between piers	Quick and easy; familiar building technique	Average
Modified stud wall	Continuous, platform or beam between piers	Allows smaller glazing framing while using familiar building technique	Average
Post and beam	Continuous, platform, post or pier	Smallest glazing framing for best light levels	High
Preformed truss	Continuous, platform, post or pier	Strongest frame for severe wind or snow loads; allows most prefabrication	High
Rib truss	Continuous or beams between piers; needs foundation below common wall	Rib truss doesn't require structural support from house	Average
Laminated arch	Continuous, platform, post or pier	Curve strengthens materials; minimum use of materials in arches	Average

just the arches, from Gothic Arch Greenhouses (see Appendix 2).

Several framing styles have been explored and described in some detail in this chapter and are summarized in table 10-3. The last two styles, trusses and arches, are quite distinct from the others, but when you look at the stud-wall, modified-stud-wall and post-and-beam methods, you find that they are all really points along a continuum. By using thinner studs in the stud-wall method you start to approach the modified-stud wall or post-and-beam methods; or having a solid roof on a post-and-beam frame starts to look like a modified-stud-wall frame. The nominal divisions used here are intended to show various techniques, but when you build your greenhouses, you may end up modifying the techniques shown to come up with a blend that best meets your requirements.

Chapter 11

GLAZING

There are many, many types of glazing on the market, with new materials appearing all the time as the market for conservation and solar energy increases. In this chapter, we'll describe some of the available glazing materials and the installation techniques that work with each type. These glazings cover a range of costs and a variety of installation methods that require different levels of construction skill. First, though, here are some general rules of thumb to follow when buying and installing glazing:

• Installation should be done according to the manufacturer's specifications and instructions (an absolute necessity for any warranties to be valid)

• Don't hesitate to write or call the technical information departments of glazing manufacturers to answer questions and solve problems

• Install glazing carefully, since it will be the most visible part of the greenhouse

• If possible, install glazing on cool days for your personal comfort

• Make sure the glazing is compatible with the sealant and glazing system (some systems require a *gasket seal,* others a *wet seal*)

Whether a gasket or wet seal is required depends on the *coefficient of expansion* of a material, which describes how much it expands and contracts with temperature change. You will see it expressed in manufacturers' literature, in inches of expansion per lineal inch of glazing per degree Fahrenheit (or Celsius) of temperature change (abbreviated as in/in-deg F). Acrylic glazing, for example, has a coefficient of expansion of 0.00004 in/in-deg F, which means that a 100-inch-long piece will expand 0.4 inch over a 100°F temperature rise (100 inches × 100°F × 0.00004 in/in-deg F = 0.4 inch). Glazing temperatures will range from over 100°F (up to 120°F in the summer if the vents are left shut) down to whatever the coldest winter temperature is in your area. If this were −30°F, the range would be 150°F. This would result in a maximum change in length of as much as 0.6 inch. This is more movement than any caulk can handle, so a gasket seal would be needed. Glass, at the other end of the spectrum, has a coefficient of expansion of 0.000005 in/in-deg F, about one-eighth that of acrylic. The length of a 100-inch piece of glass would only change 0.075 inch (a little over 1/16 inch) over a 150°F temperature change. A properly installed wet seal can easily handle this amount of movement.

Whatever sealing system you use, remember the principle of overlapping layers: Use a caulk (a wet seal) or gasket seal but don't rely solely on it to keep water out. Layers should be lapped like shingles to shed water. If they can't be lapped, such as where the bottom of a double-glass unit meets the top of another, you'll have to provide a way out for any water that does get by the seal. Trapped water can break the seal on double glass, rot any wood it sits on, and if it freezes, it literally can force things apart. In the illustrations, *weep holes* are shown for this purpose. They are small, easy to incorporate and essential for a good, long-life seal.

If a large area of the house roof dumps rain onto the area where you will be building a greenhouse, it is a good idea to install a gutter to redirect the water. This minimizes the amount of water your glazing seals will have to resist, and it keeps the house's roofing materials from getting the glazing dirty. This is more than an aesthetic problem, since dirt on the glazing can easily cut your available solar heat by 10 percent. If trees drop their leaves on the house roof and then the roof drains onto the greenhouse, the leaves, particularly from an oak tree, can stain the greenhouse. If the greenhouse has a solid roof, a gutter can be placed along its bottom edge, rather than on the house roof, though this won't work if the greenhouse roof and glazing are on the same plane. You could also install an aluminum or galvanized sheet-metal diverter near the low end of the solid roof. This is a simple way to direct runoff to one or both sides of the greenhouse.

The illustrations of the various glazing systems are shown with a solid roof above and with a particular framing system. The framing system shown was chosen simply as an easy one to illustrate, to avoid complicating the drawings: Any of the glazings can be used with any of the framing systems presented earlier. In these illustrations, the top of all the sloped glazings are shown with a solid roof in the same plane as the glazing. Since this is one of the more difficult waterproofing details, it was chosen for illustrating. If the framing changes pitch at the bottom edge of a solid roof, the roof can overhang the glazing. If there is a vent above the glazing, the flashing from the vent curb will cover the top of the glazing. (This is covered further in chapter 12.) So while the illustrations standardize much of the framing and glazing, they are by no means inflexible to changes in overall design.

Sealed Double Glass

Sealed double glass has become a standard premium glazing for solar greenhouses. It performs well for both solar heating and horticulture, has the best appearance, and the glass itself, if not the seal, has virtually unlimited life span. Installing these units requires quite a bit of precision and attention to details, from the foundation all the way to the finishing details, so first-time builders should work with someone who's had some experience in all this. Higher transmittance units made of low-iron glass are also available in standard tempered glass sizes, and their performance is high enough to warrant the extra cost where the extra solar gain is needed. Double low-iron glass transmits about 82 percent of the sunlight striking it, while standard double glass transmits about 70 percent. Sealed units that incorporate energy-conserving inner films or coatings are also beginning to be available in standard sizes for green-

Photo 11-1: This greenhouse uses standard 46-by-76-inch tempered glass units for the lower part of the slope and ship-lap-pattern FRP for all the rest of the glazing. This saves materials cost and labor for the triangular and trapezoidal pieces, while making use of the economical standard glass size where possible. *(Photo courtesy of the Memphremagog Group.)*

houses. Their overall thermal performance is as good as double glazing with night insulation, but they do reduce incoming light somewhat, making them a better choice for sunspaces intended for solar heating and solarium uses than for purely plant-growing greenhouses. This section shows how to handle standard double-glass units, but the construction detailing is similar for the other types. Go over your proposed installation method with your glass supplier, not only to get his approval for warranty purposes, but to glean some of his experience. The glaziers trade is an art and a science, and the suppliers experience can be a useful resource.

Tempered glass is recommended for any sloped glazing and for glass at floor level, where someone or something is liable to bump into it. It is much stronger than regular annealed glass (used in most windows), and if it does break, it breaks into tiny pieces that usually won't hurt you. Some installers won't use anything but laminated safety glass (used in car windshields) over any place where people will be, and some building codes require laminated glass for overhead applications. Many builders feel this is unnecessary and use annealed glass for odd-sized vertical glazing and tempered glass overhead, but you

should check your local building code for guidance. Tempered glass is also nicer to handle than annealed glass because the edges are sanded smooth and because the glass is stronger and less likely to break in handling.

Using standard sizes of tempered glass will reduce costs. The most common sizes, including 34 by 76 inches and 46 by 76 inches, are manufactured in mass quantities for the sliding-glass-door industry, so they are usually available for a relatively low cost. Sometimes 28-inch widths and 92-inch lengths can also be found as a standard size. Standard sizes run from three to four dollars per square foot, for the complete sealed unit, depending on the quantity and the supplier. Of course, the larger the quantity, the lower the price, so if you can arrange a cooperative purchase with others you can often get a substantially lower price. Tempering custom-size pieces is very expensive, often costing over six dollars per square foot. Check with your glass suppliers early in the design process, so you can design for the standard sizes. The greenhouse shown in photo 11-1 was built on a limited budget, so it was designed to use standard 46-by-76-inch units for the glazing at eye level for a view out, and lower-cost fiberglass glazing with an inner polyethylene

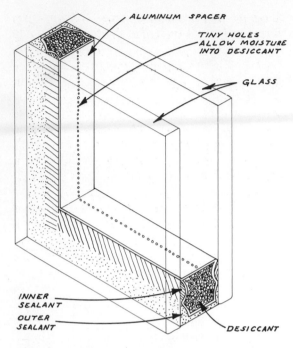

ALUMINUM SPACER

TINY HOLES
ALLOW MOISTURE
INTO DESICCANT

GLASS

INNER
SEALANT

OUTER
SEALANT

DESICCANT

Figure 11-1: Factory-sealed glass units consist of an inner and outer piece of glass, an aluminum spacer filled with desiccant and one or two sealants. The one shown is a double-sealed unit. Care must be taken in installation to avoid physically stressing the seal and to protect the seal from direct sunlight, rain and snow.

layer for the odd-shaped pieces above, below and on the end walls.

Sealed units consist of an inner and outer "light," or layer of glass, and an aluminum spacer that is filled with a *desiccant* (a moisture-absorbing powder) with one or two sealants holding it all together (see figure 11-1). Whether a single seal using one sealant or a double seal using two, gives the best protection, and which sealants are best are matters of much discussion. The technology of sealed units continues to evolve as improved sealants are developed. Of the double-sealed units, a butyl inner seal with a silicone outer seal is a common combination. Urethane single seals

have recently come into use in this country, with manufacturers claiming a long life for the seal, but these are not as widely available, at the time of writing, as the butyl-silicone sealing system. Other double-seal combinations include a polysulfide inner seal with a butyl outer seal, or a double-polysulfide seal. These aren't as durable as the butyl-silicone seal, according to some manufacturers, but can be used, as long as care is taken to shield the seals from the sun. When they're correctly installed, manufactured seals of the best-quality materials can last 20 years and more, while poorly installed or faulty units often fail within the first 2 years. You should expect to get at least 10 years of service from a sealed glass unit.

The fact that sealed glass units don't last forever is a disillusionment to many people, but they simply don't. Sloping the glass puts more strain on the seal than vertical glass, since the exposure makes the glass hotter in the summer and colder in the winter (compared to vertical glass). The temperature changes stress the seal by the expansion and contraction of the glass, such as on a sunny winter day when the inside layer is 80°F and the outside one is 40°F. The sloped glass is also subject to much more water running over it. Sloped glass also sags, or "deflects," simply from its own weight, and this is another source of tension on the seal. Snow and wind loads deflect it further. It's a good idea to use $\frac{3}{16}$-inch-thick glass (a standard thickness for the standard sizes mentioned earlier) for sheets that are as wide as 34 inches, or on slopes that are shallower than 60 degrees, since it will deflect less than $\frac{1}{8}$-inch glass. On slopes shallower than 45 degrees, the glass shouldn't be wider than 34 inches since the deflection will put more stress on the seal than is desirable. Some builders won't use glass wider than 28 inches on slopes shallower than 45 degrees, but the 34-inch width can be used if it's properly installed.

Properly supporting both layers at the bottom is critical with sealed glass. If the bottom layer is supported, but the top one isn't, the top one will want to slide or creep down the slope, stressing and eventually breaking the seal. To get the needed support, *setting blocks,* made of hard neoprene, are used at the quarter points along the bottom of the unit, as shown in figure 11-2. The blocks themselves can be shimmed, if necessary, with flashing scraps or other noncompressible material, to equally support both layers.

A good, square, level and parallel foundation will help you get the framing accuracy that glass requires. All the glass support framing openings should be quite square, with diagonal measurements across the openings coming within ⅛ inch of each other, since only ½ inch of the glass edge will rest on each support. And the opening must be a flat plane with no high or low corners or dips or rises in the rafters. (You can check this by siting across all the rafters from one side.) If the glass unit is twisted or warped when the battens are tightened down, the seal won't last long. Resting the glass right on a 1½-inch-thick rafter involves more precision in framing than is really necessary. By installing a ¾-inch-thick piece of wood flat on top of the rafter for a "glazing bed," as shown in figure 11-4, the top surface is widened enough to allow a more human amount of error. This

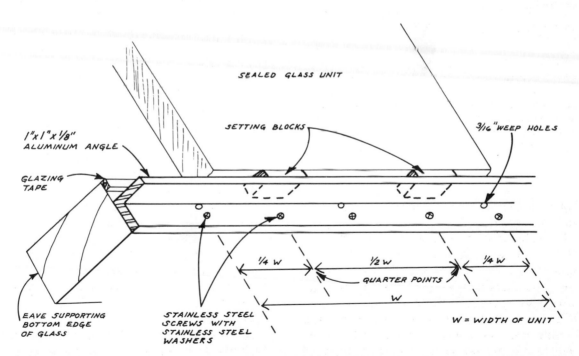

Figure 11-2: Setting blocks made of hard neoprene are placed under the quarter points of the bottom edge of a sealed glass unit to cushion it, to provide equal support for both pieces of glass and to provide a space between the glass and the glazing support. The aluminum angle glazing support is fastened to the framing with stainless steel screws (which won't chemically react with the aluminum) below each setting block and at equal spacing in between. Weep holes are needed to provide an exit for any moisture that gets in. (Flashing under the angle is not shown here.)

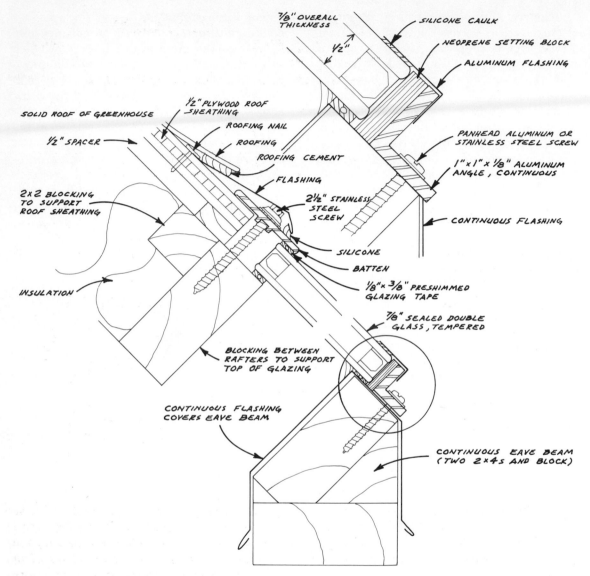

Figure 11-3: Sealed Double Glass (vertical section through eave). Double glass installation requires precision and patience, and it is useful to have an experienced hand around to help. At the bottom, the small aluminum flashing that covers the glass seal, protecting it from the sun and weather, is glued to the glass with silicone, which is an excellent adhesive and will adequately hold the flashing. The "saddle flashing," which covers the eave, is shown a little loose, for clarity in the drawing.

piece should be as wide as the battens you will use, so the battens neither shade unsupported glass, nor expose the sealant under the edge. If

the glazing bed is installed after the rafters are all up, minor framing errors can be corrected by adjusting the position of the bed. The

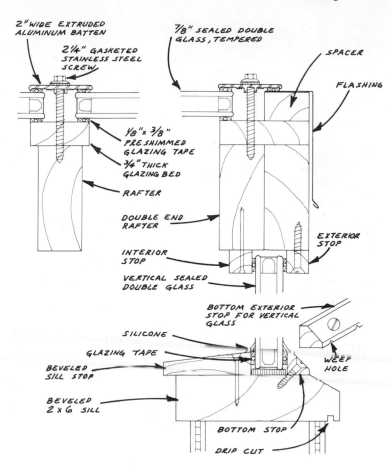

2" WIDE EXTRUDED ALUMINUM BATTEN

2¼" GASKETED STAINLESS STEEL SCREW

⅞" SEALED DOUBLE GLASS, TEMPERED

SPACER

FLASHING

⅛" x ⅜" PRESHIMMED GLAZING TAPE

¾" THICK GLAZING BED

RAFTER

DOUBLE END RAFTER

INTERIOR STOP

VERTICAL SEALED DOUBLE GLASS

EXTERIOR STOP

BOTTOM EXTERIOR STOP FOR VERTICAL GLASS

SILICONE

GLAZING TAPE

BEVELED SILL STOP

BEVELED 2 x 6 SILL

WEEP HOLE

BOTTOM STOP

DRIP CUT

Figure 11-4: Sealed Double Glass (section perpendicular to rafter). The ¾-by-2-inch glazing bed on top of the rafter can be used to take up some inaccuracy in framing. Nail the glazing bed down very securely, with galvanized box nails, since the glazing battens are held mostly by this piece. The weep holes in the exterior bottom stop on the vertical endwall glazing are cut with a knife and the stop is painted or stained on all sides before it's installed.

blocking between the rafters can also get this ¾-inch-thick piece added on top or, as shown in figure 11-3, the blocking can be raised up so the top is flush with the top of the bed on the rafters.

On sloped glazing, aluminum battens are recommended over wood for durability. While wood has a warmer look than aluminum, it will warp, crack or split, even if the highest grade wood is used and it is painted regularly. Repainting battens that cover a large glazed area is bothersome and possibly dangerous. But if the wood isn't maintained, the batten can leak, which in turn can destroy the glass seal. It's best to avoid wood battens on the sloped areas, but they are all right on vertical areas, if you don't mind the necessary repainting. The battens shown in figure 11-4 are from Solar Components Corporation (see Appendix 1), but flat aluminum bar stock can be used. These battens (made for use with Solar Components double-layer fiberglass panels shown later in this chapter in photo 11-4) are a little stronger than flat stock and won't buckle up between the screws, though as long as the screws aren't overtightened with flat stock, the waviness will be only a minor visual problem. Also the battens have little teeth

Photo 11-2: The IDEA glazing system offers the inexperienced builder a relatively easy glass installation method. It is shown here with single glass but is also designed for use with sealed double glass. The system includes an aluminum batten with EPDM rubber gaskets, and all the necessary screws and incidental hardware. Silicone is used in addition to seal horizontal joints at the bottom of sloped areas. *(Photo courtesy of IDEA, Inc.)*

under each arm to better grab the seal. Aluminum battens can be painted, as long as they are properly prepared, either by sanding or chemical etching, and the proper primer and paint are used, but ask yourself if it's worth the maintenance before doing this.

The glazing details shown here use a wet seal system, with a butyl glazing tape for the actual sealant, but there are also other methods. One system uses a prefabricated aluminum extrusion and ethylene-propylene-diene-monomer (EPDM) rubber gasket system, as shown in photo 11-2. While these prefabricated systems are somewhat easier to install, which saves labor, the materials are roughly twice the cost of those shown here. A variety of these systems are available from a number of sources, usually in a mill finish, bronze anodized or baked-on paint finish. (See Appendix 1.)

The actual seal on the system described here is made with ⅛-by-⅜-inch *preshimmed butyl glazing tape.* The shim is a ¹⁄₁₀-inch-diameter neoprene rubber cord in the middle, and it keeps the weight of the glass

and the pressure of the batten from squeezing all the butyl out. A disadvantage of the pre-shimmed tape is that it won't fill irregularities in the glazing bed. If there are dips or bumps in the wood, the shim will maintain the glass at the level of the highest bumps, keeping it from sealing uniformly along the rafter. Therefore, you should use preshimmed glazing tape with a very flat, true glazing bed, but use nonshimmed tape if there are dips or irregularities of ¹⁄₁₆ inch or deeper. (You can check the bed with a metal straightedge.) Preshimmed glazing tape can be used in either situation between the glass and the battens. The tape is laid down on all surfaces on which the glass will rest, with the paper backing left on top until the glass is laid on. The surfaces should be clean, smooth and dry and painted, stained or otherwise sealed. The bottom edge of the glass unit rests on the setting blocks, which are supported by a continuous aluminum angle at the eave, as shown in figure 11-2. Joints in the aluminum angle should be located below each rafter leaving a ¹⁄₁₆-to-⅛-inch gap for a *weep hole.* This also allows you to take up irregularities in the framing that make one glass unit slightly higher or lower than the next one. The aluminum is screwed into the eave with stainless steel or aluminum screws with stainless washers, located below each setting block (see figure 11-2) and between each setting block. Other materials cannot be used for fasteners with aluminum, since they will corrode. The bottom edge of the unit has no batten, in order to avoid catching water or snow there, but the seal must still be covered to keep the sun from degrading it. A small strip of flashing can be used, sealed to the glass with a thin layer of silicone, which is not only an excellent sealant but an excellent adhesive. The flashing will have to be taped onto the glass and/or weighted with a board for 24 hours while the silicone cures. In figure 11-2 notice the weep holes. Even if the flashing covering the bottom leaks a little, the weep holes in the aluminum angle will allow any moisture to run out. One weep hole should be drilled between the setting blocks and one where the rafter meets the eave (if the angle doesn't break there) to provide a way out for any water that gets in under the rafter batten. Be careful not to block the weep hole with the glazing tape or any caulking. (Over time, these weep holes may get clogged by insects plugging them for nests, so periodic cleaning may be needed.)

A batten is used across the top of the glass, with a strip of flashing covering the batten, as shown in figure 11-3. The top batten should run between the rafter battens, rather than running continuously across the top, so that the top flashing can also cover the top of the rafter battens.

The installation sequence goes something like this. First wait for a day when it is over 40°F outside, if at all possible. This will avoid any condensation on the glass where you want it to seal to the butyl tape. If you're racing to finish and don't have the luxury of waiting, the sealing surfaces can be dried

immediately before setting the glass in place by wiping them with an alcohol-dampened rag. Once all the framing is ready for the glass, the eave flashing and the aluminum angle are installed, and the battens are cut and drilled. The battens are long enough to just cover the upright portion of the aluminum angle. (One-quarter inch of the "feet" of the batten will have to be cut off to rest on the angle, if you use this type of batten.) The glazing tape is set on the rafters, with care taken to avoid stretching the tape. Wipe the surface of glass and the battens where the glazing tape will sit with the alcohol-dampened rag to get off any dirt or oily residues and put the setting blocks in place.

Setting the glass in place is difficult, since it is so heavy. Two people can do the job, but it's a lot easier with three. Be careful not to set the glass on its corner, since this concentrates all the weight on one tiny point and can result in a pile of tiny glass pieces. The glass is set on top of the glazing tape, with the paper backing still on the tape. (Turn back the ends of the paper so you'll have something to grab when you pull the paper out.) This allows you to center the glass, which must have at least ⅛-inch clearance on the sides and top, for expansion and contraction of the glass as well as allowing a little movement in the framing. Then the paper is peeled out from the inside, from under the glass. Have someone stabilize the glass to make sure it doesn't move while the paper is being removed. Then the top layer of glazing tape and the battens are applied, again wiping sealing surfaces with a clean, alcohol-dampened rag. Set the battens in place and then drill the rafter for the screws. Stainless screws with neoprene and stainless washers are available from the Solar Components Corporation, but any stainless or aluminum screw with matching metal and neoprene or EPDM washers can be used. The EPDM washers will last longer. IDEA is one source for a lower profile, somewhat better-looking stainless screw. (See Appendix 1 or check with local fastener companies.) Use only enough torque on the screws to slightly squeeze the glazing tape, and *don't* over tighten or you will buckle the batten slightly, making an uneven seal to the glazing tape, and you can even break the glass. The battens are followed by the bottom edge flashing, which runs between the battens. Once all the battens are in place, you can test the seal with a hose. Mark any leaks and use silicone to seal them up after the water has completely dried.

On long runs of sloped glass, you may run into the need for horizontal joints where two glass units meet. If you can get glass that is long enough to cover the whole slope, you'll save much time and effort, though a larger-than-standard piece is likely to cost more per square foot. Some suppliers carry tempered glass up to 120 inches. Tight horizontal joints can be made if need be. (One minor drawback

of horizontal joints is that condensation can drip off the blocking beneath the joint, instead of running down to the eave, but this can be remedied with a small gutter.) This joint, shown in figure 11-5, requires the same basic treatment as the bottom of a single unit: Both lights of the upper unit must be equally supported, the sealed edge of the unit must be shaded from sun and the joint should be "wept" to prevent moisture buildup. The upper unit is supported in the same way a single unit is supported, with an aluminum angle and setting blocks at the quarter points. The angle is supported on the blocking that runs between the rafters.

In order to have enough room for the aluminum angle and the setting blocks, and to have enough clearance between the top of the lower glass unit and the aluminum angle, a 2½-inch-wide-by-¾-inch-thick glazing bed is nailed onto the top of the blocking, as shown in figure 11-5. Four-inch long pieces of

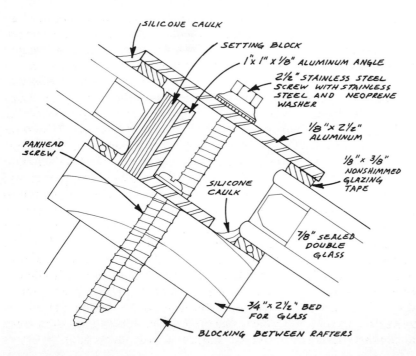

Figure 11-5: Horizontal Joint in Sealed Double Glass (vertical section through joint). These horizontal joints between sloped double-glass units require attention to waterproofing, support and weeping out moisture. The aluminum angle can be installed in 4-inch pieces to support each setting block, rather than running a long continuous piece.

1-by-1-by-⅛-inch aluminum angle are screwed into the blocking, through the bed piece, with aluminum or stainless steel screws, with two screws in each piece, to keep them from turning. (Since the angle is hidden beneath the batten, a continuous piece isn't needed.) Two-and-one-half-by-⅛-inch flat aluminum bar stock is used for a batten, running between the battens on the rafters. Any moisture that does manage to get under the horizontal batten will go to the space between the glass units, run to the rafters on either side, down the rafters in the space between the glass units and leave through the weep holes in the bottom of the aluminum angle. It's a good idea to seal the top of the glazing beds with shellac or epoxy paint. It is also important that the glazing tape between the lower glass unit and the bed (on both the rafters and the blocking) be well sealed. For this reason, be sure to use the nonshimmed glazing tape if there are irregularities in the glazing bed. It's a good idea to set all the glass in place on top of the glazing tape on the rafters, and then douse it with a hose to find leaks. When the leaks are found, mark them with a pencil, and seal with silicone after everything has had a chance to dry. Once all these leaks are sealed, you can be pretty sure that the system will be watertight once the outer glazing tape is in place for a second water seal.

The installation sequence for glass with horizontal joints goes as follows: Once all the framing is up and the paint or stain is dry, caulk all the cracks and joints in the bed pieces that are on top of the rafters and blocking and seal the top surfaces. When this is dry, install the aluminum angle pieces and the setting blocks. The glazing tape is laid down next and any joints in the tape should be sealed by mushing together the ends of adjoining pieces. Then lay down all the glass, remove the paper from underneath and press the glass firmly onto the glazing tape. If you

have any doubts about the seal between the glass and the glazing bed, run a small bead of silicone for an extra seal, right next to the glazing tape. Then hose test for leaks. Mark the leaks, but wait until all is dry to seal them. Then put on the outer glazing tape, using nonshimmed tape under the horizontal battens, so they have a lower profile and will catch less water. When installing the battens, put on the rafter battens first, followed by the horizontal battens, and lastly by the bottom edge seal covers. If the glazing tape doesn't squeeze out beyond the edge of the horizontal battens on the upper side, or if the corners where the horizontal batten meets the side of the rafter batten looks questionable, supplement the seal with a bead of silicone. Do another leak test with all the battens in place.

Site-Built Vented Double Glass

You can build your own double-glass system that relies on a different principle than the sealed units to keep the air gap between the layers dry enough to prevent condensation on the glass. Where the sealed units rely on a hermetic seal to keep out moisture and a desiccant to absorb whatever moisture does get in, this site-built system uses controlled ventilation of the air gap cavity. The inner glass is sealed to the rafter to keep greenhouse moisture from the cavity, and the outer sheet is sealed to the batten to keep out rain water. Air holes connect the air gap with the *outside* air to keep it at the lower outdoor relative humidity (lower than the greenhouse rh) and thus prevent condensation in the air gap. The outside air is allowed to "infiltrate" the air gap at a slow enough rate that the insulation value of the unit is about the same as for sealed glass. And since you can space the glass layers as far apart as

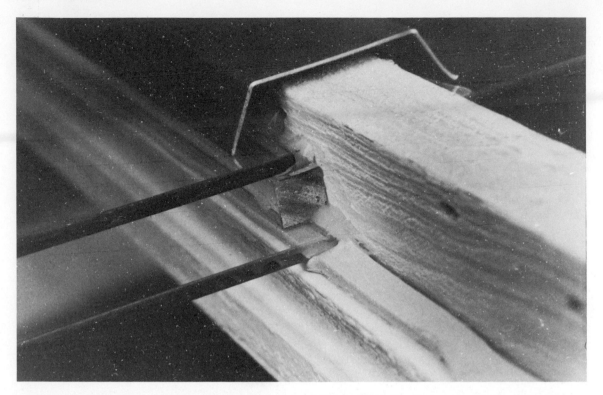

Photo 11-3: This site-built, vented double-glass system, built by Mark Ward, uses recycled cypress rafters from an old commercial greenhouse, with the rabbets cut a little deeper. The 24-by-36-inch glass is ⅛-inch-thick tempered, made for use in storm doors, putting the rafters a little more than 24 inches on center. The bottom glass layer is bedded in butyl glaziers tape, with the ½-inch square acrylic spacer set in silicone and sealed with silicone to the rafter. The outer glass is set in silicone that is put on top of the acrylic spacer and is sealed to the rafter with silicone. The cap on the rafter is shop-bent aluminum. The cavity between the sheets is vented to the outside. Since the glass sheets run only 36 inches they are overlapped ½ inch, with the laps sealed with a bead of silicone, applied very carefully to keep it looking neat. The next sheet that will be applied is an inner sheet, resting against the acrylic spacer and lapping over the inside sheet that is already installed. Then the next acrylic spacer goes on, resting on the spacer below, followed by the outer sheet, which laps over the lower outer sheet, and bears on the cap that is already in place. The next cap will overlap the cap that's there.

you like, you can choose an optimum spacing for a slightly higher insulation value than that of a sealed unit with a narrower air gap.

The big advantage of site-built double glass is the lack of hermetic seals that can fail (though this may occur only after many years of use). The materials cost for the site-built, vented system is somewhat lower than the cost of factory-sealed units, but more labor is required. The materials cost can be from one to three dollars per square foot less for site-built double glass. Vented glass requires considerable care in design and construction, to prevent chronic condensation between the lights, and there actually will be occasional condensation under certain weather conditions. For example, when it's warm and moist outside all day, and then a cold front blows in and the temperature quickly drops, the moisture in the air gap will condense on the outer glass, until enough air moves through the gap to evaporate it. This is at worst a temporary condition and doesn't hurt overall performance.

In this section one method is described for site-building vented double glass. Several methods will work well, as long as a few guidelines are observed.

• The air gap should be very tightly sealed from the greenhouse environment to keep moist greenhouse air from getting in. Wood rafters should be painted with a fairly

impermeable paint, rather than stained, to minimize moisture migrating through the wood into the air gap. The spacers between the glass should either be made of an impermeable material (see photo 11-3) or painted with an epoxy paint.

• The cavity should be vented to the outside, with provisions made for filtering the air and keeping out bugs. If the air isn't filtered, dust will find its way in and eventually reduce transmittance. Of course, the vents must be located to keep out rain.

• Before installation the glass must be thoroughly cleaned, at least on the sides that

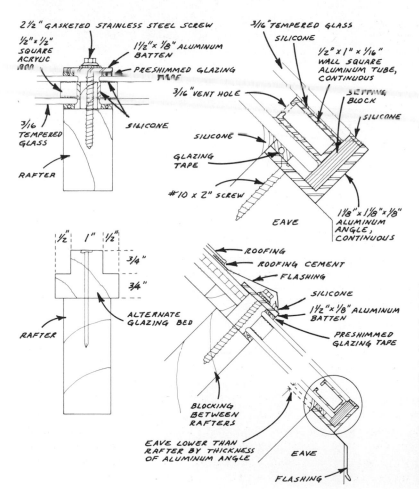

Figure 11-6: Site-Built Double Glass (sections perpendicular to rafter on left, and through eave on right). This system has no hermetic seal that could eventually fail, but it does require more labor than sealed glass. The air gap between the sheets of glass is vented to the outside air, to keep condensation from forming under the outer glass. The rafters can be rabbeted out, or, alternatively, a rabbeted cap put on the rafters to receive the glazing and spacers.

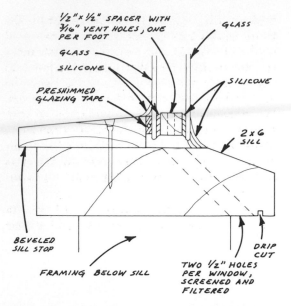

Figure 11-7: Site-Built Double Glass (vertical section). The bottom spacer in vertical site-built glass can be drilled to communicate with the space between the setting blocks, which is vented to the outside through the sill.

will face the air gap. This requires some patience, and you'll never get the very last speck of dust. It's easy to get carried away trying to clean glass perfectly, but don't go nuts. Unless you wash your greenhouse windows every week, the outsides will always be much dirtier than the insides, and you won't notice those inside specks. To do the cleaning use some nonsudsing ammonia in a pail of water or a commercial glass cleaner and newspapers or lint-free rags.

The installation system shown in figure 11-6 is similar, in some respects, to that shown for sealed double glass. The battens and the preshimmed glazing tape are the same. The aluminum angle shown is similar, but a little larger, 1¼ inches by 1¼ inches, to be able to run the angle underneath the glass, rather than below it on the eave. This allows you to fit the lower square aluminum tubing over the

eave, without having to make the eave wider. (With a wider eave, the angle could be mounted as shown for double glass.) The main differences are the venting of the air gap and the fact that you build the units in place.

The spacers used along the bottom are 1-by-½-inch square aluminum tubing with a ³⁄₁₆-inch vent hole drilled into the cavity for each foot of glass width. These tubes are continuous, with their ends continuing all the way to the outside of the endwalls. A very small, thin piece of fiberglass insulation is stuck into the ends for a dust filter, followed by insect screen as shown in figure 11-8. One easy and neat way to keep rain out of the tube is to end it behind the flashing that covers the top edge of the endwall, making sure the flashing doesn't block the flow of air, as shown in figure 11-8. Or, if you decide to use wood trim rather than metal flashing at the top of the endwall, you will have to improvise a small flashing to cover the end of the tube.

The spacers between the glass that run up the rafters and across the top are shown as ½-inch-square clear acrylic rods. These rods are precise, and unlike wood, they're impermeable to moisture. Wood spacers can be used, as long as you paint the wood with a durable, impermeable paint such as an epoxy paint. The spacers are sealed to the upper and lower glass with silicone. Acrylic rods should be no longer than about 4 feet, since the great difference in the coefficients of expansion of glass and acrylic would be enough to break the silicone seal. To allow for this difference a ¼-inch gap, filled with silicone, should be left between the pieces of acrylic rod. At the bottom of vertical glass, the spacer can be drilled to connect with the space left between the setting blocks, which connects with the outside via a filtered, screened hole through the windowsill. Vertical or sloped glazing should be vented only at one end. Venting in these details is at the bottom.

The rafters can be rabbeted on the top to

create a ½-inch-wide-by-¾-inch-deep space for the glass and spacer, or a filler piece can be added on top of the rafter, as shown in figure 11-6. This doesn't give much room for error, but if you are using a fairly narrow rafter spacing, like 24 to 30 inches and/or you are fairly confident of your ability to frame the rafters accurately, the rabbets will give enough tolerance. With wider spacings, though, you may want to use a rabbeted 1½-inch-thick piece flat on top of the rafter, as shown in the alternate detail in figure 11-6, to provide you a little wider bearing surface for the glass. Or the same bed for the glass can be

built up with a 2-by-¾-inch piece flat on the rafter with a 1-by-¾-inch filler piece centered on top of that. The single piece is a little more rot resistant in the long run, but the built-up approach is easier and can more easily be adjusted to compensate for framing errors. When installing the rafters, remember to keep all bearing surfaces for the glass in the same plane, and remember to maintain the minimum ⅛-inch gap between the edge of the glass and the rafter for glass expansion and rafter movement.

The construction process for this system requires a thorough and patient washing crew

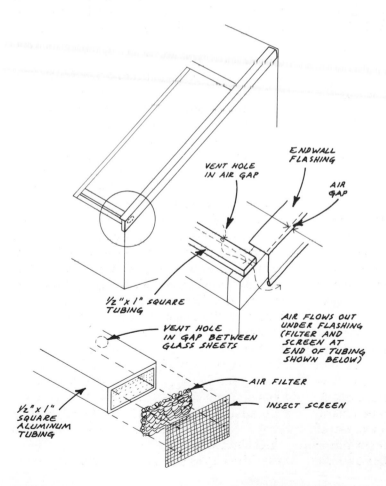

Figure 11-8: The ½-by-1-inch vent tube is filtered to keep dust out of the cavity, screened from insects and flashed to keep out rain, as shown in the details. The tube is run out under the endwall flashing to keep rain out.

of at least one person, but preferably two, who will have clean, dry glass ready at just the right moments. Two people are needed to set in the glass and apply the caulk. (Scaffolding is a must for larger glazing areas.) The person with the steadiest hand should do the silicone work to ensure a neat finished appearance. One advantage of the wider ¾-inch rafter rabbet, afforded by the two-piece or three-piece rafter, is that the spacer and caulking can sit a little inside the rabbet, so the caulking won't show if it squeezes out when the glass is installed. (Clear weather is required for installation, as rain inside half-finished glazing will make a mess of your cleaning job, though the water will eventually evaporate.)

The installation sequence starts with checking the glazing openings to make sure they're square. Then the aluminum angle is screwed into place on the eave, with stainless countersunk screws, making sure it is quite secure, since you won't be able to tighten it after the glass is in. Trim the setting blocks a shade narrower than the 1-inch dimension of the aluminum angle, so that silicone can be run above them. Then set the blocks in place. (They don't need to be glued or fastened in place.) Install the wood spacers that will support the battens at the sides of the aperture and check them for the proper thickness. Drill all the required holes in the square aluminum tubing and notch out the little part of the rafters where the tubing crosses them (or leave the filler strips short if you use the two- or three-piece rafter). The bottom of the rabbet should be flush with the top of the inner glass. Set the tubes in place to be sure they fit, and then take them out. Cut all the acrylic rod (or other prepainted spacers) and the glazing battens to length, and drill the battens. Lay the glazing tape along all surfaces on which the glass will bear, leaving on the paper backing. Then install all the inside glass pieces, which should be clean already, with their edges wiped with alcohol where the sealants

will be. Remove the paper backing from the tape, and gently push down the glass to bed it in the tape. Then run a small bead of silicone along the glass edge where the aluminum tubing will go and set the tubing in place, pushing it down enough to bed it into the silicone. Then install the side spacers, again bedding them on a small bead of silicone. Run another small bead of silicone on top of the side, bottom, and top spacers, and set the outer glass in place.

Start your glazing at one side of the greenhouse. Once the first two outer glass sheets are in place, put on the outer glazing tape, and put the battens on the first unit. Tighten the battens only enough to just begin to squeeze the silicone out from between the glass and the spacers. This must be done fairly quickly, so the silicone doesn't skin over. After all the glass is in and the silicone has had a chance to cure for 24 hours, you can go back and retighten the battens enough to compress the glazing tape a little.

When the glass is first closed in, you may see some fogging inside, depending on the weather. Don't panic! This is the moisture that was sealed in when you put the glass on. If it doesn't go away after a day, you may have put too much fiberglass in the ends of the vent tubing. Only the barest wisp is necessary for filtering. If fogging occurs after a rain, you probably have a leak somewhere to the outside. If it occurs whenever it's cold outside, you may have a leak to the inside or insufficient venting. Site-built double glazing takes patience and a steady hand, but the result is durable and you can be satisfied knowing that it will last as long as the greenhouse will.

Double-Walled Plastic Glazing Panels

There are two main categories of factory-made double-layer plastics, *fiber reinforced polyester* (FRP) sheets, often known as fiberglass, that are bonded to either side of an aluminum frame, and extruded acrylic or polycarbonate. Most panel manufacturers offer an aluminum extrusion mounting system for their product, which provides both a bed for the glazing and a batten to hold it down. The main advantage of these panels is their labor savings, since the whole glazing system is prebuilt and requires less precise framing than double glass mounted directly on wood rafters. The extruded panels also can be cut to odd sizes and shapes, saving the cost, in overhead applications, of using custom-shaped tempered units. Most of the panels available are translucent, with one available in clear. This can be an advantage or disadvantage, depending on what's outside your window. Some growers feel that the diffused light is beneficial to the plants, spreading light more evenly to more of the plant leaves, and that the ultraviolet light admitted by all plastic acrylic or polycarbonate glazings inhibits legginess and discourages mold and fungus growth. You can also get a suntan (or a sunburn) under these ultraviolet (UV) transmitting plastics, which you can't under FRP or glass. Another advantage of most of the extruded panels is that they are available in long sheets, up to 16 feet standard and longer on special order. This avoids having a horizontal joint between glazing panels.

These panels cost about as much as standard sizes of sealed double-glass units. The thinner ¼-inch-thick extruded panels are less expensive at about $1.50 to $2.00 per square foot, while the FRP and thicker extruded panels cost $3.25 to $5.00 per square foot. All the panels have such a large coefficient of expansion that they must be used with expensive extruded aluminum mounting systems, unless pieces less than 4 feet long are used. The extrusion system for the FRP panels, which uses a caulking seal, costs about $2.60 per linear foot including necessary hardware,

compared to $3.00 to $5.00 per linear foot for gasketed systems. Adding this to the $2.00 to $5.00 per square foot cost for the glazing panel, the total materials cost for a double-walled plastic panel system can run from $4.00 to $7.00 per square foot. Shipping is additional, and can be high for large, bulky glazing panels, unless you have a local distributor. If the cost of the thicker panels with their extrusions is compared to standard size sealed double-glass units with a site-built mounting system, glass has a lower materials cost, though it does require more labor. Plastics also have a limited life span, with the better materials guaranteed for 10 to 20 years. A minor disadvantage of the extruded panels is the tendency for condensation to be caught in the spaces between the layers, unless precautions are taken when installing the panels to seal the ends.

The insulation value of the double plastic panels varies from R-1.5 for the ¼-inch, double-layer panels to R-1.7 for the ⅝-inch-thick panels to R-1.9 for the newly developed ⅝-inch-thick triple layer panels. By comparison, double glass with a ½-inch air gap has an R-value of about 1.8. (These values are for vertical installations; sloped installations will have lower R-values.)

When you receive plastic glazing panels from the shipper, be sure to check for damage while the driver is present, before you sign the receipt, since plastic panels are very susceptible to damage. Make a record of any damage on the receipt itself, before signing. (If you don't have time, or the driver won't wait for you to inspect the panels on the spot, note any damage to the packing on the receipt, and note on the receipt that you have received the goods subject to inspection for concealed damage. Inspect the materials promptly, and report any damage to the shipper immediately.) Store the panels in a dry place and out of the sun, since moisture can permanently damage many plastics when panels are stacked together. The temperature in a stack of panels sitting in the sun can quickly rise above the temperature at which they'll permanently deform. Any cleaning should be done with mild soap and water, *not* ammonia, cleanser or other cleaners. In general, panel manufacturers have specific instructions for handling and installing their products. Make sure your supplier gives you all the available literature that is pertinent to your installation.

Installing FRP Glazing Panels

FRP is bonded, under heat and pressure, to a rigid aluminum frame to form double-layer glazing panels. FRP is formulated to have almost exactly the same coefficient of expansion as aluminum, 0.000013 in/in-deg F, so the two materials expand and contract together, without most of the wrinkling that happens with noncorrugated single-layer FRP installations. But over time, the panels do show some wrinkling. Solar Components Corporation, the only manufactuer of these panels, also developed an aluminum extrusion system for use with the panel. They also make a panel with two layers of clear acrylic glazing for "view windows." But the acrylic has a much higher coefficient of expansion, 0.000041 in/in-deg F and therefore wrinkles noticeably. Due to the higher rate of expansion, the acrylic is only available in 4-foot-long panels. Both the acrylic and the FRP panels are 1½ inches thick. The FRP panels cost from $4.00 to $4.50 per square foot, and the 4-by-4-foot acrylic panels cost a little over $8.00 per square foot.

The aluminum extrusion system made for mounting the panel, shown in figures 11-9 and 11-10 and photo 11-4 is the most surefire way to install the panels. The two-piece batten is used on rafters where two panels will join. The lower extrusion is screwed to rafters, and the top piece is screwed to it, with stainless steel hex-head screws with neoprene and

Photo 11-4: The Solar Components Corporation glazing system for their double-layer FRP panels makes the installation job considerably easier. The two-piece batten system consists of an inner and outer extrusion, with glazing tape for a seal, and stainless steel screws. The outer screws come with stainless steel and neoprene washers. *(Photo courtesy of Solar Components Corp.)*

metal washers. Glazing tape provides the actual seal. The relatively low expansion rate of the panels—a 12-foot panel only expands ¼ inch over 130°F temperature rise—permits the use of wet seals. The tape is applied directly onto the end rafters, eave or cross-blocking at the top of the glazing, all of which must be about 3/16 inch higher than the top of the rafters on which the two-piece batten is used, to account for the thickness of the extrusion. On the edges, a 1-by-3-inch aluminum angle is used to fasten the panel in place, with the same sealant and screws. This

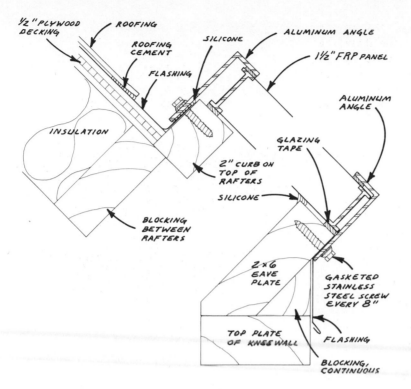

Figure 11-9: FRP Panels (vertical section through eave). Double-layer FRP panels are available with an extruded aluminum mounting system that is sealed to the panels with nonshimmed glazing tape. The panels are relatively easy to install and don't require a high level of precision.

mounting system costs about $3.30 per linear foot for the double batten and about $2.20 for the outer edge angle battens.

The whole glazing assembly sits 2 inches above any solid roof above the glazed area and any framing or trim to the sides, to provide positive drainage around the sides and prevents leaks. (While the roof above could be "shingled" over the top of the glazing, as shown with other glazings, the manufacturer recommends raising the glazing as a more foolproof method.) Flashing from the lower area runs up under the 1-by-3-inch aluminum angle around the edge of the panels. One way to arrange the framing to accomplish this is shown in figure 11-10. Be sure that the "gutter" formed above the raised glazing is free to drain to the sides. If the flashing is stiff enough, it can be run beyond the edge of the endwalls to form little drainage spouts. Alu-

minum flashing should be used, since it is in contact with the aluminum extrusions.

The rafter extrusions are placed on 48-inch centers and fastened to the rafters every 24 inches with stainless steel or aluminum countersunk screws. The 48-inch spacing leaves $\frac{1}{8}$ inch for expansion on both sides of the $47\frac{3}{8}$-inch-wide panels. The same clearance must also be left on the outside edges of the end panels. The bottom of the panel can rest directly against the 1-by-3-inch aluminum angle as shown in figure 11-9, but if the slope is over 40 degrees, an additional smaller aluminum angle should be used as a bearing surface as shown in figure 11-10. Clearance for the expansion of the length of the panel is at the top of the opening: $\frac{1}{4}$ inch for an 8-foot or shorter panel, $\frac{3}{8}$ inch for 8-to-12-foot panels and $\frac{1}{2}$ inch for 12-to-16-foot panels.

An alternative is to set the FRP panels

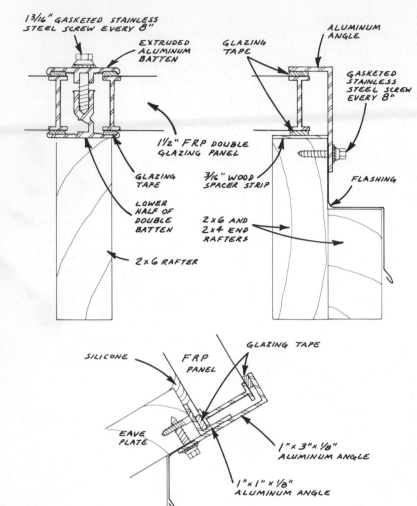

Figure 11-10: Double-Layer FRP Panels (section perpendicular to rafters above, and vertical section through steep-sloped eave below). On rafters that carry two double-layer FRP panels, a two-piece batten system is used, while on end rafters the panels lie directly on the wood and are held in place by an aluminum angle. On steep slopes, the bottom of the glazing panel should rest on an aluminum angle or other support.

directly on wood rafters, eliminating the rafter extrusion from the two-piece batten system, as long as the rafters are at least 2 inches wide on the top edge. It is important that the rafters be of sufficiently high-quality wood that they don't warp or twist over time, since this could cause leaks between the glazing panel and the batten. This system would look identical to the sealed double-glass system.

Installing Extruded Double Glazing Panels

Extruded double glazing panels are available in acrylic and polycarbonate. Both materials are quite clear when extruded in flat sheets, but the ribs in the extruded double glazing give a translucent effect. The two materials differ in physical strength and resistance to UV degradation. Acrylics last as long as 20 years or more, with Exolite extruded acrylic panels carrying a 10-year guarantee of not more than 3 percent reduction in light transmission. Polycarbonates tend to yellow and develop a surface haze from sun and weather, losing about 1 to 1½ percent of their transmittance per year. Manufacturers use either a UV inhibitor in the resin, a UV-resistant coating, a UV-resistant film on the surface, or some combination of these. Since these are relatively new approaches to prolonging the life of polycarbonate, there is no general agreement as to which is best, but some manufacturers claim they have reduced UV degradation to less than that of acrylic, while others claim that this isn't possible. Both polycarbonate and acrylic will get scratched over time, by blowing sand and dust or falling debris from trees, making them look

a little worse, and reducing their light transmission. The scratches are less noticeable in the double-walled extrusions, as visual images are already distorted by the ribbed pattern of the extrusion. Both plastics are generally tougher than glass, in terms of resistance to breaking from impact by rocks or hailstones, but polycarbonate is by far the tougher. (At subzero temperatures tempered glass is stronger than some acrylics, but at warmer temperatures, acrylic is stronger.)

Extruded multilayer glazing is an area that is changing rapidly, with many polycarbonates on the market. There is now a whole group of thin double-walled polycarbonates, with overall thicknesses of 4 millimeters (a little over 5/32 inch) to 10 millimeters (a little over 3/8 inch) as shown in photo 11-5. There are also a number of new triple-layer extrusions,

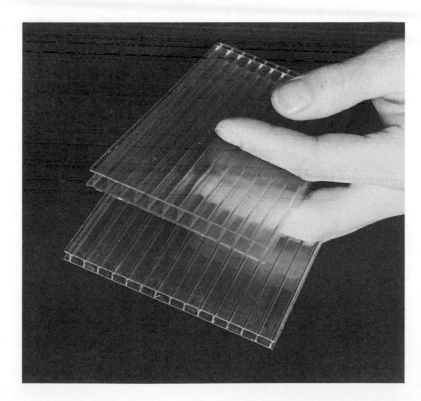

Photo 11-5: Extruded polycarbonate double glazing is made in many configurations and thicknesses, ranging from 5/32 inch (4 mm), to 5/8 inch (16 mm). Shown here are 5/32 inch and ¼ inch (6 mm).

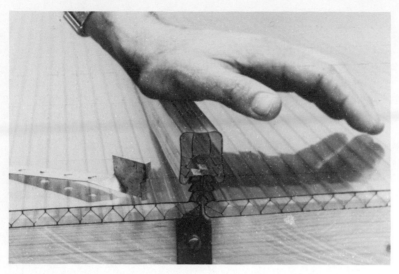

Photo 11-6: Danaplon, one of the new generation of triple-layer extruded polycarbonate glazings, is available with a polycarbonate extrusion for joining the sheets. Sheets are 15.75 inches wide (400 mm) and 0.394 inch (10 mm) thick and can be curved to a 4-foot radius. An H-shaped joining extrusion is available for doubling the material to create a 6-layer glazing. *(Photo courtesy of Polygal Corp.)*

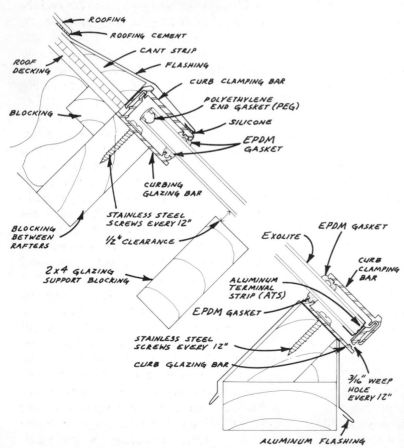

Figure 11-11: Exolite with ESGS Mounting System (vertical section through eave). Available in acrylic or polycarbonate, Exolite is one of the old-timers of extruded plastic double glazing. It is shown here with its ESGS aluminum extrusion with rubber gasket mounting system, which allows the panels the necessary room for expansion and contraction. While fairly expensive, the system does minimize labor. In plant-growing greenhouses, the ends of the panels should be sealed as shown to minimize moisture condensation between the glazing layers. Note that only aluminum, not galvanized steel, flashing should be used in contact with the aluminum extrusions. The blocking is lower than the glazing, to account for the bowing of the glazing due to greater expansion of the inner layer on cold, sunny days.

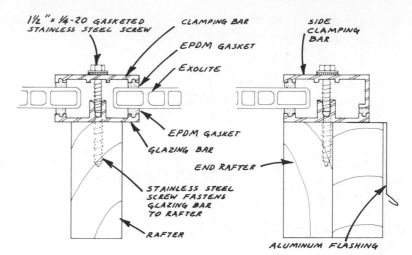

Figure 11-12: Exolite with ESGS Mounting System (section perpendicular to rafters). In this mounting system, the extrusions for the edge are different from those used on rafters that carry glazing on both sides. The screws that hold the lower extrusion to the rafter are shown dotted.

most of which have special mounting systems. One of these is shown in photo 11-6, with a polycarbonate, rather than aluminum, extruded mounting system. Plastic mounting systems like this one have the potential to greatly reduce costs. In this section, construction details are covered for one of the old-timers, Exolite, a double-walled extrusion that is available in both polycarbonate and acrylic. Detailing for others would be included if there were more space, but the basic elements of the Exolite installation—room for expansion, gasket seals, purlin supports and weep holes—can be applied to other extruded panels.

The Exolite ESGS mounting extrusions are designed to be applied on top of wood or metal framing. The extrusions themselves are rigid enough to span any irregularities in wood framing. Both the rafter and edge extrusions are shown in figures 11-11 and 11-12. They are a mill-finish (plain) aluminum, since darker colors would heat up, causing uneven expansion and stress in the panels. (Other gasket seal systems can be used with Exolite, but CYRO, the manufacturer, recommends against dark-colored extrusions, saying the temperature buildup could cause a weakening

or cracking of the glazing.) The panels and the extrusions are designed for mounting on 48-inch centers, which allows sufficient side clearance. The EPDM gaskets allow for considerable movement with no opening up of the perimeter seal. An 8-foot panel expands ½ inch over 130°F temperature rise; a 12-foot panel expands ¾ inch and a 16-foot panel expands a full inch. For panels over 16 feet long (Exolite panels can be made up to 30 feet long) consult the factory for details for a special "floating" top joint. In greenhouses where many plants are grown (or other high-humidity environments), the top end of the Exolite should be sealed with the polyethylene end gasket (PEG) that is supplied with the material and the bottom should be sealed with the optional aluminum terminal section (ATS) that CYRO makes for this purpose. When the top of the panel is cut at an angle, the PEG won't fit, so the top should be sealed with 3M's 1-inch-wide #425 foil-back tape with an acrylic adhesive. In nonhorticultural greenhouses, the ends should be sealed with the PEG at the top and bottom. In either case, the bottom edge rests on neoprene setting blocks at the quarter points (as in figure 11-11) to cushion the bottom of the panel, with weep holes drilled in the mounting extrusion to drain out any water that gets past the gaskets.

Depending on the wind and snow load conditions, the panels may need additional supports perpendicular to the rafters. With wood-framed greenhouses, this is usually done with blocking between the rafters, as shown in figure 11-11. The frequency of the blocking depends on the loads. For 35 pounds per square foot (psf) wind loads, use blocking every 6 feet for the acrylic panels and every 5 feet for the polycarbonate panels. For 50 psf wind loads, support is required every 5 feet for the acrylic and every 4½ feet for the polycarbonate. Note in figure 11-11 that the blocking is ½ inch below the bottom of the glazing. This way the glazing will only bear on the blocking when the wind is blowing hard, or the snow is piled high. The clearance between the blocking and the glazing also accommodates the bowing that normally occurs with double-layer extruded panels. When it is cold outside and warm inside, as on a sunny winter day, the outer layer is much cooler and therefore more contracted than the warmer inner layer, causing an inward bow. The blocking should be nailed through the rafters as well as toe-nailed for maximum strength.

The horizontal base extrusions are continuous. The rafter (or vertical) extrusions run on top of them, where the rafters meet the horizontals. Both are screwed down every 12 inches with stainless steel screws. The horizontal battens that hold the Exolite down onto the base extrusions also run underneath the rafter battens. The rafter extrusions are spaced 48 inches on center. The aluminum is cut most neatly with a circular saw, with a blade made for cutting aluminum or ferrous metals, along with an aluminum cutting fluid to prevent binding of the blade, or with a carbide-tipped blade. (Don't forget to wear ear and eye protection.) A hacksaw can also be used with a lot more elbow grease. Weep holes can be drilled in the bottom rail (see figure 11-11) before or after the extrusion is in place. The gaskets can be pressed in place before the extrusions are mounted. They are cut 1 inch longer than the extrusions and are inserted by hand or with a roller, starting at the middle and working toward the ends. Press the ends of the gaskets in so they are compressed a little to avoid stretching them.

The panels should be shorter in length than the opening provided in the extrusions to accommodate the expansion discussed earlier. Remember to include the end treatment, the PEG or the ATS, in your measurement. The width clearance is accounted for in the 48-inch spacing of the vertical extrusion (the Exolite is 47¼ inches wide). Panels can be cut with a circular saw having a sharp, fine-toothed (at least 10 teeth per inch) hollow ground blade (such as a plywood blade). Reversing the blade helps minimize chipping. Vacuum or blow the chips out of the channels as you cut.

Once the panels are cut, the appropriate end treatment is put on and the panels are set in place on the setting blocks. The battens are cut to the same length as the base extrusion. The panels are centered side to side in the opening, and the battens are screwed on with stainless steel screws, neoprene gaskets and stainless washers. Flashing covers the top ends of the rafter battens, as well as much of the top horizontals. Joints between the batten extrusions can be caulked with silicone.

Single-Layer Glass

When your climate and use for the greenhouse permit, a single layer of glass or FRP glazing is a much simpler and easier proposition than double-layer glazing. Both offer more flexibility in correcting for errors because they don't require quite as much precision for support and sealing. FRP can be used throughout the greenhouse. When glass

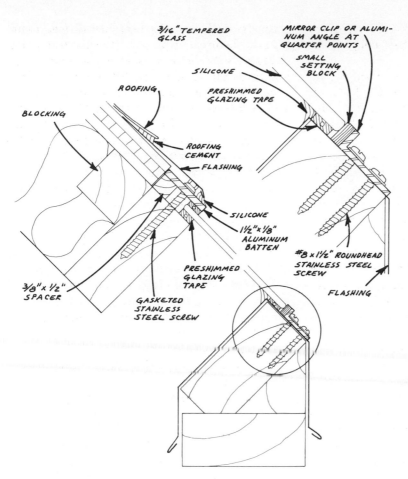

3/16" TEMPERED GLASS

MIRROR CLIP OR ALUMINUM ANGLE AT QUARTER POINTS

SILICONE

SMALL SETTING BLOCK

ROOFING

PRESHIMMED GLAZING TAPE

BLOCKING

ROOFING CEMENT

FLASHING

SILICONE

1½"x⅛" ALUMINUM BATTEN

#8 x 1½" ROUNDHEAD STAINLESS STEEL SCREW

3/8" x ½" SPACER

PRESHIMMED GLAZING TAPE

GASKETED STAINLESS STEEL SCREW

FLASHING

Figure 11-13: Single Glass (section through eave). A single layer of glass is a durable and good-looking glazing, making it a good choice for season-extension greenhouses in warm climates. The installation is similar to that of double glass, with the use of mirror clips or short pieces of aluminum angle instead of the continuous aluminum angle at the bottom edge of double glass. Silicone is used to fill any voids between the eave and the glass inside the greenhouse, to keep condensation from getting between the glass and the eave.

is used, it should be tempered for overhead installation (if local codes don't require laminated glass). Otherwise regular annealed glass can be used. Standard tempered sizes offer the same economy for single-layer as they do for double-layer applications. Check with local glass suppliers for available standard sizes.

The installation of single-layer glass is very similar to that of sealed double glass, except that you can be a little more relaxed about some of the details, since there is no hermetic seal to protect. The previous discussion about clearances for expansion of double glass and using stainless steel screws and

aluminum battens also applies to single-layer installation. Shingling everything is the key to keeping it watertight, as shown in figure 11-13. The void between the batten, the glass and the rafter is left open at the bottom to drain any water that gets in there (see figure 11-14). *Mirror clips* (shown in photo 11-7), which are simply small pieces of angle, replace the continuous aluminum angle used with double glass, since there is no need to keep the edge of single glass covered. They are placed at the quarter points and are used with a small piece of setting block to cushion the glass from the metal. Mirror clips are available from most glass suppliers, but you can also make your

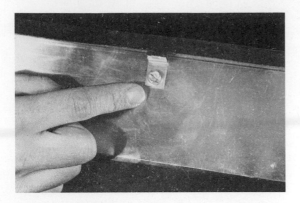

Photo 11-7: Mirror clips, as they are called in the glazier's trade, are used to support the bottom edge of single glass. Without them, or some type of stop, the butyl glazing tape would allow the glass to slip down over time.

own from aluminum angle. They can be installed with the screws outside the glass, as shown in figure 11-15, or with countersunk screws under the glass if the eave isn't wide enough. The bottom edge of vertical single glass rests on setting blocks, with a bead of silicone caulk sealing the edge from blowing rain. Note the bead of silicone on the bottom inside edge of both the sloped and vertical glass to keep water away from wood framing. This is particularly important with single glass, to avoid rot, since there will be considerable condensation on the inside.

Rafters 1½ inches thick are shown in figures 11-13 and 11-14, rather than the two-piece rafter shown with double glass, but either can be used. Sometimes the choice is decided by the overall dimension you want for the greenhouse, rather than your confidence in the accuracy of your framing. Using the two-piece rafter adds about another inch to the overall width of the greenhouse for each piece of glass. The 1½-inch-by-⅛-inch aluminum battens, shown in figure 11-14, just cover

the rafters. They are readily available from hardware stores, though they are likely to be cheaper from metal wholesalers. The screws should be a little closer together than with the Solar Components Corporation's battens (6 inches rather than 8 inches), and more care should be taken to avoid overtightening, since the flat stock will bend more easily.

The installation sequence for single-layer glass is about the same as for sealed double glass. After the glazing support framing is checked for squareness and flatness of plane, the mirror clips are installed. Be sure there are no bows or dips in the top surface of the eave, since it is only the weight of the glass on the glazing tape that seals this edge, and the shim keeps the tape from conforming to dips or bumps larger than around $\frac{1}{16}$ inch. If there are big bumps, smooth them out, or use un-shimmed glazing tape. A bead of silicone can be used in place of the glazing tape on the rafters and the top and bottom edges of the glass. The spacers at the top and sides of the aperture are installed and checked for edge clearance around the glass. Their thickness is also checked to make sure the batten will sit flat when it's tightened. The top rafter surface is cleaned and wiped with alcohol, and then the glazing tape is put in place, with the paper backing left on (or the bead of silicone is run). The small setting blocks may need to be held in place with a tiny dab of silicone, if the clips are small. Then the glass is set in and centered, and the paper backing on the glazing tape is removed from the inside. The edge of the outside of the glass is wiped down with alcohol, and the outside glazing tape (or bead of silicone) is put on. Sand the underside of the batten lightly, with a fine emery paper, for good adhesion to the sealant, and put the battens on. Leave enough room at the joints in the battens to allow a ⅛-inch bead of silicone. Tighten the battens only enough to just begin to squeeze out the sealant. *Don't overtighten.*

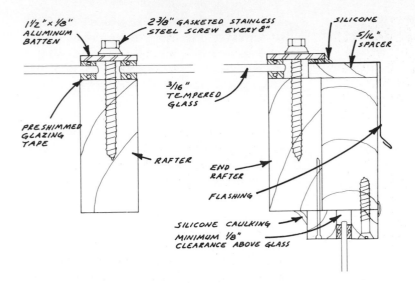

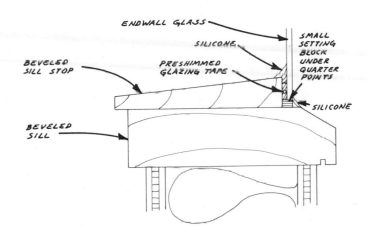

Figure 11-14: Single Glass (section perpendicular to rafter). Note the bottom edge of single glass needs no batten on either sloped or vertical installations.

Single-Layer FRP

This material, commonly known as fiberglass glazing, is a relatively inexpensive, translucent glazing material that is easy to work with and doesn't require ultraprecise framing. It's a good glazing choice for low- and intermediate-cost greenhouses and for those who are less experienced in the ways of glazing. It can be easily cut, making it ideal for odd-shaped pieces, and is fastened with nails or screws with neoprene gasket washers. It can also be coupled with polyethylene inside for a low-cost, fairly durable double glazing. The glass fibers in the FRP keep out most of the UV light, prolonging the life of the inner polyethylene layer. The glass fibers also make the material, which is only 0.040 to 0.060 inch thick, quite strong, able to withstand high wind and snow loads. The translucency of the material distributes light fairly evenly around the greenhouse, an advantage for plants, but it doesn't allow you a view out. The limited life span of this material is its one major drawback.

FRP is made of a fiberglass matt that is impregnated with a polyester resin, with ultraviolet inhibitors in the resin and/or various coatings on the surface to prolong its life. It is available in many grades, but only the best grades, which use the best UV barriers and carry a 15-year warranty, should be used. Otherwise the decrease in light transmission that will occur within a couple of years will hurt both plant growth and solar energy collection. Cleaning the glazing periodically will help extend its service life, particularly in areas with a lot of air pollution. It can be cleaned with a hose, or a soft brush and mild soap if the dirt is persistent.

When the FRP ages, the resin deteriorates, and the glass fibers are exposed to the air, severely decreasing transmittance, but a resin can be applied to the surface to regain at least some of the original transmittance. Each manufacturer has its own resin, so check with your FRP supplier for recommendations for resurfacing. FRP is made in many configurations, including flat rolls, smoothly curved and angular corrugated sheets, and shiplap pattern sheets. Its coefficient of expansion is large enough that when flat FRP is used, it tends to look very wrinkly after it has gone through its first summer. Corrugated and shiplap pattern sheets, however, maintain a neat appearance, since the corrugations maintain stiffness in the direction parallel to the ribs, and the corrugations "absorb" the expansion perpendicular to them. FRP usually costs $1.00 to $1.50 per square foot, including the materials that are needed for installation.

Installation detailing is described here for the 0.050-inch-thick shiplap pattern, made by Filon, which has the unique advantage of fitting over rafters on a variety of spacings, and has a pleasing look. It is called "shiplap" because its corrugations look a little like shiplap siding running perpendicular to the studs and rafters. Instructions on applying FRP with rounded corrugations, with the corrugations running parallel to the rafters, can be had from the manufacturer, and are also found in the New Mexico Solar Energy Association plans and the Ecotope plans listed in Appendix 2.

Care must be taken in the handling of the FRP before it is installed. It should be stored indoors in a dry, well-ventilated area, for if it isn't kept dry it can absorb moisture and become cloudy and actually lose strength. If it is wet and exposed to sunlight, the process is speeded up. Check the material when you receive it to make sure the shipper hasn't gotten it wet. If it is wet but not discolored, separate and store the panels on end so they can dry off.

The method for mounting individual panels is quite simple. Rafters can be spaced as far apart as 3 feet on slopes over 40 degrees. On shallower slopes, the 3-foot spacing is all right as long as snow won't build up on the roof, but in snowy climates, the rafter spacing should be reduced to 2½ feet. The panels cover a 14-foot-wide-by-4-foot-high area, with actual dimensions of 51½ inches by 14 feet 4½ inches. Closure strips of neoprene foam that match the shiplap corrugations are used under all vertical edges and a plain square foam closure strip is used under all other edges. When the material is cut at an angle, the square closure strip can be compressed to fit the odd-shaped holes under the ends. A thin bead of clear silicone caulking is used on top of the closure strips to make a good seal, and the FRP is held down with gasketed nails or screws. The nails, which are either galvanized steel or aluminum, have ringed shanks to increase their holding power. Screws are preferable to the nails, though, since they have greater holding power. The expansion and contraction of the rafters due

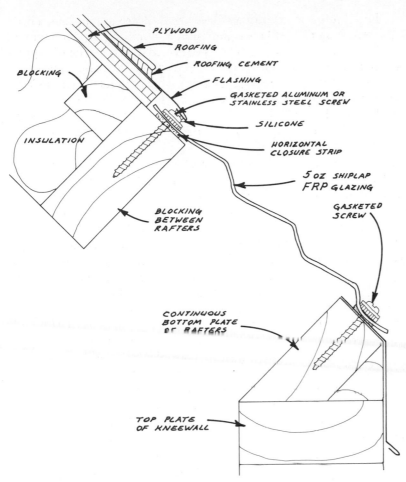

PLYWOOD

ROOFING

ROOFING CEMENT

BLOCKING

FLASHING

GASKETED ALUMINUM OR
STAINLESS STEEL SCREW

SILICONE

INSULATION

HORIZONTAL
CLOSURE STRIP

5 OZ SHIPLAP
FRP GLAZING

GASKETED
SCREW

BLOCKING
BETWEEN
RAFTERS

CONTINUOUS
BOTTOM PLATE
OF RAFTERS

TOP PLATE
OF KNEEWALL

Figure 11-15: Single-Layer FRP (vertical section through eave). FRP glazing is easy to work with, relatively inexpensive and moderately durable, making it a good choice for low- and intermediate-cost greenhouses for either the entire glazing or to fill in around standard size glass. Ring-shanked aluminum nails with neoprene gaskets and closed-cell foam closure strips make installation very easy, but the screws shown will hold better. The shiplap pattern shown is made by the Filon Company and can span rafters up to 3 feet apart.

to moisture cycling in the greenhouse can work nails loose. Holes 1/32 inch larger in diameter than the fastener are drilled into the FRP for the fasteners, to keep them from crazing the fiberglass when they're tightened and to allow for some expansion and contraction. Fasteners should be spaced every 5 to 6 inches along all the straight edges, and in every third valley on the shiplap edges. Note in figure 11-15 that the shiplap pattern is not symmetrical in the same way that rounded corrugations are, since the ultraviolet inhibiting surface is only on one side. That is, if you cut a rectangular piece on the diagonal for use on opposite triangular endwalls, you will end up

with the shiplap pattern upside down on one endwall, which is really no great catastrophe. Whatever brand or pattern of FRP you use, check with the manufacturer to see which is the UV protected side, and be *sure* to put that side out. If you cut off the label that shows which side is out, mark the outside with a piece of tape to avoid confusion.

Where the sheets overlap but aren't supported by blocking, they are sealed with clear silicone and then joined with pop-rivets with neoprene-backed washers every 6 inches, as shown in figure 11-16. FRP can be used as its own edge flashing, simply extending it over the sides and bottom edge of the aperture and

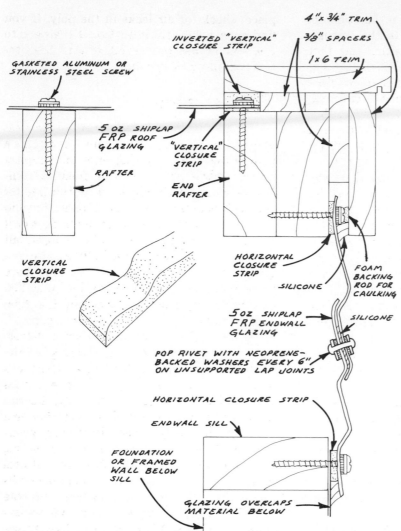

GASKETED ALUMINUM OR
STAINLESS STEEL SCREW

INVERTED "VERTICAL"
CLOSURE STRIP

4"x 3/4" TRIM

3/8" SPACERS

1x6 TRIM

5 OZ SHIPLAP
FRP ROOF
GLAZING

RAFTER

"VERTICAL"
CLOSURE
STRIP

END
RAFTER

VERTICAL
CLOSURE
STRIP

HORIZONTAL
CLOSURE
STRIP

SILICONE

FOAM
BACKING
ROD FOR
CAULKING

5 OZ SHIPLAP
FRP ENDWALL
GLAZING

SILICONE

POP RIVET WITH NEOPRENE-
BACKED WASHERS EVERY 6"
ON UNSUPPORTED LAP JOINTS

HORIZONTAL CLOSURE STRIP

ENDWALL SILL

FOUNDATION
OR FRAMED
WALL BELOW
SILL

GLAZING OVERLAPS
MATERIAL BELOW

Figure 11-16: Single-Layer FRP (section perpendicular to rafter). Horizontal joints in shiplap FRP glazing are made with pop-rivets and sealed with silicone, eliminating the need for support blocking. Vertical glazing can run right over the material below, forming its own flashing. This can also be done with the roof glazing, hanging it over the edges to eliminate the top trim, but the detail shown is neater.

running it under any solid roofing above. But wood trim and metal flashing do look a little nicer and are shown in figures 11-15 and 11-16. The detail shown for the sides of sloped glazing uses two closure strips, one underneath the FRP to make the seal, and the other inverted on top of the fiberglass to seal to the trim, to keep water and leaves or other debris out from under the trim.

Once the framing is up, the closure strips are put in place and held with a very thin bead of silicone. A tiny nail can be used as needed on steep slopes or vertical walls. Measure twice before cutting the fiberglass and put all your pieces in place before applying silicone to the closure strips. The FRP can be cut with tinsnips, or with a carbide-tipped laminate cutter. The laminate cutter is a hand tool used for scoring the FRP and is easier than tinsnips when you're cutting parallel to the corrugations. Score with a straightedge and then break the FRP by bending it back and forth. Apply only enough silicone to install one sheet at a time, as the silicone skins over pretty quickly. In direct sun, when it's warmer than 60°F, some silicones can skin over in less than one minute, so you need to work quickly. Have enough people on hand so that you can gently set the fiberglass down on the gooey silicone without sliding it around and making a mess. Don't do it on a windy day, since the pieces are large enough to catch quite a bit of wind. Another method is to hold the sheet in place with two or three screws near the center and then lift the edges to caulk underneath, after all the rest of the holes are drilled.

Start applying the sheets from the bottom and work your way up, overlapping upper over lower sheets. Drill the holes for the screws with the fiberglass in place, being careful not to drill too deeply into the wood, which would cut down on the screws' ability to hold. After the first sheet is in place, screw the second one up, but don't put the screws in the bottom foot or so of the panel, so that you can bend up the bottom edge to run a silicone bead to seal the lap joint. Drilling the holes for the rivets on the laps before applying the silicone will make the drilling job a little neater.

An inner glazing of polyethylene can be attached between the rafters with small ½-by-¾-inch wood battens, or it can be applied as one big sheet under the rafters. Having it between the rafters looks a little neater and makes it less susceptible to accidental bumps and pokes, though it may not be quite as tight as the single sheet. If it isn't carefully installed, moisture can get between the glazings and condense on the inside of the FRP. If more than just a little condensation forms under the fiberglass with the polyethylene in place, check for air leaks in the poly. If you find none, some vent holes from the air gap to the outside may be needed, as with the site-built double-glass system.

Polyethylene

Polyethylene is by far the cheapest greenhouse glazing, costing only a few cents a square foot and requiring only the simplest support structure and attachment. Greenhouses glazed with polyethylene can pay for themselves in their first year of operation and are a good choice for a minimum budget or if you don't own the house you're living in but you still want a greenhouse. Poly can also be a good temporary glazing, if you will have money for more permanent glazing later. You can build the framing to accept the final glazing and just glaze it for now with poly.

Polyethylene can easily span a 4-foot-wide opening with proper securing at the supports. Inflated, double polyethylene can span the whole greenhouse. For greenhouses that will always be glazed with poly, this can allow fewer framing members and thus less shading. Since polyethylene isn't a very good-looking glazing for a greenhouse living space, it is more likely to be used in a horticultural greenhouse. The main drawback of polyethylene is that it doesn't last very long, with the best UV-resistant types lasting two or perhaps three years. After two years, light transmission may be reduced enough to significantly slow plant growth, particularly in northern winters where growth is already limited by lower-light levels. Count on replacement at least every two years, even with the more UV-resistant brands that are supposed to last three years. Many commercial growers reglaze every year with the two-year poly and every two years with three-year poly to avoid the possibility of a midwinter tear and possible crop failure. Use the best-quality, most

UV-resistant material, such as Monsanto 603, which costs about 6¢ per square foot for 6 mil (0.006 inch thick) and 4¢ for 4-mil material. It is worth the extra cost (compared to 1¢ to 2¢ per square foot for regular polyethylene) for the longer life span and the higher transmittance over time. Your final installed cost per square foot will be higher because you'll probably have to buy a whole roll, which will be more than you need. But you may be able to share a roll with a friend, or you can save the poly for the reglazing in a couple of years. Store it in a tightly closed double plastic bag, in a dry, dark location. UV-resistant polyethylene is available through commercial greenhouse suppliers.

Polyethylene is fairly delicate, requiring care to avoid puncturing it during and after construction. Using the thicker 6-mil material rather than the 4 mil will help a little with durability, but if you are careful with the installation, 4 mil can be used successfully. Cats will climb right up polyethylene greenhouses, once they discover they can get their claws in it, so if you have cats around and can't keep them away from the greenhouse, use a different glazing material. Another disadvantage of polyethylene is its transparency to long-wave infrared radiation, making it lose heat a little faster than glass or most rigid plastics, but moisture condensing on the inside reduces this effect in horticultural greenhouses.

Many commercial growers use double-layer "inflated" poly greenhouses with a small blower that inflates the space between the layers. The air pressure puts the poly under tension, which makes it much stronger and more wind resistant. It is the flapping in the wind of noninflated polyethylene that fatigues the plastic and leads to failure. Inflated poly construction techniques can be adapted to attached greenhouses. One of the kits listed in Appendix 2 uses this system. Blowers and accessories for building your own can be obtained from commercial greenhouse suppliers. Aluminum and plastic extrusions are available for holding the edges of inflated poly, which simplifies the job of changing the plastic, but wood battens and screws will also do the job.

In this section, we'll discuss the installation of noninflated double polyethylene, using wood spacers to hold the two layers apart, and inflated double polyethylene, both with wood battens to hold the plastic down. When installing polyethylene it's important to avoid *point stress,* where a corner of wood or a nail head or any other small point is pressing on the film. Battens rather than nails or staples alone are used to distribute stress. Wherever possible, you should roll up the end of the poly around the battens or spacers and then fasten them down, as shown in figure 11-17, to further reduce stress. Duct tape can be used to relieve the strain where a nail or screw head bears directly on the poly. The duct tape should be out of the sun and weather for it to last as long as the poly. Another general rule is to make the poly easy to change.

Installing polyethylene is a simple and fairly quick procedure. After the framing is up, and before it's painted, check the wood and smooth down any splinters, sharp knots or other protrusions that could cut the poly. A disk or belt sander makes this quite easy. If you can't smooth them, cover them later with a piece of duct tape. Cut all the battens and spacers to at least their approximate lengths, sand off the rough spots and paint them when you paint the framing. Once all the pieces are painted and dry, cut the poly larger than the aperture to allow for at least one and a half rolls around the spacer or batten. Starting with the piece that covers the main opening, roll up the top side of the piece on its spacer, and tack it in place with a few nails driven in just partway, starting in the middle and working to the ends of the spacer. As you nail, pull the poly out towards the ends of the spacer to

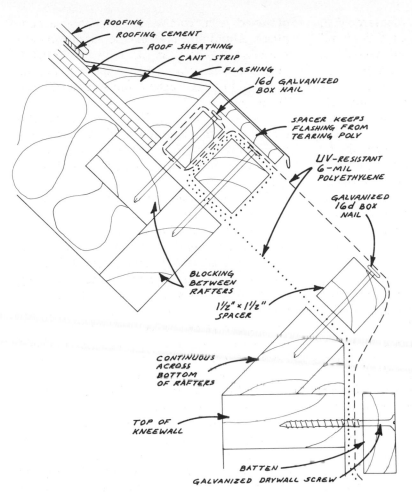

ROOFING

ROOFING CEMENT

ROOF SHEATHING

CANT STRIP

FLASHING

16d GALVANIZED BOX NAIL

SPACER KEEPS FLASHING FROM TEARING POLY

UV-RESISTANT 6-MIL POLYETHYLENE

GALVANIZED 16d BOX NAIL

BLOCKING BETWEEN RAFTERS

1½" × 1½" SPACER

CONTINUOUS ACROSS BOTTOM OF RAFTERS

TOP OF KNEEWALL

BATTEN

GALVANIZED DRYWALL SCREW

Figure 11-17: Stretched Double Polyethylene (vertical section through eave). Polyethylene is a very low-cost glazing. It goes up easily, over widely spaced framing supports, and the UV-resistant varieties will last two to three years. In the method shown, the poly is rolled up around some of the battens and perimeter spacers to give the edge extra strength. Galvanized drywall screws can be substituted for the nails shown.

work out wrinkles. (If you use nails and have to take them out, put a piece of wood between the hammer head and the poly to avoid damaging it.) Using plated drywall screws with a variable speed drill or a "screw-gun," rather than nails, speeds this process up and makes changing the plastic easier. Then roll up the bottom edge of the film on a pole or board, with the pole below the point where the spacer will go. With two or three people pulling to stretch the poly tight, screw the bottom spacer in place, again starting in the middle and working wrinkles out toward the edges.

Once the top and bottom spacers are in place, the end spacers can be put on, using the same stretching technique, followed by the spacers that sit on top of the rafters.

After the spacers are on, the process continues with the outer poly layer and the battens. The battens are placed as much as possible to keep water from collecting on them. Polyethylene should be stretched as tight as possible, to eliminate wrinkles and avoid flapping. Its coefficient of expansion is so large, about ten times that of polycarbonate, that it will be under quite a bit of tension

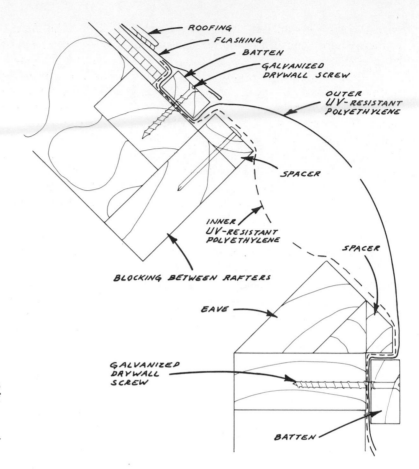

Figure 11-18: Inflated double polyethylene is much stronger than polyethylene held only by battens, since the inflated material doesn't flap and fatigue. It is secured by pulling both layers of plastic tight over a spacer, and then fastening it with a clamping batten, using galvanized drywall screws.

during winter when it contracts. This makes the poly less susceptible to flapping and tears and looks neater.

Inflating two layers of polyethylene increases their strength quite a bit, since the plastic is in tension and does not fatigue from flapping. It's also easier to install, since it only needs to be fastened around the edge. The blower and tube that connects it to the poly can be purchased from a commercial greenhouse supplier. The blower is of the type that can handle a high static pressure (up to 1½

inches of water). Check the power consumption of the blower, and purchase the smallest one that is recommended for the size of the structure you are building. Otherwise, you may end up spending more on electricity than you would like to keep the greenhouse inflated. A 125-watt blower, for example, would cost $9.00 per month to run at $0.10 per kilowatt-hour. If you can't find a smaller blower, you can use a solid-state speed control that will decrease the power consumption. Make sure the speed control is compatible with the blower and that it is the type that reduces energy consumption and slows down the speed.

Inflated double polyethylene can be installed similarly to stretched poly, but only a single layer of battens is required around the perimeter of the polyethylene, with the two sheets installed under a single batten, with the air pressure from the blower separating them. As shown in figure 11-18, the poly is drawn tight over the corner of a piece of wood at each edge and then is battened, which distributes the stress along the corner piece. The poly is stretched when it is installed, using the same trick of wrapping it around a pole and having people pull it tight while the battens are installed. The battens are snugged up against the corner pieces as tight as possible to "clamp" the poly between the two. After the battens are installed, the excess plastic can be trimmed off and the blower installed.

Recycled Wood Storm Windows

Wood-frame storm windows can be a durable, low-cost (often two or three dollars each) glazing for vertical kneewalls and end-walls. They can be installed permanently or hinged for use as vents, or they can be made completely removable for summer venting in moderate and warm climates. They can also be paired back-to-back for double glazing, if you can get enough matched pairs, or used with a polyethylene inner glazing. Storm windows tend to be a better choice than regular window sash, since they usually are twice as big, with more glass and less wood and thus more overall light transmission. (It's not unusual for a window sash to be 15 or 20 percent wood.)

The main limitation of wood windows is they can be used only as vertical glazing. They aren't designed to shed water or snow on a slope, where they would deteriorate faster and be more prone to leaking. Old windows may also need a lot of scraping and reputtying, but if the windows are installed in good shape, they'll last longer and look better.

Wood windows can be installed between or over the front of vertical glazing supports. Attaching them to the fronts means less shading from solid wood, but the choice often comes down to making the floor plan the length you want, either to fit standard overhead glazing sizes or to match the available space on the house. Putting the windows between the supports makes the floor plan wider by about the thickness of all the supports, plus ⅛ inch on each side of each window. Leaving a gap of ⅛ inch between the framing and the sides of each window makes fitting and caulking the windows a little easier. (Use a backing rod behind the caulk if the crack is larger than ⅛ inch.) The foundation type also affects this decision. With the wood-post foundation, the sloped sill in front of the posts makes an easy place to rest the windows. If you double the storms, they will have to go between the supports, since two would protrude too far from the face. The bevel on the sill should match the bevel on the bottom of the windows.

When the windows are placed between the framing members, stops are needed. They can be made from ¾-inch boards. The windows should be predrilled for the nails or screws that will fasten them to the stops or the framing. This will help prevent the glass from cracking when you are nailing. Put as few nails as are needed to hold the window securely, in the sides and the top where they will be covered with trim. Don't put any in the bottom, since they may eventually rust and rot the wood. Removable windows can be held

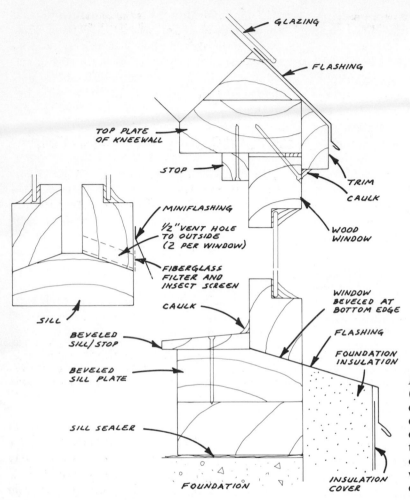

GLAZING

FLASHING

TOP PLATE OF KNEEWALL

STOP

TRIM

CAULK

MINIFLASHING

½" VENT HOLE TO OUTSIDE (2 PER WINDOW)

FIBERGLASS FILTER AND INSECT SCREEN

WOOD WINDOW

SILL

CAULK

WINDOW BEVELED AT BOTTOM EDGE

BEVELED SILL/STOP

FLASHING

FOUNDATION INSULATION

BEVELED SILL PLATE

SILL SEALER

FOUNDATION

INSULATION COVER

Figure 11-19: Storm Windows (vertical section through eave; detail of double windows at eave). Recycled wood storm windows are a low-cost, durable option for vertical glazing. They can be used for double glazing with vent holes drilled in the outer window.

in with screws, turning latches, or even old-style storm window hardware. (The fastening detail shown for removable plastic panels can also be used.) Hinged windows should be reinforced with diagonal wire supports, as shown in figure 11-20, or metal corner braces, since the windows weren't designed to be hung by one edge and will eventually come apart if they're not reinforced. Hook-and-eye latches are a low-cost way to keep the windows closed, with one located near the top and

one near the bottom of larger windows. Also needed is a way to keep the windows from flapping in the wind when they are open, such as another set of hook-and-eyes that latch the windows open or partway open. If you use hinges with removable pins, you can easily remove the windows for the summer.

Before installing the windows, check them for size in your openings, to see if they need trimming. If they do, check carefully for nails, screws and other hardware before using

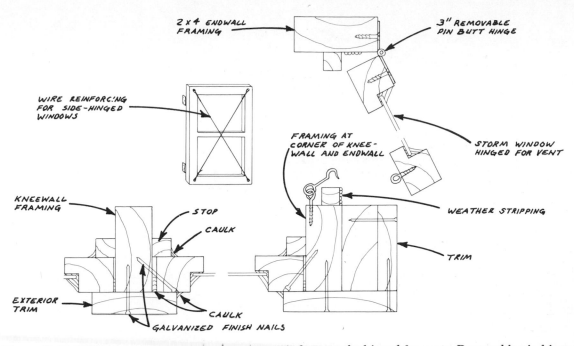

Figure 11-20: With wire or other reinforcing, storm windows can be hinged for vents. Removable pin hinges allow you to take them off for the summer and replace them with screens. If they need trimming, watch for nails used to build or repair the windows. Reputty and repaint any worn parts of the windows after you've trimmed them to size. Holes are predrilled for the toenails through the windows to avoid cracking the glass.

your favorite saw blade or plane. Then scrape, repaint and reputty, making sure to paint the edges as well as the faces. Unpainted edges will absorb moisture, encouraging rot and making movable windows hard to move. It is best to prime the stops and the glazing supports before nailing in the stops, since moisture is bound to find its way under them. Then paint or stain after the stops are in place. Also prime and paint or stain both sides of the trim before installing it, to help keep it from warping. Once all the stops are in place, put the window in place, temporarily shimming it to center it between the vertical supports. With the shims in, drill the holes for the nails, drive them in partway and take out the shims. Use a nail set to drive the nails in the rest of the way, and countersink them enough

so the trim can sit flat. (If you do have to remove a nail after it is countersunk, use a thin nail set to drive the nail all the way through, rather than trying to dig it out.) Caulk around the window, put on the trim and caulk again. Notice that there is no trim on the bottom and that the window overlaps the flashing to shed water.

Double windows should be installed back-to-back with the putty sides towards the outside and inside of the greenhouse. The cavity between the windows needs to be vented to the outside to minimize condensation between the windows. Two ½-inch holes per window, each containing a wisp of fiberglass insulation for a filter and covered by insect screen and flashing should provide enough venting.

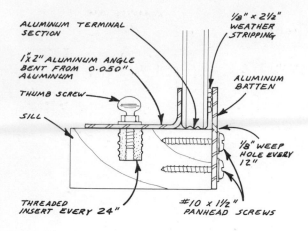

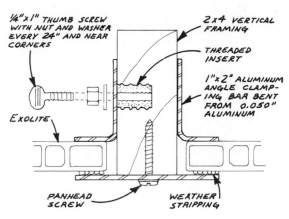

Removable Glazing Panels

In moderate and warm climates, removing some of the glazing is a time-honored solution to summer overheating, as shown by the removable storm windows on many old glassed-in porches. If you want to use the greenhouse in the summer for a screened-in patio, or if you want to keep insects out for horticultural reasons, you can replace the glazing with screens. The screens should be removed for the winter, to avoid unnecessary shading. Removable glazing panels are not a substitute for vents, since you will want to have easily operable vents for spring and fall. Removable glazing requires careful choice of materials and careful construction to make sure the seal is both watertight and airtight when the panels are closed in winter. If wood is used to retain the panels, instead of the aluminum shown in figure 11-21, it should be free of large knots and have a reasonably straight grain to minimize warping. Removable glazing should be limited to vertical areas, since making a good weather seal would be difficult on a slope. Just about any glazing can be used with this system, but whatever you choose, be sure you have a dry area that's out of the sun to store the panels out of the way for the summer.

There are many ways removable glazing panels can be held in place. The method

Figures 11-21 a, b and c (to the right and to the left): Removable glazing panels are nothing new—storm windows have been used for decades to close in porches—but the materials shown here are modern. These drawings show extruded plastic double glazing (such as Exolite) used with aluminum stops and clamping bars. The glazing has weather stripping attached to the outside and is held in place from the inside with aluminum angle clamping bars, which are fastened to the support framing with thumb screws going into threaded inserts. Weep holes let out any moisture that gets by the weather stripping and lets out rain that might collect on the sill when the glazing is out for the summer. An alternative clamping system (not shown here) uses aluminum angle as both the interior clamping bar and the exterior stop.

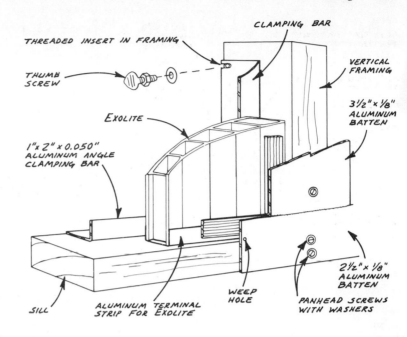

THREADED INSERT IN FRAMING

THUMB SCREW

CLAMPING BAR

VERTICAL FRAMING

EXOLITE

3½" x ⅛" ALUMINUM BATTEN

1" x 2" x 0.050" ALUMINUM ANGLE CLAMPING BAR

2½" x ⅛" ALUMINUM BATTEN

PANHEAD SCREWS WITH WASHERS

WEEP HOLE

ALUMINUM TERMINAL STRIP FOR EXOLITE

SILL

shown in figure 11-21 uses an aluminum batten fixed permanently on the outside of the glazing supports, with the glazing pressed against it from the inside. This has an advantage over systems where the glazing is put in from the outside: The thumb screws used to secure the panels are kept out of the weather. Weather stripping attached to the outside of the glazing is compressed by an aluminum angle that is fastened to the support framing on the inside with thumb screws. (Putting the weather stripping on the glazing rather than the batten gets it out of the weather during the summer.) The vertical batten shown is ⅛-by-3½-inch aluminum bar stock, which completely covers the outside of the support and

doesn't require painting or other maintenance. Or a shop-bent aluminum angle could be substituted, screwing it into the side of the support rather than on the outside face. At the bottom, this angle can have a drip edge to overlap whatever is below. If you don't like the look of aluminum, ¾-by-3½-inch wood trim could be substituted on the outside as long as you are willing to paint and maintain it. An advantage of shop-bent aluminum is that it is available in factory-painted colors such as brown and white, which can be nicer looking than plain aluminum. It is also cheaper than the extruded batten.

For the inside clamping bar, it is cheaper to use an angle bent at a sheet-metal shop

(continued on page 292)

TABLE 11-1: GLAZINGS FOR GREENHOUSES

MATERIAL	ADVANTAGES	DISADVANTAGES	COMMONLY AVAILABLE SIZES
Factory-sealed tempered double glass	Completely transparent; attractive, with good resale value; high performance, low-iron or heat-reflecting units available	Precise framing and installation required; delicate and heavy to handle; seal not as permanent as glass	34″ × 76″ 34″ × 96″ 46″ × 76″ 46″ × 96″
Site-built tempered double glass	Completely transparent; attractive, with good resale value; no hermetic seal	Precise framing and installation required	Same as above
Tempered single glass	Clear view; attractive, with good resale value	Low insulation value; for warm climates, season extension only	Same as above
Double-walled plastic glazing panels (FRP bonded to aluminum, extruded polycarbonate & acrylic)	Strong; fairly easy to install; extruded panels can be cut to odd sizes; available in long sheets to avoid horizontal joints	Extruded panels have high coefficient of expansion; high cost; extruded panels require gasket seal mounting system, which is expensive	Nominal 4′ widths; 8′, 10′, 12′, 16′ lengths
Single-layer fiberglass	Strong; easy to install; doesn't require precise framing; with inner polyethylene makes low cost, fairly durable double glazing; can be cut to odd sizes and shapes	Loses light transmission over time; lower grades deteriorate quickly; hard to eliminate wrinkling in flat sheets	Shiplap: 14′ × 4′; corrugated: 2′ and 4′ widths; 8′, 10′, 12′, 14′, 16′ lengths

*1984 costs based on glazing an 8-foot-high-by-16-foot-wide aperture, with all the glazing in a single plane, using glazing pieces as close to 4 by 8 foot as possible. The cost per square foot for glazing only is the cost of only the glazing material. The cost per square foot with all necessary accessories includes all the hardware, such as battens, screws, glaziers tape, caulking and gasketed screws or nails, that was detailed in the section on that glazing. All glazing costs are based on double glazing except single glass, single-layer fiberglass and recycled storm windows. Note that costs per square foot are higher for smaller areas, or if smaller or odd-sized pieces of glazing are used.

†Estimates are based on manufacturers' projections. Life span of plastics are for the higher-grade materials recommended in the text, assuming periodic washing, particularly in areas with air pollution.

COEFFICIENT OF EXPANSION (in/in-deg F)	COST PER FT²* GLAZING ONLY ($)	COST PER FT²* WITH ALL NECESSARY ACCESSORIES ($)	LABOR REQUIREMENTS	ESTIMATED LIFE SPAN†
0.000005	3.00 to 4.00	4.25 to 5.25 6.00 to 8.00 with prefab glazing system	High, but can be less with prefab aluminum glazing system	10 to 20 yrs for seal, glass indefinite
0.000005	2.00 to 2.50	4.00 to 4.50	High; requires precise framing and installation of glass	Indefinite
0.000005	1.00 to 1.50	2.25 to 2.75	Moderate labor; moderate precision required	Indefinite
FRP panels: 0.000013	4.00–5.00	5.50–6.50	Moderate to low; moderate to low precision required	FRP: 10 to 15 yrs; acrylic: 20 yrs; polycarbonate: 7 to 15 yrs, depending on UV inhibitors
Exolite acrylic: 0.000040	3.25	5.25		
Exolite polycarbonate: 0.000035	4.50	6.50		
¼″ double polycarbonate: 0.000035	1.50–2.00	4.00–5.00		
0.000013	1.00 to 1.50	1.25 to 1.75	Low; little precision required	10 to 15 yrs; inner UV-resistant poly: 3 to 5 yrs

(continued)

TABLE 11-1: GLAZINGS FOR GREENHOUSES (Continued)

MATERIAL	ADVANTAGES	DISADVANTAGES	COMMONLY AVAILABLE SIZES
Double polyethylene	Very low cost; easy to install; doesn't require precise framing; covers large span if edges evenly attached; available in large sizes	Better grades last only 2 to 3 years; delicate, easily punctured by sharp objects like cats' claws; higher heat loss due to high transmission of long-wave infrared radiation	10′ up to 42′ by 100′ rolls, in 4- and 6-mil thicknesses
Recycled wood storm windows	Low cost when available; easy to install; can be hinged for vent; can be paired for double glazing	For vertical installation only; may require labor to re-putty and scrape paint; some units have wide wood frames which cut light levels	Various, approx 3′ × 4½′ common

1984 costs based on glazing an 8-foot-high-by-16-foot-wide aperture, with all the glazing in a single plane, using glazing pieces as close to 4 by 8 foot as possible. The cost per square foot for glazing only is the cost of only the glazing material. The cost per square foot with all necessary accessories includes all the hardware, such as battens, screws, glaziers tape, caulking and gasketed screws or nails, that was detailed in the section on that glazing. All glazing costs are based on double glazing except single glass, single-layer fiberglass and recycled storm windows. Note that costs per square foot are higher for smaller areas, or if smaller or odd-sized pieces of glazing are used.

†*Estimates are based on manufacturers' projections. Life span of plastics are for the higher-grade materials recommended in the text, assuming periodic washing, particularly in areas with air pollution.*

from 0.050-inch aluminum than an extruded aluminum angle. Standard thumb screws hold the angle tightly against the glazing. They should be used with a nut and a washer to keep the thumb screw from gouging into the angle when you tighten it. The thumb screws go into threaded inserts in the support framing. These are available from two hardware sources listed in Appendix 1, if not from your local hardware store. The clamping bar is slotted for the thumb screws to allow you to push the clamping bar against the glazing. The bars are mitered at the corners for good appearance.

After the framing is up and painted or stained, the outside battens are put in place and the glazing is either cut, if it is an extruded material, or built to fit if it is in a frame. Take diagonal measurements of the opening, as well as height and width, so you will be sure your panel will fit. If you use an extruded material, which doesn't have to be framed, follow the directions in the section on that material for expansion allowances. If you have wood glazing frames, allow ⅛ inch on all sides for cutting error, expansion and settling of the framing. Once the glazing panel is cut and checked for fit, the clamping bars are cut,

Coefficient of Expansion (in/in-deg F)	Cost per ft²* Glazing Only ($)	Cost per ft²* with All Necessary Accessories ($)	Labor Requirements	Estimated Life Span†
0.0003	0.04 to 0.08	0.20 to 0.25 (have to buy whole roll plus accessories)	Very low; very little precision required	2 yrs
0.000002	0 to 1.00 depending on condition and availability	0.25 to 1.25 depending on condition and availability	Low if in good condition, high if need reputtying; little precision required	Indefinite

slotted and mitered. The slots can be spaced about every 2 feet. Use the slots to mark where the threaded inserts should go in the glazing supports, and install those. If you use Exolite, install the aluminum terminal strip on the bottom, with ⅛-inch weep holes drilled in it every 12 inches or so.

Put the panel in place, center it and trace a light line on the panel along the batten edge on the outside. Put the weather stripping up to this mark, so that when the panel is in place, the weather stripping is just flush with the batten edge to prevent water from getting under the battens. This is particularly impor-

tant at the bottom. The bottom batten or angle should have weep holes every 12 inches or so, to let out any moisture that gets by the weather stripping and the rain that will fall on the sill when the panels are out in the summer. Mark all the panels and battens with a permanent marker, so you will know where each one goes next winter.

A low-cost approach to removable glazing is to use wood-turning latches on the outside to hold in wood frames covered with flat fiberglass on the outside and 6-mil UV-resistant polyethylene on the inside. In very warm areas, the panels can be single glazed.

The frames can be built of 2 × 2s, with glued lap joints at the corners for a little extra strength. Turning latches will be needed at about 2-foot intervals to hold the panel tightly, and the sloped glazing above, or a flashing under it, has to overlap the top of the panel. The bottom of the panel can overlap flashing below it.

Chapter 12

VENTS AND FANS

Building functional vents is one of the more challenging aspects of greenhouse construction. Exterior vents must be easy to open yet be virtually airtight when they're closed in winter. Roof vents invite leaks, and they are subjected to the high humidity generated by plants, which can warp the wood. The potential for problems requires attention to details while you are building and to a few basic principles of building exterior vents.

Heat exchange vents into the house, on the other hand, generally don't require the same attention to tightness as outdoor vents, since the greenhouse isn't as cold as the outside, and there isn't any wind to drive cold air into the house. Still, heat exchange vents should be built with backdraft dampers in most cases to ensure airflow only in the direction you want. And if the greenhouse will be used in winter only to solar heat the house, you will probably want insulating panels to close off the vents when it's very cold in the greenhouse. Insulating panels aren't needed in greenhouses that are used for growing plants all year, since a small amount of heat leaking from the house to the greenhouse is probably needed anyway. And if you keep the minimum temperature in your greenhouse as high as 50°F (with a back-up heater) you probably don't even need backdraft dampers.

Designing Exterior Vents

There are a few basic guidelines that will help you design and build trouble-free exterior vents. The principle of *overlapping* is as important to exterior vents as it is to roofing and flashing. Everything above must overlap everything below. A corollary also applies: Use caulk, but don't rely on it instead of overlap protection to keep out water unless you really have to, since it will eventually fail and need replacing. Sometimes there's simply no way around gooping up a hole and hoping for the best, but you should try to overlap elements of the vent as much as possible. The flashings shown in the vent details are the main ways that overlap protection is main-

Photo 12-1: Commercial sky-lights take the precision work and worry out of making glazed roof vents. This greenhouse uses commercial skylights for roof vents, awning windows for knee-wall vents and a double-hung sash window for an endwall vent.

tained. If the greenhouse is placed under a house eave, the vents should be placed so that the eave overlaps the top of the vent. This will keep most of the rain or snow from getting behind the vents. Placing the vents as close as possible to the house is helpful even if there is no eave, as this decreases the greenhouse roof area that drains down behind the vents. By raising sloped vents a few inches above the roof surface with what is called a *curb,* the rain can't get close to the vent opening. (This is the same technique used for skylights in normal house roofs.) Carefully overlapping flashing, as shown in the next section, is the trick to keeping the curb itself tight. Placing the vent above the rafters also simplifies the framing, avoiding the need to cut the rafters and use headers for a flush-mounted vent. Vents in vertical walls can be built flush with the wall, with the same waterproofing and framing techniques used for doors and windows.

The materials used in the vent should be capable of withstanding the rigors of green-house life: wide temperature changes and high humidities. Save some of the best lumber in the pile for the vents. Hardware, like hinges, latches, and screws should be heavily plated either with zinc (galvanized), or brass, or should be solid brass or another noncorroding material. Standard brass-plated hinges aren't adequate for outdoor use and will often rust within a year or two. In addition, hardware and weather stripping should be kept out of the weather as much as possible. Hinges that have removable pins, "loose-pin" hinges, will make life much easier while you are building and if you ever have to make repairs.

Even if you aren't going to put screens on the exterior vents when you first build, you should at least think about them as you are designing and building so that if you ever do want them, there will be a place for them. While screens do considerably cut down the

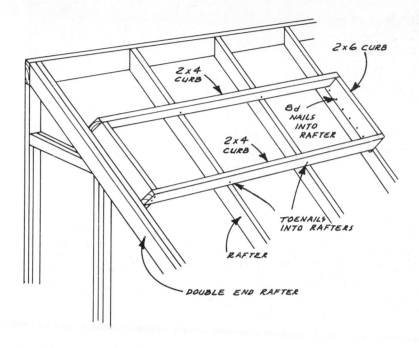

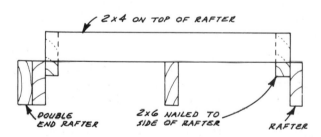

Figure 12-1: The top and bottom 2 × 4s of the vent curb can sit right on top of the rafters, with the 2-by-6 sides overlapping the rafters to provide a nailing surface. The 2 × 6s are notched for a strong joint with the 2 × 4s.

airflow rate, they can be worth the decrease for the benefit of having a bug-free greenhouse or a way to keep beneficial predatory insects inside.

If you don't want to build vents, you can consider buying commercially made operable skylights for overhead vents. These units come complete with all the hardware and weather stripping in place, and some have all the flashing. Better-quality units are expensive, but they're attractive, tight-sealing and durable. Check with your local building supply dealer for prices and options. Some are available with screens, exterior shades and motorized operators.

Vent Curbs

A curb is simply a wood frame that raises the vent opening above the roof surface and helps to direct water around the sides of the vent. If the total required length of ridge vent is more than 8 feet or so, you should probably split it into two vents, with flashing in between, to drain water from the middle as well as around the ends. The curb can go right on top of the rafters, with the horizontal pieces sitting on top and the sloped pieces nailed to the side of the rafters, as shown in figure 12-1. This arrangement eliminates the need to break the rafters at the vent. The rafters carry the sheathing or glazing on the sides of the curb, and blocking between the rafters (not shown in figure 12-1) carries them above and below. Standard 2-by-4 pieces are a convenient material for the horizontal, raising the top of the curb 3½ inches off the rafters, and 2 × 6s can be used for the ends, giving a 2-inch overlap onto the rafters for nailing. The horizontal pieces are toenailed into the top of the rafters and the sloped pieces are nailed to the rafter face. This curb can be assembled on the ground and then lifted onto the rafters. An alternative curb for glazed vents that are set right next to the house, with the top curb touching the house, is shown later in figure 12-7. It is assembled in place.

Before nailing down the curb, strike a straight line across the rafters where the edge of the curb will be, since the toenailing will tend to move the curb as you are nailing. (Clamps may be used to hold the curb while toenailing.) Sight across the top surface of the curb to be sure it is flat, so that the vent will close tightly without having to twist. If the curb doesn't sit flat, check that the rafters themselves all lie in a plane. If not, correct this before installing the curb, or shim the curb to get it flat.

Blocking is needed between the rafters, just above and below the curb, to support the roof sheathing or glazing. (The blocking is not shown in figure 12-1, for clarity in the drawing, but can be seen in the section drawings of the various sloped vents.) Where this blocking

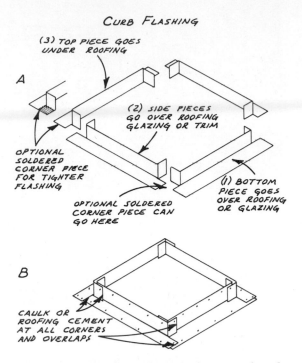

Figure 12-2: The pieces shown in A are numbered by their installation sequence. The optional corner pieces for the top and bottom pieces can be soldered into shop-bent galvanized or copper flashing. These avoid relying on caulking to seal the corners.

supports glazing, it can be as narrow as the span permits, usually a 2 × 3 or 2 × 4, to minimize shading.

Curb Flashing

The curb flashing is designed to provide continuous overlap around the curb. The *basic flashing* shown in figure 12-2 is intended for use with roll roofing, for glazed areas and for curbs that extend all the way to the endwall. The *step flashing* shown in figure 12-3 is for solid roof areas with asphalt or wood shingles. The basic flashing has identical top and bottom pieces, and identical side pieces. The bottom and side flashings go over

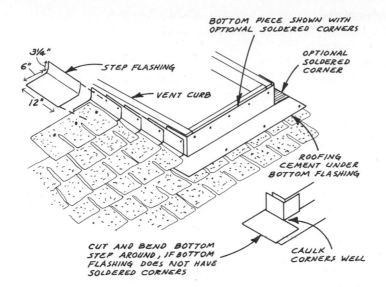

BOTTOM PIECE SHOWN WITH
OPTIONAL SOLDERED CORNERS

3¼"

6"

STEP FLASHING

OPTIONAL
SOLDERED
CORNER

VENT CURB

12"

ROOFING
CEMENT UNDER
BOTTOM FLASHING

CUT AND BEND BOTTOM
STEP AROUND, IF BOTTOM
FLASHING DOES NOT HAVE
SOLDERED CORNERS

CAULK
CORNERS WELL

Figure 12-3: Step flashing is used with shingled roofs. The top and bottom flashings are both single pieces, but the side flashing is done in steps that are interleaved with the shingles. The shingles are held back from the corner of the steps about ½ inch.

the roofing or glazing, while the top piece goes under whatever is above it. (An option for the side flashings with roll roofing is to hem the edge of the flashing that goes on the roof, and then put the flashing under the roll roofing and seal down the roofing with roofing cement. This hides more of the flashing, and the hem will act as a dam to direct any water down and out that does get in.) If the top of the vent is within a foot or so of the house, this top piece should continue up under the house siding, as shown in figure 12-4. If the curb isn't close to the house, the top flashing should extend up the roof to be as high as the top of the curb. This is so that if snow or water is ever caught in the valley above the curb, water can't back up under the roofing and get under the flashing. Fifteen-pound felt (tar paper) is laid down on any solid roof areas before any of the roofing or flashing is put in place. It should be run up the sides of the curb.

The top of the basic flashing overlaps the side pieces, which overlap the bottom, as shown in B (figure 12-2). If the optional extra piece is soldered into the corners of the top

and bottom pieces, there is an excellent overlap. If you have your flashing made up at a sheet-metal shop, the additional pieces can be soldered in the shop. (Remember that copper or aluminum rather than galvanized should be used in acid rain areas.) The best time to make up the flashing is after the curb is in place, and, for glazed areas, after the lower glazing and any trim on the sides of the curb are in place. (There will be trim on the sides if the curb goes to the end wall.) This is so you can measure the flashing to fit what is actually built, rather than what you might anticipate. Once the flashing is made, place it around the curb without nailing it to check the fit. Mark around its edges to give you a mark for where to lay the sealant and remove it. Otherwise, the caulk or roof cement will make a mess as you guess where it's supposed to go. After caulking place the flashing, starting with the bottom piece, then the sides, and finally the top piece. Use roofing cement where the flashing contacts solid roof or the curb, butyl or silicone caulking where it contacts trim, and silicone where it contacts glazing or glazing battens.

Ideally, nails should only go through the flashing where they will be away from water, such as at the top of the curb, or under an overlap. This isn't always possible, so roofing cement is again relied on. With the cement or caulk underneath, nails that penetrate will be fairly well sealed, but it doesn't hurt to give them another dab after you nail them in. A more secure option is butyl-gasketed roofing screws (available from roofing suppliers), which seal well and resist pulling out better than common nails. If the bottom flashing

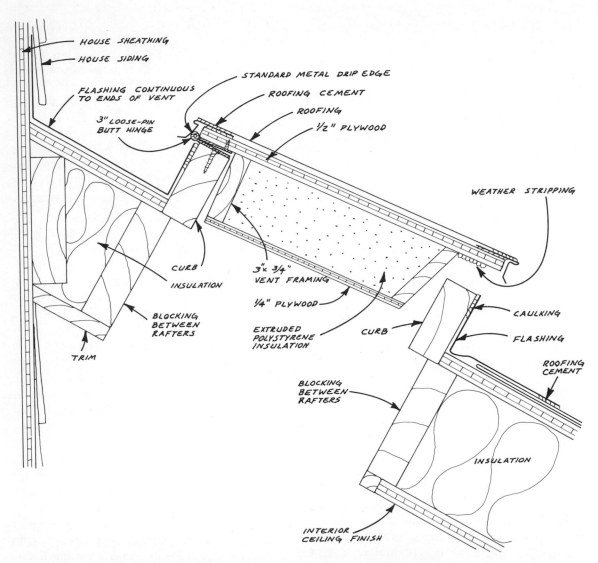

Figure 12-4: Solid Roof Vent (vertical section). This vent can be built to fit inside the curb, on top of the rafters. This allows a large vent while avoiding breaking up the rafter framing.

overlaps glazing battens, seal between the flashing and the battens with silicone caulking after both are in place. Without the optimal corner addition to the top and bottom flashing, the corners indicated in figure 12-2 are vulnerable, and will need careful caulking to keep out water. Liberal amounts of silicone or roofing cement should be applied underneath with the flashing pressed down onto it. After some years, these corners may need recaulking.

With shingled roofs, the step flashing allows proper overlapping all the way around the curb and hides the flashing under the shingles, with the exception of the bottom edge. The soldered corner addition is also best used here to eliminate a potential leak spot. But you can get a good seal without it if you are careful. The shingles are brought up to within an inch or so of the curb. No nails or screws need be exposed, except below the curb at the bottom. You have to watch the sequence as you go, roofing up to the bottom of the curb, putting on the bottom flashing, and then alternating shingles and step flashing up the side. The top flashing is nailed and tarred to the 15-pound felt on the roof sheathing or run up under the house siding if the vent is close enough to the house.

Vents for Solid Roofs

Placing roof vents in a solid roof section simplifies the glazing somewhat, allowing all the roof glazing to be uninterrupted. This also allows the vents to be placed at the highest point in the structure for best ventilation, and as close to the house as possible for minimum rain and snow drainage above the vent. The vent cover (which we'll simply refer to as the "vent") should be framed out of the lightest-weight material possible, so the least effort is required to open and close it. Standard 2-by-4 framing with ½-inch plywood sheathing creates a surprisingly heavy vent. One-by-four

framing, with ½-inch plywood on the outside and ¼-inch on the inside, as shown in figure 12-4, is plenty strong and cuts the weight considerably. The ½-inch outer sheathing is thick enough for attaching hinges and gives a good, solid nailing surface for roofing or flashing. It's a good idea to glue and screw the vent frame together and to use expanded polystyrene insulation inside rather than fiberglass, which may settle with repeated opening and closing. Note in figure 12-4 that the side of the framing away from the hinges is beveled to allow the vent to pass by the curb without hitting it, as shown in figure 12-5. Also, allow for a ⅛-inch gap between the vent and the curb to keep it from sticking when it gets moist and expands.

Weather stripping is usually placed on the underside of the outer plywood, all the way around where it contacts the top of the curb. Where the hinges would interrupt the weather stripping, it can be placed inside the curb. Attaching the weather stripping to the vent rather than the curb keeps it out of the

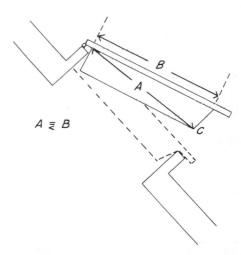

Figure 12-5: In order for a solid vent to operate without corner C hitting the curb, the diagonal A must be no longer than dimension B across the top of the insulated portion.

sun. By placing the hinges on top of the curb and under the outer plywood, rather than routing out the wood to place the hinges flush with the surface, there will be space for weather stripping. Figure 12-4 shows the vent covered with roll roofing (asphalt shingles can also be used) with a commercially available drip edge all the way around. This is an effective, low-cost approach with roofing cement sealing the drip edge to the plywood and the roofing to the drip edge. Another very effective way is to have a one-piece sheet-metal cap made up for the vent, complete with soldered corners and edges that come down over the curb flashing. Whatever type of flashing you use, be sure it overlaps the curb flashing at least ½ inch, and preferably more, when the vent is closed. This flashing also keeps the hinges out of the rain, but shouldn't

hide them so much that it is difficult to get the hinge pins in or out. If you can't find a standard drip edge tall enough to overlap sufficiently at building supply or roofing dealers you will have to make one or have it made.

The vent should be assembled on a very flat surface, or it will be warped when it is finished. After it is assembled, it is quite rigid, so be careful to keep it square while assembling. Paying extra attention to cutting all the pieces quite square also helps keep the frame flat. Once you have the vent and the curb assembled, you can fit them together, install the hinges on the ground and then remove the hinge pins. The vent can also be painted or stained much more easily on the ground. After all is dry, install the curb, being careful to keep the curb straight as you nail it. The vent

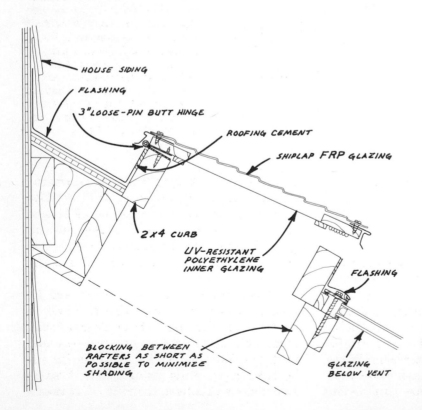

Figure 12-6: Glazed Roof Vent on Standard Curb (vertical section). Glazed vents can sit on top of the same type of curb shown for solid vents, with the drip edge flashing on the vent overlapping the curb flashing. The top flashing runs up under the house siding if the vent is close enough to the house. (Glazing details are shown in figures 12-10 and 12-11.)

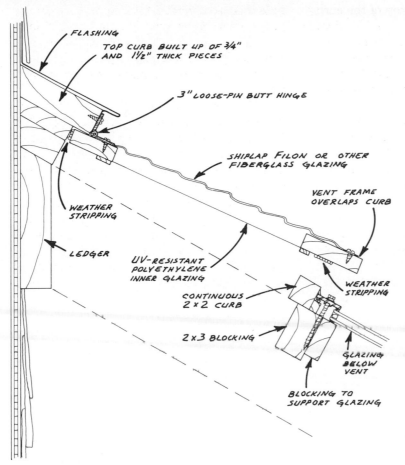

FLASHING

TOP CURB BUILT UP OF ¾"
AND 1½" THICK PIECES

3" LOOSE-PIN BUTT HINGE

SHIPLAP FILON OR OTHER
FIBERGLASS GLAZING

VENT FRAME
OVERLAPS CURB

WEATHER
STRIPPING

LEDGER

UV-RESISTANT
POLYETHYLENE
INNER GLAZING

CONTINUOUS
2 × 2 CURB

2 × 3 BLOCKING

WEATHER
STRIPPING

GLAZING
BELOW
VENT

BLOCKING TO
SUPPORT GLAZING

Figure 12-7: Glazed Roof Vent with Curb at Common Wall (vertical section). If the top of the curb can be right next to the house, a shorter curb can be used. In this case, the vent frame is slightly larger than the curb, to provide overlap at the sides and bottom and eliminate the need for flashing on the vent itself and on the bottom of the curb. Flashing over the built-up top of the curb directs water running down the side of the house over the top of the vent. Glazing details for vents and for the flashing to the roof glazing below the vent are shown in figures 12-10 and 12-11.

can then be put into place and the hinge pins installed.

Vents for Glazed Roofs

Glazed roof vents can use the same curb system as solid vents, but with the vent sitting completely on top of the curb, as shown in figure 12-6. If the top of the vent is right next to the house, then the top of the curb can be attached to the house, and the curb can be lowered, since it won't have water behind it, as shown in figure 12-7. In this case, water running down the side of the house is directed over the vent by flashing that extends over the top edge of the vent glazing. The vent also overlaps the curb an inch or so on the bottom edge. Flashing is eliminated on the vent and on the bottom of the curb, and, if the vent is as wide as the greenhouse, on the sides of the curb.

The framing for the vent should be matched to the kind of glazing that will be used: Double glass needs the most rigid frame, to minimize flexing that would stress the seal, while the frame for polyethylene glazing can be lightweight. After using the vent sizing guidelines in chapter 4, the actual dimensions

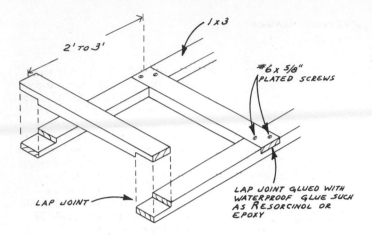

Figure 12-8: This light-duty vent frame is for flexible plastics including fiberglass, polyethylene and 4- to 10-millimeter-thick extruded double-layer polycarbonate or for thicker double-layer plastic panels with aluminum extrusion mounting systems that strengthen the frame. The lap joints are put together with waterproof glue and wood screws. The frame should be hinged and supported by a vent operator arm every 2 feet.

Photo 12-2: This glazed roof vent is right next to the house and uses the shorter curb. When the vent is closed, it sits almost in the same plane as the rest of the glazing, making for an aesthetically pleasing line.

of the vent will be determined, in part, by the standard size of the glazing, or by the size of any scraps you might have left from the rest of the glazing, particularly with the more expensive extruded plastic glazings. Figures 12-8 and 12-9 respectively show light- and heavy-duty vent frames. The lighter frame is appropriate, in general, for flexible glazings, including fiber-reinforced polyester (FRP), polyethylene and the thinner, 4- to 10-milli-meter-thick extruded double-layer polycarbonate. It can also be used with the double-layer extruded or FRP panels with extruded aluminum frames, since the extrusions give extra strength to the vent frame. The heavy-duty frame is more appropriate for single or double glass, or for double-layer extruded plastic panels that are small enough to need only a wet seal. The depth of the rabbet depends on the type of glazing, but in general

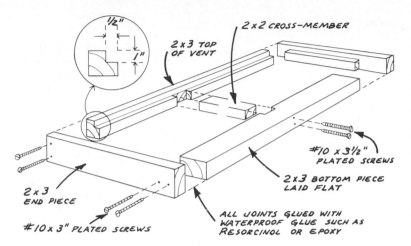

1/2"
1"

2 x 2 CROSS-MEMBER

2 x 3 TOP
OF VENT

#10 x 3 1/2"
PLATED SCREWS

2 x 3 BOTTOM PIECE
LAID FLAT

2 x 3
END PIECE

ALL JOINTS GLUED WITH
WATERPROOF GLUE SUCH AS
RESORCINOL OR EPOXY

#10 x 3" PLATED SCREWS

Figure 12-9: Heavy-duty vent framing for double glass and extruded plastic panels with a wet-seal mounting is shown with 2×3s, but other sizes can be used, depending on the spacing between the hinges and between the supports of the vent opener. Vent operators should be attached to the vent near the cross-members, and good-quality, kiln-dried wood should be used to prevent warping.

it is about 1/8 inch deeper than the glazing material. It is shown in figure 12-9 as 1 inch deep, for 7/8-inch-thick double-glass units. The number of hinges and operators to be used also determines how heavy the frame needs to be. A light frame needs hinges and an operator at least every 2 feet. The thicker frame can be built with 2×2s or 2×3s laid flat, if every 2 lineal feet of vent is supported by a hinge and an operator; 2×3s can be used on edge (as shown in figure 12-8) if the vent has a hinge and an operator every 3 feet, and 2×4s can be used if there is hardware every 4 feet. The hinges and operators should be attached at or near cross members, and near each end.

Both frames are strengthened with waterproof glue and screws. Since this frame will be somewhat exposed to the weather, interior grade wood glue shouldn't be used. Note in figure 12-9 that the bottom rail is shallower than the others to allow the glazing to overlap the lower edge. The glazing details are essentially identical to those for fixed sloped glazing (see figures 12-10 and 12-11). The FRP glazing is shown in figure 12-10 with a drip edge all around the vent to protect the edge of the wood and overlap the curb flashing. When the vent frame overlaps the curb

Photo 12-3: This glazed roof vent is being glazed with shiplap pattern FRP. The vertical closure strip, which matches the corrugations in the FRP, has already been attached to the vent frame, and a bead of silicone has been applied to seal it to the FRP. Note that the vent frame is already painted.

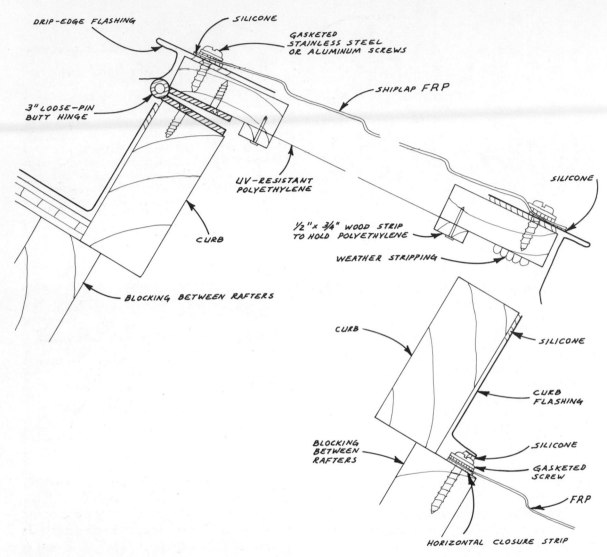

Figure 12-10: FRP Glazing on Roof Vent (vertical section). A low-cost, easily built vent with FRP outer glazing and polyethylene inner glazing is shown here on a full height curb. Standard drip edge is used around the vent to overlap the curb flashing and cover the hinges. (Glazing details are the same as shown in chapter 11 except where differences are noted.)

below, this drip edge may be omitted, and the fiberglass can be extended over the edges of the vent frame ¾ inch or so for a drip edge. In

both figures 12-10 and 12-11 the curb flashing overlaps the glazing below it and is sealed to the glazing or batten with silicone.

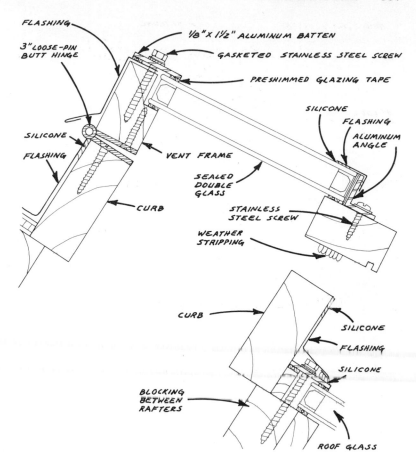

FLASHING

3" LOOSE-PIN BUTT HINGE

1/8" X 1 1/2" ALUMINUM BATTEN

GASKETED STAINLESS STEEL SCREW

PRESHIMMED GLAZING TAPE

SILICONE

FLASHING

ALUMINUM ANGLE

SILICONE

FLASHING

VENT FRAME

SEALED DOUBLE GLASS

CURB

STAINLESS STEEL SCREW

WEATHER STRIPPING

CURB

SILICONE

FLASHING

SILICONE

BLOCKING BETWEEN RAFTERS

ROOF GLASS

Figure 12-11: The frame for this sealed double-glass vent is made with 2 × 3s. The detail for the bottom edge of the glass is the same as shown in chapter 11. The vent frame overlaps the curb flashing, which overlaps the top batten of the roof glass.

Vents for Solid Walls

Wall vents can be built flush with the wall with relative ease. The opening is framed like a conventional window or door opening, though more care should be taken to make it square, since this is a finish opening. The bottom of the frame is sloped to shed water and allow the vent to close easily. The vent shown in figure 12-12 is hinged at the top, which allows the vent to shed water even when it is open. This arrangement has the disadvantage of making it heavier to open than a side-hinged vent, but you don't have to worry about closing the vents when it rains.

The vent itself is framed with 3/4-inch-thick wood, except for the side with the hinges, which is 1 1/2 inches thick for a better hold on the hinge screws. Three-inch butt hinges with loose pins are used. The vent is sheathed with 1/2-inch exterior grade plywood on the outside. It overlaps the finished opening about 1/2 inch on the sides and bottom (not the top) to provide a place for weather stripping. When the vent is pulled tightly closed, the weather stripping will tend to push the plywood off the frame, so it is important that it be securely glued and nailed. If siding isn't used over the plywood, a small piece of flashing, shown in figure 12-12, should be attached

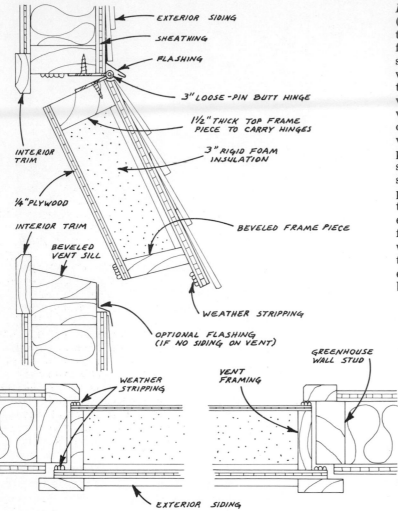

EXTERIOR SIDING

SHEATHING

FLASHING

3" LOOSE-PIN BUTT HINGE

1½" THICK TOP FRAME PIECE TO CARRY HINGES

3" RIGID FOAM INSULATION

INTERIOR TRIM

¼" PLYWOOD

INTERIOR TRIM

BEVELED VENT SILL

BEVELED FRAME PIECE

WEATHER STRIPPING

OPTIONAL FLASHING (IF NO SIDING ON VENT)

WEATHER STRIPPING

VENT FRAMING

GREENHOUSE WALL STUD

EXTERIOR SIDING

Figure 12-12: Solid Wall Vent (vertical section above; horizontal section below). The rough framing for a solid wall vent is similar to that for doors and windows. The vent itself is built the same way as a solid roof vent. The outer plywood on the vent overlaps the wall framing on the sides and bottom to provide a place for weather stripping. A second line of weather stripping can be put on the inside edge of the vent to compress against the inner trim. If the outside plywood isn't covered with siding, a small piece of flashing should be used to direct water over the exposed edge of the plywood wall sheathing. All exposed plywood edges should be carefully sealed or covered.

to the bottom edge to keep water from running down onto the top edge of the plywood below the vent. To minimize air leaks, a second level of weather stripping can be put on the interior trim around the inside of the opening on these same three sides. The hinged side should have the weather stripping between the opening framing and the vent framing, where it will be compressed when the vent closes. The hinges need not be rabbeted

into the opening or the vent to leave room for the weather stripping.

The vent is assembled in the same fashion as the solid roof vents, and the same care should be taken to ensure that the unit is assembled flat and square. The edges of the plywood, on the vent and on the wall sheathing around the vent, should be well sealed, since they will be exposed to the weather. One way to do this is to smear caulking on them

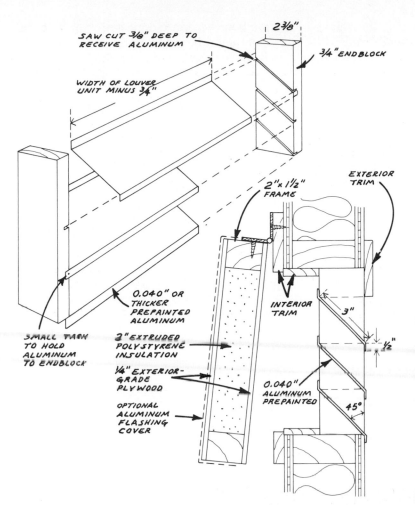

SAW CUT 3/8" DEEP TO RECEIVE ALUMINUM

2 3/8"

3/4" ENDBLOCK

WIDTH OF LOUVER UNIT MINUS 3/4"

2"x 1 1/2" FRAME

EXTERIOR TRIM

0.040" OR THICKER PREPAINTED ALUMINUM

INTERIOR TRIM

3"

SMALL TACK TO HOLD ALUMINUM TO ENDBLOCK

2" EXTRUDED POLYSTYRENE INSULATION

1/4" EXTERIOR-GRADE PLYWOOD

1/2"

0.040" ALUMINUM PREPAINTED

45°

OPTIONAL ALUMINUM FLASHING COVER

Figure 12-13: Louvers can be used to keep rain out of openings for vents that swing in. You can build them yourself by first having pieces of heavy-gauge prepainted aluminum or galvanized sheet metal bent for you. Fit these into endblocks, of cedar, redwood or pressure-treated wood, which you slot to accept the metal pieces. The louver units are assembled with small tacks driven through the vertical face of the sheet metal into the face of the two endblocks. The assembly is then put into the framed opening with the top trim covering the opening slightly. Also notice the relative positions of the louvers, which keep blowing rain from getting through.

after the vent is assembled, but before it is painted. Another, better protection is to glue and nail 1/2-by-3/16-inch or 1/2-inch half-round trim on the exposed plywood edges before painting. Be sure the edges get a good coat of primer and two coats of finish paint or stain when you paint or stain the rest of the vent.

Another approach to solid wall vents is to hinge them to swing inward. This does take up some inside space, but if they swing into an unused area, such as under a bench, then no

useful space is taken. Fixed louvers can be placed over the opening, to keep rain out, as well as to provide security when you want to leave the house and need to leave the vent open. Photos 12-4 and 12-5 show a louvered lower vent that extends under a planting bench. (The bench for this space will be slatted wood, to allow cool air entering through the vent to be drawn up through the slats and between the pots. The vent door has been covered with flashing to protect it from any spilled water that drips through the slats.) The door will be opened manually and will swing up and latch to a hook under the bench. The main drawback to louvers is that they reduce the effective area of the opening. Shorter units can reduce the area by about 50 percent, as do the units shown in figure 12-13, but most units are built taller than these. Taller louvers don't block as much, but any reduction in effective opening should be considered when you size the vent.

Louvers can be fabricated fairly easily, at a much lower cost than purchasing them complete. Figure 12-13 shows the necessary pieces and how they go together. The sheet metal should be around 0.040 or 0.050 inch thick—and can be galvanized steel (except in acid rain areas) or prepainted aluminum. This gauge is too heavy for do-it-yourself bending

so you'll have to get it done at a shop. The end blocks should be cut from rot-resistant wood, such as redwood, cedar or pressure-treated lumber. The slots are simply saw cuts in the wood.

Note the placement of the louvers to keep the rain from blowing in. The bottom slot ends at the corner of the block, allowing the bottom metal piece to overlap the bottom of the opening on the outside. This is helpful in waterproofing the bottom, as well as giving you a little wider tolerance in the fit between the louver and the opening. The sheet metal is tacked to the inside and outside faces of the blocks. Insect screen can be tacked over the back of the unit once it is installed. The opening for the louver can be slightly taller than the louver itself, with the louver installed in the bottom of the opening, as

Photos 12-4 and 12-5: Site-built louvers, built as shown in figure 12-13, let in ventilation air, but keep rain and people out. Inside, the vent doors swing up and will eventually hook up under a growing bench.

shown in figure 12-13. Once the unit is in place, vertical trim can cover the blocks on the sides, and horizontal outside trim overlaps the top opening enough to keep rain out.

Vents for Glazed Walls

The construction of glazed wall vents is just about identical to that of glazed roof vents. The frames are identical, with light- and heavy-duty frames used with the same glazings and support requirements as described for the roof vents. As with roof vents, glazed wall vents are also more easily mounted outside the framing than between framing members, as shown in figures 12-14 and 12-15. This allows larger continuous vents to be built in one piece, which also decreases the number of vent edges that need to be sealed. Placing vents outside the framing has another advantage for horticultural greenhouses: When the vents expand because of high humidity, they won't get stuck in their frames. Continuous vents also tend to have less solid framing and more glass, resulting in less obstruction of sunlight. Placing the cross-members of the vent frame directly in front of kneewall framing members also decreases shading.

Commercially made windows can also be used for vents. These may be more economical than custom-built units in cases where labor costs are high. You can often find windows that match those on the house. In the end-walls, or in taller vertical kneewalls, there is usually enough room to use whatever type of window you want or can afford. In shorter kneewalls, awning-type windows—hinged at the top to swing outward—or hopper-type windows—hinged at the bottom to swing inward—are often used.

Commercial windows are installed as in regular house construction, in a rough opening slightly larger than the window frame. This can create a lot of solidity near the growing areas, a place where you would like the most light possible, but this can be an acceptable trade-off where design dictates a particular type of window or appearance. If you do use commercial windows, be sure they are easy to operate. If they have crank operators, be sure you will be able to reach them comfortably. Casement windows can usually be ordered with the crank on either side, so choose the side that will allow you to reach it once the beds and benches are in place. Double-hung windows could be difficult to open if you have to reach over a 3-foot-wide bench. Awnings or hopper windows can be had with either crank or push-type operators. (Operators for pushout windows and for site-built vents are discussed later in this chapter.) A note about buying commercial windows: Since they fit inside their frames, they are susceptible to sticking when the greenhouse gets humid. For this reason, you should buy good-quality windows that have a weather-stripping system that is tolerant of expansion and contraction. Window installation isn't discussed here, since standard construction techniques are used. It's suggested that extra care be given to installing the frames square and true, to minimize problems with the window sash sticking against the frame.

Vertical vents don't require curbs, since the flashing above them can direct water over the top. An eave member can be attached to the outside of the framing, with the vent hung below it, as in figures 12-14 and 12-15. The lightweight framing and glazing is shown in figure 12-14 with stud-wall-type framing, and the more heavily framed glass vent is shown with truss framing in figure 12-16, although either type of vent may be used with any framing system. The double glass vent is shown with ⅝-inch-thick sealed units. These are thinner than optimum, for insulation value, but allow you to use 2-by-3 lumber flat for framing them, and 2 × 4s for the eave member

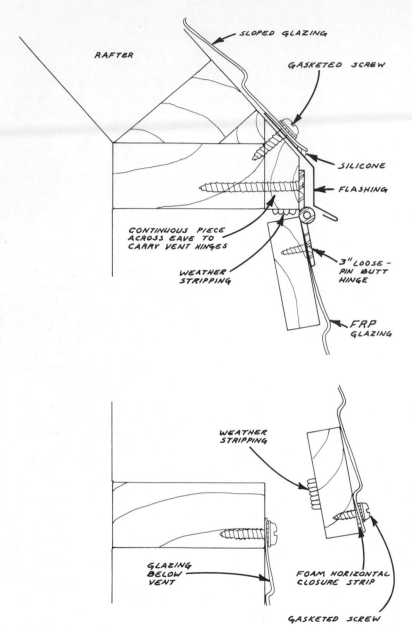

SLOPED GLAZING

RAFTER

GASKETED SCREW

SILICONE

FLASHING

CONTINUOUS PIECE
ACROSS EAVE TO
CARRY VENT HINGES

WEATHER
STRIPPING

3" LOOSE-
PIN BUTT
HINGE

FRP
GLAZING

WEATHER
STRIPPING

GLAZING
BELOW
VENT

FOAM HORIZONTAL
CLOSURE STRIP

GASKETED SCREW

Figure 12-14: Lightweight
Glazed Wall Vents (vertical section). Glazed wall vents sit outside the structural framing and
are hinged to a length of wood
fastened to the greenhouse
frame. The wood screws that
hold the hinge onto the eave are
long enough to go into the eave
framing member. Flashing under the sloped glazing covers the
vent hinge and bends out
enough to keep the hinge out of
the rain while still allowing the
vent to open. The FRP glazing
shown here forms its own flashing at the bottom, overlapping
the glazing below. The framing
for the vent is the same as for
roof vents (see figure 12-8).

to which they are attached. With the trusses, the eave member that carries the vent also forms the bottom support for the glazing. With post-and-beam framing, the eave member can be made wide enough to extend beyond the vertical framing members and over the top of the vent, or another piece with the hinges attached to it can be added to the outside face of a narrower eave. The added eave piece has the advantage of allowing you

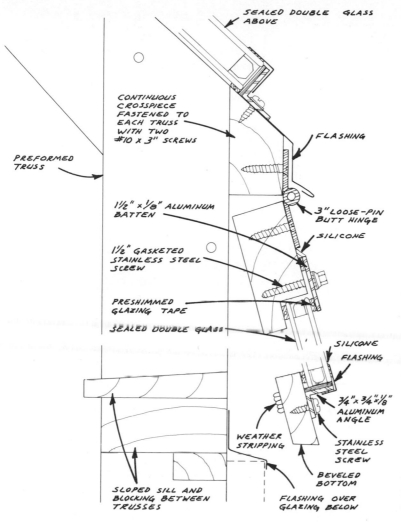

SEALED DOUBLE GLASS ABOVE

CONTINUOUS CROSSPIECE FASTENED TO EACH TRUSS WITH TWO #10 x 3" SCREWS

PREFORMED TRUSS

1½" x ⅛" ALUMINUM BATTEN

1½" GASKETED STAINLESS STEEL SCREW

PRESHIMMED GLAZING TAPE

SEALED DOUBLE GLASS

SLOPED SILL AND BLOCKING BETWEEN TRUSSES

FLASHING

3" LOOSE-PIN BUTT HINGE

SILICONE

SILICONE

FLASHING

¾" x ¾" x ⅛" ALUMINUM ANGLE

STAINLESS STEEL SCREW

BEVELED BOTTOM

WEATHER STRIPPING

FLASHING OVER GLAZING BELOW

Figure 12-15: Sealed Double Glass Wall Vent (vertical section). A glass-glazed eave vent is shown here with ⅝-inch-thick overall sealed double glass. These thinner air gaps don't insulate as well as 1-inch units, but they do result in a thinner vent. The framing and glazing details for the vent itself are the same as for the glazed roof vent (see figures 12-9 and 12-11). The vent is shown here at the eave of a greenhouse framed with pre-formed trusses, with the hinges attached to a 1½-inch-thick crosspiece that is screwed to the trusses. If the bottom of the vent is beveled, water will be directed over the glazing or whatever is below.

to install the hinges before the eave piece is installed.

The upper flashing runs from underneath the glazing above the vent and forms a drip edge that keeps water from running onto the hinged edge, but still allows the vent to open fully. With fiberglass glazing below the vent, the vent frame overlaps the glazing below, as shown in figure 12-14. With glass or other glazing that has some thickness below the vent, the bottom of the vent should be beveled, as shown in figure 12-15. If the bottom of the vent is at the top of the foundation, the vent will close onto the top of the foundation flashing.

Operating Hardware for Vents

Vent operators can involve using elaborate automatic systems that open the vent in proportion to the amount of venting required at a given temperature, or they can be as

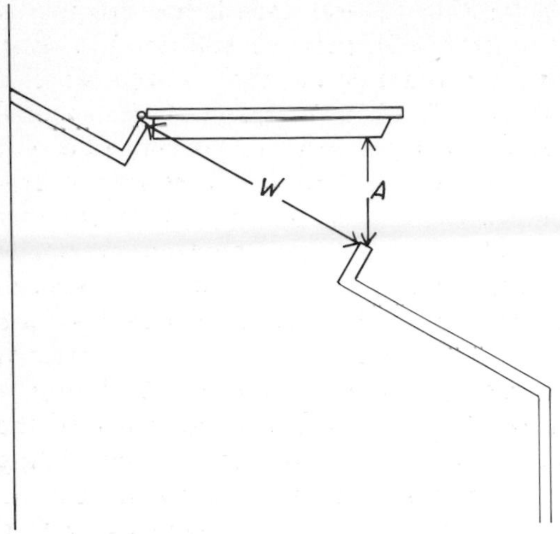

Figure 12-16: The actual area open for ventilation is the distance the vent opens (A) times the length, plus the total of areas of the two open triangles at the ends of the vent, approximately the width of the vent (W) times A. If the vent doesn't open very far, the total may be smaller than the area of the vent hole itself. Watch for this as you are planning your ventilation.

simple as a stick with a hook that you use to push and pull the vent. In this section we'll first discuss a couple of general issues and then look at some simple manual operators, heat piston operators, and manual and motorized gear-driven systems.

How far the vent actually opens, rather than the size of the vent hole will usually determine the effective opening. If for example the opening for your vent is 2 feet wide (see figure 12-16) but the vent can only open enough that dimension A is 1¼ feet, the effective opening is actually 1¼ feet times the length of the vent, plus the area of the two open triangles formed at the ends of the vent. Thus if the vent is 8 feet long, the open area would be 1¼ times 8 plus the area of the two triangles, each of which is about 1¼ square feet. This gives a total of:

$$(1\tfrac{1}{4} \times 8) + (2 \times 1\tfrac{1}{4}) = 12\tfrac{1}{2} \text{ square feet}$$

Again, by just looking at the opening in the roof for the vent, you would think you had 2 feet by 8 feet, or 16 square feet of vent opening. If the vent could be opened enough that dimension A were 1½ feet, the effective area would be:

$$(1\tfrac{1}{2} \times 8) + (2 \times 1\tfrac{1}{2}) = 15 \text{ square feet}$$

So by increasing the travel of the vent to a little over 1½ feet, the effective opening in this case is about equal to the framed opening. Opening the vent any wider won't gain you any additional area. The amount of travel needed to create the maximum effective opening depends on the length and thickness of the vent. If the vent is only 2 or 3 feet long, the open triangles at the ends are a bigger portion of the effective opening, and the vent need not travel as far for the open area to approach that of the framed opening. If it is longer, it will have to travel farther.

The other factor affecting how far you can open a vent is rain. It is best to have the maximum open position of the vent slightly sloped downward to the front of the greenhouse, so that if it rains, water will drain off the front, rather than behind the curb. With wall vents this is no problem, since opening them even 60 degrees (which makes the travel measurement "A" equal to the width of the opening measurement "W") still leaves them sloping downward for drainage. Roof vents are a little more difficult. Unless the roof is very steep, opening them 60 degrees will cause rain to drain behind the vent. This area should be completely waterproof in case this happens. And if the roof of the house drains onto or behind the greenhouse vents, a downpour could very well bring in enough water to overwhelm this little gutter, and some water

Another general issue is how frequently the operator is going to support the vent. With a manual crank, such as the recycled unit shown in photo 12-6, or motorized geared operator, as many arms as needed can be put onto the rotating shaft, but most other operators push only at one point. This means that the vent frame itself must be strong enough to be supported at one spot when it is opened, and to close tightly when it is closed. Having a tight closure is not of as much concern as supporting the open vent against buffeting by the wind, since latches, in addition to the operator, can be used to close the vent tightly in winter. Solid vents are quite strong and need an operator arm only every 4 or 5 feet. For glazed vents, use the spacing guidelines discussed earlier in the section on vents for glazed roofs.

Poles and Push-Sticks

One of the simplest ways to open a vent is to push it with a pole or stick. By hinging the stick to the outer edge of the vent at the top and giving it a series of notches at the bottom to rest it, the vent can be left in one of several positions. Some type of restraint is needed since the wind can easily lift even a heavy vent, and then drop it shut. One scheme for pole openers is to have a screw or nail sticking out of the side of a post that the pole runs by, and a series of holes at various heights in the pole. This can also be adapted to vertical vents.

Storm Window Hardware

Another variation, for lightweight vents, is to use the operator hardware that is used on wood storm windows. It is similar to that used on folding table legs, and turns the vent into a simple awning window. The hardware locks the vent all the way open and can be operated

Photo 12-6: This hand crank mechanism opens 80 pounds of double-glazed eave vent with a twirl of a finger. This unit is recycled from an old glass commercial greenhouse, but similar ones are available from some of the prefabricated greenhouse manufacturers.

could spill into the vent. So achieving a maximum effective opening must be balanced with keeping out the rain. Steeper sloped roofs and smaller vents make the problem easier to solve, but with shallower slopes and larger vents you may lose some of the area of the hole in roof in order to keep the rain out. Consider this when you design your vents and be sure your effective open area is large enough to satisfy your ventilation needs.

TABLE 12-1: HEAT PISTON VENT OPENERS

PRODUCT* (manufacturers/ distributors)	MAXIMUM FORCE AT LIFTING POINT (lbs)	MAXIMUM EXTENSION (in)	COST (suggested list price in dollars)
Bayliss MK III Autovent (Superior Auto- vents, Ltd.)	14	about 12	78.95
Bayliss MK V Autovent (Superior Autovents, Ltd.)	10	about 12	54.95
Thermofor Select (Bramen Co.)	15	12	59.50
Thermofor Sovereign (Bramen Co.)	15	12	49.50
Solarvent (Dalen Products, Inc.)	4½ 5 (with counter-weight accessory)	7½	34.95
Heat Motor Model 50 POR (Heat Motors, Inc.)	50	6	80.00

SOURCE: *Adapted from Sellers,* Automatic Vent Opener Report. *Data based on manufacturer's specifications.*

The addresses of the manufacturers/distributors of these products are given in Appendix 1.

remotely with a hooked stick. This system has the advantage over the pole method of not having a pole in the way when you aren't operating the vent.

Heat Pistons

A heat piston consists of a piston in a cylinder that is partially filled with a paraffin oil that has a high coefficient of expansion. The oil expands and contracts quite a bit over a very small temperature change and causes the piston to move. This motion is transferred to the vent by one of a variety of linkages. In

Photo 12-7: Shown here is a Bayliss heat piston vent operator.

Temperature Range and Adjustment	Features and Comments
Adjustable to start opening from 60 to 80°F; moves to fully open in about 25°F temperature rise	Twin arm construction offers balanced lifting action; sturdy construction; internal springs assist in closing vertical vents and dampens wind buffeting; 1-year warranty
Adjustable to start opening from 55 to 75°F; moves to fully open in about 25°F temperature rise	Same as Mark III, but arms are not quite as sturdy
Adjustable to start opening from 55 to 80°F; moves to fully open in 20°F temperature rise	Built-in return spring to help close vents and dampen wind buffeting; easily detached for manual control; 5-year warranty
Same as above	Same as above, except more easily disconnected for manual operation; needs more headroom than the Select model
Starts to open at 68°F and is fully open at 75°F; range not adjustable	Overrun springs prevent overload damage and help to close vertical vents; counter-balance spring to increase capacity available as option; 5-year warranty on thermal element
Adjustable to start opening from 50 to 90°F; moves to fully open in 60°F temperature rise; moves 1″ per 10°F temperature rise	Large, heavy-duty, direct action cylinder; piston rod pushes directly on vent; restraining chain and spring recommended to protect against wind buffeting; piston should be shaded from direct sunlight; 5-year warranty

some brands, the piston pushes directly on the vent, while other brands use more or less elaborate linkages. Some have overrun springs, which allow you to latch the vent closed without disconnecting the piston, no matter how warm it gets. Other systems require disconnecting the piston from the vent. Overrun springs also provide a damping action against wind buffeting. Heat pistons and other automatic operators are usually used on the top vent only, since automatic venting is required only during the swing seasons, when the outside air is cold enough to cool the greenhouse through the top vent alone. When it's so warm that both bottom and top vents are needed, all the vents can usually be left open. Table 12-1 summarizes the specifications of the heat pistons on the market today.

The operating temperature range of different heat pistons varies. One brand might start to open at 70°F and be fully open at 80°F, having a 10°F range, while another might start at 70°F but not be fully open until it gets to 100°F, a 30°F range. The temperature at which the piston *begins* to move the linkage is adjustable with most of the pistons.

The power and travel of different piston systems, or how much weight is moved how far, also varies. Some brands can push 10 pounds 12 inches, while others push 50 pounds 6 inches. All of the systems require the weight of the vent or a return spring to close the vent, since the piston itself is only capable of pushing, not pulling. With some systems the overrun spring provides some return pull for using the pistons with vertical vents. Counterweights can also be used to help close vertical vents, or to help open vents that are too heavy for the piston to move by itself.

In choosing a piston, consider both the force required to move the vent, and the distance that you wish to move it. The force required depends on the weight of the vent, as well as its width, and where you attach the piston. As shown in figure 12-17, the force required, F, is:

$$F = \frac{W \times w}{2d}$$

where

F = force

W = the total weight of the vent

w = the width of the vent

d = the distance from the hinge to the point of attachment of the linkage to the vent

For example, if a vent weighs 20 pounds (W) and is 24 inches wide (w), and the operator is attached at the middle of the vent (d = 12), the force required to open it is:

$$F = \frac{Ww}{2d} = \frac{(20)\,(24)}{(2)\,(12)} = 20 \text{ pounds}$$

If the piston were attached at the edge oppo-

site the hinges (d=24), the force required would only be:

$$F = \frac{Ww}{2d} = \frac{(20)\,(24)}{(2)\,(24)} = 10 \text{ pounds}$$

Note, however, that the same extension of the piston can move the vent twice as far when it is attached in the middle. Also note that this formula doesn't include friction. If the vent sticks in the curb, more force is required to begin to move it. Pistons are most effective on lightweight, easily opened vents.

You should choose an opener that has a little more power than will actually be needed, since a smaller piston may tend to operate more slowly and sometimes start to move at a higher-than-rated starting temperature when fully loaded. Table 12-2 will help you determine what your vent will weigh.

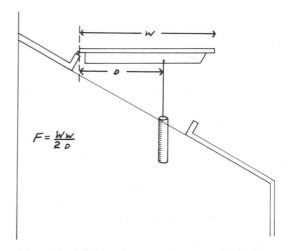

Figure 12-17: The above formula is for calculating the force, in pounds, needed to lift a vent. F = Ww ÷ 2d, where W equals the total weight of the vent; w equals the width of the vent; d equals the distance from the hinge to the point where the vent opener is attached to the vent. This *doesn't* include force needed to unstick a vent that is sticking in its frame.

As an example, take a 2-by-6-foot solid roof vent, built as shown in figure 12-4. The weight of the materials used is calculated in table 12-3. From this table you can see how the weight of solid vents builds up quickly. Only the most powerful heat piston listed in table 12-1 would have the strength to lift it. It could push on the middle of the vent, halfway between the hinge side and the opening side, and open the vent 12 inches over its full throw. If twice this area of top vent is required, you might consider building the vent in two pieces, with one operated by a large heat piston for use during the spring and fall, and one operated manually that can be left open during hot weather. It will also become obvious when you figure out the weight of glazed vents that it is better to use lightweight glazing with heat pistons. If the above vent were glazed with 6-millimeter double-layer polycarbonate, and the same 1-by-4 framing materials were used, the finished vent would weigh just 20 pounds.

TABLE 12-2: WEIGHTS OF COMMON BUILDING MATERIALS

MATERIAL	WEIGHT PER CUBIC FOOT (lbs)	WEIGHT PER SQUARE FOOT (lbs)
Wood		
Fir	40	
Pine	30	
½″ plywood		1.5
Glass		
⅛″ thick		1.17
³⁄₁₆″ thick		1.75
Plastic		
Single-layer fiberglass, 5 ounce		0.31
Exolite, acrylic		1.15
6-mm double-walled polycarbonate		0.27

TABLE 12-3: WEIGHT OF MATERIALS FOR EXAMPLE ROOF VENT

MATERIAL	QUANTITY	VOLUME OR AREA	WEIGHT/UNIT	TOTAL WEIGHT
1 × 4 pine	2 @ 6′	$\left(\dfrac{2 \times 72'' \times 0.75'' \times 3.5''}{1{,}728 \text{ in}^3/\text{ft}^3}\right) = 0.218 \text{ ft}^3$	$\times 30 \text{ lbs/ft}^3$	$= 6.54$ lbs
1 × 4 pine	4 @ 2′	$\left(\dfrac{4 \times 24'' \times 0.75'' \times 3.5''}{1{,}728 \text{ in}^3/\text{ft}^3}\right) = 0.146 \text{ ft}^3$	$\times 30 \text{ lbs/ft}^3$	$= 4.38$ lbs
½″ plywood	12 ft²		$\times 1.5 \text{ lbs/ft}^2$	$= 18$ lbs
¼″ plywood	12 ft²		$\times 0.75 \text{ lbs/ft}^2$	$= 9$ lbs
Insulation			negligible	
Total weight =				38 lbs

Electric Vent Operators

There are many motorized vent operators on the market, but most are designed for opening large commercial-scale greenhouse vents. These systems usually connect to the geared hand crank-type operators used in the old commercial greenhouses, with the motors essentially replacing the crank. They occasionally can be found used, but new systems are quite expensive, in the $400 to $1,500 range. They are available from many of the manufacturers of larger glass greenhouses and from greenhouse suppliers. Smaller motorized operators work on several different operating principles and cost from $220 to $500. In general, motorized operators are more costly than the heat pistons, but they do provide faster vent movement to prevent excessive temperature rise, more precise control of the temperature at which the vent operates and more lifting power.

One system, made by the Gleason-Avery company, uses a linear actuator motor, which consists of a thermostatically controlled electric gear motor that drives a straight shaft with teeth on one edge (a *rack*). The motor pushes the rack until the vent is completely open, and then the motor stalls. The motor is designed to stall, so this doesn't hurt it. When the thermostat calls for the vent to be closed, power is shut off to the gear motor, and the weight of the vent pushes the rack back down. An optional counterspring or a counterweight is needed with vertical vents. The motor uses only 10 watts whenever the vent is open, which might amount to only 20 kilowatt-hours (kwh) per year. Also, a pin can be inserted in the rack to keep the vent all the way open, so that no electricity need be used in the summer. The motor pushes with a 25-pound force and is available with a 3-, 6½- or 11⅞-inch reach. The rack can also be pinned to decrease its travel during colder months when you might want the vent to open only a little. A complete system, with two motors (6½-inch travel), a thermostat and mounting hardware, costs around $300. A single motor (6½-inch travel), with mounting hardware, is $118. You can supply your own line-voltage thermostat.

Advanced Greenhouses, Ltd. (AGL) makes a vent operator based on a different type of linear actuator, using a rotating threaded shaft rather than a toothed rack. A 12-volt direct-current (DC) gear motor moves the shaft in and out as shown in figure 12-18. The shaft pushes on an arm that is connected to a shaft, causing the shaft to rotate. The rotating shaft moves arms that are connected to the vent, similar to those used in the old crank-type vent openers, to push the vent open or pull it closed. The 12-volt DC gear motor can use a regular automobile battery charger for power. A two-stage thermostat activates the control box, which controls the motor. It then opens the vent partway at the first set point, and then opens it farther if the temperature rises to the second set point. The amount that each set point opens the vent is adjustable right on the system control box, avoiding the need to climb up a ladder to adjust a pin or connect or disconnect a piston. The system is "position limited," which means that a microswitch on the shaft tells the control box when the vent is all the way open or closed. If the vent either is frozen or latched shut, the motor will stall, causing a thermal circuit breaker to cut the power supply, avoiding damage to the vent or motor. A variety of motor sizes and arm/shaft systems are available for different vent sizes and weights. A typical AGL system that would drive a glazed vent up to 40 feet long including the linear actuator, power supply and controls, but excluding shafts and opening arms would cost around $900, in Canadian dollars. (AGL quotes prices for shafts and arms on request, since these vary considerably from one greenhouse to the next.) The exchange

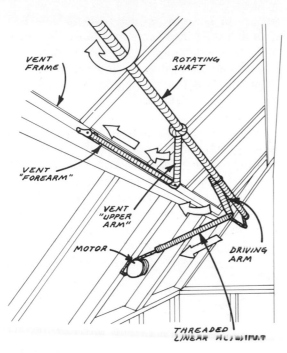

Figure 12-18: This motorized operator system uses a linear actuator to push an arm on a shaft, which rotates the shaft. Arms attached to the shaft then push open the continuous vent. A thermostat controls the motor and limit switches tell it when to stop.

rate currently makes this 20 percent lower in United States dollars. A battery charger costs around $30. AGL also makes motors and controls that can be adapted to manual vent operators. National Greenhouse Company also makes a motorized vent operator that uses a 115 VAC linear actuator, with an operating principle similar to the AGL unit.

Aluminum Greenhouses, Inc., makes a motorized vent operator based on a *damper motor*, which is made to control dampers in air ducts in large forced-air heating and cooling systems. These are gear motors that rotate an arm anywhere from one-quarter to one-half of a turn. In this system, a rod connected to the arm of the damper motor pushes another arm on a shaft, which rotates

the shaft. A set of arms on the shaft, connected to the vent, pushes the vent open. The rod travels over a range of about 2¼ inches and has about 80 pounds of force. This could translate into about 6¾ inches of vent movement with about 27 pounds of force, depending on the size of the arm rotating the shaft and the size of the arms moving the vents. More movement can be had with less force, or less movement with more force. The model SAV-1 vent opener (with the thermostat, the damper motor, the rod and arm for the shaft, and some mounting hardware) costs $280. It is intended for use on several of the company's own greenhouse kits, but it can be adapted for use on others, as long as you supply the shaft and arms for the vent and devise mounting hardware for your situation.

Motor drives for attaching to skylights, casement and awning windows are also available. These can be used to automate existing units or new ones. Sources are listed in Appendix 1.

Exhaust Fans and Air Intake Vents

Fans and intake louvers are simpler to install than most vents, since they are typically located in vertical walls and since the penetration through the wall is generally smaller than for a passive vent. Fans do require though, a tight-closing door or push-in foam plug over the inside for winter, in addition to the louvers that keep rain out. Insulated doors can fit over the opening, rather than inside it, making installation relatively simple. Push-in foam plugs are even easier to make and use. A thermostat controlled fan is an excellent addition to any greenhouse that doesn't have automatically controlled vents, to protect the inside environment from overheating.

Most fans are manufactured with a mounting flange that is simply screwed inside or on the face of a framed opening. Check the size of the fan frame before framing the end-walls, but if you have any doubts about the size of the fan when you are building the walls, oversize the opening. It's a lot easier to fill in an opening that's too big than to make a small hole larger. The fan in figure 12-19 sits far enough outside the endwall to allow an insulated door to be built flush with the inside wall. Along with the standard framing for the opening a little outside roof is needed to cover the fan. The inside door is built the same way as a roof or wall vent, except that it doesn't need to be beveled, since it closes against the

surface of the wall. It can also be sheathed with lighter ⅛-inch tempered Masonite or ¼-inch plywood, since it doesn't require the strength or durability of any exterior vent. Perimeter weather stripping and a tight-closing latch minimize air leaks. A standard sash lock for double-hung windows is good for this. A stick can be hinged to the door to prop it open, if the fan is low enough to be easily reached. If it is too high, a rope can be attached to an eye screw in the door and run up through a pulley near the roof and down to a cleat at a convenient spot.

The fan shown in figure 12-19 has the

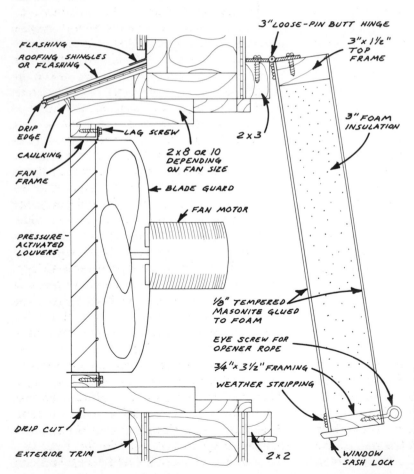

Figure 12-19: Exhaust Fan (vertical section). An exhaust fan with an insulating door can be mounted in a frame that protrudes outside the greenhouse, taking up less space and allowing the insulated door to shut onto the face of the inside wall.

motor mounted on the blade guard grille and has pressure actuated louvers mounted on the fan frame. Aluminum louvers are preferable to painted steel, since they won't rust. Using a preassembled fan is easier than assembling the various pieces, but a preassembled unit isn't always going to be available in the size you want. The wiring should be surface-mounted to avoid interrupting the vapor barrier. The vapor barrier should be installed before the frame for the fan is installed. This allows you to wrap the vapor barrier around the wall opening and cover it with the protruding frame and with trim inside the frame. Extra pieces of polyethylene should be taped in place where needed to make a continuous barrier around the fan opening. The fan door and the 2-by-2 and 2-by-3 frame that it closes against can be built as a unit on the floor and installed after the fan is in place. Using loose-pin butt hinges will facilitate this.

Air intake louvers are installed much the same as fans, but they are easier, since they don't require extending the frame beyond the outside plane of the wall. Pressure-actuated louvers must of course be installed so they face the inside and will open when the fan runs. If, however, you are using motorized louvers, they must face the outside so that the motor is kept out of the rain. Intake louvers should also have either an inner door or a push-in foam panel to seal them when ventilation isn't needed.

Interior Vents

Heat exchange vents and fans in the common wall are easier to install than exterior units, since they don't have to withstand the weather. As with exterior ventilation, fans are usually simpler to install than vents, since they involve a smaller hole in the wall. If the existing doors and windows in the common

wall don't provide enough vent area (see chapter 6 for sizing guidelines), you may want to add windows or a glass door, rather than a vent, to enhance your view into the greenhouse. However, a vent may be the appropriate solution when an opening is needed near the floor, or where a view would be blocked by furniture or by beds or heat storage units in the greenhouse. A vent is also more easily fitted with a backdraft damper than is a door or most types of windows (although a large version of the damper described in this section can be fitted to a sash-type window). If you need to add a vent wider than the spacing of the studs in the common wall, you can simply let the exposed stud run through the opening, whereas a window would require cutting out the stud and supporting it with the window header. The window, therefore, often involves more labor than would be needed for a similar sized vent, but if no studs need to be cut and supported, the labor to install a window is about the same as that required for a vent. Materials costs are, of course, less for a vent than for a new window.

The backdraft damper shown in figure 12-20 can be used for upper vents with the flap on the greenhouse side and for lower vents with the flap on the house side. Although having a damper on only the upper or lower vent will considerably decrease airflow in the wrong direction, compared to leaving both top and bottom completely open, it is best to have dampers on both vents. The damper box is built from ¾-inch-thick wood—1 × 8 is wide enough for most situations—with beveled wood strips at the top and bottom and square wood strips on the sides to support ½-inch hardware cloth at an angle. This mesh supports the thin plastic flap that blocks air that isn't moving in the desired direction. Plastic cleaner bags or the thinnest plastic "drop cloths" provide the right flap material (½- or 1-mil polyethylene). Half-mil

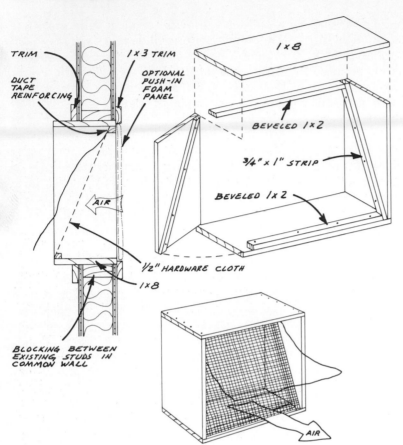

Figure 12-20: Backdraft dampers for heat exchange vents can be built with ¾-inch-thick wood. One-half-inch hardware cloth, tacked onto small wood strips on the inside of the box, supports a thin plastic flap that allows airflow only in the desired direction. A frame can be built around the inside trim for a push-in foam insulating panel. Shown here are a cross section of a damper (left), an exploded view (above right) and an assembled damper (below right).

Tedlar, which is a little stiffer than polyethylene, is another more durable material (see the listing in Appendix 1 for a source). The stiffness of the Tedlar helps make a tighter closure when the flap closes, but thin polyethylene is usually adequate. The top edge of the plastic is reinforced with duct tape so you can tack it to the beveled wood strip at the top. The whole damper can be completely built and then fitted into the framed hole in the common wall. If your vent covers more than one stud cavity, you'll need a separate damper for each hole. Weather stripping would be needed to seal the box to a window frame.

If you decide to make new vent holes, be sure to check for any electrical or plumbing lines in the wall while you are still planning where the vents will go. It's much easier to move the vents on paper than to move pipes or wires after you've cut into the wall. The width of the vent hole will be the distance between two studs, or double or triple this, if you need more vent area. The height can be whatever you need to get enough vent area. Remember that the effective area of the vent will be about 3 inches smaller than the rough hole in height, and 3 inches smaller in width because of the thickness of the box and the mesh support strips nailed to the inside of the box. The mesh further reduces the effective opening by 20 percent. If the box is tall, two flaps, each covering half the opening, will lift a little easier than one large one.

The exact placement of the vent is usually determined by its placement on the house side of the common wall, where it will be close to the floor or the ceiling, while avoiding baseboards or other trim. Vent position in the greenhouse is usually less critical. Before cutting a hole, measure carefully to be sure that the vent ends up where you want it on both sides. Cut away the inside wall surface, then drill holes through the exterior sheathing and siding to locate the greenhouse side of the hole. A utility knife is usually good enough for cutting through wallboard on the inside, though after you've taken off enough wallboard so that you're sure there are no wires or pipes inside, you can finish it with a saber saw. A circular saw can be used on wood sheathing, with the blade set just to the depth of the wood, to avoid cutting the studs. Once you've cut the hole, measure for the blocking that goes between the studs at the top and bottom of the hole. These blocks are a little tricky to install, since they go between the studs, where there is nothing to back them to keep them in place for nailing. Cut the block a little long, so that it's a tight fit and won't fall down the stud cavity. Prenail the blocks with the toenails that will go into the studs. Finish nails make the toenailing easier, since you'll want to countersink the nail heads out of the way. A screw-gun and drywall screws are very helpful in getting the blocks in place, so you can screw through the sheathing into the block on both sides to hold it in place. Then you can put toenails into the studs on either end of the block. If you drill for the toenails through the block, and just a touch into the stud, you won't move the block so much when you're hammering.

If you are installing a single-piece vent or a fan that is bigger than the space between the studs, the stud in the middle of the hole can be cut out after the sheathing on both sides is cut away. The wall sheathing will, usually, support the upper part of the stud that you want to cut until you get a header in place. Check with an experienced remodeler if you have any doubts. (The header should be the same size as would be used for any wall opening, usually a double 2 × 6 with a ½-inch plywood spacer sandwiched between for 2-by-4 walls where only one or two studs are cut out.)

With the blocks or header in place you can install the damper box with finish nails driven into the studs and blocking. The inside and outside are finished with whatever trim is appropriate. A push-in foam insulating panel, made of foil-covered isocyanurate foam, can be made to fit inside the trim covering the edge of the box as shown in figure 12-20. An inch of isocyanurate is usually enough insulation, unless your walls are very heavily insulated, you are in a very cold climate and you are abandoning the greenhouse in midwinter, in which case you may want to put thicker trim around the vent to accommodate the thicker foam. If you don't like the idea of a push-in panel, the trim can be extended into a U-shaped track for the foam to slide in. This avoids the problem of where to put the foam when the vent is open, but offers no better insulation than the push-in panel.

Air Exchange Fans

Installing an air exchange fan between the house and greenhouse is a simpler proposition than exhaust fan installation. See chapter 6 for guidelines on fan placement and sizing. After the planning issues are considered, minimizing fan noise is perhaps the most important goal of a good installation. The fan will be quieter if it is mounted to something solid and heavy, rather than something lightweight. If you have any choice, locate it next to a corner of the house, next to the intersection of the common wall with an interior partition wall, or next to a chimney. A flimsy stud wall can actually amplify fan noise. If you can mount the fan directly to a masonry wall, the mass of the masonry will absorb some of the vibration and noise.

With frame walls, the problem almost always arises that you want a bigger fan than will fit between two studs. You can remove a section of a stud to get the size opening you want, but this isn't worth the trouble if the fan needs to be just a little bigger than the space between the studs, which is usually 14½ inches for 2-by-4 studs 16 inches on center. Fans up to 18 inches in diameter can simply overlap the opening a little. Or if the fan needs to be a lot bigger, a stud can run through the middle of the opening, if cutting the stud would be difficult in your situation. The "interfering" stud(s) will have only a small effect on the fan's performance and will allow you to use a slower-running, quieter fan.

The hole for the fan is cut out and blocked in the same way as for a passive vent. If the fan is larger than the opening, a 2-by-4 frame can be built up on the outside to carry the fan. This can be preassembled and then nailed onto the wall. Toenails through the frame into the studs and blocking in the common wall are usually sufficient to carry the weight of the fan, but you can also drive lag screws into the wall studs. Once you have the frame up, put in the 1-by-6 trim pieces inside the opening. The top and bottom trim won't interfere with the flow of air, since they are above and below the circle of the fan, but if the fan is wider than the hole, use as thin

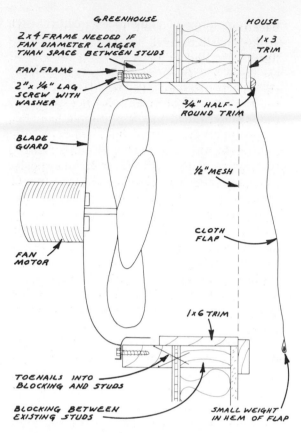

Figure 12-21: Air Exchange Fan (vertical section). If the air exchanger fan is wider than the space between the common wall studs, a frame is needed to move the fan out from the wall, as shown here.

trim as you can on the sides, such as ¼-inch plywood. Then the trim can be put around the frame inside the house and inside the greenhouse. A push-in insulating panel, the same as shown for the passive vents, can be used with a fan.

There are several options for finishing the house side of the fan hole. Figure 12-21 shows ½-inch hardware cloth for a guard and a cloth flap that serves to direct the air and as a backdraft damper. Half-inch hardware cloth strikes a good balance between safely keeping fingers out and minimizing pressure against the fan. The flap can be cloth, rather than the thin plastic used in backdraft dampers, since the fan has enough power to lift the heavier weight. If needed, small weights can be put in the bottom hem to keep the cloth from flapping excessively and so that it closes more or less tightly when the fan is off. By putting the weights off-center, the air stream can be directed more to one side than the other. The screen can be tilted, as in a passive backdraft damper, if you want to minimize warm air leaking from the house to the greenhouse. Another option for the inside is a commercially made grille with either stationary or adjustable louvers. If the fan is near a sitting area, this is preferable for directing air across the ceiling.

The metal fan frame is screwed to the 2-by-4 frame after all the trim is up. The frame shown in figure 12-21 curves in around the fan blades. This is a *Venturi* frame. The smoothly curved opening is more efficient at moving air than a plain hole cut in a flat frame and is worth the extra cost, if you can find a fan with this type of frame. The fan shown has the motor mounted on the blade guard, which is typical of smaller, lower-power fans.

The return air vent for a fan system is essentially identical to the passive vents previously described. The return vent should be the same size as the opening for the fan and should have a backdraft damper. This flap can also be cloth, since the fan will have enough power to lift it, though it probably won't need any weights. The flap will direct the air stream across the floor of the greenhouse, which is better than across the glazing, since this would increase the heat loss through the glazing. If louvers are used in the return vent, they should also be directed toward the floor.

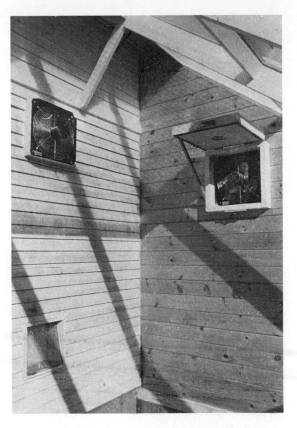

Photo 12-8: The air exchange fan is at the upper left on the common wall, and the air return vent is at the lower left. The exhaust fan, with its insulating door, is on the right. The height of the heat exchange fan and return are dictated by the house interior: the fan is at the inside ceiling and the return at the inside floor.

Installing the fan or vents into the house is usually done after the greenhouse is finished, and when they go in you can really begin to feel the solar heat coming from the greenhouse into the house. It's particularly dramatic with a fan, when the thermostat turns it on and it very noticeably begins delivering solar heat.

Appendix 1
PRODUCT DIRECTORY

CHAPTER 1
Solar Growing Frames

Rodale Press, Inc.
33 E. Minor St.
Emmaus, PA 18049

Solar Survival
P. O. Box 275
Harrisville, NH 03450

CHAPTER 4
Horticultural Supplies

Charley's Greenhouse
　Supply
12815 N.E. 124th St.
Kirkland, WA 98034
　Charley's sells small
quantities of most of the
products available at commercial greenhouse sup-
pliers. An informative cata-
log is available for $2.

Insulating and Shading Curtain Systems and Parts

Automatic Devices Co.
2121 S. 12th St.
Allentown, PA 18103

Sarlon Industries Inc.
775 N.W. 71st St.
Miami, FL 33150

Simtrac, Inc.
8243 N. Christiana Ave.
Skokie, IL 60076
　These companies sell
custom curtain systems and/
or parts for systems including fabric, track systems and
edge seals.

Solar Staircase Parts

Saunders & Co.
15 Ellis Rd.
Weston, MA 02193

Solar Staircase Plans

Circuit Engineering
15 Ellis Rd.
Weston, MA 02193

CHAPTER 5
Corrosion Inhibitor

Zomeworks Corp.
P. O. Box 25805
Albuquerque, NM 87125

Foundation Insulation

Owens-Corning Fiberglass
　Corp.
Attn: Josh Kelman
P. O. Box 415
Granville, OH 43023

Insulating Curtain Fabrics

Duracote Corp.
350 N. Diamond St.
Ravenna, OH 44266
　Manufacturer of Foylon,
an aluminum foil/fabric laminate, with high reflectivity.
Various Foylon fabrics are
available, but the ones with
the actual foil surface, such
as Style Numbers 7018 and
7137, rather than aluminized
polyester, are more reflective. Number 7137, with a vinyl backing, is less porous
and therefore better suited
for attached greenhouses but
is more expensive.

Metalized Products
37 East St.
Winchester, MA 01890
　Manufacturer of various
metalized films and lami-
nated metalized films.

Low-Temperature Phase Change Heat Storage Units

Boardman Energy Systems, Inc.
P. O. Box 4299
Wilmington, DE 19807

Type 58 tubes have a melting point of 56 to 60°F and store 1,600 Btu each over the phase change, not including heat stored above or below that temperature. Type 67 tubes store 1,800 Btu per tube at 65 to 70°F. Stainless steel tubes are 22 inches long and 5¼ inches in diameter.

Suncraft, Inc.
P. O. Box 236
Hinesburg, VT 05461

Clear Heat tubes, made of clear polyvinyl chloride, have a melting point of 68 to 76°F and store 68 Btu per pound, or 2,000 Btu per tube at the melting point. They are 7 feet 9 inches long and 3¼ inches in diameter.

Magnetic Tape and Mating Steel Tape for Edge Seals

Graber Industries, Inc.
7549 Graber Plaza
Middleton, WI 53562

Magnetic Tape for Edge Seals Only

3M
Electro Products Div./IEP
Bldg. 225-4N
3M Center
St. Paul, MN 55144

Nightwall

Zomeworks Corp.
P. O. Box 25805
Albuquerque, NM 87125

Plastic Edge Extrusions for Push-In Foam Panels

Aerius Design Group
RFD 1, Box 994B
Kingston, NY 12401

Star Technology Corp.
P. O. Box 1187
Carbondale, CO 81623

Water Containers for Heat Storage

One Design, Inc.
Mountain Falls Rt.
Winchester, VA 22601

Water Wall: 48 inches square by 7 inches deep, 53-gallon, translucent high-density polyethylene modules designed to fit between studs 24 inches on center. $180 each ($3.40 per gallon).

Solar Components Corp.
P. O. Box 237
Manchester, NH 03105

Fiberglass Solar Storage Tubes: 12-inch diameter by 4 or 8 feet high, 18-inch diameter by 5 or 10 feet high, from 23 to 128 gallons. About $60 for the 12-inch-by-8-foot tube ($1.28 per gallon).

Solar Cycle Corp.
3309 Gayhart St.
Racine, WI 53406

Econo-Rod water cylinders are 3½-inch inside diameter plastic rods, in 3½- or 6-foot lengths, holding 1.44 and 2.64 gallons each. Available in black and translucent, costing about $5 for the smaller units and $9 for the larger ones, with discounts for large quantities ($3.41 per gallon for the larger size).

CHAPTER 6

Air-to-Air Heat Exchangers

The Air Changer Co., Ltd.
334 King St. E.
Studio 505
Toronto, Ontario M5A 1K8
Canada

DesChamps Laboratories
P. O. Box 440
E. Hanover, NJ 07936

Memphremagog Heat Exchangers, Inc.
P. O. Box 456
Newport, VT 05855

CHAPTER 9
All-Weather Wood Foundations

American Plywood Assn.
P. O. Box 11700
Tacoma, WA 98411

Design information for preserved wood foundations entitled *APA Design/Construction Guide: All-Weather Wood Foundations* available. Request form A400.

National Forest Products Assn.
1619 Massachusetts Ave., NW
Washington, DC 20036

The All-Weather Wood Foundation System: Design, Fabrication and Installation Manual is available.

Foundation Insulation Coverings

Akona Corp.
1570 Halgren Rd.
Maple Plain, MN 55359

Conproco Corp.
P. O. Box 368
Hookset, NH 03106

Insulcrete Co., Inc.
4311 Triangle St.
McFarland, WI 53558

Silpro Masonry Systems Inc.
P. O. Box 219
Tewksbury, MA 01876

Thoro System Products
7800 N.W. 38th St.
Miami, FL 33166

The companies listed above provide fiberglass-reinforced trowel-on insulation coating, with acrylic modifier to increase adhesion and increase ability to expand and contract with the foam. Supplied with fiberglass tape for seams.

Trend Products, Inc.
P. O. Box 327
Waupaca, WI 54981

Insulgard, reinforced fierglass panels to cover insulation; joint moldings, inside and outside corners and caps available.

CHAPTER 11
Extruded Double and Triple Glazing

CYRO Industries
155 Tice Blvd.
P. O. Box 8588
Woodcliff Lake, NJ 07675

Exolite polycarbonate and acrylic ⅝-inch-thick double-wall; aluminum extrusions available.

General Electric Co., Sheet Products Dept.
Lexan Products Div.
1 Plastics Ave.
Pittsfield, MA 01201

Single- and double-layer polycarbonate.

Polygal Plastic Industries
P. O. Box 272
Edgerton, WI 53534

Four- to 10-mm-thick double-wall polycarbonate and new ⅝-inch triple-wall polycarbonate; polycarbonate and aluminum mounting extrusions available.

Ramada Energy Systems Limited
1421 S. McClintock Dr.
Tempe, AZ 85281

Temglaze double-wall polycarbonate with mounting system: system allows glazing to be removed and replaced with screens for summer.

Rohm & Haas Co.
Independence Mall West
Philadelphia, PA 19105

Tuffak Twinwall ¼-inch double-wall polycarbonate.

Structured Sheets, Inc.
196 E. Camp Ave.
Merrick, NY 11566

Manufacturer of Qualex, 4- to 16-mm double-wall polycarbonate, available through PolyGrowers Inc., Box 359, Muncie, PA 17756.

Factory Sealed Double-Glass Units

Check for local suppliers in the Yellow Pages and in solar magazines. Glass is heavy and expensive to ship.

Fiberglass (FRP) Glazing

Filon Division of Vistron
  Corp.
P. O. Box 5006
Hawthorne, CA 90250
    Shiplap, corrugated and
flat FRP and accessories.

Glasteel Tennessee, Inc.
Highway 57E
Collierville, TN 38017
    Corrugated and flat
FRP and accessories.

Philips Industries
Lasco Div.
3255 E. Miraloma Ave.
Anaheim, CA 92806
    Corrugated and flat
FRP and accessories.

Solar Components Corp.
P. O. Box 237
Manchester, NH 03105
    Sun-Lite FRP, in rolls of
flat material in various sizes
and thicknesses, and of double-layer panels; carries a
large line of supplies, including aluminum battens and
other extrusions, stainless
steel, neoprene gasketed
screws.

Heat-Retaining Films Used in High-Performance Glazings

Southwall Corp.
3961 E. Bayshore Rd.
Palo Alto, CA 94303
    Manufacturer of Heat

Mirror heat reflective film
that is installed in factory-
sealed double-glass units.

3M
Energy Control Products
224-55-17 3M Center
St. Paul, MN 55144
    Manufacturer of Sun
Gain high-transmission film,
used in two layers inside fac-
tory-sealed glass to make
Quad-Pane.

Heavily Galvanized Drywall Screws

Philstone Nail Corp.
35 Turnpike St.
W. Bridgewater, MA 02379
    Contact the manufac-
turer for your local wholesale
distributor of Weather Chal-
lenger exterior galvanized
drywall screws. You may
have to have your hardware
store or lumberyard order
these. They are available in
1, 1½, 1⅝, 2, 2½, 3, 3½ and 4
inches. These are not the
same as thinly plated Uni-
chrome drywall screws,
which are intended for indoor use.

Laminate Cutters (for Cutting FRP)

Brookstone Co.
Vose Farm Rd.
Peterborough, NH 03458

Prefabricated Aluminum Extrusion/EPDM Gasket Systems

IDEA Development, Inc.
P. O. Box 44
Antrim, NH 03440
    IDI extruded aluminum
battens for mounting glass or
plastic double-glazing panels;
bronze anodized, mill finish,
or polyurethane enamel finish, 2½ or 3½ inches wide.
EPDM gaskets under batten,
EPDM pad or various size
glazing tape available to sit
on top of rafter. Also a source
for stainless hex-head and
Phillips pan-head screws and
washers, with or without
bonded EPDM gaskets. Bat-
ten with gaskets and EPDM
pad for rafter run from about
$3.30 per foot for 2½-
-inch-wide mill finish, to
$4.75 for 3½-inch-wide anod-
ized (polyurethane finish
higher). Necessary hardware
extra.

New Jersey Aluminum Co.
P. O. Box 73
N. Brunswick, NJ 08902
    Manufactures a bronze
painted aluminum system
with upper and lower extrusions, 3⅛ inches wide, for ⅝-
or 1-inch-thick glazing; distributed (and privately labeled) by the following:
Abundant Energy, Inc., 116
Newport Bridge Rd., War-
wick, NY 10990; Brother
Sun, Inc., 1301 Cerrillos Rd.,

Santa Fe, NM 87501; Evergreen Distributors, P. O. Box 128, Hwy. 26, Burnett, WI 53922. Costs run from $4.50 per foot and up (stock lengths of 12, 16 and 20 feet), not including shipping or needed accessories, such as screws, silicone and touch-up paint. Price with accessories is about $6.00 per foot.

Solarium Systems, Inc.
200 W. 88th St.
Bloomington, MN 55420
    Thermalite glazing system; bronze color. From $5.75 to 7.20 per linear foot.

Weather Energy Systems, Inc.
P. O. Box 968
Pocasset, MA 02559
    One piece EPDM gasket with vulcanized corners and lock-strip that seals a whole plane of glazing. This is the same technology that is used on automobile windshield gaskets. Available for three to eight 46″ × 76″, 1″-thick sealed glass units. Gaskets, which seal to the wood frame with an aluminum framework system, are exposed to the weather. A system for four sealed double glass units (16-foot-wide aperture) costs $895.00 ($14.24 per linear foot).

Tapes

3M
3M Center
Industrial Tape Div.
Bldg. 220-8E
St. Paul, MN 55144
    Tapes for polyethylene and for end treatment of extruded double glazing.

Single-Tempered Low–Iron Glass

AFG Industries
P. O. Box 929
1400 Lincoln St.
Kingsport, TN 37662

General Glass International, Inc.
542 Main St.
New Rochelle, NY 10801

Hordis Brothers, Inc.
825 Hylton Rd.
Pennsauken, NJ 08110

Threaded Inserts and Plastic Knobs

Albert Constantine and Son, Inc. (inserts)
2050 Eastchester Rd.
Bronx, NY 10461

Mutual Hardware Corp. (inserts)
5–45 49th Ave.
Long Island City, NY 11101

Reid Tool Supply Co. (knobs)
2265 Black Creek Rd.
Muskegan, MI 49444
    Threaded inserts to provide threads for thumb

screws in wood support framing for removable glazing panels; plastic knobs with studs are an easier-to-use substitute for thumb screws and are used with removable glazing panels.

Ultraviolet-Resistant Polyethylene

Ethyl Corp.
VisQueen Film Product Div.
P. O. Box 2448
Richmond, VA 23218
    Manufacturer of UV-resistant polyethylene, number 1450. Available through commercial greenhouse supply houses.

Monsanto Engineered Products Co.
800 N. Lindbergh
St. Louis, MO 63167
    Manufacturer of UV-resistant polyethylene, numbers 602 and 603. Available through commercial greenhouse supply houses.

CHAPTER 12

Heat Piston Vent Openers

Bramen Co.
P. O. Box 70
Salem, MA 01970

Dalen Products, Inc.
11110 Gilbert Dr.
Knoxville, TN 37932

Heat Motors, Inc.
635 W. Grandview Ave.
Sierra Madre, CA 91024

Superior Autovents, Ltd.
17422 La Mesa La.
Huntington Beach, CA 92647

Motorized Vent Openers

Advanced Greenhouses, Ltd.
R.R. #2
Baden, Ontario N0B1G0
Canada
    Low-voltage DC linear actuator motor rotates shaft with arms to lift vents. Amount vent opens adjustable on control box.

Aluminum Greenhouses, Inc.
14605 Lorain Ave.
Cleveland, OH 44111

Damper motor actuated rotating shaft with arms to lift vents.

Gleason-Avery Division
John G. Rubino, Inc.
P. O. Box 635
Auburn, NY 13021
    Linear actuator motor pushes directly on vent.

National Greenhouse Co.
P. O. Box 100
400 E. Main St.
Pana, IL 62557
    115-volt AC linear actuator motor rotates shaft with arms to lift vents.

Texas Greenhouse Co., Inc.
2761 St. Louis Ave.
Fort Worth, TX 76110
    Damper motor actuated rotating shaft with arms to lift vents.

Truth, Inc.
P. O. Box 427
West Bridge St.
Owatonna, MN 55060
    Motor drive for awning and casement windows and for skylights.

Plastic Film for Backdraft Dampers

Hot Stuff Controls, Inc.
P. O. Box 306
406 Walnut St.
La Jara, CO 81140
    One-half-mil Tedlar, $2 per square foot. Also custom-made sheet-metal convective dampers and stock size forced-air backdraft dampers.

Appendix 2

GREENHOUSE KITS AND PLANS

Kits

    Most of the greenhouses listed below have a wide range of options including night insulation, skylights, thermal storage, heat exchange fans and controls, exhaust fans, screens, heaters, summer shading and ventilation systems, to name a few. Be sure to inquire regarding options. The letters indicated in the shape category refer to figure 7-7.
    Many manufacturers offer other standard shapes as well as custom shapes. What is included as the "standard" ventilation system varies quite a bit, with some manufacturers

providing a complete vent or fan system in the basic price and others treating it as an option.

Abundant Energy Inc., 116 Newport Bridge Rd., Warwick, NY 10990

Name of kit: Radiant Room
Shapes: A and L
Frame material: laminated wood beams with extruded aluminum glazing system (see chapter 11 for details)
Glazing material: tempered double glass
Ventilation system: optional exhaust fan, doors and endwall windows

Advanced Greenhouses, Ltd., R.R. #2, Baden, Ontario N0B 1G0 Canada

Name of kit: Dutch Light and English Style
Shapes: B (all glazed), Dutch Light; and G, English Style
Frame material: aluminum with thermal break
Glazing material: extruded double polycarbonate
Ventilation system: full ridge vent, eave vents and doors

Advance Energy Technologies, Inc., P. O. Box 387, Clifton Park, NY 12065

Name of kit: Zeroenergy Room
Shape: A, with glazing almost vertical
Frame material: steel-cased urethane foam panels
Glazing material: low-iron tempered double glass
Ventilation system: heat exchange fan

Aluminum Greenhouses, Inc., 14605 Lorain Ave., Cleveland, OH 44111

Name of kit: Everlite
Shapes: D and G with curved eave
Frame material: aluminum
Glazing material: double-strength glass
Ventilation system: continuous ridge vent, endwall doors

Brady and Sun, 97 Webster St., Worcester, MA 01603

Name of kit: LivingRoom
Shape: A
Frame material: laminated pine beams, bronzed aluminum glazing system and aluminum trim
Glazing material: tempered double glass
Ventilation system: kneewall awning windows, endwall window and insulated door

Charley's Greenhouse Supply, 12815 N.E. 124th St., Kirkland, WA 98034

Name of kit: Sol-Star Sunroom
Shapes: B and G
Frame material: redwood/fir laminate
Glazing material: tempered double glass
Ventilation system: exhaust fan and motorized intake louver with thermostat and variable speed control

Creative Structures Inc., R.D. 1, Box 173, Quakertown, PA 18951

Name of kit: CSI Solar Greenhouse
Shapes: D, G and custom
Frame material: redwood
Glazing material: tempered double glass
Ventilation system: awning windows and doors in kneewall or endwalls

English Greenhouse Products Corp., 11th and Linden Sts., Camden, NJ 08102

Name of kit: Florex ITB
Shapes: D and G with curved eave
Frame material: aluminum with thermal break
Glazing material: tempered double glass
Ventilation system: awning windows in kneewall and sliding glass end door

Evergreen Distributors, P. O. Box 128, Hwy. 26, Burnett, WI 53922

Name of kit: Evergreen Room
Shapes: A, B (with all-glass roof), and F

Frame material: laminated red cedar, with extruded aluminum glazing system with thermal break
Glazing material: tempered double glass
Ventilation system: skylights and door

Four Seasons Solar Products Corp., 910 Route 110, Farmingdale, NY 11735
Name of kit: System 4
Shapes: D and G with straight or curved eave
Frame material: aluminum
Glazing material: tempered double glass, combination tempered and laminated overhead, fully tempered glass curved eave
Ventilation system: automatic patented Ridge Pow-R-Vent system, awning windows

Gamman Industries Inc., 360 Farmer Industrial Blvd., Newnan, GA 30263
Name of kit: The Solarium
Shapes: D and G
Frame material: aluminum with thermal break
Glazing material: tempered double glass
Ventilation system: one sliding door in vertical kneewall

Garden Way Solar Greenhouses, 324 Ferry Rd., Charlotte, VT 05445
Name of kit: Sunroom/Solar Greenhouse
Shape: B
Frame material: laminated pine arches
Glazing material: tempered double glass, with Exolite in shallower roof glazing
Ventilation system: 3-part ventilation system including automatic window opener, control panel and exhaust fans; choice of door or window in each endwall

Gothic Arch Greenhouses, Box 1564, Mobile, AL 36633
Name of kit: Lean-to Gothic Arch
Shape: H

Frame material: redwood arches and cedar purlins
Glazing material: 4-ounce corrugated fiberglass (single glazed)
Ventilation system: door in endwall

Green Mountain Homes, Royalton, VT 05068
Name of kit: Solar Shed
Shape: A
Frame material: precut lumber
Glazing material: tempered double glass
Ventilation system: door in endwall

Habitat, 123 Elm St., S. Deerfield, MA 01373
Name of kit: Habitat Solar Room
Shape: A
Frame material: laminated cedar
Glazing material: tempered double glass
Ventilation system: air exchange system with the house

Harvester All-Weather Greenhouses, Division of China & Garden, 257 Main St., Chatham, NJ 07928
Name of kit: Harvester Lean-To
Shape: G
Frame material: aluminum
Glazing material: double-wall polycarbonate
Ventilation system: ridge vents and 1 lower louver

Horizon Products, Inc., 9301 E. 47th St., Kansas City, MO 64133
Name of kit: Sunworks
Shape: G
Frame material: redwood
Glazing material: Exolite overhead, double-glass walls
Ventilation system: sliding glass door

Lindahl Cedar Homes, Inc., P.O. Box 24426, Seattle, WA 98124

Name of kit: Sun Rooms by Lindahl
Shapes: B all glazed, D and G
Frame material: cedar or fir
Glazing material: tempered double glass
Ventilation system: optional

Lord and Burnham Division, Burnham Co., Box 225, Irvington, NY 10533

Name of kit: Insulated Imperial (other models available)
Shape: G with curved eave
Frame material: aluminum with termal break
Glazing material: double glass, tempered overhead, double strength on walls
Ventilation system: continuous ridge vent

National Greenhouse Co., P. O. Box 100, 400 E. Main St., Pana, IL 62557

Name of kit: Sunspace
Shapes: B all glazed, and G
Frame material: aluminum (with thermal break on Solaroom models)
Glazing material: single glass (double on Solaroom)
Ventilation system: continuous ridge vent plus doors; Solaroom model has sliding door plus awning windows

J. A. Nearing Co., Inc., 9390 Davis Ave., Laurel, MD 20707

Name of kit: Janco Solaroom
Shapes: D and G (also makes other models with shape B)
Frame material: aluminum with thermal break
Glazing material: double glass
Ventilation system: sliding glass door in endwall (other models have continuous ridge vents)

Northern Sun, 21705 Highway 99, Lynwood, WA 98036

Name of kit: The SunSpace
Shapes: B all glazed (gambrel) and G (vertical wall)
Frame material: cedar
Glazing material: tempered double glass
Ventilation system: door in endwall or fan system

Pacific Coast Greenhouse Manufacturing Co., 8360 Industrial Ave., Cotati, CA 94928

Name of kit: Sunroom
Shapes: D, F and G
Frame material: redwood and Douglas fir
Glazing material: tempered double glass
Ventilation system: door in endwall; optional continuous ridge vent, skylights, exhaust fan

Pella/Rolscreen Co., Pella, IA 50219

Name of kit: Pella Sunroom
Shape: G
Frame material: aluminum-clad wood
Glazing material: double glass, tempered overhead and in sliding door
Ventilation system: sliding glass door; operable windows

Santa Barbara Greenhouses, 390 Dawson Dr., Camarillo, CA 93010

Name of kit: Lean-To
Shape: G
Frame material: redwood
Glazing material: corrugated fiberglass (single layer)
Ventilation system: sliding vents in endwalls and door

Solar Additions, Inc., 15 W. Main St., Cambridge, NY 12816

Name of kit: Solar Addition Room
Shape: A
Frame material: redwood
Glazing material: tempered double glass
Ventilation system: door in endwall

Solar Components Corp., P. O. Box 237, Manchester, NH 03105
Name of kit: Sun-Lite Greenhouse Solar Collector
Shape: B all glazed
Frame material: aluminum
Glazing material: double fiberglass panels
Ventilation system: none (see options)

Solar Resources, Inc., P. O. Box 1848, Taos, NM 87571
Name of kit: Solar Room
Shape: B all glazed
Frame material: aluminum
Glazing material: 6-mil ultraviolet-resistant inflated double polyethylene
Ventilation system: doors in both ends

Solarium Systems, Inc., 200 W. 88th St., Bloomington, MN 55420
Name of kit: Solarium Systems Sunspace
Shape: A
Frame material: laminated pine with aluminum glazing system with thermal break
Glazing material: tempered double glass
Ventilation system: none (see options)

Solcan Ltd., R.R. #3, London, Ontario N6A 4B7 Canada
Name of kit: Solcan Lean-to Solar Greenhouse
Shape: B all glazed
Frame material: aluminum-clad cedar
Glazing material: double polycarbonate
Ventilation system: door in endwall; basewall vents

Sturdi-built Manufacturing Co., 11304 S.W. Boones Ferry Rd., Portland, OR 97219
Name of kit: Garden-Sun Room
Shape: G
Frame material: redwood
Glazing material: glass outer glazing with inner fiberglass or acrylic

Ventilation system: ridge vents, base wall vents, and endwall door

The Sun Company, 3241 Eastlake Ave., Seattle, WA 98102
Name of kit: Sunroom
Shape: G, with or without curved eave
Frame material: Douglas fir with extruded aluminum glazing system
Glazing material: double glass, tempered overhead
Ventilation system: 1 door and 1 awning window

Sun System Prefabricated Solar Greenhouses, Inc., 50 Vanderbilt Motor Pkwy., Commack, NY 11725
Name of kit: Sun System Solar Greenhouse
Shape: G with curved eave
Frame material: aluminum with thermal breaks
Glazing material: tempered double glass on front and sides, tempered and laminated safety glass overhead, tempered glass curves
Ventilation system: awning vent windows, thermally broken sliding glass doors

Suncraft, Inc., P.O. Box 236, Hinesburg, VT 05461-0236
Name of kit: Suncraft Inc.
Shapes: D, G and B
Frame material: aluminum with thermal break
Glazing material: tempered double glass
Ventilation system: sliding doors, windows, Vent Axia fans, WES roof fans

Sunglo Solar Greenhouses, 4441 26th Ave. W, Seattle, WA 98199
Name of kit: Sunglo Lean-to
Shape: G
Frame material: aluminum in mill finish or bronze annodized

Glazing material: 2 layers of acrylic; inner layer corrugated (vacuum formed)
Ventilation system: exhaust fan, endwall vents and door

Sunwrights, Inc., 334 Washington St., Sommerville, MA 02143
Name of kit: SuniKit
Shape: A, with glazing sloped 60, 75 or 90 degrees
Frame material: redwood
Glazing material: tempered double glass
Ventilation system: 2 sloped awning windows at top of sloped glazing, plus door

Texas Greenhouse Co., Inc. 2761 St. Louis Ave., Fort Worth, TX 76110
Name of kit: Winter Gardener Lean-To
Shape: B all glazed
Frame material: redwood with aluminum battens
Glazing material: single glass
Ventilation system: roof vents and door in endwall

Turner Greenhouses, P. O. Box 1260, Hwy. 117, Goldsboro, NC 27530
Name of kit: Lean-to
Shape: B all glazed
Frame material: galvanized steel and aluminum
Glazing material: flat fiberglass
Ventilation system: endwall vent and door

Vegetable Factory, Inc., P. O. Box 2235, New York, NY 10163
Name of kit: Vegetable Factory Solar Structure
Shapes: B all glazed, and I
Frame material: aluminum
Glazing material: double-wall fiberglass or clear acrylic panels
Ventilation system: door in endwall, top vents

Vista-Room Manufacturing, Inc., 2419-A Mercantile, Rancho Cordova, CA 95670
Name of kit: Vista-Room
Shapes: G and H
Frame material: aluminum
Glazing material: single or factory insulated tempered safety glass, curved tempered glass
Ventilation system: overhead roof vent, sliding doors and windows, electric fans

Plans

Complete greenhouse plans which relieve you from the task of designing your greenhouse are available from a number of sources. The content of the plans varies. Some have detailed instructions for the novice builder, and others have only drawings and a few comments for the experienced builder. Some include every detail and complete materials lists, while others concentrate only on the most difficult details. The comments with each listing below indicate the shape of the greenhouse, and they indicate what is included with the plans.

Domenic Bucci, 42 Tremont St., Cranston, RI 02920
Name of plans: *Laminated Arch Greenhouse Construction Tips*
Shape (see figure 7-7): H
Glazing material: ¼″ extruded double polycarbonate
Materials list: yes
Instructions: yes
Price: $15
Pages: 8 (8½″ × 11″)
Comments: inexpensive construction (pictured in photo 10-5 and 10-6) consisting of laminated arches made of two glued 1-by-3

furring with a third 1-by-3 as a batten strip on approximately 4-foot centers

Center for Maximum Potential Building Systems, 8604 Webberville Rd., Austin, TX 78724

Name of plans: *The Max's Pot Greenhouse Brochure*

Shape: F

Glazing material: fiberglass, corrugated above and flat on vertical wall

Materials list: not included

Instructions: minimal included

Price: $4.50 plus $1.00 postage and handling

Pages: 38 (5½" × 8½")

Comments: rib-truss construction; vertical glazing removable for summer for screened porch use; combination night insulation and summer shading panels for overhead glazing; includes some design information; incorporates use of recycled materials; designed for community-scale production

J. Coleman Building and Design, R.D. 2, Box 396C, Goodenough Rd., W. Brattleboro, VT 05301

Name of plans: *Solar Greenhouse Construction Plans*

Shape: A, with vertical awning windows below sloped glazing

Glazing material: tempered double glass

Materials list: included

Instructions: not included, but has extensive notes

Price: $25

Pages: 3 (18" × 24") *filled*

Comments: details very clearly drawn in this improved 2d edition

Cornerstones, 54 Cumberland St., Brunswick, ME 04011

Name of plans: *Attached Passive Solar Greenhouse*

Shape: A, with passive collector extending down below level of floor

Glazing material: tempered double glass

Materials list: included

Instructions: not included

Price: $25

Pages: 6 (17" × 22") including 2 pages of renderings and 1 of insulating shutters for the greenhouse

Comments: glazing details pending revision by Cornerstones

Ecotope Group, 2812 E. Madison, Seattle, WA 98112

Name of plans: *A Solar Greenhouse Guide for the Pacific Northwest*

Shape: B all glazed

Glazing material: corrugated single layer fiberglass roof and single glass steeply sloped south wall

Materials list: included

Instructions: included

Price: $6 plus $1 postage and handling

Pages: 92 (8½" × 11")

Comments: includes design and growing information and a window-box greenhouse design; well written for novice builder; includes some design and food-growing information; relatively low-cost construction

Richard Feerey, P. O. Box 1698, Durango, CO 81301

Name of plans: *Sunflake Sunroom Plans*

Shape: L

Glazing material: Sunflake's prefabricated tempered sealed double glass/sliding shutter combination units.

Materials list: included; in architectural language, taken off drawings, not summarized

Instructions: not included

Price: $17

Pages: 2 sheets (24″ × 36″) and 7-page
(8½″ × 11″) materials list; also 4 pages
Sunflake specifications
Comments: with R-12 shutters and mostly
vertical glazing, this is a good sunspace for
very cold climates; Sunflake glazing units
available from Sunflake, P.O. Box 28, 325
Mill St., Bayfield, CO 81122

**New Mexico Solar Energy Associa-
tion,** P.O. Box 2004, Santa Fe, NM 87501
Name of plans: *Building Your Solar Green-
house*
Shape: B
Glazing material: corrugated and flat fiber-
glass
Materials list: not included
Instructions: included; very detailed; good for
novice builder
Price: $6
Pages: 73 (8½″ × 11″)
Comments: includes brief plans for building
curved laminated arch greenhouse; book

**New York State Energy Research and
Development Authority (NYSERDA)
Add-on Plans,** 2 Rockefeller Plaza, Albany,
NY 12223
Name of plans: Manuals #4 and #5: *Sun-
space Plans* and *Greenhouse Plans*
Shape: sunspace is shape A with solid knee-
wall that incorporates 2 awning windows
for vents; greenhouse is shape C, with awn-
ing windows in kneewall
Glazing material: tempered double glass
Materials list: included; extensive
Instructions: included; clear step by step for
novice builders
Price: $10 for both
Pages: 4 (24″ × 36″) and 30 (8½″ × 11″)
Comments: sunspace has post foundation,
with platform floor; greenhouse has continuous concrete block foundation

Rodale Press, Inc. 33 E. Minor St., Em-
maus PA 18049
Name of plans: *Gardener's Solar Greenhouse*
Shape: G
Glazing material: tempered double glass and
double-layer extruded polycarbonate
Materials list: not included but detailed specifications given for all materials
Instructions: included; extremely detailed for
novice builder
Price: $14.95
Pages: 157 (8½″ × 11″)
Comments: plans are for building this as a
freestanding greenhouse, but with its vertical north wall, it could easily be adapted to
attaching to a house; included are on-grade
or below-grade foundation and active heat
storage under the growing beds

Solar Applications & Research Ltd.,
3683 W. 4th Ave., Vancouver, B.C. V6R 1P2
Canada
Name of plans: *Solar Greenhouse Plans*
Shape: B all glazed with vestibule entrance
on side
Glazing material: tempered glass outer; poly-
ethylene or other film for inner glazing
Materials list: not included
Instructions: not included
Price: $25 (Canadian dollars)
Pages: 2 (24″ × 36″) and 23 (8½″ × 11″) siting
and operation guide; 1-page heat-storing
steel water tube installation guide
Comments: includes exterior overhead reflec-
tor/night insulation

SolarVision, Inc., 7 Church Hill, Harrisville, NH 03450
Name of plans: *Easy to Build Solar Sunspace*
Shape: A

Glazing material: tempered double glass
Materials list: included
Instructions: included; good for novice
builder
Price: $9.95
Pages: 1 (18″ × 24″) both sides and 19
(8½″ × 11″)
Comments: includes list of tools needed, de-
tails very clearly drawn

Solstice Designs, Inc., Box 2043, Evergreen, CO 80439
Name of plans: (1) *Universal Retrofit Passive Solar Greenhouse Plans* and (2)
*10′ × 20′ Single Story Attached Passive
Solar Greenhouse Plans*
Shape: (1) A, B, C, F and G; (2) B
Glazing material: (1) Exolite, tempered double glass and single layer acrylic; (2) corrugated fiberglass on roof, flat fiberglass or
tempered glass on steeply sloped area and
flat fiberglass endwalls
Materials list: (1) not included; (2) included
Instructions: (1) not included but detailed
notes on all drawings; (2) included, plus
detailed notes on all drawings
Price: (1) $35.00 plus $3.50 shipping and handling; (2) $22.00 plus $2.20 shipping and
handling
Pages: (1) 10 sheets (18″ × 24″); (2) 8 sheets
(18″ × 24″)
Comments: detailed construction drawings
with many options; (1) several designs to
adapt to various sites and houses; (2) very
complete treatment

Sun-Tel, 1270 S.W. Parrish St., Lake Oswe-
go, OR 97034
Name of plans: *Sun-Tel Sunspace*
Shape: L some endwall glazing; E as alternative
Glazing material: tempered double glass or
double glazed acrylic

Materials list: included for 10′ × 20′ sunspace
Instructions: included
Price: $17.50 postpaid
Pages: 4 sheets of detailed blueprints
(22″ × 30″)

**Tennessee Valley Authority (TVA) In-
formation Office, Publications,** 400 W.
Summit Hill Dr., Knoxville, TN 37902
Name of plans: 3 booklets: *Introduction to
Solar Greenhouses,* and *Sunspace Con-
struction Details,* and *Sunspace Opera-
tions*
Shape: 3 shapes described, A, C and K
Glazing material: tempered double glass on
vertical areas, glass or flat fiberglass with
inner polyethylene on sloped areas
Materials list: included
Instructions: not included
Price: no charge for 1 copy
Pages: 81 total for all 3 booklets
Comments: little detail on sloped glazing de-
tails; booklets more informational than
how-to-build; TVA may have toll-free 800
number in your area

Vegetable Factory, P. O. Box 2235, Dept.
NSP, New York, NY 10164
Name of plans: *Vegetable Factory*
Shape: A (roof glazing optional)
Glazing material: uses Vegetable Factory's
double-wall fiberglass or clear acrylic dou-
ble glazing panels
Materials list: includes lumber list only
Instructions: included but brief
Price: $3
Pages: 2 (17″ × 22″)

WES Contracting, P. O. Box 631, Fal-
mouth, MA 02541
Name of plans: *Sun Haus*
Shape: A
Glazing material: tempered double glass
Materials list: can be derived from plans

Instructions: included
Price: $15
Pages: 12 (8½″ × 11″)
Comments: uses WES's gasket glazing system, which is neoprene rubber gasket/lock-strip arrangement, just like automobile windshield gaskets; gasket is made up in 1 piece, with vulcanized corners, for 3 or more 46″ × 76″, 1″-thick sealed double-glass units

Appendix 3

SUN PATH CHARTS

Figures A-1 through A-8: These sun path charts are for latitudes of 28 to 56 degrees north latitude (NL) in intervals of 4 degrees. Source: Adapted from Edward Mazria, *The Passive Solar Energy Book* (Emmaus, Pa.: Rodale Press, 1979), with the permission of Rodale Press.

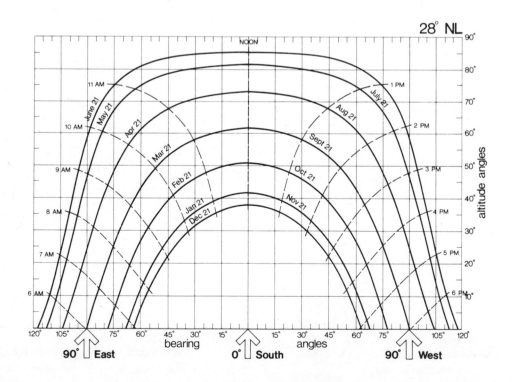

Figure A-1

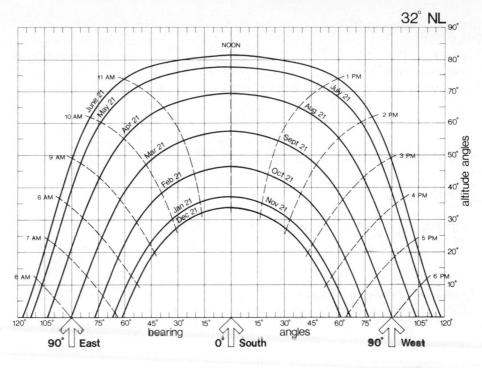

Figure A-2

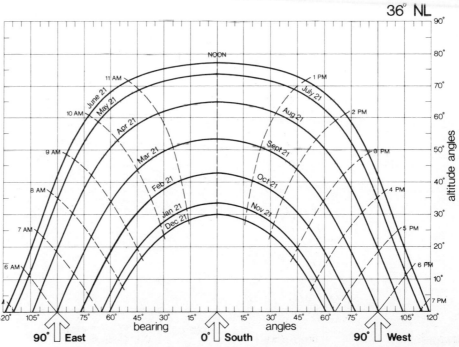

Figure A-3

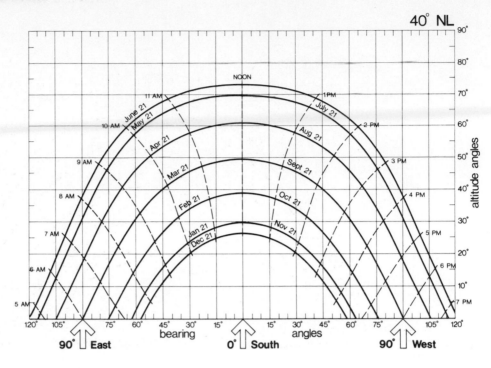

Figure A-4

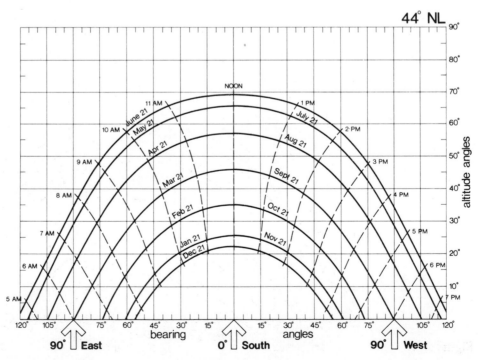

Figure A-5

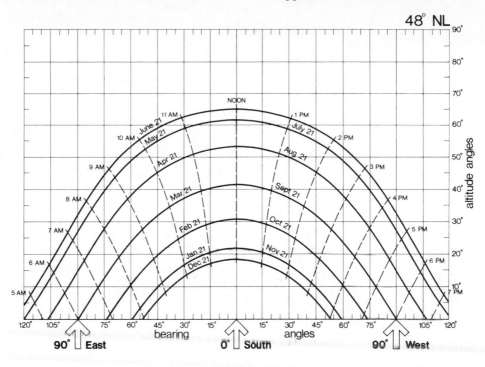

Figure A-6

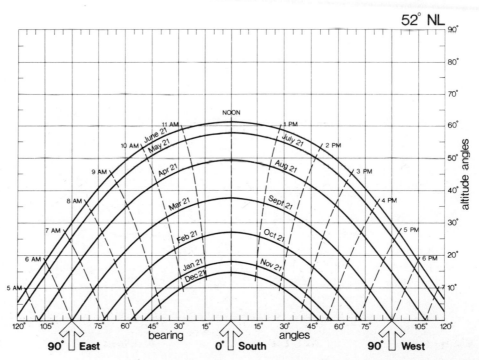

Figure A-7

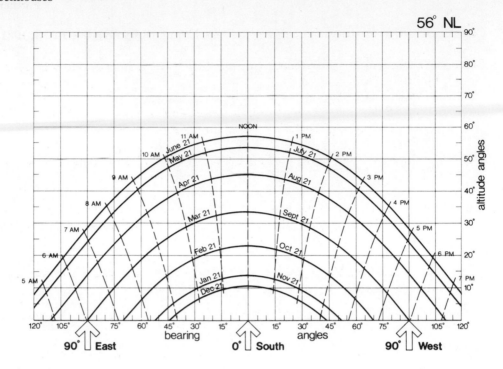

Figure A-8

FURTHER READING

Abraham, George (Doc), and Abraham, Katy. *Organic Gardening Under Glass.* Emmaus, Pa.: Rodale Press, 1977.

Adams, J. T. *The Complete Concrete Masonry and Brick Handbook.* New York: Van Nostrand Reinhold Co., 1983.

American Plywood Association. *APA Design/Construction Guide: All-Weather Wood Foundations.* Tacoma, Wash.: American Plywood Association, 1978.

American Society of Heating, Refrigerating and Air-Conditioning Engineers (ASHRAE). *Handbook of Fundamentals.* Atlanta, Ga.: ASHRAE, 1981.

Anderson, Bruce, and Riordan, Michael. *The Solar Home Book.* Andover, Mass.: Brick House Publishing Co., 1976.

Carter, Joe, ed. *Solarizing Your Present Home.* Emmaus, Pa.: Rodale Press, 1981.

Ecotope Group. *A Solar Greenhouse Guide for the Pacific Northwest.* Seattle, Wash.: Ecotope Group, 1979.

Environmental Sciences Services Administration. *Climatic Atlas of the United States.* Springfield, Va.: National Technical Information Service, 1968.

Journal of the New Alchemists. Available from Stephen Greene Press, Box 1000, Brattleboro, VT 05301.

Klein, Miriam. *Biological Management of Passive Solar Greenhouses: An Annotated Bibliography and Resource List.* Butte, Mont.: The National Center for Appropriate Technology, 1979.

————. *Horticultural Management of Solar Greenhouses in the Northeast.* Newport, Vt.: The Memphremagog Group, 1980.

Langdon, William K. *Movable Insulation.* Emmaus, Pa.: Rodale Press, 1980.

Leckie, Jim; Masters, Gil; Whitehouse, Harry; and Young, Lili. *More Other Homes and Garbage.* San Francisco: Sierra Club Books, 1981.

Los Alamos National Laboratory. *Passive Solar Design Handbook.* Vol. 3. Washington, D.C.: Department of Energy, 1982. Order no. DOE/CS-0127/3.

Mazria, Edward. *The Passive Solar Energy Book.* Emmaus, Pa.: Rodale Press, 1979.

National Forest Products Association. *The All-Weather Wood Foundation System: Design, Fabrication and Installation Manual.* Washington, D.C.: National Forest Products Association, 1982.

New Mexico Solar Energy Association. *Building Your Solar Greenhouse.* Santa Fe, N.M.: New Mexico Solar Energy Association, 1980.

Saunders, Norman B. *Solar Heating Basics.* Published by and available for $13.00 postpaid from the author, 15 Ellis (RP), Weston, MA 02193.

Sellers, David. *Report on Automatic Vent Openers.* Emmaus, Pa.: Rodale Press, 1981.

Shurcliff, William A. *Thermal Shutters and Shades.* Andover, Mass.: Brick House Publishing Co., 1980.

Smith, Miranda. Work in progress on horticultural practices in solar greenhouses. Emmaus, Pa.: Rodale Press, forthcoming.

Smith, Shane. *The Bountiful Solar Greenhouse.* Santa Fe, N.M.: John Muir Publications, 1982.

Wolf, Ray. *Gardener's Solar Greenhouse.* Emmaus, Pa.: Rodale Press, 1984.

————. *Solar Air Heater.* Emmaus, Pa.: Rodale Press, 1981.

Yanda, Bill, and Fisher, Rick. *The Food and Heat-Producing Greenhouse.* Santa Fe, N.M.: John Muir Publications, 1979.

DESIGN CREDITS

The credits are listed by photo number followed by the name of the designer(s) or company and the state.

1-1, 7-9: Keith Kemble and Dan Flannigan, Mont.; 2-1, 4-1, 12-6: Brown University Urban Environmental Lab, R.I., Beckman, Blydenburg and Associates, R.I., Robert Ornstein, Architects, R.I. and Mark Ward Greenhouses, Mass.; 2-2: WES Contracting Co., Mass.; 3-2, 7-11, 8-1, 9-2, 10-1, 12-8: Andrew M. Shapiro, R.I.; 4-2: Jeremy Saywell, Mass.; 5-1: Richard Long, Architect, R.I.; 5-2, 5-3, 7-1, 7-5, 12-1: Mark Ward Greenhouses, Mass., Andrew M. Shapiro, R.I. and Peter Scott, Mass.; 5-4: Guy LeFebvre, R.I.; 5-5: Laurence Renner, N.M.; 5-6: Windlestraw Herb Farm Greenhouse, R.I.; 5-7, 7-10, 7-11: Kirk and Rachel Badeau, R.I.; 5-8, 5-9, 11-1: Blair Hamilton and Beth Sachs, Vt.; 5-10: Heartwood Builders, Mass.; 5-11, 7-8: Paul St. Amand, R.I.; 5-12, 6-2, 7-3: Jeremy Coleman, Vt.; 6-1, photo on page 190, 9-6: Mark Ward Greenhouses, Mass.; 7-2: Val Bertoia and Shelter Design Group, both of Pa.; 7-12: Del Porto, Mass.; 7-13: David Baerg and Mark Ward Greenhouses, both of Mass.; 7-14: Mary Pea, R.I.; 7-15: Paul Russel, Pa.; 9-1: R.W. Chew and Co., R.I.; 9-5, 10-3, 12-2, 12-4, 12-5: Mark Ward Greenhouses, Mass.; 10-4: Mark Rosenbaum, N.H.; 10-5, 10-6, 10-7: Domenic Bucci, R.I.

INDEX

Page numbers in **boldface** type indicate tables, illustrations and photographs.